The Indian Economy *Problems and Prospects*

1901–1971

The Indian Economy *Problems and Prospects*

selected writings of D.R. Gadgil

edited by Sulabha Brahme

OXFORD
UNIVERSITY PRESS

OXFORD
UNIVERSITY PRESS

22 Workspace, 2nd Floor, 1/22 Asaf Ali Road, New Delhi 110002, India

Oxford University Press is a department of the University of Oxford. It furthers the University's objective of excellence in research, scholarship, and education by publishing worldwide in

Oxford New York

Auckland Cape Town Dar es Salaam Hong Kong Karachi Kuala Lumpur Madrid Melbourne Mexico City Nairobi New Delhi Shanghai Taipei Toronto

With offices in
Argentina Austria Brazil Chile Czech Republic France Greece Guatemala Hungary Italy Japan Poland Portugal Singapore South Korea Switzerland Thailand Turkey Ukraine Vietnam

Published in India
by Oxford University Press, New Delhi

First published 2011

ISBN-13: 978-0-19-806945-4
ISBN-10: 0-19-806945-6

Typeset in Warnock Pro 10.5/12.5
by Sai Graphic Design, New Delhi 110 055
Printed at Manipal Technologies Limited ,Manipal
Published by Oxford University Press
22 Workspace, 2nd Floor, 1/22 Asaf Ali Road, New Delhi 110002, India

Contents

IV PROBLEMS OF INDUSTRIAL AND AGRICULTURAL DEVELOPMENT

V INCOME POLICY

VI ISSUES IN CO-OPERATION AND ECONOMIC DEVELOPMENT

VII SOCIO-ECONOMIC DEVELOPMENT IN NEW STATES

VIII SOCIAL AND ECONOMIC THINKING OF GADGIL *An Appraisal*

Acknowledgements

Selected articles by D.R. Gadgil included in this volume are taken from the following publications of Gokhale Institute of Politics and Economics (GIPE), Poona:

1. Chapters 3, 4, 5, 8, 9, 14, 15, 18, 22, and 24 are from *Planning and Economic Policy in India*, D.R. Gadgil, GIPE, Poona, 1962 (second edition).
2. Chapters 2, 6, 16, and 17 are from *Planning and Economic Policy in India*, D.R. Gadgil, GIPE, Poona, 1972 (fourth edition).
3. Chapters 7, 10, 12, 13, and 21 are from *Writings and Speeches of Professor D.R. Gadgil on Planning and Development* (1967–1971), A.R. Kamat (ed.), GIPE, Poona, 1973.
4. Chapters 25, 26, 27, 28, 29, and 30 are from *Writings and Speeches of Professor D.R Gadgil on Co-operation*, GIPE, Poona, 1975.
5. Chapters 1, 11, 19, 20, 23, 31, and 32 are from *Writings and Speeches of Professor D.R Gadgil on Economic and Political Problems*, Sulabha Brahme (ed.), GIPE, Poona, 1981.

Introduction*

I

This publication contains a series of articles, notes, memoranda, and so on, written by Professor Gadgil from 1951, the beginning of planning in India, till 1970, the formulation of the Fourth Five-Year Plan. They are connected with planning in India and the policy of the government. A number of these were written for the Panel of Economists of the Planning Commission during the formulation of the Second Five-Year Plan, and a large number prepared by Gadgil during the period 1967–70 in the capacity of Deputy Chairman, Planning Commission. These include papers, notes, and speeches addressed to the Planning Commission and its sub-committees, the National Development Council, and other related bodies, and articles and speeches at various fora, addressed to wider audiences at different levels all over the country, discussing and expounding various aspects of planning in India in the context of the Fourth Plan or economic planning in general and problems relevant to Indian Planning.

The justification for reprinting the papers, notes, and so on, written on specific occasions, forty years back, is their historical value as well as their current relevance. The problems discussed in these writings and the issues

* The Gadgil Centenary (10 April 2000 to 10 April 2001) Celebration Committee was set up under the Chairmanship of Professor Madhu Dandawate in January 2000. Under the auspices of the Committee, the preparation of centenary volumes covering Professor Gadgil's selected writings and his life and work was taken up with the support of the Planning Commission. We gratefully acknowledge the support extended by the Planning Commission for the project, the keen interest taken by the late Professor Madhu Dandawate in the work, the permission granted by the Officiating Director, Professor Rajas Parchure, to reprint in the centenary volume, Gadgil's writings published by the Gokhale Institute of Politics and Economics (GIPE), Oxford University Press for taking the responsibility of publication of this centenary volume, and the colleagues and friends who helped in the preparation of this work.

raised are still with us in much the same form today. In almost every direction, little progress in action or in thinking is apparent. For example, in a number of contexts, the problem of distribution of income and wealth was discussed by Gadgil in these papers. The planned development, instead of effecting any movement in the direction of a more equal income distribution, has led to the accentuation of inequalities that have reached alarming levels in recent times. Gadgil had urged for a comprehensive foodgrains policy, production planning, buffer stocks, remunerative prices, and fair distribution of foodgrains to meet the basic needs of all sections of the population. He regarded price stability as an essential condition for development planning. But there has been deliberate shilly-shallying with regard to food policy to protect the interests of the rural moneylender–trader and the wholesale dealers in agricultural commodities. The license given in recent years to speculative trading in agricultural commodities, and the permission given to the companies for direct purchases has encouraged hoarding and led to the skyrocketing of the prices of foodgrains.

In Gadgil's opinion, the basic reason for the failure of Indian planning is a total absence of a policy frame and a regulatory framework. He attributed this to the growing influence in the government of the vested interests with a *laissez faire* bias. As a consequence, the plan resources have been used to enhance the profits of private groups rather than for national development. This has resulted in growing inequality and the concentration of economic activity in metropolitan centres, where, on the one hand, the numbers of slum and pavement dwellers swell and, on the other hand, there is a mushrooming of places of feasting and entertainment and palatial buildings on the most extravagant international standards. In his opinion, the policy decisions, or their absence, in relation to Indian planning, could be explained in the light of the interests of the classes or groups in power.

It will be of interest, in view of the experience of the last two decades under globalization that is leading to growing unemployment, widening of inequality, increasing insecurity and distress, deepening agrarian crisis, and massive displacement of peasants, fisherfolk, and tribals from their traditional occupations/habitat, to look for measures that could help the crisis-ridden working masses of India to meet the challenge. In this context, all the basic principles advocated by Gadgil, viz., planning with a regulatory frame, controls, active role of the government in promoting co-operative institutions and industry, self-reliance, food self sufficiency, and an employment orientation of planning become all the more important. The penetrating analysis he made of the Indian socio-political and economic situation, and the policies he propagated for amelioration, could provide valuable insights to the political and social activists engaged in organizing the toiling masses struggling for the assertion of their Democratic Rights.

II

Gadgil, a representative of the institutional economists, followed a multidisciplinary approach. His analysis of the problems of economic development and social change in India is penetrating as it is firmly anchored in a historical perspective and the complex social reality. He had evolved a holistic view of socio-economic transformation, keeping in mind the specific characteristics of the Indian social reality. Integration of the factionalized Indian society, decentralization of political power, and integration and co-ordination of policies for a socially-oriented economic development could be broadly described as the main tenets of Gadgil's approach to socio-economic transformation of Indian society. The problem of social integration has to be considered in the context of the salient features of Indian society and culture. The unity of India has not been associated with the existence of one polity. A common religion or a common history or a common language also has not acted as the cohesive principle for the Indian society. The special characteristic of the unity of Indian culture has been the unity in diversity. Indian society has been all along fragmented and compartmentalized into a large number of social groups. The identities of diverse communities are maintained because of the flexible and accommodative character of Indian culture. This has ensured a continuity in tradition despite the extinction of certain groups and the addition of new communities.

Indian society is fragmented into a number of factions on a variety of bases. The caste hierarchy compartmentalizes the society into exclusive groups. Further, the social groups identify themselves by sub-castes. At the same time the regional and language differences segregate the various groups in the society. The regional and language differences can be traced to the geographical separation of these groups. But even among the people of the same region, and speaking the same language, the caste differences and religious sectarianism are weakening the fabric of social life. The hierarchical social relations aggravate the problem and lead to social tensions and social disintegration. The only way to de-emphasize such differences and avoid social disintegration is to make the regional social groups as homogeneous as possible and emphasize the idea of neighbourliness and regional unity. Gadgil believed that it is only through a federation of a number of such homogeneous, regional communities, united on linguistic basis, that the basic unity of identity of Indian society, along with all its diversities, can be truly attained.

Decentralization of political power is another important tenet in Gadgil's social philosophy. According to the Indian tradition, the religious and economic power centres did recognize the sovereignty of the state but were never subordinated to it. In fact, autonomy of these spheres was recognized and considered important for maintaining the social equilibrium. Equally important is the balance of power between the various strata of social hierarchy. The individual in a society is a member of various social and political institutions such as a family, a village community, a state, and a nation, and each of these relationships involves a set of duties and loyalties. It is possible for an individual to function without any conflict of loyalties as long as none of these institutions encroaches upon the area of any other. The encroachment, by the lower strata, on the jurisdiction of the higher ones, could lead to anarchy; totalitarianism might be the outcome if the higher-level institutions encroach upon the area of operation of the lower-level ones. It is, therefore, essential to maintain the autonomy of these levels within their own agreed areas of jurisdiction in the interest of a peaceful and fruitful social life. It is important that political power be systematically decentralized and the areas of jurisdiction of institutions at various levels be carefully delineated.

India attained independence through a peaceful transfer of power. There was, consequently, relatively little change in the form and structure of administration. The change of rulers was also not accompanied by any large changes in the arrangements connected with the manifestation of political authority. The peculiar circumstances of British rule in India led to the development of a structure of administrative services which combined the rigid separation, characteristic of a caste society, with the careful gradation, characteristic of a class society. Little change has been effected in the structure of administrative services in the post-1947 period. The government continues to attach an even greater importance to maintaining the prestige of the high officials rather than to taking the public into confidence. The dominance of the VIPs, and the richer sections of the society, in all projects and programmes, continues to be a marked feature of the Indian situation. The difficulties encountered by the poor, and those without any backing, in obtaining access to and attention from administrative personnel remain almost as great as before. In spite of a large extension of programmes with educational and welfare intent, the manner and pace of operation of the administrative machinery remain substantially unchanged. There is a stranglehold of a single All India Administrative Service (IAS), not only in the state and central administrations, but also in the departmental undertakings, public sector enterprises, and statutory bodies. The lack of imaginative policy in recruitment and training of managerial personnel, and the lack of autonomy in planning and operating the enterprises, impedes dynamism in functioning.

A retrogressive development in the socio-economic situation in independent India has been the increasing domination of the economically powerful groups and the growing alliance between the high-level bureaucrats, the political leaders, and the economically powerful business and industrial groups. Subtle and surreptitious transactions are operative between the bureaucracy, who have large discretionary powers in relation to the regulation of economic activity, the political leaders, who are the policymakers, and the leading private economic interests, who control, in a large measure, the covetous ranks in the economy. These three power groups are collaborating for obtaining the largest possible share of the national income. In the process, the weaker sections of the community are getting further impoverished.

Political and economic stability can be ensured only if the benefits of economic development accrue to the people at large. The economic policy of the state has to enthuse confidence in the people that the government is trying to implement economic policies for assuring a minimum standard of living to the masses, and that the conspicuous consumption by the richer sections of the community is being effectively curbed in the interest of better utilizing the productive resources for the economic well-being of the community as a whole. Gadgil believed that the operation of the mixed economy can be so oriented as to approach these objectives but stressed that there are a number of conditions which must be fulfilled for the implementation of such a policy. He emphasized the need for the reduction of uncertainties in the economy for the effective operation of a mixed economy. The principal factor that gives rise to uncertainty is the instability in agriculture, the mainstay of the India economy, due to the dependence of farming on the vagaries of the monsoons. To rectify this situation he advocated the development of irrigation, the introduction of agricultural modernization through the promotion of an integrated co-operative institutional network with state participation, and the regulation of prices and trade in agricultural commodities. On the basis of sustainable and stable agricultural development that Gadgil placed at the centre of the problem of economic development, agro-processing and industrial development could be set on a sound and stable foundation.

For planned development of the economy, he considered it crucial to formulate an integrated policy for the regulation of productive activity, credit, and the prices. This implies setting up priorities in production and curbing the monopoly and concentration of economic power in industry. For preventing malpractices in the big industrial houses he suggested the nationalization of the audit services in the country. He emphasized the need for a proper price policy for maintaining the levels of consumption of the populace as well as for arresting the speculative tendencies in the economy. He had specially emphasized the need for monopoly procurement of important crops at statutory prices, for ameliorating the uncertainties in the farm business. He considered it equally important to set up a machinery for the proper distribution of foodgrains and other essential commodities at controlled prices.

He stressed the need to regulate private investments so as to control the speculative use of capital and the frittering away of the valuable monetary and physical resources of the nation into luxury production and to check the concentration of private industry and business in metropolitan centres. Gadgil considered it essential to make substantial investments for the development of agriculture, rural infrastructure, and dispersed industrialization. This would help raise the rural incomes. In the context of industrial development the choice of an appropriate technique was considered to be of crucial importance. In view of the relative scarcity of capital, the adoption of labour intensive techniques of production, so as to generate adequate employment in the economy, was considered desirable. Modern capital intensive technology may be adopted only in industries where it is inevitable on technological considerations, and these big industrial units will have to be in the state sector. During the process of modernization and industrialization, which Gadgil considered integral to economic progress, technological changes and exogenous shocks disturb the traditional production and employment. The duty of the state is to put in operation such measures as to minimize the hardships imposed on the working masses due to technological progress. This could be achieved through the protection and rehabilitation of traditional village and urban artisan and handicraft industries and their technological upgradation to ensure continuous economic progress and the promotion of rural industrialization on the basis of agricultural, forest, livestock, and other products available in the rural areas. In addition, to support the unemployed and the under-employed, he stressed the need for continuous as well as seasonal public works programmes, designed to conserve and enrich the land, water, and forest resources that would enhance agricultural productivity, and to provide social and economic infrastructure in rural areas that would help decentralized industrialization.

Regional balance in economic development and the development of the economy through co-operative organization were considered by Gadgil as the two essential elements for economic development under Indian conditions. Gadgil emphasized three aspects of the programme for regional development. First, the regional development programmes should include schemes of encouragement and assistance for increasing the productivity of the productive assets in the region, and special schemes for those who possess neither any means of production nor any specialized skills. Second, it should include schemes for providing industrial and social infrastructure in the form of transport and communication, power, water supply, education, and training, and so on, for promoting industrial activity in the region. Third, it should include schemes for the conservation and augmentation of natural resources to enable a sustained development of the region. He had also emphasized the need for the creation of a co-operative organizational set-up for development, such that the large numbers of people from various strata should be able to participate in, and derive the benefits from, the development process.

In the context of regional development, Gadgil had taken special interest and put in considerable effort for the establishment of the first sugarcane-producing farmers' co-operative sugar factory in Maharashtra, which played a transformative role in rural Maharashtra. It helped retain the surplus that was being drained by the well-entrenched *gur* merchants and private sugar factories. To replicate this model he considered it necessary to study the special features of the natural endowment of each region, identify the potential growth promoting industries, and concentrate on developing these through farmers' co-operatives, with the state providing the necessary economic aid and infrastructure. Regional development on these lines would help strengthen the economic base at the village level and change the current power balance in the countryside. It would be necessary for the regional units and the local population to increase their productive power and economic strength with the assistance of the state government, because then alone would they be able to function effectively as counterbalancing forces and help curb the concentration of power.

Co-operation could help the millions of small units that exist in India in farming, fishery, industry, business, and so on, to obtain the advantages of modern technology and scale of operation. The modern co-operative order has to be, essentially, a planned order. However, the structure of a co-operative economy would be able to modify the operation of centralized planning in those respects in which the centralized planning is supposed to be defective, that is, in respect of the dispersal of authority and of the ability to take account of local circumstances. The emphasis of the co-operative economy is on organizing all economic activities for mutual advantage at a series of levels, right from the primary level group in the village to the highest possible level—the state.

The Co-operative Movement, as envisaged by Gadgil, was to encompass a very comprehensive field of operation in an integrated manner. He had advocated co-operative rural credit and a statutory procurement and distribution machinery for agricultural produce with a view to loosening the grip of the moneylender/trader on the cultivator. He had also emphasized the need for the extension of the co-operative activity, so as to integrate agricultural and industrial activity through the co-operativization of the agricultural processing industries, thus enabling the primary producer to participate in industrial activity. A national network of consumers' co-operatives would have to be organized and integrated with the co-operative production network. This alone would loosen the hold of the intermediaries and the monopolies and organize the economy in the mutual interests of both, the producers and the consumers. These co-operatives would be organized at the village *taluka* and the district levels and their working would be co-ordinated at the state level. Such a comprehensive network of co-operatives, at various levels and in all the fields of economic activity, would enable an effective decentralization of political and economic power and the organization of a truly decentralized Co-operative Commonwealth.

It is important, in a mixed economy, to regulate and control the operations of the private industry and business so that the co-operatives are allowed to take root and extend their areas of operation. With this view, Prof. Gadgil had advocated financial support to the co-operatives by the state in the initial stages and the regulation of private business operations. The successful establishment of a large number of co-operative bodies, in a variety of fields, viz., production, processing, and distribution in a dispersed manner, would, in his view, help establish a balance in economic–political power which is concentrated, today, in the hands of a few in the country. Co-operation was considered by Gadgil as the only path which would help take economic progress to the people at large and also help ensure their active participation in the development process. Co-operation is, thus, the pivotal element in organizing the socio-economic development of a country like India, with diversified, fragmented, and unequal communities. Under such heterogeneous conditions, the establishment of dispersed and small co-operative units, and their systematic federalization, can alone span the variegated society and bring it within the ambit of the Co-operative Commonwealth.

III

We have noted earlier Gadgil's views on socio-political restructuring and economic planning to effect socio-economic transformation in Indian society, as reflected in the articles, papers, and speeches included in this volume. He was very critical of the composition, role, and functions assigned to the Planning Commission, the lack of regulatory framework, and the manoeuvring of the plan by the monopoly houses–bureaucrat–politician nexus to promote their interests. Yet, he was forced by the circumstances to accept the responsibility to head the Planning Commission in 1967, because the country was at that time plunged into a deep political and economic crisis and planning had been virtually abandoned. He felt duty bound to try to rejuvenate planning and hoped that this could be attempted with the support of the people.

Gadgil viewed the Planning Commission as a body of experts providing well-reasoned advice to the government on matters of planning and development and, as such, he did not harbour any illusions regarding what could be achieved through a plan, given the entrenched interests. The most that he hoped to achieve was to introduce a variety of ameliorative measures.

This is reflected in his addresses and writings of that period. He placed before the people, in a variety of fora, the problems and the policy measures required for mobilizing support to planning.

The Fourth Plan laid special stress on multi-level planning so that each state, district, *taluka*, and group of villages would take the responsibility to achieve the development of local resources and the realization of local potentialities, to be ensured through the diffusion of initiative, decision making, and people's participation at each level. The local area plans of physical resource development had to be integrated with district plans of socio-economic infrastructure and the state plans that were expected to control metropolitan growth and promote decentralized industrial development, employment intensive techniques, land reforms, co-operative organization, development of weaker sections through district-level plans of productive employment, joint farming organization of marginal and small non-viable farms, support to supplementary livestock, fishery, forest-based economic activities, supportive credit structure through extension of need-based credit through a co-operative and nationalized banking structure, co-operative network of farm services, marketing, processing, and consumer co-operatives, support pricing, buffer stock, and public distribution system. To achieve this, Gadgil emphasized financial autonomy of the states so that decentralized regional planning could be introduced. He was keen on ending the centralization of planning in Delhi and with this aim, the centre–state financial relations, with respect to plan funds, were reorganized. The central plan assistance was no longer controlled by the Planning Commission but was worked out on the basis of objective criteria, viz., population, development, special problems, and so on, known as the Gadgil formula, which stood the test of time. The advantage of this decentralization was taken by a state like Kerala with a Leftist government. Demand for separate states is being raised in recent times, primarily because of uneven regional development. Decentralized planning, with transfer of funds to the sub-regions of the states, on the basis of the Gadgil formula, could help meet the problem to some extent.

Gadgil was not an armchair social scientist. He was personally involved in grass-roots level studies to gain a full grasp of the ground-level reality, and the needs and problems faced by the people. Ameliorative measures were worked out in consultation with the people and put into practice with active participation of the concerned groups. On the basis of the experience of such projects, elements of a generalized programme were worked out. This helped in the formulation of a realistic policy that was made available to the people through his writings and speeches, both in English and in Marathi language, and to the government through notes, memoranda, and committee work. The methodology of fact gathering and analysis, policy formulation, and the measures necessary for progressing towards the aims set when India embarked on planning, viz., raising the standard of living of the people, or 'inclusive growth' in today's parlance, runs deep through Gadgil's writings in this volume.

There has been a continuous shift to rightist policies all over the world from the early eighties. This trend got accentuated with the collapse of the Union of the Soviet Socialist Republics. In 1991, the Nehru model of planning, and the role of the public sector and government controls, came under attack and the Indian economic policy veered its direction fully towards *laissez faire*. Higher growth rates, as compared to earlier decades, are being experienced; this is inevitably accompanied by widening inequalities between regions, and between the rich and the toiling peasants. Not only are inequalities widening, but social distress has also become deep and widespread. The problems of unemployment, food insecurity, and the displacement of tribals, peasants, fisherfolk, and artisans from their means of livelihood in the name of 'development' have assumed serious proportions. It is in this context that devising a proper regulatory framework and new institutional structures, necessary to the efficient functioning of the system, by understanding the economic processes at the grass-roots level becomes necessary. Such a policy frame that Gadgil laid stress on all along becomes as necessary in a market-driven economy as in a planned economy, and could be of use to the policymakers. The social philosophy, business ethics, and discipline required in organizing and operating co-operative institutions, as advocated and practised by Vaikunthbhai Mehta and Gadgil, could provide an ideal and inculcate faith in the Co-operative Commonwealth among the dedicated social workers and inspire them to develop an integrated co-operative structure encompassing the adivasis, peasants, artisans, and workers who are being pushed into impoverishment and distress, due to liberlization and globalization.

Gadgil's writings provide an incisive analysis of the socio-economic situation in India that is relevant even today, and his methodology for working out ameliorative alternatives could be helpful in developing programmes, keeping in view the specificity of the local problems and the needs and aspirations of the people.

Gadgil's writings could prove to be enlightening, as they provide a critical assessment of Indian economic problems and the Indian development experience in a historical perspective, and help inculcate a sense of social purpose among students, peasant and worker activists, and social activists striving for a just and equitable socio-economic order.

This volume presents at the outset, an introductory note, followed by a brief biographical note that discuses Gadgil's social philosophy and economic praxis. The opening article on 'The Political Economy of D.R. Gadgil', by Professor P.R. Brahmanada, delivered as the Gadgil Centenary Memorial Lecture at the 84th Annual Conference of the Indian Economic

Association on 30 December 2001, succinctly sums up Gadgil's perspective on Indian economic development and planning. The selected articles and speeches by Gadgil are grouped under eight sections and arranged chronologically within each section. The first three sections deal with the rationale of planning, the approach to planning, various issues and problems relating to planning in India, and the different aspects of planning at the regional level. This is followed by three sections that cover specific questions in the sphere of industrial development, village industries, agricultural development, price policy, income policy and co-operative finance, sugar co-operatives, and co-operative social order. The seventh section discusses social and economic challenges in relation to change and development in the new states. The last section includes seven articles by eminent social scientists and thinkers, reflecting upon the relevance of Gadgil's social philosophy and approach to planning under changing conditions in India.

A Biographical Note on Gadgil

The Gadgils hailed from Manjare, a village in Pedne *taluka*, Goa Province, adjoining the then Sawantwadi state and Ratnagiri district in the coastal Konkan region of Maharashtra. Bhargav Laxman Gadgil, the grandfather of D.R. Gadgil, left his priestly vocation and Manjare village in the 1860s and together with a friend migrated to Nagpur, the capital of the Central Provinces and Berar. Having been educated up to matriculation he was able to secure a job as a *Nazar* in the Civil Court in Nagpur, and by subsequent promotions, reached the position of a Judge. His son, Ramchandra (Gadgil's father), was an advocate practising in the High Court at Nagpur. He was very honest and upright and had a good practice. He was also recognized as a legal expert. Gadgil's mother, Sitabai (nee Mathu Pendse), who came from a distinguished family of scholars, was an able, resolute, and socially motivated woman. She practised in life—within the scope available to women in the 1920s—what she considered as social duty. Her father—Kashinath Balwant Pendse (1850–1910)—was a brilliant, versatile, and well-known Sanskrit scholar and an authority on the interpretation of the Vedas. In 1872, he was a Fellow at the Deccan College, Poona and among his students was Lokmanya Tilak, with whom he later developed a close friendship. In 1872, he joined government service as *mamlatdar* and during 1897–1906 he was the City Magistrate at Nashik. Gadgil was born on 10 April 1901 in Nashik at his maternal grandfather's residence. He was the only child of his parents but received no special treatment as he was brought up in a joint family along with his uncle's five sons and four daughters, all of whom were treated equally by Sitabai.

Gadgil completed his high school education at Patwardhan High School, Nagpur. He should have appeared for the matriculation examination in 1916. However, he would not have yet completed sixteen years, and the prevailing rules did not permit him to appear for the examination.

Therefore, he left the school and in December 1916, appeared for the Senior Cambridge Examination with subjects which qualified him for entrance to Cambridge University. However, because of the ongoing World War, he could not immediately proceed to Cambridge. Finally, after waiting for almost one and a half years, he arrived in England in October 1918 and immediately secured admission to Queens' College, Cambridge University. Gadgil's parents had sent him to Cambridge with the idea of his joining the prestigious Indian Civil Services. However, Gadgil had decided not to join the alien government service, but to, instead, pursue research in economics to help initiate a process of socio-economic development in the interest of the Indian masses. In view of this aim, he opted for History tripos Part I and Economics tripos Part II and obtained the B.A. degree in 1921. The newly-instituted M.Litt. degree required two years of research, for which he registered in 1921, submitted his thesis in May 1923, and immediately in July returned to India. For his M.Litt. thesis, he worked under the supervision of Professor Hubert Henderson. The subject of his thesis was 'Industrial Evolution in India in Recent Times.' It was published by the Oxford University Press in 1924, with subsequent editions in 1929, 1933, 1942, and 1971.

On his return to India, he explored the possibility of establishing a research unit to study economic and political problems of India, in one of the colleges in Poona, viz., Fergusson College (established in 1885 by Tilak) or Tilak's Kesari—Maratha Trust. However, the plans could not materialize for want of adequate funds. Hence he accepted, lacking an immediate opening in the academic field, an appointment in the Finance Department of the Government of Bombay as Acting Additional Assistant Secretary, which he held barely for one year (1924–5). Thus began a long academic career. He was Principal of the Maganlal Thakordas Balmukunddas (M.T.B.) College, Surat, for five years (1925–30), and then became the first Director of the Gokhale Institute of Politics and Economics, Poona, which he was able to establish on the strength of a generous donation from his father-in-law, the late Rao Bahadur R.R. Kale of Satara, while the facilities of library and office building were made available by the Servants of India Society, established in 1905 in Poona by Gopal Krishna Gokhale. (He was married to Susheela Kale in May 1927.) In spite of numerous opportunities he never left the Institute and remained its Director for the full tenure until March 1966, when he completed 65 years. On his retirement, he was appointed Professor Emeritus in the Institute and continued to work regularly at his desk at the Institute. Even before he had retired from the Institute, he was called upon to accept the Vice-Chancellorship of the University of Poona. He was nominated as a member of the Rajya Sabha in May 1966. He relinquished all the official positions he held on 30 August 1967, to join the Planning Commission on 1 September 1967, as its Deputy-Chairman.

Teaching and guiding research students in economics was his lifelong commitment. He engaged undergraduate classes during 1925–30 in Surat, and in the early 1950s when the University of Poona was established. Despite heavy demands of economic research, committee work, and numerous public responsibilities, he was regular in teaching M.A. classes and guiding the students for the M.A. and Ph.D. degrees by research from 1930 to 1967. He was very methodical, his exposition was crisp, clear, and incisive. To look beyond the obvious was the burden of his teaching.

He nurtured in the Gokhale Institute a tradition of critical intellectual culture, commitment to socially relevant research, democratic functioning, and humanist worldview. He was an ideal committee man, be it the academic or administrative committee at the Gokhale Institute, or the Board of Directors at the Reserve Bank of India, or in the Pravara Sugar Co-operative factory. He would listen patiently, argue softly, veering the discourse skilfully towards a consensus, and managing to arrive at a decision that he deemed rational. He was respected because he was upright, outspoken, with fearless commitment to integrity, and would never compromise on his principles in public or government committee work.

There was a harmonious blend of Indian-ness and cosmopolitanism in his personality. He upheld the rationalist, tolerant, secular tradition of intellectual heterodoxy of India and blended it with the modern values of egalitarianism and democracy. In spite of his weighty public responsibilities, he would always find time for family, friends, and relatives. He was a dutiful and caring son, a devoted and loving husband, an affectionate and supportive father, very generous and helpful to relatives, friends, and students. He treated all as his equals without any discrimination by caste, religion, sex, age, or status. There was a total consonance between what he advocated and what he practised. He considered the use of the mother tongue, in administration, business, law, and education, as a medium of instruction from primary to university levels, to be a prerequisite for the functioning of democracy, and strove for it at the government and university levels. While in England, he published his first article in Marathi in 1923. He published, subsequently, hundreds of articles and delivered public lectures on economic issues, in chaste Marathi. Unlike the Western university educated class of his times, he always dressed in the traditional Marathi style—*dhoti*, *sherwani*, black cap, and *chappals*—a dress well-suited to the climatic conditions of western India, and was a vegetarian and a teetotaler; while in England, he had suitably adopted to the Western modes. He had a passion for scientific research, for nature, music, and sports, and a passion to struggle for an egalitarian, just, co-operative social order.

There were three clear influences that shaped the personality, philosophy, and the life-mission of Gadgil. His upbringing, in a family with a high standard of learning and a rigorous code of social behaviour, provided a firm ethical code and intellectual commitment which was reinforced by his deep and thorough study of the *Geetarahasya*, Lokmanya Tilak's interpretation of the *Geeta*. The essence of the *Geeta*, as interpreted by Tilak, is *Karmayoga*, that is, discipline in action based on knowledge coupled with selfless devotion. The action directed in the service of the society has to be carried out with a detached view so that success does not lead to conceit and failure to abandonment of the pursuit of the goal. Tilak's interpretation of *Geeta* fits in with the ideal ethic of the scholarly tradition—to be learned, virtuous, and restrained, with high morals and a selfless pursuit of knowledge, 'high thinking and simple living' being their motto. These ideal values and mores were internalized by Gadgil during his childhood, and were strengthened by his poring over Tilak's *Geetarahasya* during the three months-long hazardous voyage to England. The other important influence was that of the formative years spent at Cambridge for graduate and post-graduate studies. His social and economic philosophy was shaped by Marshallian economics, Fabian socialism, co-operative ideology and practice, humanism, and democratic values. He absorbed Marshal's method of substantiation with historical and empirical studies. These played an important role in shaping his worldview and mission. Though trained as an economist, he maintained a holistic view of social sciences and could, just as convincingly, be described as a historian, sociologist, political analyst, and educationist. Like Marshall, he was of the view that, 'Without facts we can do nothing: but with facts, until they have been passed through the mill of thought and their lessons educed from them by reason, we can still do nothing.' 'It is a method, an organ of enquiry, that can be turned on to particular problems as they arise; that, in different conditions, will yield different answers to similar questions; but it does not, in itself, consist of any body of answers or any scheme of dogma.'

Gadgil was not a subject-specialist but a method-specialist. What distinguishes him from other social scientists is his method and approach to a problem. His method is marked by a rigorously logical framing of the issues, an objective assessment of the available evidence, and a vigorous formulation of conclusions within a broad framework of social values and objectives. His analysis was based on historical method and empirical investigations. Out of his own experience and practice over the years, he organized a course in Social Science Research Method and for several years, had offered it regularly to the pre-Ph.D. students at the Institute.

Gadgil had taken a deep and keen interest in the organization and administration of university education. He acquired first-hand experience in this matter at a very young age when he was the Principal of the M.T.B. College at Surat. He issued a pamphlet on the subject of Bombay University reforms in 1926. He was a member of the Senate and a Fellow at the University of Bombay from 1927 to 1952. He was also a member of the Senate and Syndicate on the S.N.D.T. Women's University (1931–40).

Gadgil played an important role in the formation and establishment of the Poona University and, later, in its organization and administration. He was the Secretary of Maharashtra University Working Committee (1932–46) and a member of the Poona University Advisory Committee (1948–9). After the establishment of the University of Poona in 1949, he was deeply involved in the organization of centralized teaching and research in various faculties. He was a member of the Court and the Executive Council (1949–58) of the University.

In the field of political science, Gadgil was actively engaged during the 1940s with the then burning issue of federating India, constitution-making, and the delineation of federating units. As a part of the same endeavour, one should note his efforts for the establishment of the linguistic state of Maharashtra to help build a constitutional structure which, in his judgement, was the most appropriate for the development of the Indian personality. The subject was at his heart from the mid-1920s. Gadgil wrote *Federating India* in 1945 and became a member of the Expert Committee on Constitution-Making, set up by the Indian National Congress (1946). With the establishment of the Samyukta Maharashtra Parishad, he became its member (1946–60) and also the Chairman of its Drafting Committee (1954–5). On behalf of the Parishad, he issued a number of pamphlets. He drafted the representation submitted by the Parishad to the Dhar Commission (1948), and the memorandum submitted to the States Reorganization Commission on behalf of the Parishad (1954). After the report of the Commission was published, he commented on it (1956). He viewed Maharashtra as a federal unit of India and advocated the constitution of similar other units, language being the primary determining factor.

Economics, for him, was the handmaiden of ethics, not an end in itself but an instrument to be perfected and appropriately used to serve the aim of establishment of an egalitarian and just social order. Gadgil viewed the process of socio-economic change in a historical perspective, keeping in view the economic, political,social, and cultural heritage of each country and the influences from outside. He viewed social transformation as, necessarily, a gradual and evolutionary process, because a society takes decades to adjust and absorb the new and to discard the old values, culture, and habits. A revolutionary upheaval may give a jolt and a sudden break from the past but it will not have an everlasting effect since the society cannot change overnight, and the dislodged old values and modes may reassert over time. Gadgil was a student of economic-social history and in this perspective, he put forth four tenants for bringing about socio-economic transformation in Indian society. These were social integration of the fragmented caste-ridden Indian society, decentralization of political power through multi-tier democratic institutions to realize participatory democracy, mass education and enlightenment to facilitate effective operation of democracy, and efficient functioning of co-operatives and people-centred economic development, with co-operation as the main vehicle of people's organizations since the majority of agricultural and other producers in India are small, weak, and scattered over 638 thousand villages.

Gadgil maintained that in the context of Indian society, which is fragmented into castes, creeds, and religious groups, and where civil society is not formed, radical social aims cannot possibly appeal to and unite the masses. The peasantry is isolated, illiterate, and steeped in the religious ideology of individual salvation and superstitions. Unless sustained efforts are put in for mass education and for institution building—institutions like co-operative societies, which help create mutuality, need to work in the interest of the collective and towards the mingling of members of various castes and religion—the basis for unity cannot be created. With this view he strove for education and training, decentralization, democratization, co-operative institution building, and working at the grass-roots level with the masses.

Gadgil considered mass education, training, and institution building on the basis of the toiler's collective efforts as the basic building block for breaking the fetters of caste-ridden feudal society and for moving towards a modern, decentralized, democratic society. He, therefore, was closely associated with and fully supported the mass educational endeavour of Bhaurao Patil through the Rayat Shikshan Sanstha, established in the 1920s in Satara district. Gadgil respected the work of outstanding leaders of the downtrodden masses—Mahatma Phule, who urged the masses to revolt against Brahminical hegemony and tyranny, Bhaurao Patil, V.R. Shinde, and B.R. Ambedkar who instilled confidence among the erstwhile untouchables and inspired them to get educated and to unite and struggle for human rights and dignity. Gadgil clearly saw the limitations of the social reform movement led by the Brahmin leadership whose influence remained confined to a tiny section of the upper castes. Their attempt to achieve through preaching what was denied to the economy was contradictory. Under the imperial rule, it was not possible to put into effect a socio-economic programme of productive economic renewal. The hold of fatalism and superstition on the peasants and other toiling masses crushed under economic exploitation could not possibly be loosened by propaganda so long as the material conditions remained slavish and wretched. Hence, during the colonial period, Gadgil restricted his work mainly to study and research of the ground-level socio-economic conditions. He got actively involved in programmes aimed towards socio-economic transformation when India attained independence.

Gadgil had plans to work with Lokamanya Tilak, not in the political movement but in the supportive economic sphere. He considered that paying attention to the political aspects of the problems with which the economist is confronted was of equal importance. However, Tilak passed away on 1 August 1920 and there was no more a possibility of coupling the political and economic work. There was little prospect of the release of forces of industrialization and agricultural development during the colonial rule. Gadgil, therefore, decided to concentrate on in-depth field studies at the grass-roots level, to deepen his understanding of Indian economic problems and participated in working out ameliorative schemes for famine relief, price control, and rationing during the war time. He also served on official committees that could help provide redressal to the people, for example, Textile Labour Enquiry Committee (1937–40), Provincial Food Advisory Board, Bombay (1943–50), and Agricultural Finance Subcommittee (1944–5). He also actively participated in bodies dealing with primary, secondary, and university education. He was a member of the Board of Directors of the Bombay State Co-operative Bank (1946–60). He advised on planning as Chairman of the State Development Committee for the Princely States of Kolhapur and Sangli.

As soon as India attained independence, there opened up possibilities of creating an appropriate institutional base so as to bring about changes in the material conditions of the peasants and other toiling masses and set in motion a process of economic progress aiming towards a rational, just, and egalitarian social order. With this view, he initiated, using as a base his rich insights into the ground-level realities acquired through field studies in rural and urban Maharashtra, the experience of working with official and other committees, banks, and other institutions, the integration of research, policy formulation, and implementation of the same through establishment of appropriate institutions. On the basis of such innovative experimentation he arrived at broad generalizations for wider application of the model. This is exemplified in a variety of fields in which Gadgil had taken active lead.

Gadgil was deeply concerned with the issue of credit and banking—the lifeline of agricultural and economic development. Freeing peasants and artisans from the clutches of the moneylender–trader by providing alternative channels of adequate credit was a prerequisite for rural development. The studies of farm economics, carried out during the 1930s by Gadgil through the Gokhale Institute in rural Maharashtra, had brought out the various facets of this problem. This was coupled with his grass-roots level practical experience. He was a member of the Poona District Central Co-operative Bank (1937–42, 1946–8), and its Chairman from 1947 to 1948. He was Chairman of the Poona District Purchase and Sale Union (1945–50). On the basis of the synthesis of his research and practical experience he prepared and submitted a note to the government on 'Basic issues in view of the Government's policy of canalising trade in essential commodities, especially in rural areas, into co-operative channels.' The note outlined his concept of regulated distribution of all essential consumer goods through co-operative channels. In 1947–8, he actively formulated detailed proposals for the reorganization of co-operative credit and in 1949, drafted the crop-loan policy resolution for the Board of the Bombay State Co-operative Bank. He became a member of the Bombay Area Committee of the Reserve Bank of India in 1941, then, a member of its Western Area Local Board (1942–52), and, finally, a member of its Central Board of Directors (1952–62). Following the Report of the Rural Credit Survey (RCS), the Imperial Bank of India was nationalized in 1955 and the State Bank of India was established. Gadgil became a member of its Board of Directors. It was the experience of working with the Reserve Bank of India and the co-operative banks and the operation of the crop loan system that enabled him to substantiate and elaborate it by means of the Report of the Rural Credit Survey of the Reserve Bank, the Committee of Direction of which he was a member (1951–4). This report constitutes the manifesto of the revolution in rural banking.

The RCS Committee recommended state partnership and the reorganization of co-operative credit, and the processing, storage, and marketing structure, through the setting up of a three-tier rural credit co-operative system—state, district and viable primary units, central- and state-level warehousing corporations and Land Mortgage Bank, and nationalization of the Imperial Bank. These were accepted by the government and put into operation in 1954. Through the responsibility for co-operative development that the RBI accepted and the initiative that Gadgil had taken as Chairman, Maharashtra State Co-operative Bank (1960–7), it was possible to develop a three-tier system of credit co-operatives, crop loan system and consumption loans for weaker sections, and support to rural industrial development.

Gadgil had taken up, through the Gokhale Institute, a pioneering study of economic effects of irrigation from Pravara and Godavari canals in 1938–40. The study brought out clearly that the benefits of irrigation could reach the peasants if they set up a co-operative sugar factory. This was an uphill task. Gadgil was a member, Board of Directors, Bombay State Co-operative Bank (1946–60) and Member, Board of Directors, Industrial Finance Corporation (1948–53). With the active involvement of the co-operative bank staff and the local leadership, it was possible to prepare a viable proposal for setting up a co-operative sugar factory and mobilizing the support of the peasantry to contribute to the initial share capital. Gadgil could secure financial support from the State Co-operative Bank, the Industrial Finance Corporation, and the government, through the active support of Vaikunthbhai Mehta, the minister for finance and co-operation, for the setting up of the sugar co-operative factory at Loni (Rahata *taluka*, Ahmednagar district). The factory was set up in 1949 and Gadgil was appointed the Chairman of the Board of Directors of the Pravaranagar Co-operative Sugar Factory. He shouldered this responsibility till 1960. Gadgil was able to attract competent and upright technical and managerial personnel, who helped establish the factory as an efficient business enterprise. All the loans and the share capital provided initially by the state government were repaid in eight years. The working of the factory and agricultural development in the factory area, through a decentralized committee structure that Gadgil had set up, helped wide participation and democratic functioning. This total experience, according to Gadgil, 'appears to suggest that it pays first to work deliberately and cautiously with a pilot and only afterwards to attempt rapid multiplication.' The pattern of organization, financing, and operation, evolved by the Pravara Project, served as a model. Gadgil and Vaikunthlal Mehta persuaded the Government of Bombay to restrict licensing of sugar factories only to the co-operative sector and extend financial support for the establishment of co-operative sugar factories. To help the spread of sugar co-operatives, the Federation of Bombay State Co-operative Sugar Factories was organized with Gadgil as its first Chairman (1956–9). He was, later, Chairman of the National Federation of Co-operative Sugar Factories (1961–7). He worked assiduously for the healthy growth of the co-operative processing industry in India. Gadgil propounded the Co-operative Commonwealth as the model for development in India. He considered it ideal for India because of the complex problem of organizing into viable economic units, lakhs of small peasants, artisans, fisherfolk, small business and service functionaries, and dispersed households toiling under a variety of socio-cultural conditions spread over the then 20 odd states of India. He envisaged co-operatively owned and operated farms, sale and purchase unions, rural industries, urban undertakings, banks and other service industries, housing and consumer co-operatives, with large-scale industries and services chiefly in the hands of the public sector. His ideas on the Co-operative Commonwealth were presented in a series of lectures delivered at the University of Punjab in Chandigarh in 1961. The Co-operative Commonwealth was preferred in comparison with State Socialism because the former is based on the voluntary union of small producers functioning democratically. The units of operation are decentralized and small, receiving support and aid from the state but not under direct control of the centralized state.

Throughout his long and sustained effort in the co-operative field, his senior colleague was Vaikunthbhai Mehta, whom he held in the highest regard and esteem. Gadgil was closely associated with Mehta in yet another field, namely, the village and small-scale industries. He visualized the development of these industries, using intermediate technology together with the modern and mechanized sector, under the aegis of the public sector. He stressed the need to restrict the growth of metropolitan cities and urged for decentralized industrial development and balanced regional growth.

Gadgil was a keen student of world history and a champion of the cause of the Afro-Asian countries. He viewed the present domination of the Afro-Asian countries by the Western powers as no more than a transitional phase in world history. He believed that, in the not too distant future, the Afro-Asian countries will occupy their rightful position in world affairs.

Gadgil was active with development issues much before most others in India and quite characteristically at the bottom. He was a member of the Consultative Committee of Economists (1942–7) and was a signatory to the 'Manifesto by Indian Economists on the Recent Economic Policy of the Government of India' (1942). He served as a member of the United Nations Expert Group to report on the 'Measures for Development of Under-developed Countries' (1951). He did not view the First Five-Year Plan very favourably and thought of it as no more than a list of schemes and projects. At the beginning of the preparation of the Second Five-Year Plan, the government appointed an Economists' Panel. Gadgil was, initially, a member (1955) and later, the Vice-Chairman (1959). For the Panel, he prepared his basic paper on 'Policy Decisions in Plan Making' and a number of other notes on various subjects.

During much of the Third Plan period, Gadgil devoted attention to the preparation of the Plan at the district level and prepared a concrete plan for Wardha district, Maharashtra state. During the period, he was also a member of the Planning Commission for Goa and spent considerable time in the preparation of the plan. The period was also marked by the establishment of *Panchayati Raj* Institutions at the district and lower levels in Maharashtra. With the help of these institutions Gadgil tried to put into action district planning.

In his opinion, the basic reason for the failure of Indian planning is, what he calls, a total absence of a policy frame and a regulatory framework. He attributed this to the growing influence in the government of the vested interests with a *laissez faire* bias, and of the technocrats. In consequence, in his opinion, the plan resources have passed into the hands of vested interests and have been employed in market-oriented uses. This has resulted in a failure to maintain stability, reflected in the unchecked increase in prices and the growing inequality in the economy. He believed that in order to achieve price stability, the essential requirements are restraints on luxury consumption and a price policy supported by much greater control over production, trade, speculation, and banking. He attributed the growing inequality in the economy to the lack of a regulatory frame, the failure to achieve diffusion of the effects of development, and the neglect of the employment aspects of development planning.

It is against this background that Gadgil accepted the responsibility of the Deputy Chairmanship of the Planning Commission in September 1967.

He was aware that it was an uphill task and that the task was as much political as economic. Nevertheless, he accepted the task with a sense of national dedication, as the country was plunged in 1967 into a deep political and economic crisis due to a series of disastrous events—the humiliating defeat of India in the border dispute with China in 1962, the death of Prime Minister Nehru in May 1964, the war with Pakistan in 1965, sudden demise of the Prime Minister Lal Bahadur Shastri at Tashkent in January 1966, the severe famine of 1965–6 and the increasing domination of the World Bank and the US government on policy decisions, the consequent steep devaluation of the Rupee in June 1966, infighting in the Congress Party and its defeat in the 1967 elections in seven states and a slim majority at the Centre, the abandonment of planning in 1965, severe food shortages, rising prices, and a spate of mass protects. As the influence of right-wingers, in and outside the Congress, was increasing, Prime Minister Indira Gandhi felt the need to take a radical posture and for this purpose economic planning had to be rejuvenated. She, thus, needed a person acceptable to the various political parties and to the people. With these considerations, Gadgil was invited to head the Planning Commission.

Gadgil had all along criticized the composition, role, and functions assigned to the Planning Commission. He was of the view that the function of the Planning Commission is to provide expert advice to the government in the matters of planning and development and the Commission should not have executive functions, and that it should include only experts in natural and social sciences, technicians, and economists. When these conditions were met, Gadgil agreed to take the responsibility of Deputy Chairmanship. He was fully aware that given the entrenched interests of the big business–politician–bureaucrat nexus, the regulatory framework that he considered basic to planning would not be accepted. The most he could achieve was to rehabilitate planning and to introduce a variety of ameliorative measures, and the devolution of plan funds on an objective basis so that the states can formulate their plans in a decentralized manner keeping in view the variety of the regional-level problems. In the aftermath of the 1971 parliamentary elections, the Planning Commission resigned in mid-March 1971 and the charge of Deputy Chairmanship was handed over by Gadgil on 30 April 1971. On 2 May, Gadgil set on the journey home from Delhi to Bombay but met with a fatal heart attack and died in the train around 11 A.M. on 3 May 1971.

The Political Economy of D.R. Gadgil*

P.R. BRAHMANANDA

THE MODERN TRINITY OF INDIAN ECONOMISTS

This is the centenary year of the birth of Dhananjaya Rao Gadgil, one of the members of the great trinity of Vakil, Gadgil, and V.K.R.V. Rao, who have been associated with the founding of three important institutions of training and research in economics, the first in Mumbai (the Bombay School of Economics), the second in Pune (the Gokhale Institute of Politics and Economics), and the third in Delhi (Delhi School of Economics, the Institute of Economic Growth, also at Delhi, and the Institute of Social and Economic Change at Bangalore). Vakil, Gadgil, and Rao also contributed to the development of economics in India, producing important literature in economics by themselves and jointly with others. They also, positively and negatively, influenced the thinking on economic policy and planning in India. All the three of them were intimately associated with the historic Economic Association of India. The Association took initiative in celebrating the centenary of C.N. Vakil at the Mysore Economic Conference by a special lecture. It is now similarly celebrating the centenary of D.R. Gadgil. The Association also discussed the contributions of each, Vakil, Gadgil, and Rao, in technical sessions in Mysore, Gwalior, and Hyderabad. I am, indeed, greatly beholden to Dr Bawa and

* Excerpts relating 'The Political Economy of D.R. Gadgil' from D.R. Gadgil Birth Centenary Memorial Lecture by P.R. Brahmananda delivered at 84th Annual Conference of Indian Economic Association on 30 December 2001 held at Vellore. Published in the *Indian Economic Journal*, Vol. 49, No. 2, 2001–02, pp. 82–94. Reprinted with permission of the *Indian Economic Journal*.

Dr Bajpai for asking me to deliver the Gadgil Centenary Lecture at this Conference.

GADGIL AS ECONOMIC HISTORIAN

The most famous work of D.R. Gadgil is *The Industrial Evolution of India*, first published in 1924. This book was based on the thesis written by Gadgil for the M.Litt. Degree of the University of Cambridge. The remarkable fact about Gadgil's book *The Industrial Evolution of India* is that it has very few references to the earlier works by Indian scholars on the above and related themes. There is no reference either to Ranade or to G.V. Joshi. There is, also, no reference to V.G. Kale, who had earlier written on industrial problems in India. Gadgil hardly makes any reference to the impact of the drain. *The Industrial Evolution of India* has been among the most successful books written in India. It ran into several editions. The hallmark of the work are the extraordinarily incisive observations at the micro levels on different aspects of the Indian economy. These observations are all from a neutral angle. There is no overtly or covertly a strong Indian standpoint. The book states categorically that, in India, the processes of change in industry were the same as those in the Western societies prior to and after the advent of the industrial revolution. There is no effort to discover any especially Indian economic characteristics as Ranade did. The hypotheses are all based on empirical data and the observations, at first hand, of the author. The treatment is thoroughly dispassionate. I may give one example—as an explanation for the large number of deaths due to the influenza epidemic, Gadgil refers to the poverty of the people, who had no capacity to wear warm clothes, as a cause.

UNDERSTANDING GADGIL

There was one, rather strong, viewpoint which Gadgil held all along. He argued that without a stable and policy-oriented relative prices structure, there would be no stable and regulated structure of incomes, especially in agriculture, and without a stable structure of incomes, there would be no security to the large masses of marginal and small producers in agriculture and small industry. But, he also pointed out that a relative prices structure implied powerful control at several points on the allocation of resources. Such control would require regulated licenses, ceilings, and permits all around. That sort of regulation required an honest and patriotic bureaucracy and an acceptance of the implications of the same by the political system. Gadgil was a strong pleader of a growing public sector in industry, banking, finance, and insurance. Besides, he wanted a state trading system in order to protect farmers from exploitation by trade and business. In the course of his continuous thinking and experimentation, he came to the view of a structure of co-operatives, especially in agro-industrial lines, as an alternative to both communism and capitalism. His experimentation in the sugar industry co-operatives in Maharashtra was the basis of the new ideology of a normative economic system, different from the other two extremes. While he was working with Deshmukh in the Reserve Bank on agriculture and the rural sector, he came to the view that the traditional thinking about co-operation, in which the role of the state was eschewed, was not suitable to the Indian environment. He wanted the state to play an active role in the promotion, financing, and regulation of the Co-operative Movement in India. He desired the Reserve Bank of India to take a lead in this respect. It was largely because of his influence that the Reserve Bank of India became a sort of a custodian of the interests of the co-operatives, especially in rural credit. Gadgil was instrumental in the initiation of periodic surveys, by the Reserve Bank, of financing channels and sources in the rural sector. As I mentioned earlier, he gradually encompassed agricultural raw material using industries in the sphere of co-operation. The farmers growing sugarcane could themselves start sugar factories in the co-operative sphere. Similarly in other agro-based raw material using activities. Agriculture was a state subject and it is here that he visualized a co-operation between the Reserve Bank and the state governments in the sphere of co-operation. The state governments, by developing the Co-operative Movement among agriculturists, could provide a countervailing power to the influence of capitalism in high industry.

STABILITY OF RELATIVE PRICES

Another contribution of Gadgil, to which I have referred earlier, was to constantly emphasize the significance of relatively low food prices as the most crucial distributional factor in the Indian scene. Careful studies of his writings bear out the important point that it is only in a federal and decentralized political system that programmes of local employment schemes can be worked out and implemented effectively. He realized that rural labour, and labour in small and cottage industries, would be largely unorganized and that in the absence of mobility, their interests had to be protected by the government through reservations of productions and arrangements for raw material, supplies, and so on. He was also for state purchases through minimum prices of a large number of agricultural products. The cotton purchase scheme of Maharashtra seems to have had his blessings. The approach of Gadgil is currently very important, particularly, in the light of the impact of WTO on Indian agriculture. Hundreds of crops are being produced in India and without a scheme of minimal state purchases at pre-fixed prices, agricultural producers and agricultural labour would have to face starvation prospects. The raw materials for industry can now be cheaply imported and it is the domestic producer who would face the crisis of emerging stock accumulation and unemployment. The state governments have no resources with them to deal with these problems.

When Gadgil emphasized the stability of agricultural prices, he was thinking of the stability of agricultural incomes for diverse crop producers. Prices are the source of incomes to the producers and the numbers involved are so large that consumption demand for many industrial products depends on the stability of agricultural incomes. Growth has to be subsumed on the foundations of stable agricultural prices.

GADGIL'S CRITIQUE OF THE ESTABLISHMENT

From an analytical angle, there were several points in Gadgil's critique, which, in my judgement, are independent of the second plan's strategy. (i) The bureaucratic process had an autonomy of its own and had not been trained to incorporate, in its functioning, the technical and policy implications of the second plan. (ii) The trade and business interests in the private sector were in a position to strongly influence both the bureaucracy and the politicians. These interests did not share either the concept of austerity in living and functioning styles, so necessary for accelerated capital formation, nor the vision of an egalitarian society. (iii) The political process was increasingly willing to getting influenced by the powerful and wealthy trade and business interests in the private sector. At the time when Vakil was the Adviser to the Planning Department, it was the bureaucracy which was a hurdle. By the time of the second and later plans, according to Gadgil, the two executing and implementing agencies, the politicians in power and the bureaucrats, had joined together in hostility to the day-to-day and longer-term implications of the policy processes of the plans, and these two governmental agencies had been literally bought over by the rich and powerful business interests in the private sector. Gadgil referred to the huge run-down in exchange reserves due to the liberal licensing in the early 1950s. He also strongly argued that the resort to deficit financing was not the cause for rising prices during the second plan. It was the absence of a structure of controls that was responsible for the rise in prices. He also believed that without a strong policy for regulating income and wage differentials and a lowering of the disparity ratio between the lower incomes and the top incomes, there would be powerful non-egalitarian processes let loose into the system, which would distort the priorities contemplated in the thinking behind the plans. He was especially critical of the emergence of strong consumerist influences in the allocation of resources and in the pattern of industrial development.

EMPIRICAL CRITIQUE OF MARGINAL PRODUCTIVITY

I may mention that in an address at Nagpur, Gadgil had examined the non-relevance of the marginal productivity theory of remuneration and of wages under Indian conditions. His point was that the payments to the government servants were the benchmark wage or salary in India and all other emoluments were largely related to the above. But the benchmark wage itself was determined arbitrarily by the government. I recollect vividly that Gadgil criticized the human capital approach as the basis for differences in emoluments, on the score that in India the payments to the government servants were the crucial determinant of all other types of emoluments. There was no question of applying the rate of return theory in the case of wage and salary differentials in India. As we are aware, the government does not suffer from the budget constraint and can determine the pay scales of government servants without reference to any concept of measures of productivity of government employees. The implications of the Gadgilian approach have yet to be examined in detail in India. Gadgil was very critical of the high emoluments for teachers and professors in the Indian system. Can any one of us say that these emoluments have any relation to the productivity of these parties? I remember the great Nurul Hasan wanted the professors to get as high emoluments as the collectors and that the UGC followed the norms set by him. This process has continued even now.

ANALYTICAL PROPOSITIONS OF GADGIL

Let me put together a brief list of the propositions on economics which can be gleaned from Gadgil's writings.

1. The fundamental motivations of the impulses governing economic activity in the process of economic and, especially, industrial development are the same in Western countries as well as in India. The differences in the pace of adaptations to technical changes are due to the constraints from the initial states, and the differences in policy perspectives of governments. Under foreign rule, interests of the rulers could be different from those of the people over whom they rule. (Gadgil took the view, in his *Industrial Evolution*, that the processes and consequences of change in India were the same as in Western countries. By this he incidentally refuted Ranade's hypothesis that the Indian circumstances were different from those in the Western countries at that time.).

2. The Indian development processes were slow because of the absence of an entrepreneurial class or an entrepreneurial spirit in the business sector of India. The latter was dominated by trading instincts rather than innovative and risk-taking propensities.

3. The distributional imbalances in the Indian economy were such that the lower strata of society, especially in rural areas, would be bearing the brunt of the adverse consequences of any economic change. The primary role of the state was to rectify the imbalances and to take special measures to insulate the lower strata from the adverse effects.

4. The bureaucratic and administrative as well as political apparatus in India was prone to be influenced powerfully by the trading and business

interests. Consequently, the distributional impact of economic changes, including those of planning, would be more and more adverse to the lower strata.

5. A scheme of permits, licences, and controls was necessary in the Indian economy to prevent the diversion of resources from accumulation to luxury consumption.

6. The failure of the changes contemplated by the second plan, and by subsequent plans, was due to the invisible links between the bureaucracy, the politicians, and trade and business.

7. Distributional aspects of economic processes were more important than the production-promoting aspects.

8. It was the rural and agricultural sectors that suffered most from exploitative processes in the economy. Hence, organizing production and distributions of activities in agriculture, and related lines, in the form of co-operatives was the most important institutional change for improving the lot of people dependant on rural and agricultural occupations.

9. Because of the absence of wealth and liquidity in the rural and agricultural sectors, it was necessary for the state to take an active role in the promotion and financing of the Co-operative Movement in India. There was also a need for state regulation of the working of the co-operatives in order to prevent the latter from coming under the sway of the exploitative processes of trade and business.

10. Under conditions of immobility of labour, difficulties in the transportation of food from the surplus regions to the deficit regions, as well as of the absence of communications between the regions, famines could be due to both deficiency of food supply in the drought-prone and rainfall deficient areas as well as deficiency of employment and purchasing power. The development of transport and communications in India, as well as a scheme of public works, both mitigated famine, especially in the twentieth century under the British rule. The explanation of why a more severe drought in most parts of India in 1920–1, than in 1899–1900, did not lead to a famine has to be accounted for in terms of the above two factors. The concept of an aggregate supply deficiency in food supplies has to be interpreted in different regions in terms of the relative obstacles to the movement of grains. (I may add that this explanation can also explain the 1943 Bengal Famine. Supplies from Burma had been stopped; even boat transport had been suspended; but, according to some, there was also an additional factor about the rigidities of food consumption habits; wheat could not be substituted for rice.)

11. Methodologically, the concept of a macro economy seems to be untenable in the conventional sense. There is a collection of different sectors of production with differences in the conditions of production among them. There is a collection of labour working in the different sectors, again, with differences in their conditions. There is a collection of regions in a

country with different conditions of production among the regions. The aggregate should be viewed in terms of a federal composite of different regions, not necessarily specializing in different branches of production. A federal aggregate of different partial categories is different from a macro economy. In that sense, each region itself is a macro category with its own specific conditions of production, social and economic class distribution of wealth and incomes, and problems thereof. The macro picture, then, is a collection of macro regional categories with a federal system of governance.

GADGIL'S CRITIQUE OF WESTERN THEORY OF ECONOMIC POLICY

In my judgement, the best analytical writing of Gadgil is his Presidential address in 1941 to the Indian Economic Association's Mysore Economic Conference. The address is titled 'Some Conceptual Issues in Economic Policy-making'. Whereas Ranade had challenged, in his 1898 lecture, the relevance of classical economics under the then Indian conditions, Gadgil challenges the foundations of the theory of economic policy as was in vogue immediately after the Keynesian revolution. The lecture has references to the great names of that period like Viner, Keynes, Harrod, and Robbins. Gadgil appreciatively refers to Keynes' contention that the monetary policies of different countries will have to be governed by the specific economic and historical contexts of these countries. He refers to Viner's critique of the popularly understood positions of Adam Smith. He has a pertinent reference to J.B. Say, who accepted the possibility of technological unemployment and desired an ongoing programme of public works to mitigate the hardships of the unemployed. Say also did not desire technological changes to be introduced suddenly. Just note how pertinent that reference is, particularly in the context of the popular impressions created by Keynes about Say's belief in automaticity of full employment! Gadgil refers to Harrod's statement of the economic criterion in which he states, 'If an individual prefers a commodity or service X to Y, it is economically better that he should have it. Similarly, if the individual prefers work X to Y, or dislikes it less, it is economically preferable that he should have it.' Gadgil refers to the case of an individual preferring drugs, say, to food. Should society allow this? Gadgil's point was that there was a social or a society's angle on the consequences of untramelled *laissez faire* in consumers' choices. He argues that Harrod's economic criterion could not be termed as a universal criterion. Similarly, the defence of *laissez faire* cannot be made on universal grounds. Gadgil supports himself by quoting Viner, who maintained that economic and political formulations in the liberal tradition are dogmas and not axioms. Gadgil asks the question: why should the preferences of individuals be taken to be axiomatically supreme and why should the criterion neglect the group or the society. He then shows that very often the interests of concerned parties who benefit by a particular measure are often portrayed as the interests of society. He refers to the cotton excise duty, which was in the interest of Lancashire. He then examines the case of the moneylender–trader nexus and the element of exploitation of the poor peasants. He shows that the rightful share in the margin for the latter is never obtained. The failure of a policy of *laissez faire* to generate corrective forces, even in the very long term, is only too obvious over the whole field of Indian rural credit. He points out how the marginal productivity theory of wages could not explain differences in the same areas in wages for similar types of work. He shows that industrial labour in most cases at that period was highly exploited and the normative conditions of remuneration and work did not obtain in most portions of India. He takes up the case of how the British transported the landlord system to India without being aware of the social conditions here. He points out that the landlords in India never functioned as pioneers of agricultural improvement. He then shows that Indian industry had no entrepreneurial spirit and was unlike the German industrial leaders. He concludes by stating that we must reject the *laissez faire* bias in economics speculations, reject the pseudo universalism, which merely consists in the assumption of a uniform set of conditions ruling in the world without an enquiry into the differing needs and circumstances of the various peoples.

Gadgil then argues that the adverse effects of the industrial revolution and technological changes in the West were transmitted to the people in countries like India. Further, without a high rate of growth and of prosperity, technological revolutions would lead to large displacements of labour and cause untold hardships. Gadgil then makes the profound observation that a changing society in the technological sphere is a society in perpetual transition and unless we devise programmes of perpetual public works to take up the dispossessed in employment there would a continuous insecurity in the country. While commending the British for the famine relief programmes, he argues that such a programme has now become continuously necessary.

Gadgil looked at equilibrium economics, with its just price concept, as relevant to a static and stationary society. Dynamically, every economy is continuously in disequilibrium in terms of techniques, commodities, preference patterns and prices and quantities. But, from a human angle, equilibrium is necessary in terms of employment and/or incomes. The Western societies have achieved minimal securities in these latter respects. We have no capacity at present to have even minimal securities in employment and/or incomes. That is why our economy, particularly after opening up, is getting lost in myriad insecurities at the local, micro, regional, and group levels from an economic angle. We have to look at Indian economics in a different way than in terms of the economics of countries like the USA and the UK. The social, economic, and political environments in India are very different from those in the developed countries where minimal securities have been obtained and the states stands ready to enforce them. In our setting, the free play of market forces, in a context of full opening to international influences and shocks with the state walking out of its traditional responsibilities, is causing anarchy in production, distribution, employment, and prices. This anarchy, in an ocean of insecurities, is simply causing enormous disruptions with absence of any healing touches. Economic lives in India are now like boats in a huge ocean of uncertainty without moorings and directions. It is a great challenge to economics in India to develop an orientation and a theoretical frame to understand our problems in the current setting. Gadgil was making efforts in this direction in the sphere of policy.

I submit that Gadgil's major contribution to the understanding of the economic process was his perception that continuous technological changes and other exogenous shocks are normal in a changing economy. Equilibrium economics, with compensating adjustments built in, holds only in a static society. Since, technological changes and shocks disrupt traditional employment and productions all around, so countries like India are in perpetual disequilibria. The role of the state is to device instruments of policy and agencies for implementation as would minimize the hardships to the poorer strata of producers in society. It is in this context that he described the Indian economy as in a perpetual transition of adjustment to influences over which it had no control. That was the main lesson he learnt from the study of industrial evolution in India during the British period. Gadgil came out with the solution of the permanent adoption of types of public works in a continuous process as mentioned by J.B. Say. He did not object to technical change or the shocks which were parametric constants to societies like India. What could be done in an independent country would be the establishment of a technological framework which could generate technical changes within. Probably, this was one reason why he supported the Mahalanobis strategy. In that context, the adjustment to shocks could be probably tamed and controlled. Even then if we accept Gadgil's hypothesis of the economic process as a continuous transition ('a traverse from a traverse to a traverse'), at the policy level, the provision of security of employment as such, and minimal incomes to all, becomes an all important duty of the state. This role of the state, in my judgement, is new and cannot be escaped by the political leaders if they have to depend on support from the people. Gadgil looked at the poor law system during the classical economists' period as having served some useful cushioning purpose. He realized that there was a resources constraint in India, but pleaded for frugality and austerity and state intervention in distribution as measures necessary over a very long period in India. He would have been appalled at the luxury consumption promotion strategy of the current phase in India. He would have probably felt that in the wake of the

WTO shocks, the economy had to undergo continuous transitions with upsets in employment, production, distribution, and prices. Consequently, a massive programme of public works, supported by savings along with low prices of essentials, would have been the components of state policy in India at the present time. His belief that a 5 per cent growth rate would solve problems was probably mistaken because we have realized that the employment elasticity of growth is becoming lower and lower and we also know that huge distribution inequities have also accompanied our market oriented growth process.

Methodologically, the concept of a macro economy seems to be untenable in the conventional sense. There is a collection of different sectors of production with differences in the conditions of production among them. There are groups of labourers, working in the different sectors, again with differences in their conditions. There is a collection of regions in a country with different conditions of production among the regions. The aggregate should be viewed in terms of a federal composite of different regions, not necessarily specializing in different branches of production. A federal aggregate of different partial categories is different from a macro economy. In that sense, each region itself is a macro category with its own specific conditions of production, social and economic class distribution of wealth and incomes, and problems thereof. The relevant macro picture, then, is a collection of macro regional categories with a federal system of governance.

1. State purchases at minimum support prices of commodities produced in agriculture and related activities.

2. State finance of activities of distribution of inputs at subsidized prices for the agriculture and related producers.

3. An RBI sponsored programme of network of rural credit agencies with re-financing at subsidized interest rates.

4. Development of organizations of farmers to develop agro-industries by the establishment of factories which would process raw materials produced in agriculture and related occupations. Knowing that the Centre would normally pay scant attention to the needs of rural producers, Gadgil favoured the establishment of state government financed and regulated co-operatives. This would also help accounting and monitoring.

5. Looking to the problem of surplus labour pressure in agriculture and acute unemployment and underemployment therein, Gadgil favoured an ongoing programme of regular public works at moderately low real wages.

6. Noting that the producers of cottage and handicraft industries, as well as of yarn and cloth, were at the mercy of demand vagaries, Gadgil favoured the reservation of spheres with regard to a number of consumer goods, so that labour-intensive and skill-intensive activities in rural areas could thrive.

7. Gadgil also wanted the macro level regulation of allocation of foreign exchange, finance, licenses, and so on, to prevent and forestall the development of luxury consumption of industries, and to insulate the economy from international shocks.

8. Gadgil wanted austerity in public expenditure, primarily, through a relatively lower level of salaries and wages for individual servants. He believed that the wages and salaries in the public sector had a powerful influence in fixing wages and salaries in industry, business, trade, and finance. He wanted the disparity ratio to be kept as low as possible. The Servants of India Society's emphasis on austerity, dedication, and hard work had impressed him.

9. Gadgil believed in fiscally strong state governments and wanted devolution of the power and responsibilities of the central government, except in crucial areas.

10. Gadgil did not want primarily an anti-poverty programme in terms of distribution. He wanted a large number of productive and related measures with activities focussed in rural and agricultural areas, supported and, if necessary, subsidized by the state. The state, in this context, would be mostly state governments working through decentralized district level administrations. To repeat, he believed very strongly in the classical motives of hard work and thrift.

Let me conclude with two thoughts on Indian economics, one on theory and the other on policy. The intertwining of macro analysis, plans, and policies with the micro and even district- and village-level specificities of needs and problems is the type of economics which is best suited for India. The theoretical framework for this is more complex than visualized in Keynes' General Theory or in the general equilibrium models. My own wage-goods model has to be integrated with the micro-level specificities in targets, channelling policies and implementations. In Keynes' 'General Theory', broadly, the aggregates of different macro magnitudes are deemed to be composed of sectoral and individual items which are largely homogenous within. This endows policies also to be free from spatial and sectoral constraints. The incidences of the underemployment problem, as well as the causes for the same, are assumed to be the same within an economy for different sectors and activities. We cannot proceed in this manner in a country like India. The aggregate problem of unemployment, or of poverty, is made up of heterogenous components notional and has to be broken into its regional and activity-wise subsets. The generalized market approach, and in a context of open economy, will simply aggravate the magnitude of the problems. At the fundamental theoretical level, Gadgil raised the question of the intersection of distribution, exchange, and production insofar as the large numbers of producers and producer–consumer categories are concerned. We cannot, then, treat price formations as independent of production and distribution. Nor can production itself be separated from distribution. Alfred Marshall himself provided a fundamental critique of the separability of exchange, distribution, and production by pointing out in an article in an economic journal dealing with distribution and exchange that a portion of distribution, and in the Indian context, often the whole of distribution, becomes a condition of production itself. Hence, the notion of exchange which enters into the determination of prices has to take into account the encompassment of livelihoods in the process of exchange itself; it is in this context that, say, producers of crops as well as of small and cottage industry products and self-employed service employees seek direct purchases of their productions and services and look up to the state to protect them in the case of failures of supplies and shocks arising from demand fluctuations. Minimum subsistence cannot be looked upon only as a result of poverty alleviation transfers or of employment schemes in times of distress. The subsistence for millions of producers has to be worked out as part of regular productions and purchase price arrangements by the state or its agencies. Theory and policy in Indian economics have to become different from those in developed countries. A study of American or British economics cannot substitute for the building up of theoretical and policy structures for the Indian economy, if at all we care about the well-being of the substantial majority of producers and people therein.

I

Planning in India

The Issues

1

Indian Economic Organization*

An attempt is made in the following to set out in brief the salient features of Indian economic organization. India is a large country and has an enormous variety of natural conditions. The stage of development reached also differs widely from region to region. In the circumstances, a brief general description necessarily involves considerable, somewhat arbitrary, simplifications. Approximately 85 per cent of the population of India lives in the countryside. About three-quarters of residents in the rural areas are directly concerned with primary production; among primary production agriculture is overwhelmingly important.

The typical unit of agricultural production is the peasant family farm. Land-tenure systems vary widely from region to region, but the scale and the organizational characteristics of agricultural production are comparatively uniform. There are states in which the ownership of land is concentrated to a considerable extent in the hands of a comparatively small number of persons; in other states, the bulk of the land is held by cultivating-owners; and there are situations and systems lying between these two extremes. In almost all states, however, the actual cultivator operates on a comparatively small scale, chiefly with the help of family labour. The status of the cultivator-tenant, owner, etc., may differ, and the burden of rent may vary, but the organizational pattern remains the same. This characteristic differentiates India from other important types of agricultural economies. Large estates do not mean, in this country, large agricultural units worked either as feudal estates or as modern farms. They

* Originally published in Simon Kuznets, Wilbert E. Moore, and Joseph J. Spengler (eds), 1955, *Economic Growth: Brazil, India, Japan*, Durham: Duke University Press, pp. 448–63.

have always been parcelled out among, and worked by, small tenantry. The abolition of landlord systems in India has, thus, not the same consequences for productive organization as in the countries of, say, southern and eastern Europe. The dominant form of capitalistic organization in agriculture—the plantation—which has become important in many under-developed countries during the last two centuries has also been confined to a comparatively small field of India. The plantation is the dominant form only in the cultivation of tea, coffee, and rubber; and the cultivation of these crops is highly localized. Within their own regions, which are for the most part mountainous regions, unsettled previously, the plantations are the most important organizational type; outside these regions their influence in agricultural production is insignificant.

The form of tenancy does not materially affect agricultural production. Crop-sharing, which is widespread all over the country, normally means the supply, by the landlord, of a proportion of the working capital. But this does not lead to a larger investment of working capital resources in crop-sharing units as compared with the farming of cash tenants.

The geographical conditions are extremely varied and the circumstances in which agricultural production is carried on are equally so. At one extreme stand large, arid regions with a scanty soil surface, a meagre supply of subsoil water, and a small and uncertain annual precipitation of rain. Agricultural production activity in these regions is highly precarious, barely profitable, and confined to only a part of the year. On the other hand, there are rich alluvial tracts where the soil is highly productive, the rainfall is plentiful and certain, and where supplementary irrigation facilities make secure an appropriate supply of water throughout the year and its intensity raised to a high pitch. Among all these varying circumstances the size of the typical peasant family holding remains small; that is, as related to the supply of labour within the family available for employment on the farm. Under favourable external conditions this leads to migration, seasonal or semi-permanent, of members of peasant families. The volume and duration of migration depends chiefly on employment opportunities available to migrants. This may be casual or seasonal labour in the neighbourhood, either agricultural or non-agricultural, or seasonal or permanent employment in distant regions. Where agricultural activity is confined to a part of the year, this may be held to generate streams of annual seasonal migrations. But seasonal migration is usually the result, not of conditions in which agricultural activity is carried on, but of conditions of living and employment in the region of alternative employment. For, in most rural regions which supply migrant labour, the extent of chronic underemployment in agriculture is so large that these could supply, in appropriate circumstances, much larger numbers of migrants, seasonal or permanent.

The capital resources of the peasant family are correspondingly small. The stock of working capital and the resources available for capital development are both limited. India is an old, settled country with a large population. Therefore, such development of land resources as can be carried out with family labour and with the implements and draft cattle available to the average peasant, has in this country proceeded very far. Similarly, the intensity of cultivation compatible with the limitation of resources is also considerable in appropriate circumstances. The technical level at which productive activity is carried on varies; but in the more settled and developed areas the traditional technique is fully exploited, and ordinarily no marked improvement could be brought about without a considerable increase in the capital resources available to the peasant family.

The pattern of productive activity is shaped by the organizational type. Broadly, there are three purposes which productive activity has to serve: food for the family, fodder for the livestock, chiefly draft cattle, and a surplus for sale. The small size of the productive unit and the differences in terms made by the wide margins at both sale and purchase make for an emphasis on domestic production, as far as possible, to serve the first two needs. Ordinarily, even with an increase in unit size and with almost complete commercialization, production for domestic needs does not vanish though its proportionate importance decreases rapidly. This is statement of merely a common characteristic. Its manifestation will be different with differing sizes of units and different crop combinations. For example, on very small farms, or among what may be called part-time farmers, the need for a cash income may lead to a cash crop being grown, or part of food or fodder production being sold, even though the remainder is not fully sufficient for family and farm business needs. In the same way, in areas where extension of cultivation of particular cash crops is widely possible, especially at times of a relative increase in the prices of these crops, cash crops may expand to the extent of making some purchase of food and fodder necessary, even on a large farm. It is not often, however, that such a position is reached. The production pattern thus contains everywhere a core of self-sufficiency. The share of production included within this aspect does not come on the market and is not monetized. Another part that is non-monetized or only partly so is that in which the primary payments are made in terms of produce. The most important part of this is the payment in terms of produce, to casual or permanent labour and to artisans. Crop-sharing in the case of the smaller landlords may also be classed with this.

The structure of the agricultural labour economy is shaped by the dominance of the peasant family unit. This means that the majority of production units in most agricultural regions do not offer employment to outside labour except at times when pressure of seasonal operation makes such employment necessary. However, the distribution of the size of cultivated holdings is uneven, and only a small proportion of units in most tracts would demand the employment of agricultural labour on a more permanent basis. This would be the more prominent, the more highly commercialized and intensively developed agriculture was in any particular region. In such regions, again, the monetization of the larger part of the economy would have brought about a greater concentration of land operation and capitalistic agriculture, on the one hand, and a permanent body of landless agricultural labour, on the other. Such regions would, however, be exceptional. For the larger part, agricultural units employing agricultural labour through the year and families of purely landless agricultural labour, would be small in numbers, and the bulk of agricultural families would employ casual and seasonal agricultural labour and would be the source of supply of such labour.

Agricultural productive units, as sketched above, would come into contact with the outside world and with modern economy, chiefly, through the monetized sector of their operations. The extent of this would be defined by the extent to which the peasant producer family, in its aspects of both producer and consumer, needed to trade with the outside world and to the extent that its economic relations with outsiders made necessary dealings in money. And it may well happen that the latter aspect may in some cases be the more important. The agriculturist would have such relations chiefly with the landlord, the state, the moneylender, and the trader. Rent, where it had to be paid in money, taxes such as the land revenue, the water charges, and the payment of interest, etc., on the debt would all necessitate converting the produce into money form. To the extent that any of these payments were inexorably timed, the sale of given volumes of produce would be enforced on the cultivator at particular times. These monetary payments, especially those in connection with debts, may also have the effect among the smaller and poorer units of monetizing an unduly large share of the economy. Many of these units find it necessary to sell a large share of total production to satisfy immediate and pressing demands at one time of the year and to buy back for consumption needs part of these sales at a later period.

Agricultural produce available for disposal would come into the hands of the producer in significant quantities only at fixed periods in the year. The requirements for making outlays, both as producer and consumer, would be more continuous throughout the year. Hence the need for credit. The funds for repayment would accrue, chiefly, through the disposal of the surplus of agricultural produce. Credit would thus be linked with the marketing of agricultural produce; and moneylending and the marketing of agricultural produce and also general trading activities would tend to be combined by one agency. In economies where the landlord holds the dominant economic position, moneylending may be connected with this class.

The smaller the scale of the peasant and the greater his ignorance and his distance from the market, the more would he be dependent on the trading-moneylending class and the greater would be the margins they would command. Apart from the scale of individual operations, the development of the transportation system of a region and the extent or demand for the product offered by the agriculturist for sale would determine the strength of position of the agricultural producer. In the extreme case of the sugar-cane producers of Bihar and the United Provinces there exists, at present, a guaranteed purchaser at prices fixed by the government, in the local sugar mill. In crops like cotton there are, in most important cotton areas, a large number of regulated markets where the producer is usually certain of obtaining a price in fair relation to current quotations on the commodity exchange. Again, in commodities like cotton and some others, agents of exporters or local manufacturers often operate in producing regions for obtaining supplies immediately after harvest. The advantage of these comparatively sensitive markets will be available only to producers who are free to sell their produce in the way they think most suitable. A wide—preferably international—market, competitive purchase, good transport facilities, and freedom to sell enable even small producers to obtain fair market prices. This entire conjuncture is, however, obtainable only in a minority of cases, and on the whole, the dependence of the producer on the trading classes at all times is considerable.

This dependence is emphasized by the fact that the processing of most products is in the hands of classes allied to the trading and moneylending classes. Formerly, some aspects of processing, such as husking and, partly, milling and decorticating, were conducted by the producers themselves; too, the whole economy was more nearly self-contained. With greater commercialization and the marketing of a large portion of some crops, processing began to be divorced from agricultural production, especially after power-driven machinery was introduced for most of these processes. Consequently, today, in all areas where the crop is an important commercial crop, husking and milling, ginning and pressing, hulling and decorticating are conducted in centralized units operated and owned by non-producers, except in the rare instances where they are co-operatively managed. The one important instance of processing still remaining mainly in the hands of producers is that of the somewhat elaborate process of the manufacture of raw sugar from sugar-cane. The key position of processors in the disposal of produce and the fact that they are usually able to combine among themselves for determination of terms of operation weakens still further the bargaining position of the agriculturist producer.

The productive organization of rural industry had many features in common with the organization of agriculture. It was conducted essentially on a family basis and drew usually on the supply of labour of the whole family. Its capital resources were meagre, it tended to be underemployed, and the income yielded by it was consequently low. Attention needs to be drawn to one aspect of Indian economic organization in which it appears to differ from other similarly placed economies. The ordinary peasant household in India is not self-contained in relation to most industrial products and personal service needs. In this respect, comparative self-sufficiency is the attribute not so much of the individual household as of the village community. The agriculturist aims at satisfying family and business needs by his own production so far as concerns food, fodder, and—one may add—fuel. For other products and services he depends on the specialized artisan or other families within the village community. The carpenter and the blacksmith, the potter and the cobbler, the barber and the washerman are all resident artisans entitled to a small part of the crop on the threshing floor. Most of the repair work on agricultural equipment is performed not by the agriculturist households but by the resident artisan families. In a large number of cases, the artisan families would also have small cultivated holdings and would thus be part-time farmers. This would be the pattern in all the large settled plains areas in most regions of India where social life was organized in substantial village communities. In mountainous areas, where isolated dwellings or hamlets were the rule, households would be somewhat more self-sufficient.

The complement of artisans integrated within the village community organization would not be the same everywhere; this would be related, in particular regions, to products and services required continuously by the peasant families. An artisan industry whose products would be demanded only occasionally or periodically would not be so evenly spread and would not be connected integrally with the organization of the village community.

From the point of view of organization, rural artisan and cottage industry may be divided into two classes. The large majority of artisans who were scattered widely over the countryside lived in close proximity to consumers of their products and services and did not face complex problems of credit and marketing. To a large extent their work was connected with the maintenance and repair of equipment; in a number of instances of original production, raw material was supplied to them by customers, and they got paid mainly for wage work. Not only would the majority of rural carpenters, blacksmiths, potters, and cobblers fall within the class but also basket- and rope-makers, and even oilmen, may be mostly included in it. Artisans of this class would also be most likely to be part-time farmers in many instances. Their field of operations would be limited to a village or a small group of villages and the non-monetized sector in their business would be considerable.

The other class of rural artisans, though located in rural areas, would face problems of productive organization similar to those of traditional urban handicraft. The most numerous among these would be weavers of all kinds. This class of artisan or handicraft industry—rural and urban—would be dependent on the trader both for supply of raw material and sale of product and would need credit for carrying stock and for sustenance during the average length of the period of production. This credit would be almost invariably obtained from the trader at either the one or the other end, except in the not unusual cases where both ends of trading would be concentrated in the same class of trader. These artisan units would be even more dependent on the trading intermediaries than the peasant agricultural families, for there would be no element of self-containedness in their economy. In this class, also, transition would be made from organization on the family basis to the basis of a workshop; there would then emerge capitalistic owning of equipment and the employment of artisans on wage work away from their homes. Even when this capitalistic form of organization emerged, most of the artisans and handicrafts industries operated as long as it was traditional, within specially circumscribed limits.

These limits were set by technical considerations. In this respect, the position of Indian artisan industry differed from that of Indian agriculture. At least as far as the domestic market was concerned, Indian agriculture was not faced with competition from production which was the result of superior technique of agricultural units either within the country or outside it and, barring the notable case of indigo, domestic production of particular agricultural products had not been affected by technical industrial advance. Traditional Indian industry, on the other hand, had faced for a century or more, and continued to face, a market which was continuously shrinking at a varying pace as the result of increasing variety and cheapness of machine products. The continuous pressure of the competition of machine industry had compelled traditional Indian industry to adapt its methods, readjust its stages, and limit the variety of its products; but whatever the equilibrium reached at any time by these processes, it was liable to be upset afresh by further extension of the field of machine products, forcing traditional industry to further limitations and fresh adaptation. The survival, within given limits, of the traditional industry was itself dependent on taking partial advantage of modern industrial technique. Thus the weaver used machine-spun yarn; the metal worker, machine-produced metal sheets; and the leather worker for the major part, leather produced in modern tanneries. And where improvements for strengthening the competitive position of traditional industry were proposed, these involved taking further advantage of modern technique. Such were proposals for setting up central reeling, winding, or sizing and warping plants for handloom weavers or for improved types of bullock-driven oil mills fitted with ball-bearing.

The most important result of these conditions was that traditional industry, whether conducted on the basis of the family or of the workshop unit, suffered continuously from underemployment or unemployment. The underemployment suffered by peasant agriculture was the result of limited land resources and a growing peasant population, giving a small and diminishing holding per family unit. The underemployment in artisan industry was the result of a diminishing field of demand for the products of that industry. In both cases the situation was revealed in the low income per worker; all calculations indicated that the average income of the small scale artisan industry unit in India was as low as the average income of the peasant agricultural unit.

The Industrial Revolution affected Indian agriculture primarily through increasing commercialization and monetization of agricultural economy. The first impact was through the increased demand created for agricultural products like cotton. The transport system in regions where these products could be grown was rapidly developed, and the incentive of a large money income led to the extension of cultivation of particular crops in these regions. Beginning with a few crops and regions the movement became, in time, widespread. As pointed out above increased commercialization or monetization did not essentially change the unit or organization of productive activity. It did not, also, materially influence technique. Some new crops were introduced, the varieties in many were improved, in particular regions a new implement like the iron plough made progress; but there was no technical revolution. The most important change was in the relative economic strength of the landlord, trading, and moneylending classes. The disappearance of the older political and social regulations and the establishment of the British judicial system strengthened the position of all these classes vis-à-vis the agriculturist producer and affected, correspondingly, the distribution of the increased incomes due to the commercialization of agriculture. During the last three decades legislative regulation has greatly undermined, in a number of regions, the position of the landowning classes. However, in spite of seeming policies to the contrary, the position of the trading and moneylending classes is as strong as ever, and they continue to derive the greatest benefits from every improvement in the terms of trade of agriculture.

The nature of the impact on traditional industry has been already indicated. The first influence was the increasing imports of products of machine industry. This led, in course of time, to the disappearance of many old handicrafts, urban and rural, and the continuous narrowing of the field for most others. The efforts at survival of these led to many adjustments in production and adaptations in technique.

For the impact of foreign influences the initial process was the opening up of the country. The most important aspect of this was the construction of a railway system connecting the main ports with important agricultural regions. This was done by British capital either private or borrowed by the government. At the same time the road system was developed, and improved types of bullock carts were introduced. Thus, within a few decades, a revolution from the older system of pack-animal transport for internal trade was brought about. The main immediate effects of the development of this transport system were the distribution of imported machine-made goods throughout the country and the export of important raw products in increasing quantities. Indian traders participated from an early stage in the distribution of imports and the collection of raw produce for exports; the foreign side of the trade was throughout the nineteenth century in European hands. Ancillary to trading activities were the credit institutions of the modern type, especially banks, mostly in the chief ports, established from the early days by the British. The first excursions, in modern production activity, were plantations—tea and coffee. In connection with the export of agricultural products, certain processing activities were begun. Then followed the exploitation of minerals and lastly, manufacturing industry. Indians played almost no part in the nineteenth century in the development of plantations or mining. However, together with internal trade, from the start, Indian trading communities undertook processing activity in a large measure. One important feature of the development of industry in India was that in western India, with Bombay as the nucleus, manufacturing industry developed in Indian hands from the very beginning. The chief reason for this seems to have been the presence of old established financial and trading houses and communities in Gujarat, Kathiawar, and Kutch which were ready to take advantage of the new opportunities. As a result, the cotton industry, which developed chiefly in western India, was always predominantly in Indian hands.

Till World War I the policy of British Government in India was dominated by somewhat peculiar 'liberal' concepts which led to the imposing of a counterbalancing excise on Indian cotton manufactures, the moment a small revenue duty was imposed on imports of British cloth and to the banning of even the establishment of an Industries Department by the government of a province. There were many other difficulties such as those in obtaining prospecting licenses, etc., in the way of progress of modern business in Indian hands. At the beginning of World War I, economic activity of the modern type was very limited in India. Manufacturing industry was represented chiefly by the cotton and jute textile industries, plantations chiefly by tea and, and only to a very small extent, by coffee, mining by coal, begun chiefly by, and for, railways, and general engineering chiefly by railway workshops. There was also the processing, and a small number of minor, industries. All these, except the cotton textile and processing industries, were predominantly British owned and managed. Modern banking was represented by the Presidency Banks of British origin and the branches of foreign banks; insurance was conducted mostly by foreign companies and coastal shipping by steamers was carried on mostly by British firms of either Indian or British registration.

During the first decade of the twentieth century Indian banks and insurance companies were first established and some change in policy of the state was brought about after World War I. Modern business in Indian hands steadily increased in volume and diversity during the interwar years. The Indian beginnings in each line were usually with the smaller scale operations; the British still continued to do the pioneering in most new fields. An important new development during this period was the establishment of subsidiaries by important international groups or units; this was part of a world-wide movement. Concerns like the Imperial Chemical, Unilevers, Dunlop (tires), Westinghouse Electric, General Motors, etc., established either completely owned subsidiaries or allied concerns in collaboration with Indian capital. During the interwar years activity of British and other foreign business interests did not recede. They continued to hold their main, developed positions in the older fields and initiated many new ventures. However, Indian business grew at a much more rapid pace; hence, its proportionate share had become substantial in most fields on the eve of World War II. Apart from the older fields of jute manufacture and coal mining and plantations where Indians obtained significant shares, they made special headway in new lines such as iron and steel, hydroelectricity, cement, and sugar. Their growth in banking and insurance was vigorous; they began to participate in coastal shipping and took a substantial direct share in foreign trade. The number of stock exchanges in 1914 was three; of these, Europeans dominated only the Calcutta Exchange. During the interwar years stock-exchange business, mostly in Indian hands, grew in a large measure. And in all important centres in the country a number of commodity exchanges, in which the speculative element was important, also sprang up.

A more radical change in the situation came about in the forties as accompaniment to the withdrawal of British political power. Many Indian capitalist groups made large gains during wartime and were willing to offer favourable terms for the acquisition of British interests in all types of business. The somewhat uncertain future induced many British businessmen to seize the opportunity, and there was fairly large-scale transference of ownership and management from British to Indian hands. It is, however, possible to exaggerate the total effects of this transference. Details regarding transference of ownership are difficult to ascertain. However, British interests still continue to control the major portion of the jute, coal, and tea-plantation industry and have large and important units in most other manufactures. The activities of foreign banks and insurance and shipping companies continue to be important, and the sphere of operation of subsidiaries or Indian collaborators of the dominant international units or groups is not decreasing.

The existing structure of Indian economy contains within itself a large number of divergent elements. In each aspect it has, in particular, an important residue of pre-Industrial Revolution forms and usually also an important element of the most advanced industrial technique and organization. In transport, for example, side by side with the aeroplane, steamship, railways, and mechanical road transport, there exist country craft and bullock carts; and the share of the latter continues to be very considerable. In finance and banking, the indigenous system had been well developed in pre-British times for the conduct and finance of an extensive long-distance internal trade; money changing and a system of trade and financial bills were fully operative. With the extension of trade in agricultural products, a connection had been established between urban indigenous banking and traders and agents in rural areas. Today there is, in the country, a modern monetary and banking system; there is a central monetary and banking authority in the Reserve Bank of India; and the Imperial Bank, whose growth has been state-sponsored, has an intermediate, somewhat anomalous position; the finance of international trade is still largely in the hands of branches of foreign banks, and within the country, banking has developed in the direction of the concentration of deposits and business in the hands of a small number of giant concerns with a wide-spread network of branches. Even so, the banking system has not reached the smaller centres of trade and the ill-defined policy of the government towards co-operative forms has not enabled co-operative marketing, processing, and banking organization to cover any substantial part of the field. The primary field of trading and finance still continues to be occupied, therefore, by surviving parts of the older system. The relation between the two systems is, however, not well articulated; and this makes for difficulty in proper regulation, and in the implementation of positive policy.

The development of modern industry has been on the usual lines of extension, mainly in textile and other consumer-goods industries such as sugar and vegetable oils. Because of specially favourable conditions, and of tariff protection, an important iron and steel industry and a cement manufacture have been established. Heavy chemicals, production of machinery, electric equipment, and other capital-goods industries are still in their infancy. The future progress is dependent on planned effort, whose direction and extent are, however, yet unclear. Today, though industrial production is much more diverse than it was two decades ago, its total extent is small in relation to the size and requirements of the country. Employment afforded by modern industry is very small; the vast bulk of industrial employment is still in other forms. The total proportion of urban population—approximately 15 per cent—is itself an index of under-development. Apart from modern large industry, towns afford employment in a large number of miscellaneous industries such as *bidi* or country cigarettes, bakeries or flour mills, or various branches of building trades; they also give occasion for a considerable body of modern types of workshop activity for repair, maintenance, etc. The main industrial employment, however, still comes from the traditional artisan industry of the types described above. In special instances new intermediate forms of industry, such as the power-loom industry, have arisen; but they are confined to few industries and localities and are not numerically important. Between the two fields of traditional and modern industry there is, however, little integration. Two types of rationalized arrangements have, for example, been reported from countries like Japan. One relates to the division of markets between the two types of industry and the other is the accommodation of traditional skill, cheap human labour, and domestic working by division of production by processes, some of which are allotted to domestic industry, in the structure of modern industry. Intelligent action on either line is not evident in India; hence the haphazardness of the process of transition and its associated social and economic costs are both enhanced.

In the early stages of industrial development, capital and management as well as technical personnel were all foreign. The displacement of foreign influence has come about in all lines; and today, excepting a small number of highly specialized experts, technical personnel are normally Indian. There are no special difficulties in the way of recruitment or training or in bringing about an adequate increase in the supply of such personnel. Experience during war also shows that, when required, the minimum technical training of industrial labour, even for munitions factories, can be accomplished rapidly through intensive methods. The strength of trade unions in India is also not considerable and unless backed by state and legislative support they would, in the large majority of cases, find it difficult to stand up against employers and their associations. The total potential supply of industrial labour is very large indeed. The main difficulty in the way of its proper utilization seems to be the conditions of living and employment in the main centres of industry. The important point to notice in this connection is the heavy concentration of modern industry in India in particular centres and regions.

The initial development of the transport system was such as to lead to a concentration of modern business activity in the main ports. First developments in manufacturing industry also took place chiefly in the port areas. With later growth concentration in the ports, especially Calcutta and Bombay, has become particularly intense, and within the other centres in the country there has been an equal tendency to concentration and overdevelopment. This means that not only are there a small number of centres of modern industry but also that they are unevenly distributed; the economic life of large regions is thus practically unaffected by the forces of industrialization. It also means that the social problems in the industrial centres are especially acute. Housing conditions are very bad, and family living is practically impossible for the bulk of industrial labour in most industrial concentrations. There is an entire absence of social-security services such as sickness or unemployment insurance or old-age pensions; this further makes it impossible to build up a permanently settled industrial labour force even in the largest cities. Ill health, instability, unnecessarily large and frequent movements of labour between the cities and rural areas of origin are natural consequences.

Another feature of the development of modern business is the concentration of trading and entrepreneurial activity in comparatively small sections of the total population. Because of the dominance of caste in Indian social life there has always been a high specialization of occupational distribution. The trading and financial castes have always been highly urbanized and have rarely undertaken directly agricultural or handicraft productive activity. However, it is these communities that had the resources and acquaintance with business technique required to venture in fields opened by modern business. A small number of these castes, therefore, chiefly supplied and continue to supply, in the main, those who occupy the field not only in trading and finance but also the entrepreneurial role in modern manufacturing activity. Caste and community bonds help to maintain and accumulate strength gathered in particular fields and also the extension of activities to others. As pointed out above, the crucial economic position in relation to agriculturists and artisan industry is also occupied by the members of these communities. Members of the industrial labour force and the technical personnel usually belong to entirely different sets of communities.

The Indian business castes have been habitually traders, financiers, and moneylenders. The demarcation between trade and finance was never sharp in India, and a large number of individuals and firms combined both functions. Because of the fairly rigid association of occupations with caste, none of these castes have traditionally engaged in what might be termed direct productive activity. They have always been highly urbanized, and their contact with agricultural activity has been confined to moneylending and trading. They have, also, not been directly engaged in handicraft or artisan activity. They traded in the raw materials required and the finished goods produced by artisans, and they might lend money to artisans or, perhaps, finance the whole field of activity in particular handicrafts. In the last case they would take on the entrepreneurial role; but this would not involve any direct participation in productive processes or activities, which would be left entirely in the hands of members of the traditional artisan castes.

Parsis alone among the important Indian business communities had a background which was in marked contrast to this. In pre-British times they had little share in banking or finance and were engaged, to a considerable extent, in both artisan industry and agriculture. Their entry into trade chiefly followed on their association with the British, and it is noteworthy that their first entry into modern industry, in Bombay City, at the beginning of the nineteenth century, stemmed out of their initial employment as master carpenters in the shipyards by the British. The Parsis had the advantage of not being fettered by any of the numerous taboos and prohibitions associated with members of Hindu castes, and they adapted themselves quickly to new conditions after the advent of the British. They were employed largely as agents for supply and other needs by the British and were among the first Indians to enter modern industry.

Others who followed have mainly belonged to the traditional Indian moneylending, trading, and financing classes. The earliest among these were trading and financing classes from Gujarat. Gujarat's cities were known for many handicraft industries; and Gujarat had, always perhaps, been one of the most urbanized regions in India. In agriculture also Gujarat was one of the richest and comparatively one of the least overpopulated tracts. The spread of activities of business communities from Gujarat in the modern field within their home region, in Bombay City, and in special fields all over the country has therefore been large. In a similar manner, trading and financing communities from among other parts of India entered modern business and industry in successive stages. To a small extent members of new professional classes which arose under the British entered this field, especially in the first decade of this century during the *Swadeshi* Movement and after. They have, however, not yet effectively occupied a large part of the field of modern business.

At the present moment the most dominant single class in Indian business is that of Marwaris. These have been comparative late-comers into the field of modern industry. The term 'Marwaris' usually includes Jain and Hindu Bania communities originating in parts of the geographic area called Rajaputana or Rajasthan. The Rajaputana region is mostly arid and has not been able to support a flourishing agriculture or a large population. Also, it does not lie on important international or internal trade routes. The economic activities for which Marwari communities are noted thus take place almost entirely outside the home region of these communities. Though they are found to be specially concentrated in certain regions, the Marwaris are more generally spread over the whole country than the Gujaratis or any other group of business communities. Another important fact regarding them is the part played by them as rural moneylenders in many regions of India. Members of other groups of business communities are usually not found as village moneylenders outside their home region. In most parts of India whenever there is an important alien element in rural moneylending this is usually that of the Marwaris. Some decades ago the chief centre of Marwari activity in modern business was Calcutta. Since 1914, their share in modern business in northern, central, and western

India has rapidly increased; and they have recently made considerable headway even in Bombay City.

The differing traditions and backgrounds of different sections of Indian businessmen are important because they continue, largely, to mould the attitude and behaviour of their members in the conduct of modern industry and trade.

The bias towards financial manipulation, rather than production performance, has been greatly accentuated by the general prevalence of the 'managing agency' system. British companies who pioneered industrial and economic development in India on modern lines during the nineteenth century were usually formed and incorporated in England while their actual business was carried on in India. In the then prevailing conditions of transport and communication it was impossible for a British company directly to conduct this business. In the circumstances, there arose a practice by which British firms in India having British personnel continuously residing in the country undertook the actual conduct of the business in India on behalf of British companies. For this they were paid a commission and an allowance. This arrangement was called a managing agency, and in time the important British firms in India—chief centre was Calcutta—came to hold managing agencies of a number of companies and in various businesses. It also happened that initiative for floating British companies for particular projects was taken by the managing agency firms themselves. In this case, the prospectus of the company would itself state who the managing agents of the company were intended to be, and the reputation of the agency firm would help the promotion of the company. The institution of managing agents thus arose out of a peculiar situation. When Indians and Indian companies entered modern business, the institution was naturally adopted from the British in India. In the early days, when the capital market was undeveloped and Indian personnel experienced in managing modern business limited, the agency system had some justification, even though the business and the company were not separated by large distances. Also, in the days before the growth of modern banking, Indian managing agents, who were in origin mostly financing or trading firms, were useful in the supply of working capital to industry. Today the situation has changed completely and it is no more difficult for a company in India than in the United Kingdom to manage its business through a manager or a managing director. But the managing agency system is by now strongly entrenched, and it has in recent years served as a device by which rising financial groups have brought under their control established companies in a variety of industries and trades. Legislation was passed in the thirties which put a term—renewable, of course—to all managing agency agreements and which indicated a basis on which commissions might be determined. Events of the last decade show that this legislation has not much effect. Fresh legislation is at present under contemplation, but is encountering much opposition.

This feature of the situation gives a very peculiar turn to Indian developments. It helps to retain control of the productive organization primarily in the hands of financiers. And it leads to agglomerations or combines of a peculiar type. The trend in India is not, as elsewhere, for either horizontal or vertical combines around a central productive activity. Instead, there arise, because of the operation of the managing agency, large financial combines with a very mixed composition, since the link between the various members in the group has not been technical production or trading considerations but only financial opportunity. It has been calculated that towards the end of World War II the seven biggest managing agencies in India (four of which were British controlled) gave employment to more than 7 per cent of the total employed persons in modern plantation and manufacturing concerns in India and that the corresponding percentage for the first twenty was more than 14. It will be realized that concentration of this type made action as pressure groups much more effective than when the sphere of individual combines was confined to particular spheres of economic activity. The effect was intensified by the control, by many of the biggest managing agencies, of banks, insurance companies, and also newspapers.

Another feature of the Indian situation which helps concentration of economic power is that no legislation in restraint of monopoly has even been enacted, or even contemplated, in India. Not only are there no laws comparable to the anti-trust laws of the USA, but even nothing on the pattern of the postwar anti-monopoly legislation of the United Kingdom has been thought of. As a matter of fact, the government has found it convenient to deal with trade and industrial associations, has encouraged their formation, and has sometimes given them legislative recognition in such matters as price-fixing procedures. This has given an impetus to the formation of producer and trader associations in each important field of modern business, and the more influential of these have freely indulged in price-maintenance and price-raising activities.

2

Notes on the Government of India's First Five-Year Plan*

The following are brief notes on the draft outlines of the First Five-Year Plan. They are intended to bring to notice certain important gaps and points of criticism. In these notes the plan has been examined chiefly from three points of view: (i) The programme of investment that has been set out and the manner of its determination; (ii) The measures proposed for attaining targets and production plans, their adequacy and efficiency; and (iii) The social directives in the Indian Constitution and the possible economic and social results of the plan.... (p. 1)

PROGRAMMES OF INVESTMENT

The main investment outlays are concerned with agricultural production; and chief among these are the irrigation and power schemes. It is not clear how the list of irrigation and power schemes included in the plan was made up. There could, for example, be two important criteria used in locating expenditure on irrigation developments. Firstly, expenditure on irrigation works could be concentrated in regions where insecurity on account of scarce or uncertain rainfall is heavy; or expenditure could be concentrated in regions where additional production brought about because of investment in irrigation gave the largest returns. In practice, some consideration may be given to both these criteria.

An examination of the actual works finally included in the five-year plan in relation to, for example, Bombay State, shows, at least apparently, a disregard of both these criteria and can be explained in relation to no obvious

* Submitted to the Planning Commission in September 1951, published in *Economic Development and Cultural Change*, Chicago, March 1952. Reprinted in *Planning and Economic Policy in India*, D.R. Gadgil, GIPE, Poona, 1972, pp. 1–21.

tests on which the final decision could be supposed to have been based. ... (p. 1) It should be noted that this area contains one of the most extensive tracts of peninsular India liable to famine. Irrigation expenditure in this tract secures not only protection but also leads to increased production in a specially large measure per acre because of the low utilization capacity previous to irrigation. Both these special advantages have been recognized since the days of the Irrigation Commission (1900) and a large number of projects have been in an advanced state of preparation for a long time. The entire elimination, progressively since 1944, of irrigation works in this tract, excepting for one work on which nearly one-third of total expenditure has already been incurred, is presumably based on reasons which have nothing to do with economic or social objectives. ... (pp. 1, 2)

An additional criterion for investment expenditure on development could be disparity in regional development. The poorer regions should obviously be allotted special priority in development investment if such investment can profitably be made in them. From this point of view again, the allocations made in Bombay State are difficult to understand. The Bombay State allocations have been specially referred to because I have personal knowledge of comparative conditions within the state. Nothing is, however, said in the plan to indicate that in framing the plan of irrigation investment in other areas also any set of criteria or tests had been adopted.

What is said regarding irrigation seems to apply equally to investments for generating electric power. ... (p. 2) A plan of development of electric power which is not integrated with a plan of development of industries, with special reference to their location, is thus completely meaningless. At present, investment in electric power generation appears to be proposed merely because certain engineering possibilities exist. Obviously in this respect, as in schemes of irrigation, a series of criteria and tests must be laid down for testing priorities of investment expenditure.

A necessary corollary of generating electric power in regions where there is no demand for it or where *pari passu* proper industrial development is not planned is that the power is diverted to distant centres of existing industrial concentration. This further intensifies regional disparities by diverting the developed resources of backward regions for the increased benefit of the already well advanced. Thus, here, as elsewhere in the plan, it is assured that those who have, get more.

Another aspect of plans of irrigation and electric power development is the planning of the subsidiary and ancillary works that are necessary for the proper utilization of water and electricity. It has been the experience both in India and the USA that without the previous planning of such works an unnecessarily large time elapses between provision of water and electricity and its full use, and even when full utilization is reached, it does not, when left to chance, necessarily take the most desirable directions. It does not appear that this aspect of the problem has been at all attended to in the schemes drawn up for the five-year plan.

We may next consider another main aspect of investment expenditure, that of industrial investment. A plan for industrial investment may be framed in relation to a number of criteria. These criteria, it may be expected, will be explicitly stated in the plan for the first five years, of what is presumably a long term development process.

There is some discussion of priorities in planning in the sphere of industry, chiefly from the short period point of view, in the plan. From this discussion it would appear that the development of producer goods industries is related chiefly to the development plan of agriculture, irrigation, and electricity. Curiously enough, generation of electricity itself is nowhere considered as having special significance only in relation to a plan of potential industrial development. Even with a recognition of the fact that conditions in India are favourable for the expansion of steel, cement, and fertilizer industries, no substantial provision for investment in these industries is made in the plan. Similarly, though it is recognized that the development of other producer goods industries is useful from the point of view of establishing some sort of balance in the industrial structure, no special provision for the expansion of these industries has been made. The same gap is evident in relation to pig iron, though the report places more emphasis on it. As a matter of fact, the additional industrial investment visualized in the plan is very limited and the increase in production of even important consumer goods industries is to be achieved chiefly by utilization of fuller capacity. ... (pp. 3–4)

In the entire field of large scale private industry, the total new investment is expected to be of the order of Rs 125 crores. This, together with the requirements of the accumulated need for replacements and renovation, is expected to require a total investment of about Rs 250 crores. The figure of Rs 250 crores is in addition to the Rs 80 crores that are provided as investment on account of government in the field of large scale industry but is inclusive of an indefinite sum, of the order perhaps of Rs 35 to 40 crores, which may be provided through semi-official agencies like the Industrial Finance Corporation or directly by the government. It is thus clear that the five-year plan visualizes only a very limited expansion of industrial equipment or employment, and that further it does not plan this development in such a way as to lead to any progressive expansion of employment or an elaboration of the industrial structure in subsequent periods.

In relation especially to a country like India, it is obvious that importance should be attached to an increasingly complex structure of economic society and the generation of a rapidly increasing pace of non-farm employment. The plan of industrial development should properly have been presented in the light of some such general considerations. The fact that it is not so presented makes it difficult to pass an informed judgment on it. In all countries at an early stage of development special emphasis is placed on the rapid growth of basic industries on which the later development of industrial structure depends. (This is emphasized by the almost equally urgent consideration of defence industries.) In countries in which the fundamental conditions are not favourable to the increase of basic and capital goods industries special efforts are made to force their growth. It is thus surprising that in spite of the favourable conditions for production of basic materials such as pig iron and steel no large planned provision is made for their expansion. Thus apart from the details of the plan of industrial development, the relative weight attached, in the plan, to agricultural and industrial investments, is itself difficult to appreciate. ... (p. 4)

The picture of the industrial employment plan becomes even more confused and less intelligible when one considers the section on small scale and cottage industries. The total expenditure by the government on these industries provided in the five-year plan is less than Rs 16 crores. At the same time, however, these sectors are relied upon to provide the main avenues of additional employment of the future. The development of small scale and cottage industries is supposed to be capable not only of providing additional employment but also of building up local industries capable of expansion and of developing domestic markets. It is unfortunate that a sector on which so much is supposed to depend is treated most unsatisfactorily in the plan. ... (p. 5) The basic problem of economic development in a country like India has been described as that of underemployment; and it is the lack of continued employment in agriculture together with its inadequate equipment that is supposed to be responsible for its very low productivity. It needs to be emphasized that the productive efficiency of the small scale and cottage industries is equally low, and that the low product per worker in all cottage and most small industries is also due to inadequate equipment and underemployment. The problem of small scale and cottage industry has to be consequently treated essentially in the same way as that of agriculture; only there are two circumstances which make the task of development of rural, cottage, and small scale industry even more difficult than that of agriculture. There are no possibilities, such as that of irrigation works in agriculture, of the intensification of exploitation in the field of small scale and cottage industry. Secondly, the position of these industries is being continuously undermined, to an extent unknown in agriculture, by competition with the products of large scale industry.

The rehabilitation of these industries is thus a delicate problem which has at least three important aspects: (i) finding out ways of technical and economic reorganization which would make production in these industries much more efficient than at present without altering its social character; (ii) investment in capital and technical training required to bring about this reorganization; and (iii) guaranteeing, for a given period, a sheltered market for the product of these industries so as to make the reorganization possible and durable for a minimum period. Without these three steps a proper rehabilitation of small scale and cottage industries cannot be contemplated. Even when all these steps are taken employment in these industries is not likely to increase. All that could be done would be to stabilize the employment by stages at progressively lower levels, but attain, at the same time, higher productive efficiency.

Not only is additional employment in small scale and cottage industries difficult to visualize if their productive efficiency increases but also all the three steps indicated above require action and investment which are not visualized in the plan. With the measure of expenditure given in the plan and the steps contemplated in it, an increase, neither in employment nor in the levels of earnings in these sectors of industry, seems to be possible. ... (p. 6)

PRODUCTION PLANS

We may now turn to the production targets set up in the plan and the manner in which they are expected to be attained. ... (p. 6)

The only means of planning agricultural production contemplated in the plan is that of village production councils. The village production council is obviously not a suitable agency for overall decisions like general regional crop plans or targets of production. Unless crop plans for comparatively large homogeneous areas are worked out in the broad and legislative or other regulatory devices framed for directing cultivation or laying down lower and upper levels of particular crop allocations there is no guarantee that the targets in the plan will be attained. With an area crop-plan backed by regulatory powers and devices, village production councils may prove useful; but without it the energies of these councils are not likely to be specifically directed, and their performance is likely to vary enormously with local circumstances. ... (pp. 6, 7)

The main reorganization proposal in relation to agricultural production is that for the promotion of co-operative farming societies. It is no exaggeration to say that there are today, in most states of India, no co-operative farming societies proper in existence and that the formation of these has been found to be one of the most difficult problems in co-operative organization. The pooling together of existing holdings of land and forming a joint co-operative productive organization has been realized everywhere to be the most difficult and logically the last step to be taken in agricultural reorganization. There are a number of steps which would have to be taken to increase the income of the agriculturist and to influence his productive methods and efficiency before going on to complete co-operative organization of production. The most serious handicaps of the agriculturist and the largest sources of his loss of material income are the marketing and processing activities. Even in times of boom the largest advantage is obtained by the intermediate merchandising and processing agencies. Also these agencies are chiefly instrumental, through a variety of practices, in making difficult the progress of co-operation and the operation of state measures of direction and control in all sectors of rural life. It is surprising, therefore, that the plan nowhere makes any reference to the important part played by marketing and processing activities in agriculture and the possibilities of reorganization through their being nationalized or being brought into the co-operative fold. ... A programme by which all marketing of agricultural products comes within a period in co-operative hands is a *sine qua non* of agricultural advance. There is also a strong case for nationalization of agricultural processing activities. ... When processing is nationalized and marketing comes into co-operative hands it would be found easy to influence productive activities of individual agricultural producers and gradually conditions may be created in which a further step forward, i.e., in the direction of co-operative farming, may be taken. ... (pp. 7, 8)

We may next turn to proposals relating to industrial production. Almost all large scale industries are left in the private sector. The programme of suggested expansion in this sector is said to be based on previous discussions with private industrialists. Presumably it reflects the judgments or expectations of leaders of industry in that sector. It is, therefore, not a programme drawn up by the Planning Commission in relation to certain overall objectives and trends determined by the Commission, but only a summary of what the private industrialists think may well happen during the next five years. Perhaps this curious species of planning is the only one possible in the Indian type of mixed economy. ... (p. 9)

There are two main aspects to the industrial development programme of the Planning Commission. There is, in the first instance, an increase to be brought about through fuller utilization of existing capacity. In most existing industries, increased production is estimated to come about much more through a better use of present capacity than through increase in installed capacity. It is obvious that this expectation could be fulfilled only if extensive measures in such directions as the rationalization and standardization of production could be enforced by the government on industry. There is no discussion in the report of the Planning Commission, of action required for the utilization of the private capacity, and regarding the powers of the government there is only a reference to the Industrial Development and Control Bill. This Bill, as it has emerged from the Select Committee, is an obviously inadequate instrument for the enforcement of a plan. ... (p. 9)

The unrealism of the whole production plan becomes even more marked when the proposals for production planning in relation to small scale and cottage industries are taken into account. The whole plan regarding the development of small scale and cottage industries is dependent on the ability of the government not only to direct the production of small scale and cottage industries but also to delimit the markets of large scale, small scale, and cottage industries respectively. Such delimitation involves control on the production pattern and quantitative performance of domestic and large scale industry and of imports in specific direction. There is nothing in the report of the Planning Commission to show that the Union Government or the state governments will be given powers on this behalf or indeed to show that the Planning Commission considers any such powers essential for the fulfilment of its own plan. ...(p. 10)

No reference is made in the report of the Planning Commission to policy relating to industrial prices. In so far as the Planning Commission depends on an integrated price policy as the chief instrument of directing production in agriculture, and presumably in industry also, it would have been expected that the Commission would discuss some of the more difficult problems of devising a price policy which could be effective for this purpose. ... (p. 11)

SOCIAL EFFECTS

A third important point of view relates to the social effects of the plan. The Planning Commission claims to have been guided by the directives set out in the Constitution of the Indian Republic. It is necessary to see how far this claim can be sustained. Comment may be made on a preliminary defence that is likely to be offered. It may be argued that the First Five-Year Plan is in the main a production plan and that the planners will turn to specific social objectives after production has been significantly raised during the period of the First Plan. The validity of such a distinction between a production and a distribution plan must be challenged. A production plan is necessarily based on a specific productive organization of society. A plan of development, while increasing productive activity, must necessarily strengthen the important economic and social elements in the existing production structure. If, therefore, there exist strong vested interests or dominant or ruling groups in the production structure, a production plan which pays no attention to social or distributive effects will inevitably increase the economic strength and social and political power of the vested interests and the governing elements. The operation of such a production plan would make it not less but more difficult to frame and carry out a plan for attaining social objectives at the end of the period of the first plan. It is, therefore, essential that the social directives of the Constitution be paid attention to during the period of each plan. This is apart from the consideration that no plan is likely to arouse the enthusiasm of the majority of the population, which all planners desire, unless it is expected and demonstrated to make an immediate beginning towards attaining of a more just and equal order in society. ... (p. 12)

The Planning Commission contents itself with a vague statement of abstract policy relating to agricultural credit. The large problem of financing the rehabilitation of depressed areas and classes it entirely ignores. Even for the financing of the smaller body of creditworthy farmers it suggests nothing concrete. ... An integrated system of agricultural credit will require drawing upon the resources of all existing financial agencies and institutions. It is symptomatic of the present trend in Indian economic policy that thought should be now concentrated on subsidizing private commercial banks and the Imperial Bank of India for extending activities in rural areas, rather than on how a co-operative-cum-state system could draw upon the resources in private hands to finance agricultural industry in a systematic manner all over the country. The Imperial Bank has been helped in the past to increase its activities and currently holds large governmental funds. The nationalization of the Imperial Bank is obviously an important and necessary step in building a countrywide system for the finance of agricultural production and marketing. ...(pp. 13, 14)

Indian rural society presents today a picture of a mass of uneconomic and poor production units that are ordinarily and without help unable to reap much benefit from such a phenomenon as the rise in prices. The benefit of an investment or development programme in such a society, will equally be unavailable to the large mass of poor producers, unless special efforts are made in that direction. ... (p. 14)

What is necessary, however, is to emphasize that in all under-developed economies where lack of resources and ignorance are so widespread, as among the majority of producers in Indian agriculture, a development plan is bound to result in increasing inequality of wealth and distribution even without a bias in favour of the rich such as is reported to have been avowed publicly by the Bombay Irrigation Minister. The experience of the *laissez faire* regime of the British period confirms this conclusion which one would expect even on *a priori* grounds. It was necessary to draw attention to this issue with some emphasis as there is nothing in the agricultural plan of the Commission which could counteract this strong inherent tendency. ... (p. 15)

It would be noted that public investment in the five-year plan is largely concentrated in irrigation projects and that the direct effect of these irrigation projects will be confined to very limited areas. In these limited areas the major benefits will be derived by a comparatively small number of specially advantaged people. As pointed out above, the plan makes no reference to marketing and processing activities, which are to a very large extent in the hands of private persons, who are the major exploiters in the rural sector. The plan leaves this aspect of the matter entirely outside its consideration. In the agricultural sector, therefore, it can be said to entirely ignore social objectives and to be content with the continued operation of present trends which make for increased inequalities of distribution.

It has been indicated above that the use of electric power generated by the multi-purpose etc. schemes has not been planned. To the extent that the power is used privately for irrigation and other agricultural purposes, it will benefit the bigger farmers who alone will be in a position to afford it. In the field of industry, increased electric power may serve social objectives only if it is deliberately used for the dispersal of location of industry or for encouraging smaller units. This could be achieved if, not only is there a previous detailed plan of industrial development and location related to schemes of generation of power, but also if the specific measures indicated above for demarcation of the field of small industry are taken.

INDUSTRIAL LOCATION

In the matter of location nothing whatever is said in the plan. ... (p. 16) It is notorious that in the absence of regulation or direction private enterprise naturally prefers location in the biggest centres, and that the private entrepreneur class, as a whole, never undertakes deliberate development of backward areas, as from the point of view of returns to the private investor these are ordinarily not attractive. The absence of a plan of industrial location and of the development of backward areas is another important gap in the five-year plan.

By neglecting to pay any attention to this aspect of the problem the plan helps the continuance of present trends of concentration of economic power and the continued increase in the riches of those classes and regions which are already comparatively richer. This trend is most clear in the attitude of the Planning Commission towards private industry. All large scale industry is to continue to remain in the private sector. At the same time, all existing plans of state aid by protection, allocations, subsidies, etc., for the growth of private industry will continue. In addition the plan makes provision for the supply by the state, directly or through semi-official corporations, of large funds to enable the largest industries to expand production and improve efficiency. It is one of the curiosities of the results of recent official policy that whereas the state, since 1947, has been giving continuous relief to industry and to the income and super tax payers, presumably, to aid further investment in industry, the biggest and the most central schemes of expansion of industry have still to fall back on the state for investment capital. It would also be interesting in this connection, to calculate the extent of the tax-relief the state has given in recent years and the results that this has had in terms of additional investment. ... (p. 17)

The continuance of the private sector is apparently not justified by performance. More importantly, it results in continuously increasing unequal distribution. A glance at the industrial growth of India during the last 30 years makes clear how almost each industry has grown through support, direct and indirect, given by general revenues or by laying burdens on the general consumer. In terms of the distribution of income and wealth in society, the process of industrial advance, which was largely the result of state policy and social sacrifice, has meant an increasing concentration of wealth and income in the hands of restricted groups and a limited number of individuals. This policy is to be, evidently, pursued through the five-year plan. When the government lends money for industrial expansion to a private concern or helps to build up or reform particular units by special technical assistance or other aids, it is, in fact, increasing wealth in private hands through expenditures and costs which are borne by the public at large. There appears no justification for this procedure. It is indeed doubly inequitable; it not only increases artificially the present income-earning capacity of particular individuals or classes at the cost of the general public, but also later when the possibility of acquiring any of these concerns by the state arises, it would have increased, by present policy, the capital compensation that the general public which has helped to build up the concerns or units will be called upon to pay. ... It is clear that either the field of industry has to be increasingly nationalized or, at least, to the extent that in any sphere industrial units continue to receive assistance directly or indirectly, this must be accompanied by suitable conditions both as regards their present incomes and future compensations. ... (p. 18)

The spheres in the Indian economy today, in which large incomes and opportunities for considerable capital formation arise, are strictly limited. These are the fields of large scale industry, finance, and trade. It is in these fields specifically that the government postulates the necessity of private operation. Obviously, therefore, all talk of social objectives in the plan is futile. ... (p. 19)

There is obviously a clear case in relation to important export industries for assumption of an export monopoly by government. This is supported by action taken in many undeveloped economies. It is also the only possible method of enforcing a proper price policy in relation to commodities of which prices on the international market are liable to fluctuate widely. However, though this view has been pressed on the government by various boards and committees since 1947, it has found no favour and the five-year plan, though making vague references to possible state trading, formulates no concrete proposal in any particular respect.

To sum up, the existing distribution of wealth in our economy is very uneven and a small number of people in each sector are placed in strategic positions; it is these people that stand to benefit most from any large public investments leading to economic development. Large public investments, in circumstances like ours, lead to all sorts of unearned increments; these accrue to a few and whatever the increase in national product that is brought about by the investment, it is distributed in an even less just manner than the distribution before. This tendency could be counteracted only if special precautions are taken in the plan of public investment itself. These precautions could be: (i) limiting, by legal action, existing rights of private property....; (ii) providing in the investment plan itself for the dispersal of investment or of the effects of investment; or (iii) fiscal policy designed to redistribute increased incomes. (i) is too radical to be considered by this government, and (ii) has not been provided for in the plan. (iii) Fiscal policy for social redistribution would have two aspects: (a) taxation; and (b) expenditure in relation to tax income. The plan makes clear that no burdens heavier than the existing ones are to be laid on the rich. The only redistribution measure specifically included in the plan is the suggestion for the imposition of death duties. This is a hardy perennial and whenever it is implemented it would require a period of decades before its distributive aspect really became prominent or effective. From the fiscal point of view there is thus no corrective to the inherent inequitable tendency of the plan indicated above. There is nothing also to indicate, on the expenditure side, that the plan may lead to a correction of social inequality by any measures of state regulation or expenditure. The plan contains a section on what are called social services; almost the entire expenditure under these is merely the summation of current expenditures already undertaken or planned by the state and central governments on such services as education and health. Even in relation to these there is no indication of a new policy or a special redistribution of the effects of expenditure. None of these expenditures are, for example, of the type that may be termed transfers, i.e., either through measures of social security or through subsidizing of particular activity or product, making for an indirect increase in the income of the poor. A possible exception is the expenditure on industrial housing. I have already indicated, however, that this expenditure is of doubtful social use. As a matter of fact, it is possible to argue that such expenditure, by making possible the continuance of location of industry in congested areas, which only benefits factories owned by industrialists in these locations, is in the long run actually inequitable. ... (pp. 19–20)

In the other direction, it may be pointed out that the whole fiscal policy underlying the plan is one that makes for increased inflationary pressure. The policy of controls and state powers outlined in the plan is not such as to hold these pressures effectively in check. Therefore, to the other trends of the plan a continuous inflationary movement may add further inequality on the distributive side. A reference may be made here also to the absence of a foreign trade plan. It has been suggested that that plan is yet in the making. It is important to note, however, on the distributive side, that in England the increased standard of living of the poor and decreased standard of the rich was brought about largely through controls of exports and imports. No such policy seems to be contemplated in the five-year plan, so that the standards of consumption of our rich will not even have the ceilings that are current for the rich in England. ... (p. 20)

It may finally be permissible to question whether the 'plan' could be at all properly called a plan. In the main, it is no more than a compilation of existing and expected plans of public investment, chiefly in irrigation and transport, by central and state governments, put together on the basis of no clear criteria; in the field of industry the 'plan' presents just a resume of discussions with private industrialists; in other spheres it mostly indicates existing expenditure, objectives, and levels on the part of state and central governments. The production figures contained in it are not the results of any detailed working out by regions or sections but are mere average calculations of the sort made familiar by the Grow More Food campaign. Nothing is suggested in the plan to see that production targets will be fulfilled either in the sphere of agriculture or large scale industry and in relation to trade and small scale industry it contains no more than vague generalizations. The plan effectively ignores all problems of social policy and does not even elaborate or deal adequately with problems of price policy, which is supposed to be its main operative instrument. Thus, in all important respects, in coverage, in concreteness, and in the degree of integration, it falls far short of what may properly be expected of a plan of economic development. ... (p. 21)

3

Prospects for the Second Five-Year Plan Period*

FORMULATION OF THE SECOND PLAN

No feature of the Second Five-Year Plan is really an innovation. The large size as well as the particular aspects have all been often advocated before. But they had not been accepted; indeed, only a short time before their definitive acceptance, they appeared unacceptable to the Planning Commission and to the government. The important implication of even the above simplified account is that the planning process in India has so far not proceeded through an intelligent preview or structured logical thinking on the part of any central influential group or authority in the country. ... (p. 48)

Was anything done in the formation of the Second Five-Year Plan which made a striking departure from the earlier practice? There were, no doubt, a number of papers produced by statisticians, and some even by economists. It does not appear that they affected materially the structure of the Plan. Ultimately, granting the policy-biases which had been evolved, the Plan-frame was based on common-sense projections out of rough available data in various directions. It was always known that there had never been any real technical examination of the individual projections. ... (p. 49)

Not only were the overall estimates and broad proportions in allocations arrived at chiefly in a rough manner with a wide range of possible variation, but this was also true of their more detailed breakdown. In the matter of allocation between states, and in the framing of the detailed plans of the states also, no great technical improvement over the methods adopted in framing the First Five-Year Plan was in evidence. The same method of

* Originally published in *India Quarterly*, Vol. 13, 1957, reprinted in *Planning and Economic Policy in India*, D.R. Gadgil, GIPE, Poona, 1962, pp. 43–61.

discussions of teams of ministries and state representatives with teams from the Planning Commission, resulting in figures which evolved rather out of negotiations than out of technical examination, was followed for the second time. Nothing indicates that within the Planning Commission or elsewhere in India any great expertise in any of the techniques connected with the formation of plans has been built up over the last five years or so. ... (p. 50)

INADEQUACIES OF THE PLAN

The most glaring defect of the Plan, as such, is the almost complete absence in it of the provision for techniques with which the Plan would be implemented. In the First Five-Year Plan the central place in this connection was given to prices. The Plan clearly laid down that 'the maintenance of the structure of prices which bring an allocation of resources in conformity with the targets defined in the Plan must be the consistent aim of economic policy.' (p. 36). In fact, no attempt was made during the First Five-Year Plan period to maintain a related structure of prices. This did not matter as no real planning was intended. In the description of the Second Five-Year Plan there is to be found a general discussion regarding the need of the techniques of planning, but there are no specific proposals. This may mean either that the Planning Commission does not think the matter as of sufficient importance or that it is not yet ready with its plan in this regard. The Second Plan is not only much larger but is also supposed, in the special context of industrial development, to represent the initial stage of a long, carefully regulated process. In this context, the omission is obviously grave. For activities within the public sector, or those completely subject to the governmental directives, no independent techniques need be elaborated. However, in the very large field of agriculture and private industry, attention must be paid to the manner in which it will be ensured that adequate amounts of various types of agricultural products or of consumer and producer goods would be continuously available, and in an economy with very large numbers of small agricultural producers, crop-planning by directive would be impossible. The experience of the Growth of Food Crops Act during the war in Bombay State indicates both the limitations and the possibilities of legislative measures in this regard. Therefore, the chief instrument in this field has to be the relative structure of prices. In building this up, two sets of problems are involved. Firstly, the principles on which the relative price-structure would be initially determined and the variations made in it subsequently. Secondly, the means by which the price-structure could appropriately and adequately influence the actions of the cultivator. The first has important theoretical aspects to which little attention has yet been paid. The second is related to detailed knowledge regarding the extent to which and the manner in which the cultivator's crop-plans are in fact influenced by relative prices and the variations in them.

There is agreement on the need of the government's maintaining stocks of certain agricultural products and conducting their purchase and sale. A warehousing board has also been set up. It is not yet clear whether there is any intention to invest this emergent system with price regulation and maintenance and whether it would be rapidly built up for this purpose. Attempted regulation of internal prices involves the additional problem of insulating the internal price-level from the international price-level. This is done, to a certain extent today, by the system of export quotas. However, the chief objectives to which the export control policy is directed are adequacy of available domestic supplies, and perhaps latterly, the obtaining of foreign-exchange resources. Unless to these is added the equally important objective of the maintenance of the relative price structure, export controls may in fact operate as disturbing influences rather than as instruments of support of the agricultural price policy.

In relation to industry there exist today a number of controls such as on the import of capital goods, on the licensing of new establishments and extensions of certain activities, and on the supply of certain basic materials. But all these are again oriented to specific objectives, and nothing has been done or said so far to indicate whether and how they could be used collectively in getting the Plan-targets of production, etc., implemented. With development tempo reaching a given level, the problem of the slackening of activity may not arise in the near future in modern industry. However, there would still be left problems relating to alternative uses of production capacity in particular industries and assuring production in the direction and to the extent required by the Plan.

The problem of production by the small-scale and cottage industries is even more complex. Production in this sphere is liable to many breaks and many periods of under-employment. The Plan appears to assume the maintenance, in continuing production at an even pace, of all existing producers and establishments, and their systematic and gradual technical improvement. It may be stated as a general rule that unless the small producer in this sphere is freed of all responsibilities other than production, a steady level of production throughout the year by the very large number of small producers would be difficult to maintain. The problems of finance, of the supply of materials, of technical help, and of marketing of products are too great and too much time- and energy-absorbing for the small producer to function effectively for a large part of the year. A system corresponding to the possible system for agriculture, viz., warehousing, floor and ceiling prices, purchase and sale activities by state boards, etc., has to be evolved for the needs of cottage industry. The idea of evolving a co-operative structure for small industry on these lines has been generally accepted. It does not, however, seem to have been realized that the structure is immediately required for the fulfilment of the Plan, that at the back of the co-operative structure, even when fully set up, must stand a governmental structure of purchase and sale and storage authorities connected with a system of floor and ceiling prices. It is necessary, further, to remember that while prices for the products of cottage industry must be remunerative enough to keep present producers in constant employment, they must not be so high as to induce any significant number of new recruits to take to production at the lower levels of technique. This again is an objective of policy for which an appropriate technique in implementation must be found. ... (pp. 52, 53)

INADEQUATE INSTRUMENTS

Turning attention to instruments, we may present the basic administrative problem in India in the following terms. The entire administrative system of British India was framed for the unified governance of a very large country through a very small number of British personnel stationed in each district. The structure of administration and the functions it could undertake effectively were determined by these conditions. The task today is entirely different. Ideally, it may be described as of maintaining living contact in all areas of effort, embracing every aspect of socio-economic life affecting the lives of the people of all strata, and invoking both understanding and co-operation of the bulk of the people. Obviously, a structure evolved during the British regime cannot be expected to function successfully under these radically changed conditions. ... (p. 54)

The present system operates through a select service, mostly chosen and trained in a uniform manner, in which through the maintenance of the monopoly of positions and privileges, the mental attitude of members of a high Hindu caste have been built up. .... All the highest jobs in the country have been virtually concentrated in this service, and the consequence of this restricted choice and universal in-expertness of members of the service has at times proved serious and threatens to become much more so in the future. Moreover, the complete denial of the highest opportunities to all other ranks, services, and suitable outsiders has even more serious consequences. ... (p. 54)

Obviously, the present system is extremely unsuitable for a democratic structure. It is obvious that the country requires personnel in the higher services recruited in much more diverse ways and from among many more diverse strata. ... This would require much greater elasticity in recruitment and, particularly, in creating opportunities for persons who have acquired valuable experience and expertise in activities outside government service. Also, the monopoly of position, the single-track channeling of authority, the sharp differentiation in status, etc., between members of one service and all others, are features which must be abolished. Apart from the enormous psychological damage, these features have a highly discouraging effect on members of the other services, because of the knowledge that whatever their record an inexpert from the caste service would gain precedence merely by virtue of membership of the privileged class. ... (pp. 54, 55)

The other feature which also flows out of our history during the British period, is the idea that for being effective a government servant must consider himself as external to the society in which he functions. ... At present, we still appear to be in two minds. One is the British view of Indian society as a conglomeration of different communities with conflicting interests among whom the officer judged and over whom he impartially ruled. The proper democratic concept is that the government servant is, like anybody else, an integral part of society, with specific functions to perform. There are yet no clear signs of the democratic concept having been accepted at least theoretically by officers, or even by ministers the change in practice has been slow so far. This necessarily affects performance in all, particularly developmental, activities where the government agency carries a large part of the authority and the initiative. The adverse effect is most noticeable in respect of the volume and quality of public co-operation. ... (p. 55)

Another specific deficiency relates to the supply and training of experts and managers for economic activity in the public sector. ... The progress of the public sector depends in a large measure on the availability of such personnel, and on establishing an appropriate technique of running a public enterprise. The whole of this important question is connected intimately with the structure of the service and the methods of recruitment to it. ... (p. 56)

INAPPROPRIATE ATTITUDES

The third class of deficiencies pertains to the attitudes and approaches. The major factor in this is an insufficient appreciation and knowledge of the conditions in the field on the part of those in ultimate authority. The extent of this may be best illustrated by the fact that it is possible for highly-placed persons in Delhi to talk about a social revolution brought about in India by community projects. There are no signs of even an impending large change anywhere in the country. The most that may be said to have happened during the last 15 years is that in selected areas in the country the class of substantial peasants has made headway through the better returns obtained by the more secure and profitable production systems in agriculture; there has further been in evidence in this class some consciousness of new political power. There has also taken place some shift in the balance of power amongst urban classes, i.e., as between the professional and intellectual classes on the one hand, and the trading and financing communities on the other. The considerable importance of the former in the past has been notably reduced, and in general the influence of the latter has very greatly increased. However, the aborigines, the Scheduled Classes and Castes, the landless labourers, and the class of small holders of land have, at the most, all become somewhat more conscious of their own more depressed position than before; but in no large area are there any clear signs of improvement in their position, social or economic. ... (p. 56)

While the extent of change that has come about in the country is often grossly overestimated, the extent of real poverty, unemployment, and under-employment is not adequately realized. ... There is not only an inadequate appreciation of the economic situation, but also a facile belief that the announcement of large plans and eloquent speeches from Delhi are sufficient to enthuse the population. In this context it is apparent that we suffer from certain historical traditions. The imperial tradition associated with Delhi, of great ostentation, magnificent buildings, and splendid living by the rulers, and the social attitudes springing from the socio-economic structure of the Zamindari areas, are obviously formidable barriers in the way of an appreciation of the situation by those at the top. There is, in concrete terms, no realization that a really bold plan must involve considerable sacrifices all round, especially by the rich and the middle classes, and that the response of the masses will depend on the examples set by the leaders and the upper classes, and the sacrifices that they seem to make. In this regard there are a number of conflicting influences. There is the older tradition of a highly stratified society. There is the new standard set by foreign businessmen for their fellows in India, and the standards spreading in official and semi-official circles through international contacts and assignment. ... (pp. 56, 57)

In the Plan no significant steps have been proposed regarding checks on consumption, salaries of officials, or scales of government expenditure. In the provision of public services it is not realized that restraint on standards of consumption means restraint on standards of public amenities also. ... (p. 57)

Another inappropriate approach that appears general is the tendency to concentrate attention on the volume of total expenditure incurred rather than on the directions in which or the care with which it is incurred. Possibly this is one of the by-products of the mechanistic beliefs flowing from the concentration on mathematical relations and statistical ratios. Economic management of investment, and the technical efficiency of processes seem to have diminished in importance. ... (p. 57)

No discussion of the relative merits of extra expenditures in various directions is to be found in the Plan. An illustration or two from the field of educational expenditure will make clear what I consider to be the wrong priorities, and consequently, wasteful expenditure. The Planning Commission finds it difficult to commit itself to financing recurrent expenditure in future years. Therefore, it offers very large grants for immediate capital expenditure. These can be most easily spent on buildings and equipment. So, without relation to the future maintenance of expanded activities, and leaving unsatisfied certain primary needs today which should be satisfied before any expansion is undertaken, a large building- and equipment-programme, including programmes for swimming-pools and open-air-theatres, is under way. ... By another programme of educational expenditure very large amounts have been earmarked for the purpose of raising the salaries of teachers, especially university teachers, in particular categories. ... In face of the large unemployment amongst the educated classes it seems obviously unjustifiable to raise substantially, as part of the Plan, the emoluments of particular groups. The immediate national requirement is to use such resources as are available for training and employing additional personnel. For example, the low level of the teacher-pupil ratio in Indian educational institutions is even more striking than the level of the salaries of any groups of Indian university teachers. When, as it happens, the beneficiaries of this are among the better-paid among the teachers the almost overt class bias of the procedure becomes highly pronounced. ... (pp. 58, 59)

AN ASSESSMENT OF PROSPECTS

Development, in a country like India, depends chiefly on larger investment and better technique. We have today a serious problem of urban unemployment; we are very short of capital resources, and large numbers of the working population are working with obsolete equipment and methods; also ours has to be a plan for long-term development. Therefore, the new capital has to be so utilized as to add to the basic resources and systems required for development without rapidly throwing out of work the existing equipment and personnel. The construction of our development plan is essentially a problem in phasing the adoption of technique in various directions by appropriately rationing the capital investment. The emphasis on agricultural production methods, irrigation and power projects, the transport system and social overheads, the establishment of heavy industry, and the insistence on going very slow with further mechanization of fields occupied by traditional industry, all logically hold together. The prominence attained by co-operation and decentralization is also partly related to these. The building up of a large co-operative organization, especially in activities in which large-scale operations are necessary, follows upon the rejection, on the one hand, of high capitalism and, on the other, of state socialism. It is also the appropriate form of organization for a decentralized pattern of society. Decentralization, apart from its socio-political merits, is urgently needed to start the development process all over the country. Such development as took place during the British rule was very lopsided, and today there are striking disparities in the levels of living and the stages of economic development within the country. It is an almost universal experience that economic development is concentrated largely around the nuclei of modern trade and industrial activity. Even development throughout the country can take place only when such nuclei or centres are widely spread in large numbers. ... Secondly, a poor country with no prospects of a general security system can give relief only by providing work, and this can be done in a planned way only in a highly decentralized system. ... (pp. 59, 60)

The prospects are best described in terms of the parts of this structure, which are likely to be adequately built up during the next five-year period. Private, modern large business may be expected to fulfil in fair measure its allotted share; the performance of the government in the fields in which government agencies are accustomed to work, a field such as construction works, may also be adequate. In respect of the big industry programme, both public and private, and of the economic and social overheads to be provided through public expenditure, the Plan may be expected to be reasonably fulfilled. It is chiefly in respect of those parts of the Plan in which a new departure is involved, or where it is necessary to work against the grain that all the inadequacies recounted above will be acutely felt. These will then be felt in building up the co-operative organization and even more in bringing about effective decentralization; and it will affect the programme for cottage and small-scale industries and for the poorer agriculturists and the agriculturist producers in the backward areas, which is in effect to say that where an activity has been already established and something is happening its extension may not prove difficult, but great poverty and backwardness in technique and organization are obstacles which in the existing situation may not be easily surmounted. Also, where the effort has to be at centres in a few places the administrative machinery may deal with it successfully, but not at all as well when it is dispersed all over the country. Thus it is highly likely that within the Second Five-Year Plan period the trend set in motion during the last three years will continue. Certain urban centres and classes, and particular agricultural regions, will continue to develop while the disadvantaged will fall, relatively, farther behind. Cottage industry, the unemployed, and the agricultural poor, i.e. the classes in whose favour pressures for the large Plan developed, are precisely those who are least likely to profit from it immediately. ... (pp. 60, 61)

4

The Approach to the Third Five-Year Plan*

This note is intended to bring out briefly what I consider to be the more important issues to which attention will have to be paid in framing the Third Five-Year Plan. I consider planning in India to be essentially a politico and socio-economic process. Planning for economic development involves an attempt to force the pace of the economy and to lead it over a period of years along certain preconceived routes. The essential operative element in this effort is organized action at all levels by governmental authorities, public and private associations, and individuals. To urge that forcing the pace of economic development and regulating its direction by the joint planning-efforts of state authorities, associations, and individuals is undesirable or non-feasible, is tantamount to suggesting the giving up of planning for economic development. ... (p. 132)

Planning for economic development is based, apart from institutional and psychological changes, on deliberately increasing the rate of savings and regulating the channels of investment. With severe limits to further taxation efforts, this necessarily involves some kind of deficit financing. In this respect, planned economic development in under-developed countries has close parallels with the financing of war. As war finance has never been possible except with the debasement of coinage, forced loans, printing of notes, or inflationary expansion of credit, in forcing the pace of economic

* Memorandum submitted to the Panel of Economists, Government of India Planning Commission, in August 1959. Published in *Planning and Economic Policy in India*, D.R. Gadgil, GIPE, Poona, 1962, pp. 132–59.

development, poor countries also must have recourse to some such means at least in the initial stage. Therefore, to say that the plan should be limited by the extent of resources in sight is also to recede from planned development efforts. However, deficit financing is bound to prove self-defeating in the long run unless appropriate policy-measures accompany it. Holding this view of the nature of the effort, I consider that the basic decisions are politico-economic and socio-economic in the sense that the size and structure of the plan will depend on the ability of the government and the society as a whole to sustain and agree to a heavy taxation programme, to the setting-up of a regulatory regime which prevents the inflationary effects of deficit financing from becoming significant, and which is able to achieve desirable levels of investment according to a structured programme through a long period. ... (p. 132)

In the circumstances, I consider it inappropriate to begin a consideration of planning in India with targets such as the rate of increasing national income, etc. The consideration of the plan should start from the definitions of governmental policy, what the government wants and is prepared to do, and the response it expects and will obtain from the public. Consciously or unconsciously, through the last ten years, this issue has been dodged. We have, no doubt, a theoretical formulation of policies incorporated in official plans, but there has never been a co-ordination of these policies with a view to implementing the plan as a whole. The avoidance of such co-ordination and overall framing has been so consistent that it is necessary to enquire into the reasons for it and the results of it in some detail. This note sets out a view of the events of the last 10 years and an interpretation of governmental acts of commission and omission. ... (pp. 132, 133)

During the First Five-Year Plan period, the size of expenditure undertaken by the government was relatively modest. The international situation was favourable and harvests were unusually good; because of this conjuncture, planning-problems never came to the surface. One thing, however, was made clear, viz., that the extent of the effort undertaken in the First Five-Year Plan period was very inadequate, to ensure, even moderately, full employment of labour resources. At the time of the framing of the Second Five-Year Plan, it was possible to take an optimistic view of the future; as the economy was running at a low tempo, we had not lost any of our accumulated foreign resources, and no inflationary effects of planned deficit financing had appeared. The result was a large plan, the implications of which, though fully stated in the abstract, were perhaps not fully brought alive to politicians because of past history and current easy conditions. The difficulties then faced were not primarily due to high inflationary pressures created by deficit financing but, in the main, to lack of policy and failure to implement the plans, especially on the foreign-exchange and the food front. ... (p. 133)

UNEVEN DEVELOPMENT

Whereas there appears to have been some increase in per capita national income during the period, the results of this have been evidently spread very unevenly over the society and the economy. The cities have profited as compared with the agricultural regions. The rich agricultural regions have done well, but not so the poor ones, and in all agricultural regions, it is only the top farmer strata that appear to have made any net improvement in their position. Agricultural labour has distinctly deteriorated in its position, and this, most probably, is also what has happened in the case of rural artisans and casual labour, and the labour employed in unorganized industry, trade, and transport. Even the earnings of factory labourers have not made any significant progress if 1959 is compared with 1951. The salariat which, next to labour, is important in the cities, appears to be in a stagnant, even perhaps a slightly difficult position. It is only the traders and the industrialists who appear to have consistently done well, and among them, the bigger and those in the largest cities with the largest organized business appear to have done the best. ... (p. 137)

An obvious explanation of most of the above-mentioned phenomena may be that owing to the non-integrated character of our economy, the benefits of development expenditure and increased economic activity do not easily pass on from one region or sector to other regions or sectors in the economy. The result is that activity or improvement confined to certain regions or sectors may take place as against the background of general stagnant conditions. ... Considered in terms of the numbers affected or the proportion of population having benefited, the effects may be small and the overall aggregates may not, in the average, register any improvement. In a predominantly *laissez faire* economy, therefore, developments on the lines of recent Indian developments may not cause surprise. In efforts at planned development, however, measures are supposed to be taken to prevent or counteract them. It is my contention that, in spite of all claims to the contrary, planning as such does not operate in India today. There are only schemes of public expenditure or of aid to private or co-operative enterprise. There is no co-ordinated, conscious effort to lead development along pre-defined lines. As a consequence, development proceeds largely as if in a *laissez faire* regime, and the features to which attention has been drawn, follow. Moreover, to the extent that official policy is active, it aggravates the total effects by loading the dice in favour of the traders and of large organized business. This is brought out below through an examination of official policy as related to the operation of the mixed economy, fixation of import and export quotas, the stabilization of agricultural prices, etc. ... (p. 140)

PLANNING IN A MIXED ECONOMY

The main features of a mixed economy, where economic development is being planned by the state, should be: relative elimination of risks from private enterprise through stable prices, buoyant demand for most products, and special aid and protection afforded to private enterprise in particular direction; this would be balanced by restrictions regarding fields of operation, and the existence of a regulatory regime. The total objective may be taken to be to afford private enterprise the needed security and assistance without which it cannot develop rapidly, and to guarantee on the other hand that such assistance does not result in an increasingly favourable distribution of the national product in favour of the private entrepreneur. It would be the purpose, presumably, of the regulatory regime to see that profits and gains are not high in relation to risks and costs, and the regulatory regime may also be supposed to fulfil such other constitutional objectives as to prevent the concentration of economic wealth and power. It does not appear that in India these expectations have been fulfilled. There are a number of complaints, on the one hand, that the regulatory regime is unnecessarily detailed and that it obstructs legitimate development. On the other hand, it is equally clear that the government has not succeeded in preventing undue gains from accruing to the private sector. ... (pp. 140, 141)

That in India, the most important prices in relation to products and services of modern, large, organized business are administered, may be taken to be an established fact. The government exercises little or no control in the determination of these administered prices, or in the fixation of their levels. In the area of consumer goods, in an important category like sugar, the government's inability to control extra-ordinary profits by traders and manufacturers has proved notorious. Equally important is it to observe that, where the government gives special assistance or privilege, the benefits accruing there from are compounded into assets of the party assisted by the government without any social claim or public interest being created within it. So that, as against the possibility of the government's stepping into the field in the future, current public assistance results in making acquisition of interest in the field by the State more difficult than before. That is, there is no *quid pro quo,* present or future, for liberal assistance given by the government. This is particularly harmful to national interests at that level where organized business has highly concentrated control and can and does operate as a quasi-monopolist. ... (p. 141)

There is no corrective, as government policy operates today, to this one-sided operation of the mixed economy in relation especially to large organized business. Attempts must be made to ensure that the operation is more fair to society as a whole. Firstly, a somewhat generalized system of price control and of distribution of crucial supplies has to be adopted to act as a restraining force. Secondly, it must be provided that assistance by the state leads to the creation of an appropriate measure of public interest in the unit assisted. Thirdly, suitable conditions must be created in each sphere for the government to take over certain units, if this becomes necessary to keep up production and employment. ... (p. 142)

REGULATION OF FOREIGN TRADE

It has always been recognized that inadequacy of foreign exchange is likely to be a chronic problem with most under-developed countries planning development. ... In the circumstances, it becomes necessary to regulate imports carefully and to stimulate exports. Essentially, the policy in this regard has to be a long-term policy which is carefully designed in relation to the total long-term plan. Curiously, Indian foreign-trade policy does not appear to have any such long-term design. The lack of its co-ordination with the total plan was exposed dramatically by the sudden and rapid running-down of sterling resources during the first two years of the Second Five-Year Plan. Even after that experience, however, it does not appear that greater care has been taken in co-ordinating efforts. ... The total requirements of imports of necessaries, of materials for productive activity, and of capital goods for development, must be closely related to the particular phases of the plan and fairly accurately dictated by them. In such conditions any adventitious gains of foreign exchange must not be dissipated by immediate *ad hoc* liberalization, but must be added to the reserve for emergency. On the other hand, any minor worsening of the situation should not lead to changes of policy, but to drawing temporarily on reserves. Instead of a basic long-term policy which changes only in relation to changes in the plan or the total situation, Indian policy is determined almost entirely in the short-term. ... (pp. 142, 143)

Export-quotas appear to be determined largely in the light of the price fluctuations at home. It appears that this results in our exporting the largest amounts at times when the international prices are the lowest. It is not clear that such mechanical operation of export-quota policy ever served any important end in relation to the operation of the plan of the national economy. This feature, again, is obviously the result of no attempt being made to evolve a long-term export-policy in relation to planned economic development. Apart from this built-in inability to take advantage of favourable terms of trade, variations in import- and export-quotas operate as disturbing influences in the internal market and for producers' plans. As these variations are chiefly determined by traders' advice and prejudices, they sacrifice the interest of the internal producers, especially the agriculturist-producer. The notorious export of groundnut-cake is an important instance of this. ... When a resource important in increasing production and maintaining the fertility of the soil was exported, much more was lost than the export. ... (p. 143)

It is obvious that all this changing and chopping is thought to be justified and useful only because there is no consistent durable frame in which the total plan of economic development is related to a long-term export- and import-policy. It is notable that the policies redound chiefly to the benefit of the trader and the intermediary. ... (p. 144)

The regulation of imports and exports creates a shortage of supply on the one hand, and special opportunities on the other. ... The government has to ensure that any harmful effects of restrictions on import and export are minimized through the regulation of the distribution of supplies and control of prices and that through this the planned ends are properly fulfilled; the only alternative is to allow intermediaries to exploit consumers and to obstruct productive processes and thus defeat, ultimately, the very purpose of export–import regulation. The same reasoning applies in other fields also, i.e., wherever forced economic development creates a situation which calls for intelligent regulation. The stepping-up of savings, in whatever way, must mean restraint on consumption. Direction of investment or of other economic activity in particular directions must mean the regulation of supplies of a number of goods and services, and a regulatory system in relation to these has to be conceived of and built as operating over long stretches of time for serving planned needs. If such a regulatory system is not created, the Plan cannot be fulfilled. ... (p. 144)

STABILIZATION OF AGRICULTURAL PRICES

We may also examine in this context the refusal of the government to do anything in relation to the stabilization of agricultural prices. Stabilization of agricultural prices has been an accepted plank in government policy for almost a decade. Its need in under-developed economies has been widely accepted and the adoption of measures of stabilization advocated by international organizations like the ECAFE and the FAO. The Ford Foundation Team of American agricultural specialists, which submitted a report recently, has also advocated it as being needed for increased internal production of food. In spite of all this, the government has consistently opposed and avoided in practice the adoption of a policy of stabilization of agricultural prices. While there is a good deal of talk about what may be done to increase the production of food, the simple expedient of guaranteeing in advance for each season a minimum price for food crops has been carefully avoided. The other part of the same policy of stabilization is to put a ceiling to prices, but this, which is extremely important from the point of view of industrial and other costs, is also not undertaken. ... (p. 145)

It is possible to interpret this amazing behaviour only on the basis that the stabilization of prices of agricultural products is side-tracked because of certain consequences flowing from it which are not liked. A programme of stabilization could be undertaken through, either the entry of government, in a substantial way, in trading in agricultural products, or a rapid co-operativization of the field combined with certain overall operations by the government. Either of these courses will affect seriously the strong, entrenched position of the moneylender-trader elements whose combination of the two occupations have given them a stranglehold on the Indian rural economy. Historically, the present capitalistic community in India has grown primarily on the rural moneylender-trader base. Any undermining of the position of this base would inevitably spell disaster to the trading superstructure in the urban areas and may damage even urban financial capitalism, i.e., affect vitally those interests which are today politically and economically the most powerful in the country. Recent government policy in the co-operative field also lends support to this hypothesis. All recent experiments which have been successful to any significant extent in transferring rural finance, marketing, and processing out of private hands to those of co-operative organizations are obviously suspected, and any programme which has set this trend in motion and made its progress possible, is being challenged and sabotaged. ... (p. 146)

An *ad hoc* operation also makes possible a proliferation of official agencies. It makes for unnecessary, obstructive, and costly bureaucratic operations which co-ordination would abolish. Thus, co-ordination which would force the emergence of a consistent policy-frame would not only lead to action opposed to general capitalistic interests and make much more difficult manipulation in individual instances, but would also reduce the numbers and powers of individual officers. Co-ordination, simplification, or decentralization of official agencies is not likely to receive support in high official circles which are again, of recent years, developing close connections with organized business. ... (p. 146)

RESOURCE MOBILIZATION

The great importance of price-control and of state-trading is further emphasized by reference to the problem of raising internal resources. At least in the initial stages, indirect taxation must play the crucial role in this matter. Internally, the most important source of indirect taxation is the excise or sales tax on goods of general consumption. It is no doubt possible to obtain some revenue through the operation of government enterprises. But this possibility is limited where the enterprise does not produce goods of general consumption. This is because the enterprises which the government conducts, such as of the production of steel or capital goods, and the services it may provide such as transport, supply of electricity, or of banking facilities, i.e., all kinds of socio-economic overheads, lie too close to basic pricing. Their prices enter widely and pervasively in all other prices.

It is also not usually possible through them to exercise any discrimination in taxation incidence. ... (p. 147)

Determination of the appropriate level of taxation of consumer goods, however, presents considerable difficulties where there is no regulation of trade or prices. ... (p. 147)

The only efficient way of obtaining resources from indirect taxation would be for the State to actually enter into trading activities at the strategic points, such as in important import- and export-commodities, and also to have under its control, a sufficient number of widespread outlets of distribution of general consumer goods so as to regulate effectively the level of their prices. If these steps are taken, the State would not only be able to build up a proper system of regulating prices and distributing supplies, but will also obtain the full fiscal advantages of all special margins and of particular opportunities created in the process of planned development. ... (p. 148)

In any country, the policies will be dictated mainly in the interest of the classes who actually hold power. Inferentially, it is valid to say that today in India real power rests with modern organized business and the trading community. All economic policies, whatever their intention, have been so administered as to benefit these classes. It is important to note that actual power is held by a relatively small group, entry into which is becoming increasingly difficult; there is considerable concentration of influence even within its ranks, and effective control has been reduced to a few hands and a very narrow social base. ... (p. 148)

STRUCTURE OF THE PLAN

Turning to a consideration of the structure of the Plan, certain elements of its general strategy were outlined in the Second Five-Year Plan. The Plan implied that the operation in relation to traditional industry was essentially a holding operation. New entrants would not be encouraged in these industries. Increased production from them would be expected through better technique and fuller employment. Also, in the long run, there would be a gradual diminution of employment in this field as the economy developed and as alternative employment opportunities became available. At the other end, beginning with the production of steel, it was the basic structure of industrialization and the preparation for the production of capital goods that was emphasized and undertaken. There is no reason to depart from these basic decisions. However, the stage has now arrived when a clearer picture of the intermediate field must be sketched. Over what period, and in what stages are the traditional industries supposed to become unimportant? On the other hand, when we are in a position to produce capital goods in sufficient variety and quantity, what are the types of the capital goods that will be produced? And what structure of consumption goods industries does the programme of production of capital goods visualize? The basic decisions in this regard relate to the extent and variety of consumer goods to be made available and the structure and location pattern of the consumer-goods industries which will produce them. Though a plan has to restrict total consumption somewhat in the initial years, it must ultimately have reference to a programme, sketching the manner in which and the rate at which the availability of consumer goods in the future is to be improved so as to raise the standard of living. ... (pp. 149, 150)

TECHNIQUE OF PRODUCTION

In addition to the problem of the type of consumer goods of the future, there is the problem of techniques adopted for their production. ...(p. 150)

The crucial immediate decision in this regard appears to be the measure of decentralization that all efforts are to be made to achieve, in consumer goods and intermediate products. This may be a matter of considerable initial experimentation and research. To illustrate from the building industry, whether cement can be produced in small unit factories, whether lime which is available generally can be used by more efficient and standardized methods than those used at present, whether in brick, tile-manufacturing, or prefabrication of parts, the possibility of the use of local material can be actively canvassed and established, are matters to which much greater attention will have to be paid if one is not to be content with the present trends towards universal and plentiful use of cement and steel and iron sheets. ... (p. 151)

Even where the most developed modern techniques have been fully accepted, it may be possible to think of future decisions being open in certain respects. Special reference may be made, in this context, to the engineering industry. ... Will the engineering industry in India evolve basically in the direction of small workshops spread round certain central units or joined together themselves by assembling centres? Or will it in essence be a large-scale centralized industry? ... (p. 151)

We are thus brought up to face the questions, at this stage, as to why it is necessary to think out afresh the problem of the Indian pattern of industrialization and why we cannot adopt the fully developed techniques in all directions. The basic reason for the need is obviously the relation between our population on the one hand, and natural resources and capital resources on the other. ... However intensive our efforts in relation to primary production, they could achieve no more than self-sufficiency in foodgrains and some broadening of the base of industrial raw materials. With the numbers on land and the growth in them, large net surpluses are not likely to be available in this sector even with intense development. This means that for the whole of the relevant future period, our plan of development, which means essentially plan of industrialization, must assume a relative shortage of natural and capital resources as compared with the work-force. ... (pp. 151, 152)

In relation to the existing problem of underemployment and unemployment, and its known worsening during the last decade, the plan of future development has to be thought of in terms of providing adequate employment opportunities. In view of the shortage of capital resources, additional employment can only be offered at work and technique which does not require much capital per person. ... Our efforts must be directed towards finding the most efficient techniques to adopt at our level of availability of capital. There is another aspect of this circumstance which needs to be emphasized. In our situation, the adoption, for any purpose, of a technique more capital-intensive than that required for efficient production in any activity in the context of the total plan, is to take away a highly scarce factor from other activities, and is an action which is not only unsocial but also uneconomic. This character of the action is emphasized when the vesting of such extra capital resources is in private and not in public hands, but it is not excusable even in the public sector. ... (p. 152)

The brief statement supports the conclusion that our industrial development must be planned on a general small-scale-industry model, with deliberate adoption of a large scale and of concentration of capital only where modern production technique overwhelmingly requires it; the corollary is obvious: that all such deliberate exceptions must be only under strict social control and should preferably be allowed only in the public sector. ... (pp. 152, 153)

The data regarding unemployment indicate a steadily worsening situation, and it is evident that present policies are very inadequate to deal with it. Unemployment or underemployment in cities and villages is growing apace, and it is obvious that large organized industry, whatever its rate of development, can absorb only a very small proportion of the growing numbers. For increased numbers to have to be accommodated in agriculture is to accept defeat in terms of development and to make future progress more difficult than before. In present Indian conditions, one cannot expect the 'tertiary' sector to absorb further work-people. The development of this can only proceed on the basis of a broad, diversified 'secondary' structure. It is thus a very large measure of industrial development that is immediately needed. In view of all considerations, it is a decentralized, dispersed industrial sector that we have to build. ...(p. 153)

As preparatory to such development, a widespread public works programme of conservation of resources and of building up of socio-economic overheads all over the country with the smaller towns at the centre of the picture instead of the metropolitan areas, is an obvious step. Further, in order that the employment situation may not worsen because of the collapse of the older industries, a holding operation on behalf of those of such industries as employ large numbers is imperative. ... (p. 153)

REGULATION OF TRADE

Nothing in this survey indicates that the size and structure of the Second Five-Year Plan were basically ill-conceived. It highlights failures mainly in three directions: (i) neglect or misdirection of official policy resulting mainly in distorting developments so as to benefit large organized business and the trading community; (ii) failure to do anything to better the condition of the most disadvantaged classes; and (iii) failure to implement programmes for increased agricultural production and to work out and implement programmes for the establishment of decentralized dispersed industry. All these relate not to the programme of any political party but to policy objectives incorporated in the Constitution, such as, preventing the concentration of wealth and providing for the employment and welfare of the masses. ... (p. 154)

In relation to the first, what is required is not so much the adoption of new policies as the effective co-ordination and implementation of those already avowed. An examination of recent events does, however, suggest an emphasis in relation to the regulation of trading. The implementation of plans of development and the attainment of proper economic and social objectives does seem to require, in particular, effective control over prices and the distribution of essential supplies. The various elements in this appear to be as follows: (i) a system of warehouses and a long-term policy of purchase or procurement of agricultural products; (ii) undertaking, through a public agency, the exports of the more important commodities (this could be managed by autonomous commodity export boards, as in a large number of primary producing countries); (iii) the import and distribution of all main supplies not imported directly by licensed consumers. (This could, perhaps, be best managed by a single independent authority); (iv) the establishment of retail outlets, to the extent of about a quarter to a third of the total all over the country, which are managed either by co-operatives or are under State control; (v) control of internal wholesale trade through co-operatives or directly to the extent needed to operate the procurement, export, and retail outlet systems. ... (p. 155)

One of the most notable features of recent developments is the stagnant, if not deteriorating, condition of the most disadvantaged classes, including almost the entire labouring population. ... All specific proposals so far made, relating to dispersal of ownership of means of production, pertain only to the ownership of land; and it is evidently felt desirable to soothe large organized business and its foreign collaborators, periodically, with promises of 'fair treatment' and concessions. In this context, it is unrealistic to propose any egalitarian distributive measures. It may, however, be in order to suggest that certain minimum steps, which even modern non-socialistic, non-planning governments would feel necessary, be immediately taken. ... (p. 155)

The highest priorities appear to be food and employment. In relation to both, some specific responsibility must be attached to all governments. ... (p. 155)

In relation to both these responsibilities it would be advisable to provide that periodic assessment, in the total context of the functioning of the economy, of the extent to which the responsibilities have been carried out, is made by a statutory authority. ... (p. 156)

DECENTRALIZED PLANNING

The largest failure of the planning effort, however, is in agricultural production and the starting of widespread industrial development. This failure has also the most widespread and the most far-reaching consequences. ... In an essentially rural and only partially monetized and integrated economy like that of India, it is impossible to expect the development process, started at a small number of places and in particular sectors, to spread by itself all over the country. With us, development will proceed successfully and at an even tempo only if it is started simultaneously at innumerable centres all over the country. I would also urge, and there is supporting experience for this statement, that emphasis on agricultural development by itself will also not be sufficient to start development. Development must be planned simultaneously in both the primary and secondary production sectors. This is not merely to reinforce the plea for widespread local agricultural and industrial effort. ... (p. 156)

At present, planning in India is a highly centralized process in which all real initiative and direction resides only in a few persons in Delhi. With a formally federal constitution, we have, in fact, great concentration of effective political power. That community development all over India is the charge of a Central Ministry is merely symbolic of current topsy-turvydom. The evil effects of extreme centralization are evident in the fields of education and co-operation. In education, the UGC and the Central Ministry put forward model schemes and as these are backed by scarce money, all universities and colleges have to accept them without thought. The result is wasteful expenditure on non-essentials, while even the basic needs of the poorer units remain unsatisfied. Or take the current debate regarding co-operative policy. The most distressing feature of the present situation is that policy is being made not through open debate, which can bring out the varying views and the need for adaptation of policy to different circumstances, but through the whims and prejudices of a few at the centre of political power. ...(p. 157)

In spite of all talk of planning from the bottom, no such thing is in evidence because of the simple fact that planning from the bottom, undertaken as a result of central directives, can never be real planning from the bottom. What is required is not a directive, but the power to initiate and act. The greatest need of the country today is thus the dispersal of power in relation to planning decisions. ... (p. 157)

That a shift in the balance of power, even without a change in formal arrangements, can bring about a change in planning policy may be illustrated by a recent experience in Bombay. While power rested completely in big business and its associates, the human costs, of the continued growth of industry and population in Bombay City were callously disregarded; immediately following some reduction in the concentration of power it was possible to set up a study group to study existing conditions; but the balance would have to tilt much further before anything really effective is done about the situation. It is too much, therefore, to expect that, while power is concentrated in a few hands in Delhi and the metropolitan areas, activities other than organized large industry, banking and transport, large schemes in the public sector, prestige expenditure, and impressive but empty model schemes will command real attention. Decentralized and dispersed industry has long been an accepted policy, but it continues to be a meaningless phrase. Even the Khadi Commission acts on the basis of model schemes which, it is surprised to find, do not work successfully. ... (pp. 157, 158)

It is necessary to put meaning and content into the empty slogans and phrases. This can be done only by an enormous-amount of experimentation again carried out in a large variety of circumstances all over the country. However, such experimentation can take place only when the experiment is consciously framed as for a concrete situation and the possibility of variation and adjustment remains continuously open. The work of 'starting' development (not copying it) can be undertaken only under such conditions. Therefore, without the setting-up of, at least, regional planning authorities and vesting them with considerable power, the real process of local countrywide development cannot begin. ... (p. 158)

The Plan can be a plan of local development in the real sense only if it is thought out locally. The matter does not rest merely with local adaptation and initiative. For its implementation, a plan of dispersed decentralized action requires, above all, organization and workers. Only local planning can draw in local leadership. The valuable unused human resources that movements like the co-operative cotton ginning and pressing societies and the co-operative sugar factories in Bombay State were able to tap, largely contributed to their success. There is also the possibility of bringing in additional resources and the ability to adjust scales of payment to local levels and needs which can prove valuable assets in implementation of local plans. ... (p. 158)

All this may be no doubt, theoretically accepted, but it is unlikely that without a real revolution in thinking it will be accepted in fact. The present mood is to talk about village democracy but to deny real power even to the states. Planning at the state-level means mere official compilation of schemes, which may prove acceptable to the Centre. ... (p. 158)

The contrast with other planning countries is very large in this regard. Decentralization of planning has been established not only in such countries as Yugoslavia, which specially championed decentralization, or Poland in the post-1956 period, but also, with recent developments, in Russia. Russia has today more than 100 planning-regions. In India, planning is undertaken for the country as a whole. What is required is not only a planning authority for each state but for each important geographical region within each state. ...If we have planning-regions with effective authority, the reform will, for the first time, bring into the centre of planning the small towns, the rural areas, and the small industries. It will act as some counter-weight to the existing overwhelming politico-economic influence of large organized business and of the top bureaucracy. It is only with some such operation that the difficulty of starting local development, rousing local enthusiasm, tapping in a special way local resources, and adopting costs to local conditions will be overcome. With such dispersal of planning control and power, one may expect, in course of time, even some diffusion of wealth and well-being. ... (pp. 158, 159)

5

An Approach to Indian Planning*

At the outset, I shall make clear the more salient assumptions made while drawing up the following note. I assume that modern science and technology are fully accepted by our society. This acceptance is involved in all vital operations of socio-economic life in India. For example, our entire system of transportation and communication, which is used by everybody and is not found to be dispensable by anybody, is based on modern technology and can be run and maintained only through the use of an immense variety of products of a number of modern industries. The present state of our public health is vitally dependent on familiarity with and the use of modern scientific knowledge and the organization of modern industrial production. One of the directives of policy incorporated in the Constitution asks the State in India to organize agriculture and animal husbandry on modern and scientific lines. Therefore, a valid objection to the use and adoption of advanced technical and scientific knowledge in any direction could be sustained only on the grounds of a lack of needed resources in terms of capital or personnel or through fear of undesirable socio-economic consequences of such adoption.

The second assumption made is that the plan for development of the entire community or society is under consideration and that the objectives, values, and principles adopted for the plan must be applied uniformly in all aspects, and further that the plans for the agricultural and industrial sectors, the production and distributive systems, and for employment and investment must be framed in a mutually consistent manner. This need for uniformity and consistency is also equally felt both in the temporal

* Paper presented at the seminar on 'Paths of Planned Economy in India' held in Poona at the GIPE in April 1961; also published in *The Economic Weekly*, Special Number, July 1961.

and the spatial aspects of the plan. Thus while the main orientation of the plans could be towards long-term development, it cannot disregard the short run. This is because many immediate developments may later prove irreversible, and may have a determining influence on long-term possibilities.

The concept of each village as an independent, autonomous unit and the concept of cities as excrescences on normal economic life also cease to be valid from this point of view. While for purposes of convenience, locational or regional divisions may be made in consideration of particular problems, the total plan must be fully correlated and co-ordinated. The notion of self-sufficiency at any level thus no longer remains a value. In relation to any unit or area, self-sufficiency or self-containedness as an aim of social or economic policy must be derived from accepted goals and principles of national policy. The full acceptance of modern science and technology would also require that no bias be entertained against division of labour or complex economic organization. The ultimate goal of the attainment of a peaceful world society emphasizes this trend of thought.

I also assume that the State is not treated as a foreign, or alien body but is, in itself, a manifestation of social will and purpose, which can be given shape and function appropriate to current needs and values. In particular, in relation to poor and undeveloped societies, I take the State to be an important agent or instrument. It is necessary to emphasize, in this context, the great danger of translating to a society riddled with privilege and inequity, concepts appropriate to a basically egalitarian situation. The refusal to use the powers of the State in highly non-egalitarian societies under the name of liberty or *sarvodaya* is tantamount to encouraging, consciously or unconsciously, the growth of evil forces and perpetuating social injustice. I assume democratic process to mean the active participation of as large numbers as possible in the shaping and conduct of social, economic, and political activity: federalism and decentralization are logically implicit in the democratic process.

I may, next, summarily recapitulate the Directive Principles of State policy in the Constitution. These, though not enforceable by any court of law, are, it is laid down in the Constitution, 'nevertheless fundamental in the governance of the country.' The most important general terms used in these directives are 'welfare' and 'social justice.' There is reference in a number of places to the prevention of 'exploitation.' The basic concern shown is that with the problem of poverty, that is, with employment and the standard of living. This is emphasized by a number of distinct references, such as to: (i) right to an adequate means of livelihood; (ii) living-wage for all workers; (iii) raising the level of nutrition and the standard of living; and (iv) securing, within limits of economic capacity and development, the right to work, to education, and to public assistance in case of unemployment, old age, sickness and disablement and other cases of undeserved want.

Next to preventing exploitation and providing employment and raising the standard of living, the directives emphasize non-concentration of the ownership of and control over material resources, their distribution as best to subserve the common good, and securing that the operation of the economic system does not result in the concentration of wealth and means of production to the common detriment. Attainment of compulsory education up to the age of 14 within the definite time limit of 10 years attached to it, underlines the importance and urgency of the spread of educational facilities up to this level, and there are references at many places to public health. In relation to specific aspects of activity, there is the directive to promote cottage industries and to organize village *Panchayats* to function as units of self-government.

All in all, the directives of policy concentrate attention on employment and the standard of living and on non-concentration of economic power.

THE FIRST AND THE SECOND PLAN

Against this background of the value system and priorities exhibited in the directives, one may look at the Indian plans as they have operated in the past and as projected for the future. On doing this the defect that becomes most evident is the almost entire neglect of the employment and the standard of living aspect by the plans. The plans have neither been oriented towards tackling these problems nor has any progress, in relation to these objectives, been evident in the last ten years. It is enough for the purpose to cite two pieces of evidence. Firstly, the calculations made by the Planning Commission which show that even on the assumptions of the Commission, unemployment has been steadily increasing through the Second Five-Year Plan period.

That the plans have failed to make any impression on the general standard of living may be emphasized by reference to the calculation of per capita availability of cereals and pulses, set out in a table in the Economic Survey for 1960–61, presented with the budget for 1961-62. The per capita net availability of cereals and pulses in oz. per day is shown in this table to be 15.4 in 1960, with a population put at 423 millions. In the same series, the per capita availability has been put at 15.7 for 1954, 15.5 for 1957, and 16.4 for 1959. With the higher rate of growth of population, as now revealed by the census, the disparity between the 1960 calculations and the calculations for the earlier years should prove to be even larger than that exhibited in this series. It would thus not be wrong to conclude that in relation to the basic component of the standard living there is a condition of stagnancy.

The problem of employment has a number of facets. In the first instance, labour has to be looked upon as a valuable resource, and the continued under-utilization of this resource points to defective planning. Humans are also a social liability in a society whose conscience is sufficiently aroused.

As it is clear that a poor country with a large volume of under-employment or unemployment has not the resources to grant public assistance to the unemployed and to those in distress, the planning for employment of all becomes a doubly important objective. Therefore, employment planning ought to have with us the first claim on resources of capital and organization.

It is important to spell out carefully the implications of this objective of employment orientation of the plan. The objective does not imply that employment, however given, at whatever cost, and in whatever direction, is to be accepted as part of the plan. The plan is essentially a plan of economic development, and employment orientation emphasizes priorities without affecting end-objectives. The achievements claimed for such plans as the Chinese in the way of labour mobilization, are essentially achievements flowing out of the emphasis on employment orientation in planning. In a communistic country, presumably, the State accepts the responsibility of feeding everybody at a minimum level. Once this responsibility is accepted, then in societies as poor as China or India, there becomes, or with a little appropriate organization can be made, available a very large reservoir of labour which can be employed in a number of directions, according to needs and possibilities. The availability of such a labour force can be a source of great strength. The planning of its use presents a difficult problem to which little attention has yet been paid in India.

Employment of rural labour lies at the core of this problem. This is not only by far the largest class in terms of numbers and the class which has the lowest standards of living but also the class which receives the largest share of all additions that result from the growth of population or from technological unemployment because of development. Employment orientation of Indian planning must therefore essentially mean a determined attempt to tackle the problem of actual or potential surpluses of agricultural labour through a programme of employment, which is in itself a part of development planning, and which will increase the basis of resources and facilities on which future plans can be built. I had an occasion recently to write a note on this problem in Maharashtra, and I shall not dilate on this matter further.

Employment orientation should give a marked turn to planning in India. People in India live, in the main, in rural areas and are scattered over a very large number of villages; and this rural population is growing apace. There is, currently, a relatively small movement away from rural areas or agriculture, chiefly because of the lack of alternative opportunities. If this pattern of dispersal of population and the costs of movement are taken into account, it will be seen that not only in the short run but also as a long-term objective, providing employment in rural areas through decentralized and dispersed economic development, is extremely important for India. The programme of conservation and development of natural resources and of the building-up of socio-economic overheads throughout the countryside which could provide employment to rural labour immediately, would also build up the needed structure—super and infra—for later dispersed industrial and other non-farm development.

In highly-developed and integrated economies it can be taken for granted that forces of development generated in one place will soon have a decisive impact on other areas and activities. This is especially evident in urban industrial economies. It is not so evident in the rural sectors even of some advanced industrial countries. The experience of the last decade in India has shown that there is very little of automatic transmission or spill-over of effects of development started in particular locations and activities. Therefore, if development is a national objective and government bears responsibility equally to all regions and communities, the plan must attempt to start or initiate development simultaneously in as large a number of locations and activities all over the country as possible. Undoubtedly this dispersal of effort will appear to yield immediately less dramatic results. But it will provide a sounder base for planning in the future and also avoid the accentuation of disparities, which is one of the most serious features of the existing situation.

PLAN FOR AGRICULTURE

If one puts in the forefront the problem of employment and of the standard of living, particularly as relating to rural labour in India, attention in the second instance must be given to the agricultural sector. In this context, observations may be confined to highlighting only a small number of points. In the first instance, it appears to be urgently necessary to arrive, as early as possible, at some stabilized pattern of the organization of agricultural production. The concept of the ceiling has been generally accepted, and it is good that recent legislation has emphasized the aspect of ceiling as limiting ownership and control of material resources rather than as a ceiling to individual incomes. If the Ceiling and Tenancy laws together lead to the creation of a large body of small but viable farmers, there will still remain the problem of the vast and increasing numbers of uneconomic holders.

Co-operative farming appears to have been agreed upon as the solution of this problem. Vigorous experimentation and explicit formulation of policy are necessary to accelerate progress in this direction. Equally, the total organization of agricultural production requires immediate attention being paid to consolidation. The appropriate utilization of land should be treated as a sub-problem of consolidation. The increasing pressure on land, resulting chiefly from increase in numbers of uneconomic holders, has led to an extension of the margin of arable cultivation to limits which are highly uneconomic, and which add significantly to the requirements of plough-cattle. Consolidation and creation of co-operative farms should result in putting such areas appropriately under scrub, forest, pastures, grass, etc.

Here the main difficulty is that connected with organization. Our very large and dispersed numbers of farmers and farming units will have to be properly organized for the articulation, implementation, and experimentation related to plans of development. If the co-operative organization is accepted as the universal type, large efforts must be made and initial organizational and capital resources invested to bring this to a minimum level of operational efficiency within a short time.

The most important problem of the agricultural sector is, however, that of stabilization of incomes. The experience of the last ten years in India and in a large number of other under-developed countries shows that if a farming community is given stability and relatively favourable terms of trade, the problems of organization, of acceptance of scientific ideas, or of investment and capital formation, become relatively tractable. The basic defect of Indian planning has been the lack of a price-policy and the large hazards to which the Indian farmer, the field-crop farmer especially of the dry areas, has been subject. Unless the terms of trade are secured at some minimum favourable level to the agricultural community, no general plan of development can be expected to succeed. It is equally necessary to insist that the full benefits of the terms of trade must accrue to the agricultural community itself. Processing and marketing play a crucial role in this context. So long as these are in other hands, the major benefits of any extra margin are unlikely to be derived by the agricultural community. This is especially so when the margin itself, because of lack of stability, is fluctuating. Stabilization of prices, which represents the main avenue to stabilization of agricultural incomes in India, is thus the central problem in relation to the agricultural sector; for, with relative stabilization of prices, progress of co-operative processing and marketing should not prove difficult. However, processing is so crucial that it may become necessary in the initial stages of the stabilization effort to transfer it immediately to the public sector.

PROBLEMS OF INDUSTRIALIZATION

A plan of economic development is essentially a plan for industrialization, and therefore, the approach to planning must define clearly the route and pattern of industrialization that is envisaged. The insistence on dealing as fully as possible, from the very initial stages, with the problem of employment of labour, especially rural labour, will lead to an emphasis on the conservation and development of natural resources all over the country and spreading widely the network of socio-economic overheads. The proper organization of the unit of agricultural production and the assurance of fair terms of trade to the agriculturists will result in better utilization of land, greater productivity, and broadening the base of agricultural production. This would still leave open the main problem of the stages through which industrialization is achieved.

The approach adopted at the beginning of the Second Five-Year Plan to this problem envisaged a differentiation of the field of industries into (i) production goods industries, and (ii) consumption goods industries. Among the latter, consumption goods industries producing products similar to those of traditional consumption goods industries were looked upon in a special manner. It was envisaged that in fields like the production of cloth, the increased supply would become available through better and fuller use of existing capital and personnel in the traditional handloom weaving industry, and that no additional investment in the mechanized industry was required. The consumption goods industries, products of which were non-competitive, or only partially competitive, with traditional industries were not put under such regulation. The path of industrialization, though never spelled out in detail, was thought to be that of beginning with economic overheads and basic industries and going on to the production of capital goods and intermediate products of all sorts.

The theoretic framework of the pattern of industrialization has never been constructed. The details of its actual progress have been worked out *ad hoc* and from time to time, in part through the Development Wing, and in part through the licensing of imports. The availability of foreign collaboration in given directions appears also to have shaped the pattern of industrialization to a considerable extent. The present situation is obviously unsatisfactory. It leads inevitably to a heavy investment in building-up particular production and consumption goods industries, without reference to any overall plan or perspective.

The most salient characteristic of a poor under-developed economy is the great relative paucity of capital resources. At the same time, modern technological developments are associated with heavy use of capital resources, and the raising of an adequate base of a modern industrial society requires initial investment, on a very large scale, in economic overheads and the basic production goods industries.

In the past, this dilemma has been solved in some countries by beginning industrialization with the relatively less capital intensive consumption goods industries and continuing to depend, for a large period of development, on imports of products of capital goods industries of other countries. However, this imposes higher costs in the long run and makes assured planning of a programme of industrialization difficult. Therefore, in the more recent types of planned industrialization, heavy capital investment in economic overheads, e.g., the transport and power systems and basic production goods industries such as steel and heavy chemicals, is undertaken at the earliest stages. This is supposed to red0uce costs, shorten the period of industrialization, and make for greater self-containedness. Unless, however, the balance is maintained evenly, industrialization brought about in this manner may impose severe unnecessary hardships on the people and may, in the long run, not even prove more speedy or efficient.

The dangers and defects brought out by the history of the last decade of industrialization in India may be noted at this stage. As pointed out above, rural labour has been starved of complementary resources, and this has happened in considerable part with agriculture also. Not only is this mal-allocation a source of unnecessary distress but it is also bound to retard the development of natural primary resources. Immediately, even a more damaging result of this mal-allocation is that it increases the concentration of control over material resources within the nation, and increases greatly the disparities in wealth and income between the capitalistic classes and others and between the town and the country.

The present plan of industrialization, in and through private hands, results in allocating an increasingly larger and larger share of scarce capital resources to a small class of capitalist businesses. It is in this class that modern finance, industry, and trade have been concentrated through historical development, and it is members of this class that are in a position to take advantage of the allocation of capital resources to the modern industrial sector. The largest surpluses accrue to this class because of the heavy allocation of capital resources and their utilization of most modern techniques, and these surpluses are naturally retained within the class. This concentration of capital resources and surpluses leads to very serious distortions.

The distortions are the results of many types of influences. In the first instance, because of inadequate planning and regulation, capital resources are used for investment in directions which obviously do not or should not command high priority in the national plan of industrialization. The classic instance in this regard is that of the establishment and expansion of the rayon industry during the Second Five-Year Plan period. Such distortion does not mean merely an initial allocation of a volume of capital resources wrongly, but does also, through creating a block of investment and interest, pre-empt a continuous stream of future capital resources in the wrong direction.

The most serious distortion, however, comes through the distortion in income distribution to which the present allocation of capital resources in the plan of industrialization inevitably leads. The allocation of heavy capital resources to certain classes, operating chiefly from the biggest cities, leads to a concentration of surplus in their hands, rapidly increasing their relative income and the incomes of those connected directly or indirectly with their activities. A progressively disproportionate share of the increase in the national income is thus inevitably concentrated in these hands.

This concentration of income increments strongly influences the nature of effective demand for consumption goods, which in turn affects the composition of productive industry. The phenomenon of a stagnant demand for coarse cloth, while the demand for rayon goods and air-conditioners and refrigerators and private cars is buoyant, is a reflection of the distortion of income distribution. This distortion naturally leads to distortion of the production system through making investment in production of air-conditioners or refrigerators or rayon goods especially profitable. The relative profitability in terms of market pricing of various investments may be a sound guide for capital allocations in a fairly egalitarian society. In a society in which inequality is great and rising, the market prices as guide for long-term capital investment are obviously completely misleading. However, at present, industrialization in India appears to work chiefly through this guide; it cannot work otherwise because of a number of basic aspects of present economic policy.

The first important aspect of present economic policy is dependence on the accrual of savings in the hands of the private capitalists, and the leaving of a number of important investment decisions with them. The decision to leave the accrual of savings in private hands necessarily gives a turn to fiscal policy. This has a number of aspects such as the levels of direct taxation of individuals and companies, tax concessions of various sorts, orientation of import licensing, etc., all of which ultimately have the same result. They increase to such a high extent the personal and corporate incomes controlled by the small group of high capitalists, that they and their associates, after indulging in the highest personal consumption expenditures by modern Anglo-American standards, yet have sufficient capital resources to invest in the private sector in modern business.

As if the distortion brought about by this basic policy was not enough, certain special accentuators have been added to it in recent years. These are: the twist to import licence policy in the supposed interest of export promotion and the role of foreign collaboration. Both the import and the export licensing have, throughout the plan-decade, been controlled *ad hoc*, and have never been explicitly connected with a path of industrialization and never been formulated in relation to long-term planning. The latest phase of import licences for export promotion leads to granting import licences in a special manner for a supposed increase in exports, the overall results and long-run future of which are doubtful and have never been examined.

The only effective result of this policy is to expand, obviously disproportionately, capital allocation in given directions, and the initial step has continuing cumulative effect. The favoured industrialists not only obtain allocation of currently scarce foreign-exchange for importing capital goods and raw materials but also, in the process, expand the base of production industry in their control; this must in future progressively attract, according to present policies, higher and higher allocation of capital resources and foreign-exchanges. The policy seemingly directed towards immediate export-promotion thus is really meant for, or at least results in, even a more disproportionate allocation of capital resources to a small class than would happen otherwise.

The other accentuator is the special encouragement given to private foreign business investment. This again inevitably leads to the concentration of capital resources in the same class as before. Foreign collaboration means a billionaire talking to a billionaire; and to the quantum of resources that are brought in through collaboration of the foreign collaborators have to be added additional allocations of internal resources to the Indian partner for completing the transaction. The results as apparent today are not surprising. The relative success of the plan is supposed to be in modern private industry. This has the amplest allocation of capital resources and can, because of its control over surpluses, command the best qualified personnel and, through foreign collaboration, the latest know-how also. In spheres other than that of modern business, the organizational problems are of immense difficulty, because it is in this sphere that mere imitation will not do. The personnel here is the most untried, and capital resources very inadequate. But the relative success of modern industry is itself considered to be a strong reason for continuing the existing patently unequal allocation of resources.

ALTERNATIVE APPROACH

Before presenting the alternative approach it may be noted that some present trends in the economy threaten to limit the possibility of radical adjustments in the future. These trends are: the concentration of capital resources and economic power in a small number of hands; the concentration of industrial population in the largest urban centres; highly disparate rates of growth in sectors and locations; absence of programmes of social security; and continuing low standards of living. There is no hope that any of these trends will be reversed during the next ten years if present policies continue, and if they are not reversed during the next five years or so, then developments will have gone too far to be reversible.

The path of planned development that we have adopted, with its emphasis on forced growth of basic and capital goods industries, is largely modelled on the experience of the communist countries. However, the programme of development along these lines in communist countries is protected by a number of concurrent measures. In the main, these are: (i) a basically egalitarian distribution of incomes and the destruction of economic power residing in private-interest groups; and (ii) detailed control over the prices and distribution of consumption goods, and detailed planning of the types of consumption goods industries set up and of consumption goods produced. This is combined with the assumption, from the beginning, of basic responsibility by the State towards minimum provision of food and consumption goods, and for finding work for all.

None of these safeguards is available in the Indian plan. The alternative path in the capitalist countries has usually led to initial investment in the less capital heavy industries so that the distortions induced by industrialization are not, at least initially, too great. Further, the much greater responsibility thrown on the industrial classes to find their own capital resources and to shoulder risks imposes on them consumption restraints, as in Japan, which keeps the inequality in distribution of incomes and consumption levels from becoming too great. The attempt in India to follow the communist route of planning combined with protection to high industries but little protection to the farmer or the consumer, has the result that we have the worst of both the worlds.

The result of continued operation of present trends will be unrestrained growth of metropolitan centres, continued disintegration of rural communities and stagnancy in many agricultural areas, and buoyancy and rapid growth in industries producing luxury or semi-luxury goods. The whole process will also be wasteful of capital resources. It may be assumed that where the demand for consumption goods is not highly varied and can be satisfied with large production of a restricted number of standardized types, the investment of capital per unit of consumption goods will be lower than where the demand embraces a large number of luxury items, where there is little standardization, and where the demand for each type is relatively small. The latter type of development is not appropriate to poor countries and they cannot afford it. It is still the type to which present trends lead in this country.

In framing the alternative approach, I accept the initial division of production goods industries and consumption goods industries contemplated in the Second Five-Year Plan. I should add a further three-fold division of the production goods industries, viz.,: (i) the economic overheads, i.e., the transport, power, and other systems; (ii) the basic industries such as steel, coal and other minerals, heavy chemicals, etc.; and (iii) industries producing the capital goods required by the consumption goods industries.

I start with the proposition that in the ultimate analysis the whole development is geared to a greater per capita availability of consumption goods and that the pattern of capital goods industries (class iii above) has to be related to the composition and technique of consumption goods industries. This, in its turn, is dependent on the extent and nature of demand for consumption goods and decisions regarding the technique and location of consumption goods industries.

Basically, therefore, in a plan, which is drawn up by reference to a stage of development to be reached sometime in the future, the central requirement is to project a picture of consumption requirements at that time in the future. This projected picture of consumption requirements has two important aspects. It involves, firstly, a projection of the distribution of incomes in society. Obviously, the demand for consumption goods with a distribution as highly unequal as that of today in India will be very different from the demand for consumption goods if we attained the equality of distribution of incomes similar to that of even the UK or Japan. The second factor is the projected pattern of industrialization, especially in relation to location and technique.

At this stage, some values and considerations which might be, in part, extra-economic have to be introduced. The main relevant value in this context, is that attached to the development of dispersed and decentralized industry. This value can be derived through the importance attached to the dispersal of population over space and the avoidance of conurbation, and to units of productive activity becoming relatively small. Alternatively, or in addition, the value can be derived, and the programme justified on the basis of the limiting conditions of development in a poor country with a large population. Our population is dispersed over rural areas mainly in units of less than 5,000 population: the population is growing fairly rapidly. The experience of the last decade shows that even with a significant increase in the production of modern industries, urbanization, as a whole, does not take place at a rapidly increasing rate. At the same time, the worst aspects of urbanization such as concentration in metropolitan areas, the mounting-up of economic and social costs such as strains on the transport systems, virtual non-existence of housing, and degrading conditions of living for large masses of urban population, are being accentuated in spite of the fact that the bulk of plan resources made available for housing and improvement of urban amenities are allotted to the largest metropolitan centres. The growing concentration in these centres, with growth of misery and stagnation in the countryside, can be avoided only by taking a radically different view of the future pattern of growth.

Unless industry is deliberately dispersed and decentralized, neither the problem of the great cities nor that of the villages can begin to be dealt with. If this is accepted and if relative equality in distribution of incomes can be achieved, the pattern of consumption goods industries of the future will become definitely oriented towards mass goods production in dispersed locations.

The chief problem here is to make this compatible with efficiency in production and with the process of development. Unfortunately, the case for this has become weak because of the almost complete failure of the Khadi Board and related organizations during the Second Five-Year Plan period. Instead of following proper developmental programmes, they wasted resources in what were not even effective relief measures. In the same manner, the common-production-programme approach was not kept in the re-organization of handloom industry so that there was neither efficient development of that industry nor any serious contribution by it towards additional supply of cloth for the masses.

The whole of this programme therefore needs to be re-examined from two points of view: The first is the strictly short-term point of view of avoiding technological unemployment. This problem is confined to a few widespread rural industries and cannot be effectively tackled by the older khadi-and-village-industries approach. The approach here has to be, on the one hand, to insist on a common production programme and, on the other, to move at a fast pace at improving the technique of traditional industries. In this sphere the main hopeful development during the last five years seems to have been in the direction of some research related to mechanization of village industries, which involves the adoption of a much wider view of the possibility of combination of techniques than before. This is best exemplified in the recent work of the Central Research Institute at Wardha. (The implications and the directions of the work are set out in brief in an article by Dr M. Sadashiva Rao on mechanization in village industries, in the February 1961 issue of Khadi-Gramodyog, published by the Khadi and Village Industries Commission.)

The technical improvement and part mechanization of a village industry may enable it to produce mass consumption goods more efficiently and cheaply, or it may, as in the case of handmade paper, be oriented towards the production of highly specialized costly goods. In the latter case, technical transformation will add an efficient source of supply for certain types of goods required in the economy, but will make no contribution towards the production of mass consumption goods.

The second and the long run point of view, which transcends the problem of technological unemployment, presents a continuing problem for the whole period of development. This is that of increasing adoption of modern techniques and scientific advance in an efficiently decentralized industrial sector producing intermediate goods and goods for mass consumption. This is a matter in which the approach adopted in village industries research has to be greatly widened. There has, in the first instance, to be some broad division of total products or goods which, in the modern context, can be produced in small units and dispersed locations, and those others which can only be produced efficiently in large-scale units employing the most capital intensive technique. When comparing, in this context, the efficiency of smaller units with the larger, allowance will, of course, have to be made for compensating advantages of dispersed industrialization. In the main, these are represented by the savings of costs and overheads such as of transport, housing and civic amenities, and may also be represented by somewhat smaller monetary wage-payments.

The general technical problem in this is that of the breaking-down of discontinuity. There is not, at present, sufficient research and experimentation regarding methods of efficient production at various levels of use of capital or scales of production. In continuously advancing industrial societies, with an already varied and large base for the economy, there is no inducement for such experimentation. It is, however, of the utmost importance in India to establish a path of continuing efficient production at various levels of combination of resources in varying sizes of establishments.

The approach thus sketched briefly accepts immediate and continuing investments in the transport and power systems and in the basic industries. It would suspend the further extension of the machine industry which produced consumption goods, and would try to meet the increased demand for consumption goods through increased production by traditional industry using improved techniques, or by new, dispersed and decentralized industry. The evolution and planning of industry producing the capital goods required by consumption goods industry would then be related to the character and extent of the new dispersed industry. This approach assumes a number of measures. It would require: (i) elaboration and full implementation of the idea of common production plans; (ii) regulation of investment in consumption goods industry and industry producing capital goods for them; (iii) vigorous experimentation in establishment of efficient, decentralized industry; and, above all, (iv) prevention of a premature increase in the demand for luxury and semi-luxury goods.

In the absence of appropriate and careful planning in this manner, future developments must inevitably proceed along present lines and lead to the development of industries producing capital goods, such as those used in the mass consumption goods industries of the Western industrialized countries. These will be increasingly associated with heavy capital investment in large individual establishments. With the low average income of our people, the number of such establishments possible will remain small. So that employment given by modern industry will remain small and concentrated in cities, and the agriculture and the rural population will greatly continue to lag behind.

POLICY REQUIREMENTS

I may conclude this note by indicating briefly the policy requirements of the approach tentatively sketched above. Instruments of control and regulation, at present possessed and used by the government, will not need to be amplified. Only their use will have to be differently oriented. In the first instance, the government will have to frame a price-policy and implement it. The primary objectives of this policy will be: stabilized prices of agricultural products, and holding the price line for essential consumption goods. The government's price-policy will have to concern itself also with essential industrial raw materials, and intermediate and capital goods, which are in short supply. For making price-policy effective, the government will find it necessary to undertake directly, or through co-operative or corporative channels, a measure of distribution of essential consumption goods and of allocation of some goods and services required by industries.

The regulation of foreign trade will have to be related to a long-term policy, and the system of licensing which causes frequent disturbances to markets, and provides for extra profits for speculators and favoured parties, will have to be changed. In all these matters, no more than effective implementation, or certain adjustments, of existing policies is needed.

In some other respects a radical departure from existing policies will be required. This is chiefly to achieve a more equal distribution of incomes and to route major savings through public agencies. We are not concerned in this context with the savings-investment effort at the level of the agriculturists below the ceiling or the small businessman. The problem relates to savings required for investment in large-scale modern business. Even today these are derived to a large extent through government-controlled institutions like the Industrial Finance Corporation of India or the Life Insurance Corporation. However, even the fractional dependence, in this matter, on savings formed in private hands, weakens and warps the State policy. For, as pointed out, this makes adequate control over the levels of consumption impossible and gives a wrong turn to fiscal policy.

Government policy must be oriented to seeing that incomes left with individuals after taxation do not exceed the maximum permissible levels of consumption expenditure, and that all major finance required for modern organized business is obtained through public-regulated institutions. It may be necessary even to see that investment of own savings of corporations is subject to regulation. It follows that either directly or through taxation there is fairly strict limitation of levels of individual incomes and of salaries both private and public. Without these measures it will be impossible to achieve a proper long-term plan for dispersed industrialization, or to prevent grave distortions of the productive system through upsurge of demand of luxury types of consumption goods. When these measures are adopted it will be easier to standardize and rationalize the production of consumption goods.

The policy will require, on the other hand, the assumption of some responsibility on the part of the government for the provision of employment opportunities and for guaranteed distribution of food. With an effective price-policy and a controlled purchase-and-distributive mechanism, plan targets can be framed chiefly in terms of real availability in physical quantities of food and essential consumption goods, and with these assured, problems of deficit financing will become tractable.

The new approach will also require a different attitude on the part of the governments and the people to a number of questions. In matters of public service, for example, adequate performance at levels appropriate to a poor country rather than prestige and show expenditure among general squalor would be the goal. Again, if real progress is to be made towards decentralized industry, the governments of States will have to give up their present scramble for the location of giant industrial units, public or private, within their border. The establishment of such lone units solves no problems for the economy of the State as a whole. In most cases, the only result of the scramble is to hasten further the progress of large-scale industry and to secure for it not only extra allocations of capital resources but to reserve for its use valuable resources of raw materials. This latter phenomenon in particular, greatly undermines possibilities of the growth of small-scale industry.

The policy in relation to industry implied in this programme does not lead to wholesale nationalization or to the abolition of private property in means of production. Agriculture, after the operation of a ceiling, and all kinds of small business, will be almost unaffected by this approach, except that in each sector co-operative effort will be encouraged. The operation of the new policy will be directed only towards large organized modern business, especially the centres of concentration among them. (It may be noted parenthetically that the large concentrations in Indian business today are comparable to the Japanese Zaibatsu which were forcibly broken up by the American Occupation authorities.)

Two sets of measures appear to be needed in this context. Firstly, the adoption of a ceiling applied to the ownership, either directly or through partnership or shareholding, of means of production by individuals and families. In view of the large scarcity of material resources within the country and the adoption of the concept of the ceiling in relation to agricultural land, such a measure becomes necessary. In this context, however, the resources, ownership of which comes into government hands through operation of the ceiling, need not be redistributed. Obviously, in large modern organized business, ownership is divorced from control and operation, and the structure of the operational unit will not be disturbed through a further dispersal of ownership or through some assets vesting in government. The dispersal will be a measure chiefly helping more egalitarian distribution of wealth and income.

To affect the operational units of big business, the State will have to act in another manner—by taking seriously its responsibility as a substantial financier of or shareholder in most of these. Through guaranteeing loans, and through the institutions it controls, the State is already in the position of a guarantor, substantial creditor, or owner of large business, and will become increasingly so. It is, however, not necessary for the State to control policies of the individual companies. All that is necessary is that their operations are conducted as befitting the concerns affected by public interest. This can be done through the imposition of uniform accounting systems, through the appointment of independent auditors owing nothing to the directors, and through other measures of surveillance by government directors, which will ensure that acts of evasion, avoidance, collusion, etc., intended to defeat legal regulation or State policy, are prevented.

If concentration of power or control in the hands of individuals or small groups can be avoided through operation of the ceiling and the public character and open conduct of business of large companies enforced through action of government directors, no steps towards nationalization need be taken. It will be observed that the measures suggested are no more than the minimal necessary to fulfil the directives of the State policy of the Constitution.

Another direction in which special policy measures are necessary is that of urbanization. In large metropolitan cities, historical forces have centred many activities and services which in turn attract streams of new activity. Most of these cities are now overgrown and the costs of adequately maintaining them are rising rapidly. However, in this instance, these increasing costs cannot be transferred, in a sufficient measure, to the operators within the city, and there is glaring divergence between individual and social benefits and costs. Even the measure of making some large new units provide for part housing of labour does not adequately compensate for the total effects of the establishment of a new additional unit in cities like Bombay.

Therefore, immediate policy must act in three directions: effective stoppage of any further expansion in the largest cities; increasing costs of establishment and operation in some large cities; and increasing the supply of services and reducing their costs for the towns and small industrial centres. All this has to be combined with a programme of re-organization of village layouts and of rural housing. Part of the latter will fall under the measures for providing employment to rural labour, but the total programme has to be meaningfully co-ordinated. If possible, special incentives may be afforded for industry to move out of certain areas and into certain other areas.

This note has been confined to indicating the most salient economic aspects of what, in my opinion, constitutes the right approach to planning in India. However, before concluding, a brief reference may be made to some other aspects. Firstly, there is the re-organization of administration. The chief problem here appears to be that of the hierarchical and caste structure of the services and the problem of the dominance everywhere of the non-expert administrator. Without a radical change in the recruitment, organization, and definition of mutual relations of the various services, this problem cannot be solved.

The second is the problem of decentralization. The decentralization of planning is at least as important as the decentralization of administration. The only observation I should make in this context is the great potential danger of focussing exclusive attention on the village and treating it as an independent autonomous unit. Whether in planning, in operation, or in general administration, an integrated structure of a tier of area-authorities, organized on the federal principle, has to be aimed at. I welcome in this context the recommendation made by the recent Maharashtra Committee to experiment, in the first instance, with substantial devolution at the district level.

Beyond administrative arrangements there lies the problem of the centre, or centres, of power in society and the current use of that power. There is little doubt that our society, especially the portion that constitutes the urban middle classes and the political and economic ruling strata, is corrupt and callous and is becoming increasingly so. What I mean by being callous is exemplified by avowed Gandhians violently opposing measures for restraining the further growth of Bombay City, or the Food Minister congratulating himself on having solved the problem of food when all that had happened was that the level of per capita availability of food in the country had been barely maintained through increased imports from abroad.

The main source of existing corruption in society is the concentration of economic power and resources in the hands of a small group of capitalists. The corruption was laid bare, most explicitly, when the ruling political party provided by law for contributions from public companies. But it is all pervasive and operates equally powerfully whether in the case of high-placed administrators looking, in the future, to jobs for themselves or, in the present, for their sons and relatives in private business, or in that of the station master booking a wagon for consideration. A poor, overcrowded society, in which opportunities are scarce and rewards very uneven, can be easily corrupted by those who hold concentrated economic power. Therefore, no progress is possible unless the concentration is broken down. When this happens and we are able to take a total view of all elements and of both town and country, the approach of beginning with employment and rural labour commended here can receive attention.

6

Planning without a Policy Frame*

This note is intended to present a point of view regarding the present working of the Indian economy and the possibility of giving it a definitive direction. It is necessary, for the purpose, to present a comprehensive and an integrated picture; limits of space and time make it impossible to do this in full detail. Also, it is not possible to argue each point. Inevitably the note will appear to be full of summary jottings and *obiter dicta*. An advance apology is tendered for this defect.

The Indian economy of today is a very mixed economy. There exists within it, a great variety of forms of organization and of techniques; also, it presents an amazing medley of restrictions and regulations and of undirected and uncontrolled economic activity. The economy is not open as almost all aspects of its financial and commercial dealings with the rest of the world are closely regulated. Levels of internal costs and prices have, therefore, no necessarily predictable relation with those in other countries. Internally also, a great variety of prohibitions, directions, and regulations exists. These are most pervasive in the field of establishment of modern industry, but operate to some extent in every sphere. However, to an amazing extent the formulation and operation of the regulations and controls are unconnected with each other. Each is framed with a limited specific objective and operated as such. The prices of a number of agricultural products are more or less continuously under control, such as those of sugarcane, cotton, and cereal foodgrains. The controlled levels of the different crops have never been related to each other. And it is obvious that without the definition of a frame, even the setting-up of the

* Originally published in *Economic and Political Weekly*, Vol. II, Issue 3–5, February 1967.

Agricultural Prices Commission cannot remedy this defect. Even within each field the short-term view dominates. How and to what extent this happens is made clear by the description of the full sway of 'ad-hocism' in sugar policy during the last decade in the report of the Sen Commission.

The most outstanding feature of the 'planned' Indian economy is thus, the total absence of a policy frame. It would not be unfair to say that Indian planners are deliberately avoiding the construction of such a frame and that from plan to plan, there is a definite regression in this respect. As illustrations one may refer to the full chapter on food policy in the first plan and its continuous emaciation to the very sketchy, indefinite statement in the draft outline of the Fourth Five-Year Plan; even more remarkable, perhaps, is the complete disregard of the concept of the stabilization of agricultural prices, accepted in all the previous plans, in the latest outline. The result is that in the aggregate, the economy operates as almost a *laissez faire* economy, in part, modified by the operation of particular controls. It also means that where the particular measure is in line with trends set in motion by *laissez faire* operation, the trend is accentuated; on the other hand, where it seeks to counter such trend, it is usually powerless. Thus the stabilization at a favourable level of sugarcane prices was highly effective because of the operative trend in favour of intensive irrigated crops. On the other hand, measures such as distribution of fertilizers for food-grain production proved fruitless in face of an inappropriate price policy, and programmes of rural industrialization are ineffective because of the absence of an overall integrated policy support.

It is in this context that the successes and failures of Indian planning have to be interpreted. The successes have been in the field of public investment in irrigation, power, transport, etc., and in basic industries, and to some extent, in the extension and diversification of educational and health services. These required no policy support and depended on the availability of resources and the appropriate administrative and technical skills. Therefore, even though planning might have been defective and costs high in particular cases, substantial progress has been registered. The other notable success has been in the creation of a diversified industrial complement in the private sector. Here, supporting state policy played an important part. In a few instances it was specific, relating to the finance, etc., of particular projects. Generally, it was the restrictive import policy which resulted in creating a general sellers' market for products of many industries and the large number of other concessions that private industrialists as a class were able to obtain that brought this about. In recent years, distinct encouragement given to foreign collaboration arrangements also helped. However, though there was some regulation through licensing of establishments and of imports, little control was exercised over the detailed composition of the industrial complement or over its costs to the operation of the economy in terms of prices charged for products or import requirements created in the process. The draft outline of the Fourth Five-Year Plan notes that the direction and regulation of the private sector in industry is one of the weakest areas in Indian planning.

Two areas where the performance has been partially successful also exhibit the basic characteristic of Indian planning. There has been some success in raising the level of taxation and in gathering resources in public hands. The centre has fairly insistently followed a policy of attempting to raise resources, in significant part, through taxation, and some governments of states have also done this. However, fiscal measures have failed as instruments of economic policy. They are supposed to be especially useful in two directions: as means of restraining consumption and of promoting equality. A very large part of new and increased taxation has been in the form of excises and such other indirect taxes. However, tax proposals have rarely been framed with reference to objectives such as restraint of consumption and where so intended, have not proved successful. Markets for most consumer goods, durable and others, bearing high excise duties continue to exhibit pressure of demand. The case of sugar is very instructive in this regard. The restraint on internal consumption which can be and is made effective in sugar would be the result of not the very high excise duty already imposed, but of the exercise of powers of controlling issue and sale retained by the government.

The possibility of using taxation as an egalitarian measure depends on the effectiveness of direct taxation. The failure in this field in India has been very marked. Known evasion of income-tax is so large that the tax statistics are worthless even for estimating distribution of incomes, especially in the higher ranges. The expenditure-tax was a patent failure and was given up. The wealth, gift, and estate duties together have proved disappointing even as sources of revenue and cannot obviously produce any impression on inequality.

The other field of partial success has been that of agricultural production. The overall increase in production over the years has been substantial and in some crops highly significant. However, the attempt to guide the direction of production has proved infructuous and the failure has been large in the crucial area of the increased, needed production of foodgrains. The reasons are the same as elsewhere. The government finds it possible to raise resources and make them available for use for capital investment or current inputs but is totally unable, either to ensure that these resources will reach particular categories or will be distributed in a given equitable manner, or to direct and regulate the use of the resources when in other hands. Two notable results follow: Firstly, the resources get distributed in relation to the strength of the individual units in the field and the position of vantage they command, and secondly, they are used not in the planned or desired directions but in those which the private parties find most profitable in relation to ruling market conditions.

In short, where the government in India directly undertakes large programmes of public expenditure, it succeeds best. It fails to the extent that the planned use of resources lies in other hands, especially where it is a matter of detailed multi-directional operations or where a consistent long-term policy is needed to obtain results. It is not surprising, therefore, that the most notable and fatal failure has been the failure to maintain stability. The most obvious aspect of this failure was the unchecked increase in prices, resulting in the need to devalue.

The draft outline of the Fourth Five-Year Plan appears to be based on the supposition that the tendency of prices to rise in a developing economy will be put down if you desist from deficit financing, and that financial discipline and appropriate monetary and credit policy are all the supplementary measures that are needed. Many considerations would indicate that such optimism is unwarranted. For example, if one looks at the history of credit policy during the last decade, some lessons stand out. Firstly, selective controls by themselves are useless; about the only effective measure is regulation of total bank credit, but even this has to be carried out mostly directly and not through the bank rate. Equally clearly, such regulation of the volume of bank credit raises, in an acute form, a dilemma which it is almost impossible to resolve. The continually expanding economic activity in a developing economy requires continuous increase in production credit. However, without a very much greater control over production, trading, speculation, and banking, than obtains at present, there is no way of ensuring that the general credit restraint will affect not production but only other activities. This is apart from the liberal supply of black market money in the money market which feeds by preference not production but chiefly speculative trading-activities. Nothing in the draft outline or in the recent pronouncements of the government or the Reserve Bank officials, indicates that any policy solution to this basic dilemma is available. In the absence of such a solution, credit policy by itself cannot deal with the pressure on prices unless it brings about deflation and stagnancy.

It should be noted that governments of states, in particular, face a similar dilemma. They cannot suddenly check expenditure without far-reaching effects, not only political but also economic. Moreover, their action programmes in all fields are inevitably formulated to expand year after year, and present activities and expectations are based on such continuous expansion. Many states, again, are exposed to risks, especially of natural calamities which increase the volume of expenditure suddenly and unavoidably. It is important to impress on governments of states the need to observe strict financial discipline. At the same time, once the sights and targets are fixed at the beginning of the plan period, it is highly unrealistic to expect that states will be able to revise them downwards or to prevent the expected annual increases during the currency of the plan. If they are forced to do this, adverse effects on plan performance and implementation cannot be avoided.

This is apart from the basic disparity between the demand for, and the supply of, consumer goods, created by the very process of forcing the pace of development. The large needed investment and activity in relation to development of natural resources, setting-up of basic industry, and the provision of socio-economic overheads, stimulate employment and increase incomes, but do not equally increase the supply of consumer goods. The resulting chronic short supply of consumer goods creates a pressure on consumer goods prices, in the first instance, and this is transmitted in due course to other prices. And when, as happens in the case of foodgrains in India, the supply is maldistributed over time and space, the activity of traders and speculators is able to increase greatly the effects of even a small initial shortage. An upward movement of prices in foodgrains could thus start without the previous existence of an inflationary trend and could itself lead to a higher resulting level of prices in general and of money supply. These considerations indicate that a plan of development must be accompanied by policy measures, other than fiscal and monetary measures, for holding prices in check. No such integrated policy has been evolved, even after devaluation, or included in the Draft Fourth Five-Year Plan.

It is natural to think of the balance of payments in connection with stabilization of internal prices. Devaluation was forced on us because the continuous increase in internal costs and prices made it impossible to conduct foreign trade and meet foreign obligations. Even after devaluation we are far from the stage at which a regime of revenue and protective duties will keep down the value of imports adequately. We shall have to continue for many years with a regime of prohibitions and quantitative restrictions of imports. Recent experience has highlighted certain lessons in this regard. Firstly, that the licensing of imports under existing conditions creates, perhaps, the largest area in the economy of corruption and illicit gains and that this is directly connected with the very high possibilities of gain associated with the obtaining of an import licence. Secondly, import policy is closely related to the total plan, especially of industrialization. Industrialization in the private sector has, during the last ten years, added greatly to the compulsive need of imports for maintaining the units set up; also, under the pretext of gaining or increasing export markets, capital and raw material imports have been allowed which have involved heavy net expenditure of foreign exchange. The third aspect is the continued imports of foodgrains and raw cotton. A development plan associated with continued administration of quantitative restrictions of imports thus requires: (i) an early cessation of foodgrains and cotton imports through an appropriate production policy and through measures of control and rationalization of demand; and (ii) both an integrated and detailed scrutiny of the programme of industrialization in the public and private sectors and in extreme cases even of units already set up, so that present and future imports fully, and only, serve the needs of the long-term development plan. It also requires (iii) that effective steps are taken to eliminate the extra gains obtained by private parties as a result of quantitative restriction of imports. These steps are all the more urgent as the prospects of increasing exports rapidly are very doubtful and we have to concentrate attention on limiting imports.

Two points deserve special consideration in connection with assessing our capacity to export. In the composition of our exports, jute manufactures, tea, cotton manufactures, oil and oilcake, tobacco, and other agricultural products, are still dominant. The main exports which have come into prominence during the last fifteen years are sugar and coffee, which are related to agriculture, iron ore, art silk fabrics, and machinery. However, these recent developments do not change the basic pattern of heavy dependence on jute and cotton manufactures and tea plantation and agricultural products for export earnings. For obvious reasons, the possibilities of any large increase in the international demand for these exports are slight. On the other hand, it begins to appear that the available supply for export of a number of the traditional export commodities might shrink in the future instead of expanding, if the rising domestic demand is not checked. Recent conditions in the vegetable oil market in the country have highlighted this trend. It is also clear that advantage could not have been taken of the high international prices of sugar if distribution of sugar within the country had not been fully under the control of the government. Restraining domestic consumption thus becomes an essential aspect of export policy and this might be true of new exports like machinery manufactures also.

Restraints can be placed on domestic consumption in two ways: (i) levying excises and raising prices high, and (ii) by directly controlling the physical quantities available for exports and for domestic consumption, while keeping the internal price-level moderate. The latter might require some control over internal distribution also. The second alternative will have to be accepted wherever the prices affected are of essential consumer goods of mass consumption or of intermediate or capital goods in crucial sectors. Sugar is already in this category, and any attempt to increase largely the exports of vegetable oils or their products, or of, say, coffee, would involve similar action in their regard. For a much larger number of goods, heavy excises may become necessary. In this case, the total effect of their imposition on the stability of the price level will have to be given consideration. Thus, apart from the inelasticity of the demand for our important and traditional exports, the inelasticity of the supply of our agricultural products coupled with rising internal demand poses very difficult problems of pricing and regulation if exports of these are to be maintained at a high level and, even more, if an attempt is made to expand them.

Attention may be paid to two other categories of exports. One is represented by mill-made cotton manufactures and art silk fabrics. Recent studies of these show that the policy which allowed imports of capital goods and raw material in order to stimulate the exports in this class had a negative result. They may, therefore, be written off as sources of expanding profitable exports in the near future. The other is represented by engineering goods and machinery manufactures. At the outset it may be noticed that in an economy operating with a heavy control of imports, costs of all products in which import elements enter, are likely to rule relatively high. Primary product or products, in costs of which these dominate, do not suffer from this disadvantage. In relation to others, internal prices are expected to rule high because of higher costs and also because the sealing off of imports creates a sellers' market internally. In the absence of a detailed allocation and pricing control of imported raw materials and components and of the finished products, goods in this category are unlikely to be exported in significant quantities. That this fully applies to India was shown by the need felt to devise a system of export incentives for this category very soon after devaluation. Even after a substantial measure of devaluation the internal costs and prices of these manufactures could not be brought into line with international costs and prices. Except for individual small classes of special products, this must be accepted as the general continuing situation. Therefore, little can be expected by way of contribution to export-earnings required for development plans from this category. (Even the optimistic estimates emerging from the Planning Commission did not place the total estimated value of this type of exports in 1970–71 as more than 10 per cent of the total estimated exports.) Also, unless the undesirable regime of export incentives is to be permanently maintained, the sustenance and encouragement of these exports would be possible only with appropriate pricing and allocation controls.

The failure to maintain stability while attempting development has been the largest and the most spectacular in relation to the internal price-level and the external balance of payments. However, there are other aspects where continuing imbalance may have important, long-term effects, not only for economic, but also for political and social, stability. Most of those might be described as related to growing inequality. Inequality in distribution of incomes, inequality in the pace of development of activity in different sectors, inequality in distribution of activity over space, etc. Something has already been said regarding the partial success in agricultural production and the relative failure in foodgrains production. The agricultural production programme has proved lopsided not only as between crops but also as between categories of producers. This was the result of the so-called production orientation of the programmes. This orientation, in both agriculture and industry, results in concentrating attention on those categories of existing producers who are already in the most favourable position to produce. This approach which might have some justification in the short term in an emergency, persists after 15 years of planning. Most production programmes have only partially succeeded, but whatever their benefits, these have accrued chiefly to substantial and middle farmers, mostly in the intensive, irrigated areas. Inevitably, the distance between the insecure, dry areas and the irrigated, and between the small and the large in all areas, has been greatly widened in the process. That the government and the Planning Commission have nothing to offer to the small holder is heavily underscored by the reference made in the draft outline of the latest plan to a half-baked experiment, directed to small holders' problems, in Maharashtra which has hardly started. It is often emphasized that the middle and substantial peasants, even after land reforms, cultivate more than 80 per cent of the land, but the obverse of the statement, that those who hold the remaining 15 to 20 per cent form the majority of the cultivating families should have an equal significance for the planner. If the small holder who is in possession of some land gets little benefit from the process of planned development, the landless labourer and the rural artisan is even more badly off. I am, of course, referring not to the intentions of the planners or to the writing in the reports of the Planning Commission but to actual developments.

In the entire conception and operation of Indian planning, very little attention is paid to the transmission of forces and effects within the economy. Properly speaking, this should be a primary concern of the planner. Except in a highly centralized and fully articulated development plan, action cannot be taken in every area and in every respect. Direct action has to be confined to a few strategic points, and it has to be assumed that helped by incentives and such like indirect measures, its effect will spread throughout. Therefore, appropriate visualization of transmission of force and spill-over effects should shape every plan. There are two main aspects of this visualization. Firstly, the distribution of beneficial effects, over all constituents of a sector, of action taken in relation to one constituent. Secondly, the manner in which and the extent to which development initiated at any location or in any activity spreads to other areas or activities.

The slogan 'production before distribution' is meaningful, or would be at least innocuous, in case the beneficial results of special action in favour of, say, large producers were seen to spread over fairly easily and quickly to all the participants in productive activity. However, if, in fact, this does not either happen at all or the benefits are first all concentrated into the hands of large producers and only very partially, slowly, and with struggle obtained by others, such policy is seen to have not only distributive but also ultimate production arrangement and direction effects. The same applies to consideration of transmission of effects from a large urban area to other urban areas and surrounding rural areas, and to transmission from, say, industry to agriculture. The concentration of power and wealth, which has been an obvious result of Indian planning, has to be likened to the process of unearned increments accruing to holders of land in central areas when public action begins development of an urban complex. As in this case, unless vigorous and prompt action is taken to nullify the results, there is inevitable transfer of wealth from others to the holders of privileged positions. Therefore, either the strategy of development must be such as to affect directly and simultaneously the big and the small, or corrective measures must be planned side by side. In fact, both approaches have to be adopted. The first, in relation to producers and productive activity, and the second, in relation to the large body of non-producers.

The exposition above may be illustrated by reference to the failure in respect of rural industrialization and in preventing dangerous concentration of activity in metropolitan areas. Rural industrialization has been a constant aim, but the comprehensive measures required to achieve it have never even been worked out. There are a number of aspects to this problem. An important one relates to using the skills and equipment existing in traditional industry to increase the availability of common consumer goods. This was to be achieved by affording some protection to those industries and at the same time continuously transforming their technique. A common production plan for goods produced with all kinds of techniques in an industry had to be devised for the purpose. To some extent this was done in cotton cloth production; in others no common production plan was prepared, and the Khadi Board failed to move in the direction of transformation of techniques.

Other aspects of the problem relate to processing industries and the establishment of new, small-scale production in consumer or intermediate goods industries. The programme of action, in this respect, is related to the development of the concept of 'intermediate technology' and to arranging for the supply of components and parts to big units from a series of small, ancillary establishments. The articulation of such a programme requires an elaborate policy-frame worked out consistently from the stage of licensing of imports and industrial establishments to the development of communications, power supply, etc., in rural areas. No action has been taken in this respect. The pilot rural industries projects, not backed by appropriate policy, have failed, they were expected to, and yet are to be continued in the Fourth Five-Year Plan in which the big policy issues are shelved. It cannot be too often or too much emphasized that while modern, large-scale industry receives favourable treatment from the state and has the advantage of resources and techniques, the establishment of dispersed, small-scale industry can only be achieved by well-directed and vigorous action over a number of years. To indulge in fine writing while having no plans or intention of acting is wicked in this case. Such wickedness is bound to have its reactions. They are exhibited through the emergence in the economy of a curious kind of dualism. It is this dualism that is breeding instability. Concentration of economic activity in metropolitan areas is another aspect of the same phenomenon. This concentration has now gone so far that to maintain a maximum of satisfactory conditions in the metropolitan areas requires such large resources as to make it almost impossible to initiate all-sided development of the rest of the country. Gradually, within these areas, conditions are worsening so that they will all soon become law-and-order problems. Nothing except a vigorous policy to reverse ruling trends can really contain this element of social instability.

Related to both these phenomena is the problem of employment. It has been always recognized that this is not a separate problem but an important aspect of the problem of development itself. It is because of the importance of employment in the context of making full use of available labour resources, distributing incomes, and providing social security, that insistence is laid on wide dispersal of industrial activity and on paying attention to requirements of small holders or landless labourers in the plan. The gradual solution of the problem of providing full employment is thus to be found through the proper formulation and implementation of the development plan. There is failure to appreciate this basic truth. This is evidenced, not only in the so-called 'production orientation' and metropolitan concentration, but also in the pathetic belief in the capacity of an additional rural works programme to provide a solution to the rural unemployment and underemployment problem. Obviously, any rural work, to be worthwhile has to be a part of a plan of conservation of resources or of provision of socio-economic overheads, which is integrated into the local plan. The concept of the rural works programme thus exhibits lack of faith in two directions: firstly, in proper local planning. Secondly, it can be based only on the belief that expenditure on any local work that gives employment will not be wasteful but will somehow help the development plan. This belief is obviously inconsistent with the present elaborate arrangements for preparing a national plan and underlines their great wastefulness. It should be noticed that with the rural industrialization project and many other items, the rural works programme is proposed to be continued in the Fourth Five-Year Plan in spite of its clear failure in the Third.

The extent of the failure of planning and of the growth of instability might have become very clear if we had data regarding changes in the distribution of income in society during the last 15 years. The aggregative national income statistics exhibit increase in per capita incomes. Has this increase been fairly evenly distributed? The committee appointed to investigate this problem has failed to produce a comprehensive report. The somewhat negative conclusions in the interim report of the committee are also based mostly on data relating to wages or earnings of workers in organized industry or of government servants. Data are lacking for the really vulnerable classes, the aborigines, the scheduled castes, the landless labourers and rural artisans, the very small holders; or in urban areas for the large mass of casual labourers or labourers in unorganized industries and occupations, between whose earnings and the protected earnings of labour in organized industry, there is known to be a large and possibly widening gulf. If we examine the aggregative data relating to the three basic needs, viz., food, clothing, and shelter, the results are not very reassuring. It is widely recognized that there has been steady deterioration in the housing situation; all urban and rural data point in that direction. The position in regard to overall cloth availability appears to be stable, but there is reportedly a shift in demand to better varieties. It is not clear how to interpret this. In regard to foodgrains, the position in recent years with increased imports is more or less stable. But all evidence points to growing inequality in distribution as between state and state and as between strata and strata. The most alarming new feature is reports regarding prices and availability in rural areas in deficit states which show that these are worse off than the partially protected urban centres.

All this appears to indicate a situation which is no better than before and which might in distributive terms be worse. What, however, is definitely alarming, is the declared policy of the government and the Planning Commission. The draft outline of the Fourth Five-Year Plan contains extracts from a policy statement by the government about the wages and salaries of its employees. In this, the government is explicit about the inability—almost undesirability—of giving full compensation for a rise in the cost of living. This can only mean that the financing of the plans requires a cut in the earnings, and therefore in the standard of living, of even low-paid government servants. This has far-reaching implications. The distributive effects of a rise in prices are well known; they accentuate inequality. The rise in prices in India after 1963 has been inadequately compensated for in relation even to the lowest paid government employees; it may be safely presumed that in relation to all classes indicated above as vulnerable, it has a highly adverse effect. It might be possible, in the present context, for the government to say that a sharp unexpected price rise could not be controlled by it and that, therefore, immediate compensation in a full measure was not practicable. This is very different from deliberately stating a permanent policy of not fully compensating for rise in prices. This is to make clear that the expected working of its plans is such as to require almost a continuing diminution in the standards of living of the poor. For, it is obvious that where government servants suffer, the large proportions of the less favourably placed suffer even more.

This analysis of the working of the Indian economy over the last 15 years should help to indicate the necessary corrective approach. The primary objectives of this approach would be first to maintain stability and not allow inequality to increase while implementing development plans; it should then be progressively possible to increase the welfare and egalitarian aspects and thus make progress towards satisfying the directives of the Constitution. Before recounting in brief the main constituents of this approach, some remarks on the size and structure of the plans would be in order. It should be obvious that discussion regarding size is meaningless without full statement regarding accompanying economic policy. It is necessary to emphasize this elementary fact because it is continuously ignored by Indian planners. There is no doubt that the present shape and direction of economic policy in India are largely the result of influence of vested interests. At the same time, the pushing on with a large plan regardless of appropriate policy is also in part due to the influence of physical or perspective planners who appear to believe that once a given capital investment is achieved, the economy will automatically function satisfactorily and that what is feasible just happens. While insisting on a certain rate of growth, they appear to be oblivious of the fact that instability that follows on the lack of direction and regulation will itself make growth difficult whatever be the apparent capital investment. The modified *laissez faire* bias of the capitalist and the bias towards automatism of the technocrat are the twin progenitors of the existing situation. Therefore, while acknowledging that the highest possible rate of growth is what we should aim at, it must be recognized that what is possible can be realistically estimated only in the context of a particular regulatory and policy frame.

The structure of a plan also depends on accepted objectives. For example, the strategy and route of industrialization will be moulded in a particular way if the policy of dispersal of industry is fully accepted, in another if it is accepted only notionally. Moreover, the sectoral allocations will depend greatly on how local plans are worked out. If the planning is done by working groups in Delhi, the allocation may have little relation to real need. It is only when the strategy of local or area development has been evolved in relation to known resources and accepted long-term objectives that the mutual relation of sectoral allocations becomes clear and meaningful. Otherwise, they represent no more than the summation of separate schemes of independent departments.

Regarding structure, the only worth-while comment at this stage could be in relation to the basic industrial plan. The comment is based on the assumption that it is possible to plan for varying measures of size and complexity of the industrial base depending on whether your sights are set high or low, and that self-reliance is attainable in relation to each measure, though the extent of wealth and welfare aimed at will be different. If this is accepted, the industrial plan becomes a function of available resources, of desired results, and of the time at the end of which self-reliance has to be attained. The latest draft outline appears to treat all those components as fixed and unalterable. The result is that the volume of external aid required and the period over which it must become available become non-variable. This is very dangerous. For, it mortgages our future to the giver of aid; and as recent experience has painfully underlined, it gives outsiders enormous influence in shaping our economic policy. In view of the known bias of the outsiders, this is self-defeating; because, if the required aid does become available there is every likelihood that it will be under conditions which will deflect us even further from our avowed objectives.

Therefore, the plan which defines our strategy and route of industrialization must not be put in a single, rigid frame. It must provide for a series of possible situations. It must aim at reaching self-reliance early or late, with large or no external assistance, and must define a correspondingly narrow or wide basis. Immediately, it must have an alternative ready for the most pessimistic forecast; also, to the extent that it accepts foreign aid and collaboration it must provide for their utilization only in specific, fully defined directions. In general terms, all use of foreign aid and collaboration must only be for furthering our progress towards self-reliance, and no use should be in directions in which, either immediately or with a little effort, indigenous efforts can substitute it. Also, broadly, none should be used for production of consumer goods.

Reference has been made above to a corrective approach. This is the approach that must be adopted if planned development has to be achieved with stability, and some progress has to be made towards attaining the directives of policy embodied in the Constitution or towards a 'socialistic society'. The two main objectives of stability and development are not widely separated—if stability is successfully maintained, it will be possible to undertake a larger development effort; on the other hand, the development plan must follow the route indicated by the conditions of stability. It will, at the same time, be useful if the measures needed for the two are, at first, discussed separately. Before doing this, emphasis has to be placed on the paramount need of an integrated policy and of an overall regulatory frame. It is the lack of these that is responsible for most of our troubles. Even the economies of industrialized Western countries of Europe operate today under a general regulatory frame imposed by governments, and in them the levels of incomes and their distribution are major concerns of state policy. Also, even though for the major part, fiscal and monetary measures suffice at present, in these economies, resort is apt to be had to direct price controls and physical allocations the moment signs of an inflation or a recession or of a war become evident. In comparison with these economies, the need for a full and effective regulatory frame is vastly more urgent in India; the analogy of a war economy is, in fact, more appropriate for us.

Policy for stability may be divided into two major parts: a price policy and an incomes policy, both of which are, of course, highly interconnected. Three sets of prices are immediately seen to be of the greatest importance: prices of essential goods of mass consumption; prices of agricultural products, and prices of those intermediate and capital goods which are essential for planned development and which are in chronic short supply. In the last category, imported goods and their substitutes and those goods in relation to which imports play an important part, figure prominently. The maintenance of a stable cost-of-living index depends on successfully stabilizing prices of essential consumer goods. This can be done only by arranging for a regular minimum supply of these at stable prices to needy people all over the country. The first requirement, in this regard, is a widespread network of retail outlets under public control. The second is availability of adequate supplies of the goods to enable the public system of fair-price shops to function throughout the year. The supplies required are of both, agricultural and non-agricultural products, e.g., foodgrains, vegetable oil and sugar and cloth and kerosene. Because agricultural production is scattered throughout the country and is by very large numbers of small producers, the procurement of supplies of these products presents many difficulties. However, considerable experience, particularly in relation to foodgrains, has been obtained in India during the last 25 years. The appointment, last year, of the Agricultural Prices Commission should have enabled full coverage of this field. This did not, however, occur, and the Commission did not go beyond the stage of support prices for foodgrains. A committee has recently assessed the food position in the country and has suggested a series of measures regarding procurement, buffer stocks, prices, and distribution of foodgrains. If the recommendations of this committee are adopted, a framework, in which to fit the entire policy of stabilization of agricultural prices, would be available.

While the procurement of supplies of foodgrains, oilseeds, and sugar may suffice for stabilizing the cost-of-living index, prices of other agricultural products must also be stabilized for other related purposes. Stabilization of prices of foodgrains and oilseeds cannot be successful without similar operation in relation to other competing crops such as cotton, jute, and sugarcane. Moreover, any plan of increased agricultural production in specific directions cannot succeed without the maintenance of a relative stable structure of prices of different crops. The failure of our food policy, in the recent past, was due, in part, to allowing prices of some foodgrains to reach unduly low levels. Also, as suggested above, in view of the technically weak position of the agricultural producer vis-à-vis the trader and processor, the stabilization of prices of agricultural products is a necessary measure for the stabilization of incomes of the agriculturists. Therefore, it is necessary to devise a system of purchase and/or procurement, storage, and sale and/or distribution of all the major agricultural products of the country through which adequate supplies of these products required for national policy purposes would be acquired and the prices of the products stabilized. The acquisition of supplies would be for purposes of internal distribution as well as for export.

At this stage, it would be useful to note that in a matter like this the intensity or coverage of operation would differ from crop to crop. Also, for the same crop, operations could be more or less full in particular years. What is important is to establish a comprehensive system of socialized purchase, storage, and sale of agricultural products and to hold the situation under full control. Once such overall control is established it would be possible to relax, in a large measure, if the situation is favourable and so long as it remains so. The so-called decontrol measures of the Sen Commission, in relation to sugar, were practicable because they proposed first to establish a position of lasting command in the market. On the other hand, the experience with cement decontrol was not happy, because it was brought about in the absence of such command.

Procurement from manufacturers for maintaining supplies to the public retail system should prove relatively easy. Stabilization of prices of agricultural products, as for example of cotton, should help in stabilizing prices of essential manufactured goods. In respect of industrial consumer goods, the main effort will have to be in the direction of producing, through all techniques, an adequate supply of consumer goods, as in a common production plan, and orienting effort to the production of mass consumption goods at the cheapest cost. For the latter, it would be necessary to insist on such measures as severe limitations on varieties of products and on standardization of sorts to increase production with the same equipment; it would also be necessary to make manufacturers cost-conscious.

The problem of controlling prices of intermediate and capital goods in chronic short supply is a difficult but an essential task. The existing situation is the result, chiefly, of the policy of limiting imports to save exchange and of encouraging indigenous production through a quantitative restriction of imports.

The justification for a policy of quota restrictions is that it enables you to discriminate in a more detailed manner than would be possible through protective tariff duties and, even more, that it avoids raising the price level of imported supplies in a manner that a regime of high protective duties would. The latter consideration is of special importance in the context of a developing economy. Unfortunately, however, because no follow up action has taken place, quota restrictions in India have failed to establish this advantage. A general sellers' market for industrial products, especially those in which imports play some part, has been created, and the large or small margin available in any product is fully realized and shared by producers and traders in the product in varying proportions. The internal prices of these goods rule at levels corresponding to those of high protective tariffs. Consequently, the state loses the income it would have obtained through excise duties, the consumers are mulcted and above all, the economy is deprived of those developmental effects which would have followed a regime of relatively lower prices.

The existing situation is serious because it halts development and, moreover, breads corruption. It is of the utmost importance to eliminate the extra gains available in this field of intermediate and capital goods production. The draft outline of the Fourth Five-Year Plan lays great stress on the indigenous manufacture of components, at present imported, in order to achieve early self-reliance. However, rapid and economic progress in this direction would be possible only if prices of these components and the raw materials, etc., required for these are kept under control.

This discussion of the requirements of three main elements of a stable price level would indicate how comprehensive and full the effort in this direction must be. Moreover, its success requires that the various measures of control and the various sectoral and individual prices are meaningfully related to each other. It is, thus, clear that future developmental policy requires the establishment of comprehensive price control authorities like those of war economies of the West. The OPA of the USA and the corresponding system in the UK, provide a model. As stated above, the important point is the initial establishment of an integrated and comprehensive framework.

An income policy is more difficult to articulate. For agricultural producers, as a class, stabilization of incomes has to be achieved largely through stabilization of prices. Efforts have also to be made to add an insurance element to cover risks of variations of physical production. However, there is yet little firm experience of this. The majority of self-employed in non-agricultural occupations, such as rural and other artisans, face problems, not only of prices but also of markets and of techniques of production. Their problems can be resolved only through integrating the solution in an appropriate plan of industrial development. Such a plan should aim at avoiding technological unemployment and to utilize existing skills and equipment to the utmost while continuously transforming them. Among the large number of pure wage earners in our economy, policy today looks after only the very small proportion engaged in organized industry and other aspects of modern business. The rural landless labourers, and the mass of urban casual labour and labourers in unorganized occupations have no protection. The main action that can be taken in regard to the incomes of these is to make the plan employment oriented. It is necessary to spell out the implications of this last phrase. It does not mean just creating employment; that is wasteful. But it does mean taking a long-term view of the problem, and planning the investment of resources for development in such a manner that available labour supplies are utilized to the greatest possible extent. And this is based on the view that the present production orientation, which means a concentration of resources in favour of the privileged, though apparently giving an immediate larger return, is ultimately uneconomic, because it leads to lopsided development. Moreover, such orientation of the plan is politically feasible only so long as the large masses, whom development by this method does not touch, are ignorant and acquiesce.

In the present context, there is a reverse side also to the Indian incomes policy. This is to keep in check the rising incomes of producers and traders in the advancing sectors. The justification for such a policy is that, firstly, it would augment public resources if this is achieved by fiscal measures, and secondly, it would prevent the warping of the production structure. In a poor country with unequal distribution of incomes, production of goods of mass consumption is apt to be depressed, while industries and trades in relatively luxury consumption goods are booming. In the rural sector, the most obvious and important measure for checking very high incomes is that of incorporating agricultural incomes fully in the assessment and levy of the general income-tax. A progressive personal income-tax is already levied on urban incomes. However, it is highly ineffective because of the current view regarding incentives for savings needed in the private sector. So long as the richest are expected to save largely out of their personal incomes, the levels of direct taxation must make allowance for these over and above their high standards of consumption. And there is no guarantee that these supposed savings will fructify. If, instead, it is decided that personal income-tax will be pitched so high that at the highest no room need be kept for savings, the whole approach towards personal income taxation will effectively change. This may have some effect on the capital market; but any gap on this account in capital supply can be made good through additional capital funds being made available through government financial institutions.

It might also be useful to lay down as part of an incomes policy, that governments and organized business should have the obligation to compensate at least all employees whose earnings are below the national per capita average fully for every rise in the cost-of-living index. This would, in part, act as a stabilization of incomes measure; its utility would, however, lie specially in making governments aware of their basic responsibility for stabilizing the price level.

The main purpose of the price policy is to keep inflationary forces in check, and price levels stable, and that of incomes policy to stabilize incomes in general, to augment, to the extent possible, the incomes of the disadvantaged and to curb those of the rich. Stabilization of prices should help in administering monetary policy. Credit need not be unduly restricted so long as price inflation is not apprehended.

The main instrument of monetary policy will continue to be overall limitation of the volume of bank credit. Variations in the rate of interest are not effective because of the limited extent of the organized money market; also, high bank rates are likely to have undesirable repurcussions on the more needy. Moreover, in a developing economy, policy is geared to steady maintenance of stable conditions and not to dealing with constant ups and downs.

The problem of discriminating between uses of credit will still remain and has to be dealt with in a direct manner. Success in stabilizing prices will make the operation of forward markets in commodities redundant and they can, as in war time, be suspended. This should put a considerable curb on speculative activity, and hoarding will be discouraged by government operations of procurement, storage, and sale. The suggestion made above regarding doing away with the incentives for personal savings in the system of personal income-taxation may reduce the importance of the private capital market. This needs to be further reduced by other measures. During the last decade, the private capital market has been the bugbear of successive finance ministers. Radical action has been vetoed or abandoned for fear of reactions on this market. On the other hand, its real contribution has steadily diminished. The main sources of capital are now public and private company and other institutional savings and resources of public financial institutions. Contributions of personal private savings are negligible and yet the supposed reactions in relation to these have been allowed to dominate financial and fiscal policy. The capital market is now supported to a large extent by the LIC, and the continued use of public funds, in this direction, is highly undesirable. In fact, through the LIC a group of private capitalists have obtained control over the investment of very large public funds. Once the undesirability of the bolstering of the private capital market is accepted, a much more rational use of the LIC funds, orienting them to specific national policy ends, will become possible.

In this connection, the general problem of regulating and directing the private sector in large industry needs attention. The suggestion made above regarding diminution of importance of the private capital market and the concentration of savings in public hands will make regulation easy. It will enable checking of the initial investment of capital funds. To make this more effective, some regulation of the investment of own reserves by companies may be necessary; also, Reserve Bank control should extend over the intermediate-term and long-term lendings by commercial banks. Nationalization of banks does not appear to be necessary to keep continuous watch on the operation of industry, and it is likely to have undesirable consequences. Instead, two steps might be suggested. First is the appointment and active functioning of government directors, not only where capital loans are given by official institutions, but also where the LIC holds a sufficient number of shares in any company. Through this, general supervision should be possible on the operations of all important public companies. Even more effective may be the nationalization of the profession of chartered accountants. Bringing all large companies, in this manner, within the purview of a public audit system should prove highly useful.

Finally, reference may be made to the problem of increasing cost-consciousness. During the interwar period, when the Tariff Board gave limited protection for brief periods, protected industry had to be cost-conscious. Today, protection is universal, unconditional, and permanent. The overall price control authority suggested above must, therefore, be helped by a body which continuously studies the dynamics of the process of development both in the private and public sectors through cost enquiries and through investigations into or projections of changes in structures, techniques, etc. The two together should be able not only to prevent any oligopolistic tendencies but also to indicate desirable financial, technical, and such other developments. Cost consciousness has a special place in relation to foreign collaboration. Present conditions do not induce this, especially in relation to capital outlay, in either the Indian or the foreign collaborator.

Not much need be added regarding the requirements of policy in relation to the shaping and structure of the plan. A number of points have been indicated in the discussion earlier. In agricultural production, emphasis has to shift to detailed local and area planning and planning for needs of different categories of producers in addition to planning for individual crops. Programmes like consolidation and co-operative farming have to be given very high priority. In co-operation two sets of problems deserve special attention. Firstly, programmes in relation to areas in which co-operation has not yet taken root, and programmes for the rahabilitation of the weaker sections in states where it is well established. A number of objectives have to be integrated in the plan of industrialization. In the main, these are employment and dispersal. Deliberate dispersal from the worst metropolitan concentrations and the spread of socio-economic overheads in all backward areas are most urgent; but basically the industrial plan itself must be reoriented. Further, as indicated above, self-reliance has to become an immediate and continuous concern.

7

Towards Self-Reliance*

Professionally, I have accepted a position where not only have I to think about the Fourth Five-Year Plan but I believe it is a part of my job to stimulate thinking about it. May I right now confess that I do not believe it is possible for any individual or any organization or any group of people or any single government in this country to plan for the whole country? If the planning has to be done, if the thinking has to be done, if the solutions to our problems have to be found, this will not happen unless we stimulate thinking among all our people and not necessarily only among the cream of intelligentsia gathered here this evening. It has to be done at all levels.

I have been asked to talk about the Approach to the Fourth Five-Year Plan. I propose to deal with the problem, first, in what I might call the situational sense. You are approaching this problem of defining the Fourth Five-Year Plan at a given point of time in the economy. Certain things have happened in the past. In framing the Plan, you are finding yourself mid-way in a certain stream of events. Now, this position does necessarily—and in my opinion greatly—influence the approach that you have to adopt. That is the first aspect.

As flowing from that, I propose to draw your attention to two other aspects. Those aspects relate to the definition of economic policy in the Plan. Once you adopt an approach, that approach implies a given definition of policy.

And the third aspect is equally important, though perhaps neglected. It is our approach to the methodology of planning itself. These three I am going to put before you in some measure within, I hope, not too long a time.

* Speech delivered at Bangalore on the 4 September 1968.

'PRETTY DESPERATE'

Let us look at the situation as it was last year. When a re-organized Planning Commission came into office in September 1967, the situation on almost all fronts was pretty desperate. The majority of people who offered me this office or congratulated me on accepting it also seemed to think that it was courageous of me to accept that office. That shows broadly how the judgment of the people regarding the situation was.

The situation was that until that September, for something like two and a half years, prices were constantly on the increase. We had had a succession of two bad agricultural years. Because of a series of earlier incidents, our defence expenditure had mounted. Because of this constant increase in prices, general dissatisfaction among the people, and among the salaried class especially, had so mounted that governments were no longer able to refuse demands for compensation in terms of dearness allowances. The DA burden was itself constantly increasing.

As a result of two bad years, the national economy was functioning at a low level. Demands for all kinds of products were low. *Pari passu*, the government's real resources having gone down considerably, its monetary and, very much more, real investment in development had gone down. All in all, you had a picture not only of a depressed condition and a low level economy but of an economy which looked almost driven to stagnation. You did not know how it was going to go up from here, how you are going to stop prices from rising, how the government was to have larger resources, how the agricultural incomes and demands were going to be raised.

The position was in fact such that anybody who thought in terms of planning could not think in terms of a large developmental prospect from that particular basis. In a sense, that was the main justification for the first recommendation that the Planning Commission made to the government, which was to postpone the Fourth Five-Year Plan to 1969, beginning from 1st April. The Planning Commission took the view (and I think it was the only view that the Planning Commission could take) that, as on the base of 1966–67, there was little to project. Development projection was just guessing. There was no firm basis and with that state of resources you should not do anything else but get a year's breathing space, and see what happens next.

'RAY OF HOPE'

Already in September again, it appeared that there was a ray of hope. There were fairly good rains. With the reports of successes in some of the new agricultural experiments the only hope centred round the harvest. So it was possible to say that if we had a better harvest, that could make a beginning of a breakthrough out of the vicious circle into which we had got. If you had a better harvest, the continuous rise of prices could be contained. When the effects of a better harvest were felt, a demand from consumers may increase. If you had a good harvest and if prices were stabilized, the DA claims may come to a halt so that all that particular non-plan expenditure may be stabilized and other aspects of government expenditure could also be stabilized. And if that happened, the government could act a little more boldly than before in relation to development.

So in my first news conference in the first week of September last year, what I said was that the only thing that I thought of in terms of immediate government policy was a policy centering on the stabilization of prices. I said then that, with a good harvest, there would be a natural pressure on prices downwards till March–April 1968. And the crucial stage was post-March–April. Would we keep the September 1967 prices down till next September? If we were through a year of stable prices, there was some basis on which to plan. This was the situational background.

In this situational background, how do you derive an approach to the future plan? There are two or three other factors that are already implied. I talked about government outlays not being there, no large government outlays. The consumption demand was less and therefore the economy was operating at a less-than-capacity level. The industrial base was larger than the then operation of the economy required.

INDUSTRIAL BASE

One of the things that the last three Plans had achieved, particularly since 1957–58, was to give us a much broader and a more diversified industrial base than before. It is because this base had been so diversified and was so broad that it was working under capacity. We had been producing in such areas as the engineering industry or chemical industries a number of products which were not there before. We were more self-sufficient. But when we had become more self-sufficient, the domestic demand had shrunk and we were not operating to capacity. Therefore, the national product came down.

This peculiar fact of an advanced industrial structure, side by side with a depressed agricultural economy, really gives, the clue to how you have to approach the making of the Fourth Five-Year Plan. Those of you who have read our brief Approach paper will notice that the central quantitative factor that we have used is the increment in agricultural production. The point about which we had the longest discussion in the National Development Council (and we were anxious the Chief Ministers should express themselves the most and most specifically) was the Chief Ministers' judgment about the possibility of increasing agricultural production. Because if we do get a 5 per cent increase in agricultural production, we are for a large number of other things already in a position to progress pretty fast.

NATIONAL INFRASTRUCTURE

Right from the First and the Second Plan—especially the Plan of 1956—two things we have been emphasizing. We have been emphasizing the development of national infrastructure. The railways, the roads, the ports, power—these have been stressed. As a matter of fact, they were developed as they should be developed, a little in advance of our needs. So was the industrial base. We found the moment we had a small recession that our coal and steel capacity was larger than a low-operating economy could sustain.

If you look at the obverse, this means that if the rural sector at least operates at a much higher level, you will get the whole economy moving quickly for the next two or three years without a great deal of additional investment in capital structures, with just marginal investments to utilize capacities. The central quanta in the Approach are the 5 per cent growth in agriculture and roughly 8 to 10 per cent growth in modern industry and modern business. Those two quanta are related.

The main judgment that we have to make and the main assurances that we have to get from planners, administrators, and scientists really relate to this 5 per cent growth. Because if we broadly look at it, the industrial and the infrastructure growths are matters not of a great deal of complicated new thinking; they do not present elaborate administrative problems. Setting up large industries or adding a little here or there to metals, mines, industry, railways or transport or ports, is a matter of resources. It is not a matter of detailed administration.

Agricultural production, on the other hand, is a very much more difficult matter. This, I think, we do not fully realize. It is not fully realized (when there is such a great deal of criticism about this low pace of agricultural development) that agricultural development is an extremely complicated and an extremely difficult business. It is an extremely complicated and difficult business at the scientific level, it is complicated and difficult at the administrative level, and it is complicated and difficult at the individual enterprise level. At all these three levels, it is more complicated and infinitely more difficult than industry or transport or any of the ordinary things that we talk about, even education.

Why is it so? I do not go into details, but it is necessary for people to have a full idea of these difficulties. Let us see what I mean by it being difficult at the scientific level. What has been happening through the last fifteen years? There is a lot of talk about the new agricultural strategy. Well, there have been new elements, a few here and there. But by and large those of you who have a somewhat long memory will know that from the Grow-More-Food campaign of the 1940s the agricultural strategy is more or less what it is. Fertilizers, extension, improved practices, talking about package programmes, kharif campaigns, rabi campaigns. I take it you are all familiar with the terminology. Credit, marketing—we have talked ad nauseum about them. We have done all these things.

IMPROVED VARIETIES

Yet agriculture did not get going. In the last three years it has got going. Let us reflect why it is so. During the past few years we put into this agricultural programme an element which was absent before and which alone could make the programme came alive. And this element was the entirely new types of seeds.

You could talk of the same programme earlier. You were talking of a little improved Akola bajra, for example, in Maharashtra. Or a selected jowar variety or a rust-resistant wheat. When you talked of all this, you really were talking to people who saw that any large inputs and any considerable expenditure of energy on these did not give anything like dramatic results. With even a slight change in prices, there was too much risk in adopting what was being improved and what was being pressed on the farmer.

All of us have some knowledge of how farmers behave and have experience of how, for example, improved strains of cotton have been accepted in Maharashtra area; how Coimbatore strains were not only accepted but how for the last fifteen years progressive farmers in Maharashtra have always been on the look-out for new varieties. This is without any government propaganda about the newest and best Coimbatore strains. And they have in fact adopted them before the government's extension officers have gone about. The Rockefeller Foundation started the hybridization programme a few years ago, bringing new wheat and maize and the millets. Then somebody collected the Mexican and other varieties of wheat and made a selection in Pusa and round about, and began to experiment on them. Then we had the rice. Now it is in this breakthrough in getting established the new varieties of seeds—that were not only better but are immensely better than before. They are so much better that the additional expenditure, additional effort, the pains and the risks that the farmer had to take are really thought worthwhile. So he adopted this change.

That really was on the horizon in September last year. Even with today's hindsight, I shall say that it was on the horizon, it might come through. But we could not be sure. And I say this deliberately because we should not exaggerate in fact what has been achieved.

In the light of the experience of 1967–68, what was being called a breakthrough has in fact been achieved in regard to wheat. Mexican and other varieties of wheat are so good that allowing for everything, especially for possible changes of climatic circumstances, the increase in production was in fact dramatic and so large as to allow us to believe that something has come to stay. Something took place over a wide area right from Punjab to

Bihar. Wherever wheat was grown somewhat similar results were achieved. If you get over such a large area such dramatic results, it is something you may count on.

But if you look at other things, the rice crop for instance, remember that the 1967–68 rice production was a little less than in 1964–65 when there was no great propaganda about the new varieties and in many areas still the new recommended varieties had not been fully stabilized. There are many areas where you have to withdraw varieties and substitute, and so on. So you really have in the rice belt a problem which is difficult.

In the millets, though hybrid bajra is supposed to be stabilized, hybrid jowar has not yet fully stabilized. In Maharashtra, for example, last year's bad rains or bad climatic conditions could quite seriously upset the expectations that were held out for hybrid jowar.

My point, therefore, is that even in terms of science you have in agriculture greater difficulties in achieving something. It is not, as in industry, adapting the technology which is already highly advanced in other countries. All that we have to do in industry is to borrow it. In agriculture, with even the technology of hybridization having become advanced, hybridization has to be applied to local conditions with a great deal of effort. You may then get results. Even when you get results, the local conditions differ from region to region. And as they differ from region to region, the application of results in agricultural sciences have to be split up into many sub-applications before we get results that are of wide validity over the whole country. From that point of view, even for scientists, the agricultural breakthrough is difficult.

TRANSFER OF TECHNOLOGY

From the point of view of the administrator it is admittedly difficult. Transfer of technology is an easy enough term. But what does the transfer of technology mean in this case? It means a whole set of new things to be adopted.

I would personally say that so far as the farmer is concerned, he is more educable than we think. If the demonstration effect is there, he is educable. If the demonstration effect is not there, he will not be educated at all. I mean he is stiff, stiff in his resistance. He says, when you talk to him, 'But I have been hit too many times by government propaganda to take it in easy'. One would not blame him for this.

Therefore, the administrative problem of coordination is an immense problem. I know a lot of good administrators also can achieve this easily. But the conditions differ very widely from state to state. If you have to get results all over the country, the problem of coordination of the agricultural programmes requires much more serious attention than it has received so far. It has to be incorporated in the planning process much more than it has been done so far.

From the point of view of the individual entrepreneurs, again, the agricultural problem is a very difficult problem. The large majority of the individuals have no resources, have a small base of production, and have relatively inadequate knowledge of what you would call modern technology. They learn easily, they learn by experience. But even when they learn, making the resources available, giving them the wherewithal to make much better use of their resources in the modern way than before is a problem.

THE SMALL FARMER

Why I am saying all this is because, in my opinion, this is going to be where the Fourth Five-Year Plan fails or succeeds: our ability really to get the programmes that are suitable for each crop and each region of the country. What will matter is our ability in each state to get a full coordination between the various departments, the Revenue, the Agriculture, the Animal Husbandry, the Co-operation, and the Finance altogether; all this, and to get really on the ground, the people who are interested in this programme in a meaningful manner, not only the old Community Development approach.

Much will depend upon our ability really to put this across to the farmer, especially to the small farmers of all strata. That is one of the reasons why the Approach document emphasizes the small farmer. After all, the smaller farmers command anything from 25 to 30 per cent of the area in this country. Unless they are also in it, you cannot get ahead.

The Approach to the Fourth Five-Year Plan holds as its centre this 5 per cent quantum of agricultural production. We are very much interested in this. We know that this is the most difficult programme to achieve. The achievement has not been there so far for obvious reasons. I think achievement will be there because the scientists are now alive to the problem; the administrators also and even the financial institutions. The Reserve Bank and the Co-operative Bankers are responding to the new challenge. On the whole, they are more helpful. But, again, you have a great many difficulties. We talk of the Co-operative Approach. The Co-operative Approach in the ultimate analysis depends on the strength of your primary and secondary, i.e., the district, organization. However good your superstructure may be or however nice your registrar may be, unless the primaries and the districts are really functioning, you just cannot do anything.

And you cannot reach the masses unless you do it through an organization. A small number of large industrialists you can reach easily. You can both encourage them and control them. If you have to control the sugar industry, it is a matter of, well, less than 200 units or 250 units. But to get to the farmer you want to have an organization, and an organization which has an agency in each village. Our un-evenness in the progress is one of the great handicaps.

OTHER ASPECTS: BUFFER STOCKS

I shall now touch upon other aspects. The situation was of stagnation in which the only hope was a breakthrough in agriculture. We banked on this hope. We are putting our money on this hope and we are also saying, at the same time, that the economy cannot afford to bank on it in a blind sort of way. Therefore, taken in conjunction with the extremely important food problem, we are talking in terms of stabilization of agricultural prices, of buffer stocks, of having something to fall back upon when we have a bad year.

Perhaps one of the mistakes we have done in the earlier planning is that we have relied on the averages too much. The average year is not always with us. We may have a good year, we may have a bad year also. When we have a bad year, we cannot behave the same way as if we have an average year. We have this experience in an economy where we are operating on a small margin.

A bad year means not only distress but, in financial terms, inflationary pressures. Inflationary pressures mean upsetting the stable prices. Upsetting of stable prices obstructs the development process immediately. While we are thinking in terms of 5 per cent agricultural growth, we emphasize all the means in terms of both physical supplies as well as prices to maintain a given degree of stability.

Whatever the programmes, stability and the buffer stock concept in an operative sense are an important new feature of our Approach to the Plan. It is not a non-cost operation. Building of buffer stocks means financial investment initially. Operating buffer stock means intelligent purchase and sale and distribution. These are important aspects and they will have to be worked through in details by agencies in the field. Whether it is in agriculture or the buffer stock operation or distribution, you come to realize the extremely important role that states and state administrations have to play in this.

FOREIGN AID AND FOREIGN DEBTS

The only other situational aspect to which I would refer is the foreign aid and foreign debts. All of you realize, though the details are not always worked out, that we have got into the habit of planning on the basis of fairly substantial foreign aid. We came to this point in 1957–58 when we ran through our sterling resources. Then we got or found two stand-bys. One stand-by was the Aid Consortium, the Aid India Club that got formed under the aegis of the World Bank. The other stand-by was PL-480 foodgrains.

These two stand-bys came round about 1957–59. With their help we were able to make some more ambitious plans than we could have made with our own internal resources. A much more important thing is that in

1964–65, when our economy shrank and we ran into difficulties, we still kept up the financial aspect of the development outlays by beginning to rely more and more on PL-480 and the Aid India Consortium. What has resulted—which is not fully realized—is, for example, that in 1967–68 out of a total plan outlay of Rs 2,200 crores, almost Rs 800 to Rs 900 crores was foreign aid. That is what happened after 1963–64, when the rate of domestic savings went down for a number of reasons. The agricultural harvest was bad. There was inflation. The two taken together, the rate of domestic savings went down. But if you keep the same financial outlay, it means that you are substituting foreign aid for internal resources.

When we began to think of the Approach at the beginning of this year, the Planning Commission took the view seriously that this was an impossible position to be in. This was a position which you could not sustain for any length of time. We thought we must withdraw by stages from that position as early as we can.

We, therefore, suggested two things. If, in fact, we got this agricultural breakthrough of 95 million tonnes of foodgrains or anything like that, the PL-480 food imports should be stepped down and within two years eliminated; and that for the years after 1968–69, they should be used for a major part only for building buffer stocks. Build buffer stocks and then eliminate food imports.

The other thing was that net foreign aid should be reduced to at least half of the present level—half of the 1968–69 level—by the end of the Fourth Five-Year Plan. I want to emphasize the term 'net aid'. We mean by net aid the aid that we in fact can use for development outlay. For through the last twelve years we have accumulated such a large load of public debt—internal and external—that, today, of the total aid we receive, roughly 25 to 30 per cent we spend on interest and repayment of the debt. If this piles up, we expect that within five years this proportion will go to 40. In time we should be asking for aid to repay aid!

This is a difficult position. Not only is it difficult; if you take the world's political situation, it is an impossible situation. I shall illustrate what is happening by mentioning one fact. At the beginning of the year—in January–February—we were discussing this within the Planning Commission and we were saying, a half or more but at least a half should be our target for reducing dependence on aid. There were a number of people connected with aid and so forth who said, 'Well, don't you know you are putting it too fast? Why not use a little more aid?' The position today is those very people are now taking the view that half is too optimistic. They say that even the sort of aid which will make net aid one half at the end of five years we may not, in fact, get at all.

SELF-RELIANCE

This means self-reliance. Self-reliance is an easy term but very difficult to achieve. Self-reliance means two things. Self-reliance means that you must step up the rate of domestic savings which is very important in the context of foreign aid and you must increase exports.

Foreign aid does two things. It gives you investment resources which are very useful in balancing foreign payments. Because it is foreign aid, it is available in terms of foreign currency or foreign materials. Therefore you can keep on importing much more than what you earn through exports. In a developing economy, when you try to increase the pace of your development, the need for imports necessarily increases. This is because you are trying to get in technology, capital equipment, and know-how which you have not got in the country, in order to develop your base altogether. That means your imports are increasing.

Now if foreign aid has to be cut down, your domestic savings must increase and your exports must increase. These are some of the things that you must do. In a sense it is not a new approach. Indeed, it is the old approach. But in a proper sense, properly speaking, a number of elements of the old approach are coming to the surface now, more than they did ever before. Their coming to surface is going to hit us in the eye very much more than we imagine. This is a matter over which we should all seriously ponder.

DOMESTIC SAVINGS

Raising of domestic savings is easy to speak of. What it, in fact, amounts to is certain consumption restraints. Savings, either from your financial resources, lending it to the banks or putting it in government loans and so forth or your putting in your own business, your making own investment in such a manner that the national economy develops. Now this sort of saving has to be done on a wide scale; it is a national effort. In this, everybody has to participate. If that has to come in, you come up with certain policy questions. These two other subjects I will now deal with briefly.

What is the new policy approach? What are the policy questions that are really being thrown up today? The policy questions are twofold. One of them has already come to surface. The other has not come to surface yet or strikingly, but I think we should begin to think about it. Otherwise it is going to hit us hard.

If things are going all right, anyway, you need not plan. But we think more savings must be made, these savings must be directed in certain lines and invested in a given manner. When your product increases, you must do this. Because you think of these things, a certain amount of regulation and direction has to be done. In the early days, it was fairly simple. Development, we all know, requires some things. Development requires the economic overheads, the social overheads. Unless you have your communication system, unless you have your power system, the economy cannot develop. Unless you have minimum educational facilities, unless you have minimum health facilities, your economy cannot develop. So, building these up was the main emphasis; it had to be the main emphasis.

PUBLIC SECTOR

Another major emphasis (which on the whole was, I think, the right one, though its implementation has led to a lot of criticism) was on what you call basic industries—steel and the capital goods industry. Now, all that was brought in order, mainly, to free ourselves from dependence on foreign countries; to make our own development process, so as to say, autonomous. This was a proper emphasis.

Though at some cost, we really have achieved something. I will give you only one example. One of the difficulties that we are currently facing in relation to foreign aid and are going to face increasingly, is that we now want non-project aid more than project aid. Project aid means giving the whole project to somebody. You ask the Soviet Union to put up Bhilai; you ask West Germany to put up another steel plant. You ask another country to put up an aluminium plant. They bring the whole set of technicians, they bring the whole apparatus and equipment, and they do the turn-key jobs. And you just walk in and begin to operate them. It also means that you are always dependent on their technicians, that you always buy the spares from them, you always buy components from them, so that forever you are more or less tied up.

In order that we should not be in that position, we have been trying to develop capital goods industries and all kinds of other industries. Now we have in fact so developed that we do not want projects. It is a matter of government policy—that wherever any components, parts, or important constituents and elements can be manufactured indigenously, they should not be imported. The result is that we do not now want the whole plants; a lot of designing, a lot of consultancy, a lot of scientific, technical assistance, and advice—they are all to be found in India. If that is available, that is so because of those steel and capital industry plants. Let us remember this even when we talk a great deal about mismanagement of the public sector, its high costs, and so forth. Mismanagement we need not excuse. You must remember that making it pay is one of our great jobs. And yet that was an important step forward.

Are you still in that position? Do you still want to make a large investment? Do you want to direct the whole of the economy? Or have you come to a position where you can let things up a little? Is it necessary that you should let things up a little?

CONTROL VS COMPETITION

I shall draw your attention in this context to another aspect of the manner in which we have achieved industrial development. We have achieved industrial development partly by putting up large, costly public sector projects. We have achieved industrial development for the other part by protecting the private industrialists absolutely. The moment a private industrialist was ready to produce one thing, we got an import restriction. The Director General of Technical Development said, 'Well, you can't import from outside. You must buy it from the indigenous producer and you must buy it at whatever cost the indigenous producer asks you to.'

So one of the reasons for the difficulties we face in the export market is that while we have undoubtedly built up a diversified industrial economy, it is at the same time an extremely high-cost economy. It is so high-cost an economy that from all export markets, we for most purposes are priced out. This high-cost economy is another problem that we have to deal with. There are only two ways. You can think of a strict control as was done during the War in the USA or Great Britain, where there was an overall price control and every margin and every price was scrutinized. Nobody got an extra margin. As margins were cut down, the manufacturer was constantly put on the racks, so to say.

Are you administratively in a position to do it? I am afraid the answer is 'no.' The answer is that if you look at the whole tempo of development, we are not in a position to manage efficiently such a detailed overall control. If you are not able to put down prices or force people to economize, to reduce costs through a dictat or through government directive or government enquiry, what can you do? And the reply is: competitiveness. The only other thing that you can do is to allow them to compete with each other.

And this is, very curiously, how we are coming to one policy solution or one policy directive generally. That is, try and reduce your controls to strategic points and, wherever you can, introduce competition. In the Approach, we have suggested that except where foreign exchange is involved (and foreign exchange is so scarce that control on it is absolutely essential), anybody can set up anything with indigenous equipment. If he does not want raw materials and components from abroad, do not bother about licensing. Do not bother about the capital issue. Just let him go into the field and try his luck.

The Planning Commission is interested in this because we have curiously come up for criticism. I do not know how many industrialists have come to me during the last year and have accused the Planning Commission of giving them wrong indications. A cable manufacturer among them said that the Planning Commission said so much demand would be there and therefore he set up plants. This is very curious. We always thought that the industrialist made his own calculations. But evidently he did not.

We do not want the Planning Commission to get this particular blame. There are enough other counts on which it can be blamed. We do not really want to get into a situation where, barring a few crucial industries where planning must be full and complete, not tentative or indicative, all others must be left to a great deal of this competitiveness. This is an extremely important aspect of policy.

DEMAND FOR HIGHER WAGES

The other important aspect of policy, which I said has not come in yet, is the whole question of the distribution of the product of industries and the whole question of labour and social contentment. This is a question to which even politicians are giving too little attention. I say even politicians because professionally it hits the politicians first.

You are in a situation where organized labour makes demands which the industrialist says he just cannot meet. He says, 'The product is not there; and unless productivity increases, I cannot do anything.' You are already facing up to demands like the need-based wage from the government. You are slowly going to get into a position where you do not know how just to deal with a situation in which defence expenditure increases and non-plan expenditure increases.

We can draw up plans; but that is not going to lead to anything—no movement there. Now what is to be done? This is a problem which during the last three years has slowly assumed larger and larger dimensions. And it is soon going to assume a dimension where unless you really have some much broader social understanding within the country, it would be very difficult to deal with it. But you should see it whole—it is not only the newspapers or the government or any kind of industry you take. You are getting into such a position that unless there is an understanding in the large, a mass understanding, that development is something specifically connected with productive effort, we shall not move forward.

We talk of the German 'miracle', we talk of the Japanese 'miracle': at the base of all these miracles is extremely persistent, pertinacious, hard effort on the part of individuals basically. Unless that is understood, we cannot get on our own feet.

SOCIAL INTEGRATION

But I want to emphasize equally the other aspect: that this mass understanding of the production responsibility of everybody cannot come through unless there is a mass conviction that this is a fair society, that this is a society in which the distribution of the product is being justly regulated and that everybody is participating and has a share.

This is too large a problem for me to deal with here. Perhaps it is too large a problem for me to deal with at all. In my opinion it is a basic problem. Not everybody is seeing it as a whole; everybody is seeing it as his own particular problem. The government says it is the bad government servants; the planter says, 'You know after all these agitators', and so on. But this is not as simple as that. It is not agitators; it is not politicians; it is a basic problem of social understanding, of social participation in the whole process.

This basic problem is a challenge to society. It is a challenge to integration. We talk of national integration: I think we should think much more of social integration. National integration will then be easy. Because the society is not integrated, this problem arises.

There is very little time to talk about this last theme as I have exceeded my time already. I shall merely refer to it. It is an important aspect and follows from what I have said before. It means planning is not the business of the Planning Commission alone. The Planning Commission is there to gather thoughts, to gather data, to gather the opinions of politicians, social workers, industrialists and to present to the people a frame in which all the data and all the opinions are meaningfully placed in such a manner that they prove acceptable. This is all that the Planning Commission does, no more.

The Planning Commission cannot presume to have a larger role. The role is of everybody. What, in the ultimate analysis, does development mean? National development means the effort on the part of every one of us to increase national product. And you can increase national product by two ways: by avoiding waste in consumption, by more rational consumption, and by being more scientific and more rational in your activities and by making better use of your resources.

This country is a country of small, numerous producers—it is not a country of giant enterprises though there are a few monopolies and they trouble us a little undoubtedly. But, basically, this is a country of small enterprises, small people, small producers, small houses. Let all of us say that we have to plan and this evolution in planning must begin first from the Centre to the states, so that the state governments and the state administrators feel, as they have not so far felt very much I am afraid, that the state plans are their plans. There may be a central frame, there may be a little central assistance. That is about all. It is they who have to do it.

When they have to do it, it must be on the ground. Each farmer's problem is a separate problem. I remember the other day last week, when we had a set of progressive farmers in the Planning Commission, one from each state, a body of fifteen. One of them got up and spoke on the general directions given to him. He said, 'Your people do not understand it. Each of my fields is a separate entity and I have to know each field intimately. I am a progressive farmer. I get these high yields because I know what each field requires and each crop requires, and I give it what it requires.'

This is development. So that each village, each household, each co-operative society looks to its individual problems which fully deserve all the attention that they can give. And it is only when administrators and the people at the lowest rungs feel that it is this process in which they are called upon to participate, that their participation is given meaning to at higher levels and that their ideas are considered carefully and thought worthwhile—it is only then that we can have both a better social climate and better planning in this country.

II

Institutions and Planning

8

The Role of the Planning Commission in Indian Planning*

I feel it a great honour to be asked to deliver the Laski Memorial Lecture at this institute. I consider it a privilege to be associated in this manner with the name of Prof. Harold Laski. Prof. Laski was, above all, an inspiring teacher and a great humanist. His deep sympathy for the oppressed and the disadvantaged made him a friend of Indian students and the Indian cause throughout his life. He was greatly interested in the new developments in the direction and planning of economic activity. I have therefore thought it appropriate to embark, on this occasion, on an examination, in the context of Indian planning, of the operation of the central planning institution in this country, the National Planning Commission. ... (p. 88)

I shall begin by making a few preliminary observations on the nature of the planning-effort. Planning for economic development implies external direction or regulation of economic activity by the planning authority which is, in most cases, identified with the government of the state. Planning for economic development is undertaken presumably because the pace or direction of development taking place in the absence of external intervention is not considered to be satisfactory, and because it is further held that appropriate external intervention will result in increasing considerably the pace of development and directing it properly. The decision to plan does not by itself, and cannot immediately, increase the total physical resources available to the community. Planners seek to bring about a rationalization, and if possible and necessary, some reduction

* The Laski Memorial Lecture delivered at the Harold Laski Institute of Political Science, Ahmedabad, on 24 March 1958. Published in *Planning and Economic Policy in India*, D.R. Gadgil, GIPE, Poona, 1962, pp. 88–111.

of consumption, to evolve and adopt a long-term plan of appropriate investment of capital resources with progressively improved techniques, a programme of training and education through which the competence of labour to make use of capital resources is increased, and a better distribution of the national product so as to attain social security and peace. Initially, the planning-effort starts with available resources, natural, human, and in terms of capital equipment. But with the progress of planning it is expected that natural resources will be progressively better conserved and utilized, human resources better trained and better distributed in occupational etc. categories, and capital resources continuously augmented and made more efficient. Planning, thus, is not a once-for-all effort. For it to make any impression, especially on the situation in an under-developed economy, it has to be a continuous, consistent, and forward-looking effort, sustained for decades. The main components of a programme of planned development, namely rationalization of and restraint on consumption, the training and appropriate disposition of human resources, increasing capital resources, and the adoption of improved techniques, are the characteristics which again have to be manifest at all stages throughout the period of planning, though the emphasis on one or the other may vary from stage to stage. ... (pp. 88, 89)

Planning-effort is an organizational effort undertaken systematically by an external authority. Initially, planning begins with such resources as are available, adding only better organization. This means directing and regulating individual and communal effort with intelligence and foresight so that the total result is larger and better than before. It is the continuous organizational effort that increases the quantity and improves the quality of resources at later stages in a cumulative manner and brings about development. Planning therefore means, in a sense, no more than better organization, consistent and far-seeing organization, and comprehensive all-sided organization; and the political and the administrative requirements of planning are the requirements appropriate to such effort. Directions, regulations, controls on private activity, and increasing the sphere of public activity, are all parts of this organizational effort. ... (p. 89)

The next step in considering political and administrative requirements of planning-effort in India, is to look briefly at our political system. Our political structure may be described in general terms as a federal democracy with a representative parliamentary system of government, and with executive authorities of the Cabinet type. It is in this context that the planning-requirements of India on the political plane have to be considered. The chief relevant characteristics of the political structure are the division of functions between the states and the centre, the need for the adoption and endorsement of all policies and legislation by bodies of elected representatives of the people, the joint responsibility of Cabinet ministers, both at the centre and in the states, and the stability of the Cabinet itself being dependent on the continued confidence of the majority of the elected representatives. In the context of this structure, planning-effort has to be looked upon as an effort undertaken by the government. It is an effort, legislative and administrative policy regarding—which has been accepted or is acceptable to the legislatures of the states and the centre, and an effort, the execution of which has to be the responsibility of the Cabinet of ministers. ... (pp. 89, 90)

With these preliminary remarks, I shall turn to an examination of the existing situation in India. It is in the light of the experience of the period since independence in India, more specifically, since the setting up of the Planning Commission in 1950, that I intend to discuss this question.

It is my purpose in this address to discuss the extent to which the Planning Commission in India has achieved success, and the reasons for its failure. I have defined planning above as an overall organizational effort. In the total effort, almost all organs of government at various levels, and large numbers of private individuals and non-official organizations, must participate. The Planning Commission must be considered to be at the head of this planning-effort. ... (p. 92)

In examining the performance of the Commission, it would be useful to separate consideration of the formulation and operation of the First Five-Year Plan from that of the Second. I think this necessary, because I hold that the First Five-Year Plan in India did not involve, to any material extent, what might be properly called planning-effort. It was only with the formulation and the launching of the Second Five-Year Plan that the problem of planning as such began to be faced. Therefore, in my opinion, the experience of the years since 1955 is especially relevant for judgment of the past performance and future potentiality of the Indian Planning Commission. ... (p. 93) The formulation of the Second-Five Year Plan may be said to record another high water-mark in the life of the Planning Commission. Through its various organs of committees and panels, the Planning Commission undoubtedly showed very considerable activity at this time. It also showed, as during the First Five-Year Plan, considerable ability for evolving an appropriate approach to the emergent planning-problem. ... (p. 97)

From the outside it is difficult to indicate with any assurance the contribution of different persons and organizations in the evolution of the Second Five-Year Plan of India. From all reports it would appear that a crucial part was played at the earlier stages by Prof. Mahalanobis, who was not, then, even a member de jure or de facto of the Planning Commission. The basic decisions involved at this stage of plan-making were, firstly, the determination of the size of the Plan, and secondly, decisions regarding its structure. That the size of the Plan would be nearly of the order of

Rs 1,000 crores a year was an important decision which had many serious implications. It is not known by whom, when, and under what pressure it was taken, whether it was a decision of the Cabinet, whether it originated with the Planning Commission, or whether it arose effectively from the Prime Minister, or the Finance Minister, or any of their advisers. In the second decision regarding the structure of the Plan, the important consideration was the relative allocations to different sectors, and the priorities within the sectors; in this context, the emphasis on some branches of heavy industry, in particular, implied a long-term picture of the economy developing by a certain route. In the presentation of the Plan, the insistence on defining targets in terms of related physical quantities, was an important innovation. What was new was not the discovery that this could be done (there is on record a note by Dr K.N. Raj in relation to the drafting of the First Five-Year Plan, in which a tentative approach on this line had been indicated), but the decision to use available data in order to present the total Plan in terms of physical quantities, however crude the estimation. Here, again, it is clear that the technical competence and expertise required for this effort were present within the staff of the Planning Commission itself. In all this Prof. Mahalanobis, because of his strategic personal position, appears to have acted as the person through whose plan-frame basic decisions regarding size, structure, and presentation, got expressed in a co-ordinated manner. That his role was chiefly that of a co-ordinating link is emphasized by his ineffectiveness in later years as a de facto member of the Planning Commission. ... (pp. 97, 98)

It is difficult to say what part the Planning Commission as such played in the evolution of the Second Five-Year Plan. It is, however, only fair to give full credit in relation to the formulations and the preparation of the Plan to the Planning Commission. It is, at the same time, necessary to note carefully the limitations of the total performance in this regard. As in the First Five-Year Plan, the presentation of approaches and definitions of problems show a high level of competence. However, even in this regard, there is one notable difference. In the First Five-Year Plan, the theoretic formulations were not limited by the need to refer to any large amount of factual detail. The larger size and the structure deliberately adopted imposed a responsibility in this respect in the production of the Second Five-Year Plan. It was perhaps indicative of what was to happen later that this responsibility instead of making the formulation more clear-cut and meaningful in the Second Five-Year Plan, resulted in its being blurred and indecisive. A comparison of the writing in the two plans regarding any important policy—such as that of food, prices, or controls will make this obvious. ... (p. 98)

Secondly, in relation to the targets and other figures, though the overall figures were placed in the Second Five-Year Plan in a more ordered structure, it was clear even at an early stage that neither the physical targets nor the monetary values had been built up through any realistic examination from below. Therefore, the new exercise in figures still remained abstract in the sense of its representing merely overall national estimates which, though exhibited in the appropriate columns or squares, were without any necessary operative significance, and were not based on tested relationships. ...(p. 98)

The emphasis on expressing outlays, targets, etc., in physical terms followed logically from the large size of the Plan. It was now necessary not only to provide for resources in financial terms, but also to see that what was sought to be achieved was practicable in real, physical terms. Ensuring this would require a detailed examination of the proposals from a variety of points of view. There was, for example, the obvious but vitally necessary step of seeing that the money values represented correctly the appropriate physical quantities. Much more important was to test the consistency of the proposals in physical terms in a number of directions. The test of consistency may mean, for example, estimating as carefully as possible, the total requirement of, say, steel and cement in all parts of the Plan, and examining whether they could be met with by production and/or imports of steel and cement during appropriate periods. There was also involved a more elaborate examination of targets, etc., as for example, in relation to mutual adjustment between sectors. It was a matter of dispute at the early stage of the Plan as to whether the total expenditure provided for transport was adequate to bring about the increase in transport facilities necessary for fulfilling the transport assumed by the physical targets of production, imports, exports, etc., in the other parts of the Plan. ....(p. 99)

The Plan-frame was no more than a quickly constructed overall frame, capable, essentially, of only exhibiting the main types of items involved, and indicating their possible relationships. Whether, in fact, any particular figure was appropriate or not could be determined only on rigorous technical examination in a variety of directions. The general impression at the time of the preparation of the Plan was that for the preparation of the Plan-frame, very little technical examination had been undertaken. ... (pp. 99, 100)

There is little evidence to show that this technical examination was, in fact, ever carried out, and it does not appear that the validity of the estimates and the measure of their physical consistency in the final Plan were guaranteed to be greater than those of the estimates in the Plan-frame. That the Planning Commission itself treated physical estimates very lightly was emphasized by the large revision upward, at a very late stage, of the agricultural output estimate in an attempt to meet criticism from high quarters. ...(p. 100)

This constitutes, in my opinion, the real beginning and the main reason for the later failure of the Planning Commission. This was again a failure for which the politicians could in no way be held responsible. It was a failure on the level of technical competence. The physical targets in a real plan, as distinguished from an illustrative plan-frame could not be notional and would consequently have no significance till a full technical examination of them for practicability or consistency had been carried out. In retrospect, therefore, the Plan-frame appears as a mere tour de force which made claims and raised expectations which the Planning Commission and its experts and advisers were later unable to fulfil. In the event, it may prove to have been less than useless. For, even if unwittingly, the whole series of events appears to have discredited an approach and a procedure, which it will not be possible to dispense with in any type of large or serious planning. ...(p. 100)

Another similar failure on the part of the Planning Commission requires to be drawn attention to. This is in relation to the framing of objective criteria, as far as possible, in relation to the definition of priorities of activities or schemes for being included in the Plan. When representations were made to the Planning Commission regarding, for example, inclusion of individual irrigation or power projects in the First Five-Year Plan, it was possible for the Planning Commission to say that it was not working on a clean slate. Projects included in the First Five-Year Plan, it was stated, were largely those on which commitments in one way or another had already been undertaken. The Planning Commission went on to indicate, at this time, that it would undertake the setting up of tests and objective criteria when it would begin examination of schemes, projects, etc., for inclusion in the Second Five-Year Plan. However, so far as is known, this promise was not fulfilled, and there was failure on the part of the Planning Commission to formulate any set of objective criteria for the appropriate variety of purposes. If any were formulated, they have obviously not been duly publicized. ... (pp. 100, 101)

If the Planning Commission looks upon itself as a technical and advisory body, it can make an effort to make the examination of individual proposals and its total recommendations as objective as possible. On the basis of such objective recommendations, the appropriate political authority will arrive at final decisions which are practicable in political terms. However, if in one and the same authority, both aspects of the process are inextricably mixed, one or the other must suffer. Inevitably, it is the objective approach that suffers. Both, the composition and the situation of the Indian Planning Commission, have resulted in pushing the aspect of technical expertise and objective examination into the background. To all intents and purposes, in the preparation of plans and examination of schemes or projects, the Planning Commission and its organs appear to act on the level of political practicability. This is undesirable, not in the sense that political factors must not be recognized, but in the sense that this makes it impossible to bring out, as it is important to bring out (even if only for internal record and not for publicity) in a clear manner the distinction between results obtained on an objective examination with certain externally set up criteria, and the results as finally reached by political bargaining or negotiations. ...(p. 101)

Such are some of the more important failures at the stage of the final formulation of the Plan. The failures were even larger later, i.e., as the process of execution or implementation of the Plan began. A national five-year plan is prepared, considered, and accepted largely in terms of national aggregative figures. For execution and implementation, as in the case of any other plan, scheme, or budget, it has to be expressed in terms of appropriate constituent details. An overall plan has to be broken down, for example, in terms of areas of activity as well as periods of time. Division by time is an elementary and important division. All five-year plans have to be broken down into annual plans, and all annual plans have to be broken down into allocations for different types of activities, located in different regions or areas. This is again an elementary proposition that for the proper fulfilment and the implementation of a plan, the annual plan must be framed; and also that this is the work of the Planning Commission. It appears in retrospect that the preparation of the annual breakdown of the five-year plan was, in fact, never effectively undertaken. ....(p. 102)

The most important evidence is of what happened to our foreign-exchange resources during 1956 and 1957. That the foreign-exchange position and import requirements were one of the weak spots of a large plan with emphasis on heavy industry had always been fully recognized. That careful conservation of foreign-exchange resources through avoidance or regulation of imports and through encouragement of exports was necessary had always been accepted in theory ever since the formulation of the First Five-Year Plan. ... From 1955 to the time of the greatly increased import restrictions late in 1957, the policy of licensing of imports was for all purposes uncoordinated with the requirements of proper plan-progress. It may be that the ministry granting import-licenses operated on a system or criteria of its own. It is quite clear, at the same time, that there was no well-known or established annual plan, with an import-content of the plan of each year worked out, in relation to which the ministry granting import-licenses was required to work. Further, it is clear, in retrospect, that neither the Planning Commission, nor the Ministry of Finance, nor the Reserve Bank of India, exercised any check at any point on the process of the disastrous running-down of the foreign-exchange reserve. ... What is important in this context is to note that the Planning Commission, which is presumably primarily responsible for enabling and watching the progress of the Plan, does not appear to resort to such ordinary procedures as of splitting the five-year plan into annual plans, or of defining the import content of annual plans, or of establishing channels of information through which it can keep a watch on the progress of annual plans and their more important components. ... (pp. 102,103)

I may now turn to aspects which may be considered more as matters for policy-advice than of implementation. ... (p. 103) In dealing with the activities of the Planning Commission regarding formulation and execution of policy, a difficulty arises. This is due to the impossibility of discovering what specific advice has been tendered by the Planning Commission in any particular context, apart from what is contained in the two plan reports. The difficulty arises, not only because there is no published record of the later communications of the Planning Commission, but also because the Planning Commission is active in this sphere to the extent of even advising individual ministries about matters to be placed before the Cabinet; and it continually participates through meetings in the Commission and Joint meetings with the Cabinet in final discussions of important economic issues and problems. ... (pp. 103, 104)

One particular aspect of the problem, however, the Planning Commission may be considered as being specifically charged with, is the co-ordination of measures of policy. It has been often pointed out that there is no dearth in India of regulatory powers and devices in the hands of the government. It is, at the same time, clear—this is emphasized in the memorandum of the Panel of Economists—that there has been little co-ordinated use of the various powers and measures for implementation of the total Plan. The failure to co-ordinate regulatory measures during the period of the Second Five-Year Plan continues to be as marked as during the first-plan period. ... (p. 104)

Especially remarkable, during all these years, has been the failure of the Planning Commission to pay any attention to integrating regulation of foreign trade with the plans. The continuance, for the whole period since 1947, and especially since planning has begun, of the administration of import and export quotas on a quarterly basis has been a perennial puzzle to me. The Planning Commission, in neither of its two plan reports, has given any attention to the operation of import and export controls as related to the designing and implementation of the plans. Even before the present serious foreign-exchange situation, it was clear that the quarterly licensing of export and import quotas created a privileged class of traders, a field of patronage, a source of windfall gains, all at high national cost. Moreover, it not only exerted a persistently disturbing influence on many types of consumer-goods markets, but also upset, without reason and without notice, the calculations of many classes of producers, and consequently affected productive activity. ...(p. 104)

All this would make it clear that we are not yet living in a planned economy. The First Five-Year Plan did not attempt to create a planned economy. The Second Five-Year Plan involved considerable progress towards the planned economy. However, there was a failure to execute the Plan in a planned manner, as exemplified by the non-adoption of elementary appropriate policies required, as of stabilization of agricultural prices and the absence of precautions regarding proper conservation and utilization of food and foreign-exchange resources. There are no signs that, even after the experience of the last two years, any significant improvements in this regard are being attempted or even contemplated. One might, therefore, say that though the formulation of the Second Five-Year Plan has resulted in a number of important developments in the country, the Indian economy is not yet being operated in any planned manner. ... (p. 106)

In my opinion, future progress of our country is vitally dependent on remedying this situation as early as possible, and undertaking, through intelligent and organized effort, proper shaping and execution of present and future plans. We are too poor to expect always to muddle through successfully somehow, and it is extremely dangerous to adopt a Micawber-like attitude and expect that in all difficulties, resulting chiefly from our own mistakes, something will ultimately inevitably turn up. For us there is no alternative to taking up planning seriously. No progress in this direction can, however, be made so long as the apex planning organization does not properly carry out the functions for which it was originally set up. ... (p. 107)

The main functions set down in the 1950 resolution, establishing the Planning Commission, were to assess resources, formulate the plan, define its stages, appraise progress, and make related recommendations on policy and administration. Examination of events since 1955 shows that, barring the theoretic formulation, the Planning Commission has failed in almost every respect. It failed to put together detailed and meaningful plans after due technical and other examination; it did not produce objective criteria relating to composition of programmes allocations, etc.; it failed to produce annual plans with appropriate break-downs, and failed to watch the progress of the plan even in its broadest elements; it failed to give advice insistently on right policies being followed, and at times, even participated in the adoption of wrong and inappropriate ones. ... (p. 107)

This means that the Planning Commission has failed, and continues today to fail, all along the line. The failure, it should be made clear, is not essentially the failure of its staff of experts or administrators. In such respects, as for example, the theoretic writing in the reports, or some aspects of the work of the Development Wing to take two rather divergent illustrations, the competence of the staff is shown to be of high order. The root of the failure lies in the process by which the Planning Commission, essentially only an advisory body, has come to mix itself with the actual process of the formulation of public policies, even in matters other than that of development. ... (p. 107)

It was, perhaps, the composition of the Planning Commission which made it inevitable that this should happen. It contained, from the beginning, as members, some ministers of the Cabinet. The other members also were either experienced administrators or public men of standing, almost none of whom brought to his task experience, knowledge or expertise, which were also not available among the public men from whom ministers are drawn, or among the senior administrative personnel which was chiefly responsible for co-ordination of policies and their implementation. In the circumstances, it was natural that members other than Cabinet Ministers should seek fields of action for themselves which were suited to their ability and to their inclinations. This naturally resulted in turning the Planning Commission, from its proper functions, to activities which were largely the same as those of ministries and state governments. In the result, even the expert staff of the Planning Commission lost its special character. The experts at the Planning Commission were merely experts for the time being with the Planning Commission. The ease with which not only the senior officials of the Commission but also experts changed from government department to the Planning Commission and vice versa, or combined duties in both the organizations, emphasized the basic similarity in the activities of the ministries and the Planning Commission. ... (pp. 107, 108)

It is the power complex of the Planning Commission or its members, their natural desire to exercise power and patronage like ministers, that are chiefly responsible for the neglect by the Commission of its main functions and for a needless extension of its activities over many irrelevant fields. The misdirection has been helped largely by the membership of the Prime Minister and the Finance Minister in the Planning Commission, which appears to have vested the Planning Commission and its decisions with an unnatural kind of prestige and importance. ... (p. 108)

The situation can be remedied only by going back to the functions of the Planning Commission as originally laid down and making the Planning Commission fulfil them. It is not my purpose to suggest that the Indian Planning Commission be entirely changed in character and reduced to the level of, say, a section in the Ministry of Finance. The Planning Commission as an organization, not under any particular ministry and with powers in the appropriate context to deal directly with central ministries and governments of states, should retain its present status. What is important is that it should no longer have any executive functions and should not be mixed up with the essentially political process of final policy-making. Final decisions regarding economic policy should fully rest with the special committee of the Cabinet and appropriate committees of secretaries, and in the final resort, with the Cabinet itself. It is true that there are said to exist, even today, such bodies in the Cabinet and the Secretariat, but they are apparently ineffective and the intrusion of the Planning Commission in this sphere has affected the efficiency of government itself. The shedding by the Planning Commission of its role of direct participation in policy-making may appear to reduce its importance; in fact, this is likely to increase greatly its usefulness in the first instance, and its prestige ultimately. The cutting out of executive functions will mainly affect only the Commission's special connection with national extension, etc., and with the programme evaluation organization. ... (pp. 108, 109)

Secondly, there will have to be a basic change in the manner in which the Commission deals with budgets and programmes of the ministry and the states. The proper procedure in this regard may be visualized as follows. There are two aspects to all such questions. The first is that of the proper technical examination of any individual proposal. This, on the relevant plane, the Planning Commission must carry out. The second relates to inclusions, or omissions, or size, or phasing in the light of plan size or structure. In this context, the effective decisions relating to individual ministries or states must be seen to be derived as corollaries of the basic official decisions constituting and governing the total plan. If there is an adjustment during the plan-period, this also will be on the appraisal of the Planning Commission requiring changed policy, which the government has duly endorsed. The relation of the Planning Commission with states and ministries should be that of an expert body engaged in bringing out the implications of total policy in relation to the activities of particular organizations or authorities rather than an authority engaged in bargaining with, or bullying, or being bullied by another government organization. ... (p. 109)

There are two other aspects of the Commission's existing organization relating to which a few words may be said. The first is that of panels and other advisory organizations. The Planning Commission appears to have no fixed policy regarding their use and has been active in setting them up and consulting them only at the times of the preparation of new plans. These organizations should be used more consistently for knowing what non-official expert opinion is concerned with, for giving attention to the broad problems of planning in each particular field, and for activating group-thinking in relation to the next plan stage in particular, and future plans in general. Secondly, there is the direction to which efforts of the staff of experts and administrator are oriented. The administrative staff of the Commission ought to be kept down to the minimum; its main function should be to obtain for the Planning Commission such direct knowledge of current conditions as will enable it to make a proper appraisal of the progress of a plan. The staff of experts of the Commission will, however, have to be varied in its composition. There is need for this staff to acquire, over the years, a special point of view, and a particular attitude of mind. These derive from the grounds which justify a Planning Commission retaining a nuclear expert staff of its own rather than depending on a ministry or other government experts. There are two main grounds. Firstly, the ordinary ministry or other expert inevitably takes a narrow point of view in respect both of the placing of each problem against the background of an operative national plan, and of being comparatively hospitable to novel suggestions the experts of the Planning Commission should appear differentiated. Secondly, official experts, such as those of individual ministries, are heavily burdened with day-to-day and routine work. There is no point, as happens today, in the Planning Commission experts being kept at a similar grind. If they have to be forward looking they must have leisure enough to think ahead. I may translate this in terms of what the Planning Commission economists would do. Firstly, I expect them to be engaged in producing periodical overall critical surveys of the operation of the economy such as the Council of Economic Advisers to the President of the USA produces every six months, and secondly, they would plan out a number of long-term studies such, for example, as those of the problems and the costs of the operation of the mixed economy or relative effectiveness of various types of planning techniques. ...(pp. 109, 110)

A changed view of the composition of the Commission will be necessary to bring about the re-orientation suggested above. Obviously the Prime Minister, and the Finance Minister, should cease to be members of the Commission. No minister of the Cabinet should be a member of the Commission except the Minister for Planning, if such a post is continued in the Cabinet, and he should be the Chairman of the Commission. The Deputy Chairman of the Commission should be, by preference, an administrator of wide experience. This is necessary, as the Planning Commission operates essentially through contacts with ministries and governments and their senior officers, and somebody acquainted with their ways should be the administrative head of the organization. For the rest, the members should be experts, all of whom, however, have some experience of the handling of practical problems. The expertise, chiefly required, will be that of natural scientists, technicians, social scientists, statisticians, and economists. The total membership need not be, or rather should not be, large, because after all the main expertise will be furnished by the superior staff of the Commission together with advisory bodies such as panels. ... (p. 110)

I hope I shall not be considered irreverent if I put in a strong plea for constituting, after reorganization, a relatively youthful body. Instead of thinking in terms of people above 65, it may be useful to think of the majority of members being below 55. The work of the Commission is likely to prove taxing and will need, for success, comparatively open and vigorous minds. The extremely difficult times through which we are passing make it necessary that a revitalized and properly oriented organization be at the apex of our planning-efforts. The present conjuncture may make it possible in other ways also to undertake such basic reconsideration. ...(p. 111)

9

The Finance Commission and Development Planning*

The essence of a federal system is the concurrent existence of a general government for the country as a whole and several regional governments endowed with specific powers. Formerly, the general government and the regional governments were supposed to operate in clearly demarcated spheres and to finance their activities from independent sources of revenue. With the growth of activity of the modern state, strict separation in the exercise of governmental powers and in the sources of revenue has proved difficult to maintain. Federal governments have, as a rule, written constitutions, and the division of functions and financial powers in them become relatively rigid. At the inception of the state, a conscious attempt is usually made to match the functions of each authority with the resources required to fulfil them. However, with the passage of time, there would be no guarantee that the expansion of responsibility, due to a widening interpretation of functions, would correspond closely with the elasticity of the allotted sources of revenue. Moreover, the modern trend towards greater political and economic integration requires acquisition of overall powers by the general government in many respects, including some aspects of fiscal operations. The result has been a perceptible change in federal theory and practice. Thus, while during the last two decades the federal form has proved popular among new states, rigidity in division of powers and finances is being increasingly avoided. Providing for concurrent exercise of powers in certain spheres by the general government and the regional governments has become common, and financial arrangements

* Originally published in *Opinion*, Special Number, 1961.

have been made adjustable through such devices as the sharing of revenues and the system of grants.

The main objective of a federal system is the maintenance of autonomy—relative independence of action—within defined spheres for regional governments. The avoidance of rigidity in separation of powers and sources of revenue and closeness of constant co-operation between the general government and the regional governments cannot, and should not, mean changing the basic federal concept and reducing regional governments to the status of subordinate authorities. The problem of federal finance is thus that of maintaining, through changing circumstances, needed correspondence between functions and resources without the use of any coercive power. The satisfactory working of the financial system of a federation does not depend wholly, or even mainly, on the initial division of resources between the Union and the states but on the smoothness and propriety with which later adjustments are carried out. Fortunately, the framers of the Indian Constitution had realized fully the need for providing for such adjustments. The Constitution provided, not only for a variety of combinations relating to levy, collections, assignment, and the sharing of revenues between the Union and the states, but also for a system of grants, recurring and non-recurring, fixed or variable, conditional or non-conditional, from the Union to the states, giving power to the government of the Union to vary the amounts or proportions of grants from state to state. Above all, the Constitution provided for an appointment by the President, every quinquennium, of a Finance Commission to make recommendations as to the financial arrangements between the Union and the states, including the sharing of taxes and the operation of the system of grants. The financial provisions of the Constitution have, in practice, proved fairly satisfactory. With their help, the Union and the states have passed, without any major difficulty, through many stages of re-organization. The quinquennial Finance Commissions have been so composed as to command general confidence and have done their work to general satisfaction. The Union Government has also established the convention of implicitly and promptly accepting their recommendations as a whole. The problems of federal finance that confront us are, in the event, problems arising out of developments that had not been foreseen by the framers of the Constitution, and for which consequently no provisions have been made in that document.

Even before the appointment of the first Finance Commission, the Planning Commission had been set up and the First Five-Year Plan launched. The finance of development planning has created not only a number of new problems but also a duality of authority within this sphere. Duality arises because while the plans cover both the revenue and the capital expenditure, the main function of the Finance Commission under the Constitution is to make recommendations regarding the devolution of revenue resources. The Finance Commission has to assess the needs of the states, and has, for this purpose, to make estimates of existing resources of the states their committed expenditure, the forecasts of expenditure, and the additional resources to be raised for meeting this. The Planning Commission, in drawing up the plan, has to undertake similar exercises, the results of which may or may not be deemed acceptable by the Finance Commission in particular directions. The Finance Commission of 1957, which first dealt with these problems, felt that some anomalies would inevitably arise where the functions of the two Commissions overlap, and recommended that, in order to co-ordinate the work of the two more effectively, the period covered by the recommendations of the Finance Commission should, in future, coincide with that of a Five-Year Plan.

The difficulties arising out of the overlapping of work and differences of periods may be regarded as of minor importance. The change, which has created the most serious problem, is that planning has put a significant part of the financial arrangement between the Union and the states out of the purview of the Finance Commission. This has happened in two ways. Firstly, capital expenditure, which under planning has assumed increasing importance, is not covered by the activities of the Finance Commission. The Finance Commission of 1957 was asked, specially, to make recommendations regarding modifications, if any, in the rates of interest and the terms of repayment of the Union loans to states and made valuable suggestions for consolidating and rationalizing these. It did not, however, deal with the quanta of the loans or other forms of capital assistance. The Finance Commission of 1957 did not also cover fully even the revenue expenditure of the states on development account. A system of grants or assistance for specific activities, by the Centre to the states, routed through the Planning Commission, has been developed since the inception of the First Plan. This had become very important in total finances of the states even by 1957. The following quotation from the report of the Finance Commission of 1957 throws interesting light on the resulting situation:

> Since our scheme of devolution involves substantial transfer of resources for implementing the revenue portion of the plan, which for most States is reflected in the grants-in-aid recommended for them, we considered whether we should make any part of the grants-in-aid conditional on such implementation. We would have liked to do so, if the assistance provided under our scheme had represented the major part of the expenditure. Under our scheme, the States will be receiving a little less than a third of the outlay and a little over a third will come by way of specific assistance from the Union under the plan; for the balance they will have to raise their own resources. We have, therefore, decided not to impose any condition on the grants-in-aid recommended by us.

This paragraph raises an issue of extreme importance in the context of the working of a federal government. While the Finance Commission may not be competent to cover capital expenditure, there is nothing to suggest that it need or should take a partial view in relation to the coverage of revenue expenditure. However, confronted with a situation in which a variety of grants-in-aid were already being given by the Central Government and Ministries to the states, the Commission of 1957 took the continuance of these for granted. It made estimates of total expenditure on development, which would have to be incurred by each state in the ensuing five years, made calculations about the portion of it that could be covered by a state from its current revenue and through additional taxation, etc., and further allowed for grants likely to be received from the Union during the five-year period under the existing schemes and arrived in this manner at the net assistance through grants required by a state for meeting its projected development-expenditure. Because the Commission took the existing grants-in-aid for granted, it felt that it could not impose conditions on the utilization of the grants that it recommended. The result appears to be doubly unfortunate. The Constitution of India lays down that it shall be the duty of the Finance Commission to make recommendations to the President as to the principles that should govern the grants-in-aid of the revenues of the states out of the Consolidated Fund of India. The grants-in-aid, which the Finance Commission took for granted, are made definitely out of the Consolidated Fund of India. In not examining them, and not making recommendations regarding principles that should govern them, the Commission appears to have failed in its duty. Because of this failure it did not also discuss in detail and make recommendations relating to the conditions that should be appropriately attached to grants for development expenditure.

This issue has far-reaching importance. Through the last decade, the states have come to depend on the Centre for an increasing share of their revenue resources. Apart from the fact that the expanding sources are chiefly with the Centre, considerations of administrative convenience, etc., have led to an expansion of the scope of central excises and to some reduction in the coverage of sales taxes. Further, the ability of individual states to raise loans is limited and foreign aid, importance of which has grown apace, accrues wholly to the Centre. On the other hand, in development planning, the expenditure liability of the states increases, at least, as much as that of the Centre. In consequence, it becomes necessary to transfer, through some means, substantial sums from the Centre to the states. During the last decade this has been, in the main, done through a large number of specific grants made under a large variety of terms and conditions. The characteristics of the system that has thus developed are brought out in the following quotation from a study by a high official (P.P. Agarwal, *The System of Grants-in-Aid in India*, 1959):

> What is stated in the preceding pages will show that except in regard to the grants recommended by the Finance Commission, there is a lack of coherence and conformity to any broad principles in the system of grants-in-aid at present in force in India. It is difficult to make even a broad generalization regarding the pattern of assistance at

various levels. Since during the early period assistance was given to individual schemes as and when they came up, no general principles could be framed for the country as a whole. Thus till recently, the basis of grants under Grow-More-Food Schemes for Part A and Part B States differed from the basis governing grants to Part C States. Grants for elementary education even today vary from scheme to scheme, and sometimes from programme to programme. Thus, while 50 per cent is given for ordinary schools under the special schemes relating to education of girls, 60 per cent is given for basic schools under the same scheme.

A significant fact is the comparatively heavy dependence of the State on Central resources. In the case of most of the grants considered in this study, the Centre's contribution is generally larger than that of the States. The Centre usually bears 50 to 75 per cent of the cost, though many of the schemes are primarily the concern of the States. Almost all grants by the Ministry of Education are in excess of 50 per cent of the cost of the schemes. The Ministries of Labour and Home Affairs meet about 60 per cent of the cost. In the case of the Ministry of Health, the general pattern is to give 75 per cent of the non-recurring and 50 per cent of the recurring costs.

The facts set out above present a prima facie case for a full examination by the Finance Commission of all the grants-in-aid given by the Union to the states, and determination by that Commission of the principles that should govern them and their amounts for the next quinquennium. As this proposal would appear radical to many, it is necessary to examine arguments that could be adduced against it. It may be argued that the burden imposed on the Finance Commission by the proposed requirement would be too heavy. It would have, firstly, to take an overall view of the resources and needs of each state and arrive at the size of the total expenditure, including development expenditure, which should be covered through revenue expenditure. Secondly, it would have to examine the operation of the immense number of separate schemes of grants and frame the general principles that should govern them.

The first of these tasks the Finance Commissions have, in the past, always attempted. In the context of development planning, the chief question is regarding the extent to which the Finance Commission should rely on the assessments and calculations of the Planning Commission and to what extent it should make an independent effort. The Finance Commission has a special responsibility regarding Union-state arrangements and has also to ensure fair treatment as between the states. Therefore, while it would undoubtedly be right for the Finance Commission to accept the judgement of the Planning Commission regarding the total size of the national plan, the details of state needs, allocations, etc., should be examined by the Finance Commission itself. Today, there is no well-defined arrangement for settling such vital issues as the size of the plans of the states. The Planning Commission, in consultation with individual states, largely determines these and they are finally endorsed by the National Development Council (NDC). The NDC is, however, hardly a deliberative body, and its sanction is largely a political act. The main responsibility remains with the Planning

Commission, and the size of the plan of a state is the result mainly of bilateral negotiations of the governments of states with the Planning Commission. This is hardly a satisfactory way of doing things, and it has not broken down chiefly because of the extra-constitutional factor of a single political party controlling all governments. It would, in the long run, be highly desirable to interest the Finance Commission in examining the relative sizes of the plans of the states through its responsibility of assessing quinquennially the revenue resources and needs of individual states.

The other task, that of examining the varied system of grants-in-aid, will no doubt prove highly complex and time-consuming in the first instance. However, it is on that account all the more necessary that somebody should examine, at an early date, this wild growth and systematize its structure: the body most competent to undertake this task is the Finance Commission. The present system of central grants suffers from most of the defects attributed to a bad system of grants. However, its most glaring defect is the manner in which it is insidiously undermining the autonomy of the states. This happens, chiefly, in two ways. Firstly, most state governments are tempted by offers of grants, to undertake the activities to which grants are attached and in the form in which the centrally framed scheme is presented. This often leads to serious misdirection of effort in the context of particular circumstances of individual states. Secondly, the administration of grants, with the usual examinations as to admissibility of expenditure, etc., places very considerable power, often unfairly used, in the hands of inspecting officers of the ministries and the Planning Commission. The total result is the undermining of the initiative of state authorities and the building-up of feelings of resentment. There is also the uncertainty, in some instances, regarding finance for continuance of activities already initiated. A number of these defects would be removed and the state governments would begin to operate more freely, if the basic principles governing the structure and operation of the entire system could be first laid down by the Finance Commission, the system rationalized in the light of these, and then subjected to periodic examination by successive Finance Commissions.

One need not pay much attention to the fears expressed that if the entire revenue expenditure for the quinquennium is provided for through the Finance Commission's recommendations, there would be no incentive to state governments to undertake maximum effort on their own account or that this would lead to misdirection of resources. The recommendations of the Finance Commission would themselves be based on calculations about the results of the efforts to be made by state governments. Consequently, the total resources required for the plan could not become available without appropriate and adequate effort on the part of the states. Secondly, when it is proposed that the Finance Commission should provide for all needed revenue resources, it is not suggested that they should be made available without any conditions being attached. The quotation given earlier, from the report of the 1957 Commission, indicates that that Commission was inclined to recommend conditional grants but refrained because it was providing only for partial finance. With a full provision, there need be no such hesitation on the part of the Commission.

I have raised in this article only one issue in relation to the problems of federal finance in India. However, I believe that the issue so raised is both fundamental and timely, and that if the Finance Commission could be induced to adopt the point of view put forward, a very significant improvement in the present situation would follow.

10

Planning and Administration*

In talking about planning and administration, I shall confine attention to the situation in India. In fact, therefore, the talk will be on planning and administration in India today. Also, I shall be concerned here, not with plan formulation or evaluation, but with the aspect which has closest connection with administration, namely, plan implementation.

For understanding the existing administrative situation in India it is necessary to look back at the British period. The existing administrative structure has changed very little from that developed in the British times, and procedures, methods, attitudes have to a considerable extent continued in the present from the colonial past. The main characteristics of the older situation were as follows: the total scope of government activity was then extremely limited; keeping law and order, administering justice, and collecting revenues were the main activities. Economic policy was predominantly *laissez faire* and the scope of development and welfare activities, including education and health, directly undertaken by the state was highly restricted. Lord Morley vetoed even the establishment of a Department of Industry by a provincial government. There were no set goals to achieve, as those of economic development or of social welfare. This was underlined by the inaction and the complete lack of policy in the face of the severe depression of the thirties. Discriminating protection was the only exception introduced in inter-war years; but no aspect of this was integrated into the administrative system.

The second notable feature of the situation was the exercise of power fairly directed by the top civil service itself. Before the Montford Reforms this exercise was direct. During the inter-war years, for a limited number

* Barve Memorial Lecture delivered at Delhi on 6 March 1968.

of subjects, a form of authority was vested in elected politician ministers. But, in effect, the exercise of this authority was highly limited and in very few important cases were the politician ministers in a position to ignore the wishes of the powerful civil servants. The main difference made by the Montford Reforms was to add the responsibility of managing legislators and ministers to the other work done by the top civil servants.

The top civil servants were in effect the representatives of the British in India. Till the First World War they were overwhelmingly British. During the inter-war years an Indian element was progressively introduced in the composition of the highest services but this made no real change to the structure, attitudes, or operations of the civil service. There was high concentration of total authority in this body of civil servants. As within this body there was considerable delegation of authority to the member of the service at the lowest tier. 'Trusting the man on the spot' had a specific limited meaning in British times. It meant trusting the District Collector or an official at even lower level of local authority if he was a member of the civil service. No such delegation was intended for or effected in favour of any officials outside the civil service. This had the other side of insisting upon working strictly to orders, according to a scheme or a blue-print, for all lower official cadres below the British civil servants. There was neither delegation nor exercise of independent judgment allowed at these levels.

As the official was the symbol of externally imposed authority, it was held to be of the utmost importance to maintain high his prestige in the eyes of the Indian public. This was meticulously insisted upon. To a certain extent even the Indian officials at lower ranks were vested, by a process of transfer, with this position or sense of prestige and the British system protected this aspect as against members of the Indian public.

The total operations of the bureaucracy and, in particular, of the nuclear British civil service were as those of an outsider. It was an outside element, involved neither in the affairs nor in the passions or emotions of the ruled, that was running administration.

The basic ultimate purposes of the administration were objectives and purposes of the British interest and policy. To the extent, however, that proper maintenance of law and order and of British prestige involved maintenance of certain standards of justice, etc., as between Indian and Indian, and observance of the rule of law, considerable importance was attached to these. When Indians became members of this civil service, it was insisted that they should keep themselves aloof from involvement in Indian society in order to preserve the role of functioning as outsiders.

During the inter-war years the political situation was undergoing continuous change. However, this meant no change, either in the structure of the civil service or the rest of the administrative apparatus or, in the relations of the nuclear civil service with the rest of the administration. It meant also no change of attitudes either on the part of the official or of the public towards each other. The major change was that members of the civil service found it necessary and expedient in certain contexts to conceal the basic sanction of force at the back of exercise of power by the British and to be occupied to a large extent with managing and manipulating politicians and other leading elements in Indian public life.

This environment and situation changed suddenly with the coming of independence. The most important new factor was the emergence of the Indian politician as the effective ruler. The civil servants at the top of the administrative apparatus no longer acted as representatives in India of the English crown, but had to act as servants of Indian ministers. This could have meant a very large change in the situation of civil servants and in the functioning of the administrative system. However, in effect, no large change took place immediately. This was largely because the Indian politician did not appear anxious in any way to affect the prestige and operation of the administrative system and particularly of the top operators. He did not, evidently, want to change the position of the members of the Indian Civil Service in any way and they were guaranteed, like princes, a number of privileges. Even so, the exercise of political power by ministers and later by legislators eroded gradually the privileged position of the top civil servants, and they had to learn more and more the art of management of their political masters. The change in relations between the highest civil services cadres and other elements of administration was more gradual.

The other extremely important aspect of the changed situation was that the civil servant could no longer look upon himself as an outsider or representative of an outside authority. He began, by slow degrees, to function more and more as part of Indian society. The ruler-ruled distinction did not become completely blurred but the involvement of the civil servant in public affairs, in particular groups and interests, his affiliation with regions and castes came more obviously to the surface. However, even 20 years later the transition has not been completed and in a large part vestiges of the older situation remain. The vestiges that are most important from our point of view appear to be as follows:

The 'generalist' civil service, i.e., the ICS (Indian Civil Service) and its successor, the IAS (Indian Administrative Service) still completely dominate the scene. There is an enormous concentration of power on top in this strata and new elements of specialists or managers of business still rank low in prestige and authority. The ICS and the IAS function as an exclusive club and it is openly alleged that you cannot function effectively in top positions in administration unless you belong to this group. The attitudes of the public towards officials and of the officials towards the public are still coloured largely by the older situation and this has special meaning in the context of planning and development.

The British concept of the single British District Officer, Collector, etc., co-ordinating all authority in all departments over an entire area in his hands still continues to be an important feature of the local administrative structure and colours the whole of its operation. The civil service enjoys very great effective power even today. However, an extremely important aspect is that the older combination of power and responsibility is no longer to be found. In the older regime when power vested largely in their hands, the senior group of members of the civil service also accepted the accompanying responsibility. They were responsible ultimately to the Crown for proper management of Indian affairs and always behaved with a full sense of this responsibility. Today, the civil servant no longer feels responsibility in this manner because power is supposed to reside in and directly wielded by the politician minister. The curious situation that exists at present is, therefore, that while the actual day-to-day exercise of the power rests in the hands of the civil servant, the civil servant no longer feels any overall responsibility. This, he feels, rests with the ministers who exercise it fitfully, largely on the advice of the civil servants themselves. However, as this exercise, especially in relation to personal or party matters, may be on considerations other than those accepted by the civil servant or put forward by him, the advice is likely to be disregarded in some contexts and occasions. This change seems to have relieved the civil servant from any feeling of carrying the overall burden of administration. The informal operation of a group of top civil servants as generally looking after the total situation has, therefore, vanished and the Cabinet or an inner group of ministers have not taken over this function in any effective manner; it has thus ceased to be discharged.

As against this background, one has to consider the relevance and appropriateness of the present state of administrative arrangements in India to the specific requirements of the effort at planned economic development. Apart from the results of transition to self-rule after independence, it is planned economic development that has added enormously to the dimensions of government effort. The activities of the government have increased tremendously both in width of coverage and in depth and intensity. The direct responsibilities that the government now undertakes cover large fields of social and economic life. The government takes upon itself the responsibility of erecting the structure of public services and utilities required for development of a modern industrial society and of continuously maintaining that structure. It undertakes, in addition, a large variety of welfare activities. The government owns and conducts a large number of industrial production businesses which are basic to the building of the industrial structure. The government occupies large sections of trading and it tries to regulate many other aspects of social and economic life. The number of administrators, at various levels, required in government service has increased enormously and the qualifications needed by them have become extremely varied. The contrast with the situation in, say 1939, is extremely glaring.

Not only has the sphere of direct government activity and of official regulation of socio-economic activity immensely widened, but also the conduct of operations has become extremely detailed. The task undertaken by the government, of the transformation and activization of rural economic society, is in itself immense. This, in effect, means operating on the millions of small dispersed units of farming and other rural activities. The development of agriculture and its improvement are essentially specialized tasks which must be performed in relation to every locality. In the British times, in some states the collection of revenue was related to the maintenance of detailed village records and village officials. However, in the landlord provinces, the rural administrative structure was very rudimentary. Looking at the area of the landlord provinces and of the Indian states, it may be said that for the larger part of the country an administrative structure for regulating or directing activities of individual local communities was not available at independence. This had to be constructed, widened, and strengthened.

Apart from undertaking multi-fold activities and activizing or regulating economic life all over the country, planning requires continuous maintenance of a long-term and co-ordinated direction to socio-economic developments. This is both a highly important and difficult function which is made all the more important and difficult because of the large size, the diversity, and the federal political structure of the country. Administration has to be geared to all these ends. It will be thus seen that very large ground had to be covered as between the highly limited government activity of the British times, for which the particular structure was fashioned, and the requirements of the administrative system of the era of planned development.

It must, in the first instance, be recognized that the Indian administrative system has grown rapidly, adapted itself partially to the changed situation, and tried to meet the large and manifold new requirements. Inefficiency and corruption may have increased, but there has been no real breakdown of the system and this in itself is creditworthy. However, huge problems remain unsolved and it is necessary to pay urgent attention to these. I shall deal with some indicated by the analysis above. Two major difficulties are related to the dominance and the changed attitude of the generalist ICS and IAS service personnel at the top. The first is the lack of a co-ordinated view and of a frame of considered policy. In fact this indicates a failure on the part of the Council of Ministers but it is also related to the short-term, departmental view that Secretaries and others take. This flows partly from their lack of specialization and partly from the absence of conjoint operations. The result is adhocism in policy decisions. The second, and even more important, difficulty is sheer incompetence resulting not only from the lack of expert knowledge of the generalist but also equally from the degradation and frustration of the experts and specialists in government service. The first difficulty will be dealt with later. Relating to the second action has to be divided in two parts. Firstly, even for ordinary departmental administration, much more diversified and wider-based methods of recruitment have to be adopted. This will enable direct recruitment of a certain number of specialists and technically qualified personnel for administrative posts at appropriate levels. Even more important is making it possible for them to operate side by side on similar positions of authority with members of the generalist civil service. The recent appointment of Dr I.G. Patel as Special Secretary in Finance is a case in point. Some leaven of such 'outsiders' on parallel positions could alone modify the older narrow and highly hierarchical tradition of the generalist administration.

Secondly, all operations, other than the strictly administrative, should be put outside the purview of the generalist service. The large number of public enterprises, autonomous corporations for performing a variety of specialized functions, either of research or of administration or of quasi-business activity, should be put outside the sphere of the generalist administrator. In these activities, which are essentially spheres of the managers and the experts, it should be insisted that the running would be by people who are professionally competent and are committed to a career in that particular line of activity. In business management, it is the experience even of communist countries that the manager has to have considerable power and autonomy. This is necessary in order to allow him to manage his business flexibly. It is equally necessary to enable giving him due credit or fixing blame on him for good or bad management. The present arrangements by which the generalist looks upon all these areas as his privileged preserves, into which he moves in and out at will, and regarding the mismanagement of which no responsibility is ever fixed on him, must cease at the earliest. As a corollary it follows that the power of generalist Secretaries over such branches of activity must also be abolished.

The next desirable change is essentially a change in attitudes, the attitudes of top civil servants to lower ranks and vice-versa. It is admitted on all hands that there is considerable administrative talent and considerable enthusiasm to be found among all lower ranks, especially of local administrative personnel among departmental staff all over India. However, the whole of the tradition of colonial rule has imposed a pattern of behaviour which prevents any free expression of opinion or exercise of initiative by these large elements. This is a heavy handicap especially in a society which talks of democratic decentralization. Means must, therefore, be found to vitalize the lower level of the administrative structure and, by suitable encouragement and incentives, to give scope for independent expression of views and for some types of independent action by staff at the lower levels.

Reference to the untapped potential among the subordinate official staff naturally leads to consideration of problems of local administration and local planned development. Increased requirements in these regards were met in recent years largely through the expanding Community Development administration. It may be noted that this was in essence the adoption of an older approach that was embodied, for example, in the Gurgaon experiment of Brayne, which was much publicized at one time. However, it became clear at an early stage that the Community Development approach was inadequate. For effective local development a non-official community structure had to be built up and emphasis, therefore, shifted to the Panchayati Raj institutions. The establishment of local primary co-operatives had been recognized as being necessary, even earlier, as agencies of local economic activity and development. The recognition of the importance of building up Panchayati Raj and co-operative institutions was the result of experience of successful development planning. They are not fads or ideologies but are essential systems without which planned development cannot proceed far. The difference made to rural development in various regions with different degrees of development of these agencies clearly proves this. Planning, except at a highly generalized level, has to be related to local situational variations, responses, preferences, and feasibilities. Such a relation can be established only locally. Moreover, planning also requires an agency which can communicate to vast numbers of dispersed farmers, artisans, etc., the schemes and intentions of planners and which can, in turn, interpret their wishes and difficulties to planners. Such an agency cannot be wholly official; that would be both highly costly and ineffective.

Planning at the state and district level is, thus, intimately connected with administrative problems of Panchayati Raj institutions and co-operatives. One special problem that arises out of the working of the Panchayati Raj institutions is that of co-ordination at the district level. Fortunately, Panchayati Raj constitutions mostly provide for co-ordination at the highest level through a series of area and subject committees and a superior executive committee. However, the problems of co-ordination with the sphere of the Collector and in some cases of the proper integration of the Community Development officials are still unsolved. Others are in part problems of the superior civil service and of lower ranks discussed above. They are also, in part, similar to problems of relations between civil servants and ministers. This is an area in which conventions need to be evolved based on the recognition of mutual responsibilities and limitations. Some problems also arise out of reluctance to devolve power and finance to local authorities and officials on the part of ministers, secretariat officials, and departmental heads, and out of the propensity of ministers and superior officials to interfere in the working of co-operatives. It is only when it is widely recognized that the successful establishment and healthy operation of the local institutional structure is a *sine qua non* of further progress that these problems will begin to be solved.

Finally, successful plan implementation also requires the maintenance, by the government, of a consistent long-term economic and social policy. For purposes of planning this requirement is so essential that it cannot be satisfied by the ordinary co-ordinating arrangements within a Cabinet. As indicated above, for a variety of reasons, adhocism appears to be the rule today. It is, at the same time, obvious that the ordinary day-to-day administration of various ministries, departments, and offices should not be hampered by the functioning of any outside body with a general overviewing function. The way out is specifically to ensure that all important decisions which have relevance or significance for other activities, or for future arrangements of operations, should be subject to tests of consistency with the policy laid down in this behalf or, if there is no policy already laid down, should be viewed in the possible frame of such policy. An organization which looks at policy decisions from this point of view would not only be highly useful but for any long-term detailed planning highly necessary. It does not appear essential to vest such an organization with any direct power. All that would be necessary is to ensure that in each such case informed and detailed comment in the light of accepted, co-ordinated, long-term policy decisions or perspectives should be fully expressed and should be carefully considered before action or decision is finally taken by the supreme organ of government.

At the national level, the Planning Commission could properly perform this function and does so already to some extent. If organizations for plan formulation, such as Planning Boards, are created at the state level they could be similarly used. Apart from these, it would be useful to have planning cells in all ministries and departments and planning officers at the district level. This could ensure that the planning aspect of all decisions and activities would be continuously brought to the notice of authorities and the functioning of the important organs of government would acquire a much needed orientation towards planned development.

III

Regional Planning

11

District Development Planning*

I

I find myself today on this platform in an extremely unusual position. The founder of this institute, my father-in-law, Rao Bahadur R.R. Kale of Satara, died in January 1936. We considered that an appropriate way of paying our tribute to him would be to initiate a series of annual memorial lectures. The first lecture in the series was delivered by Prof. V.G. Kale in January 1937 and since then, with the exception of an unfortunate interruption in 1947, the memorial lecture has been regularly delivered each year. We have been singularly fortunate in having secured the services of a series of eminent lecturers who have delivered discourses on important subjects year after year. The lectures are ordinarily delivered during the first quarter of the year. When, some months ago, I as Director of the Institute asked Prof. V.M. Dandekar, who was then the Joint Director, who should be invited to deliver the lecture for 1966, he suggested that I should deliver the memorial lecture myself after retiring from the post of Director on 1st April. After a little thought, I accepted the suggestion. My reasons were mainly two. In the first instance, the change in roles, from one who welcomed and introduced the lecturer every year to that of the lecturer himself would help to mark definitively and publicly the end of my administrative responsibilities as Director of the Institute. Secondly, and more importantly, it would enable me to pay my own personal tribute to the Founder.

Before doing this in the form of an academic discourse, I may be allowed to say a few words regarding the founder personally. I do this because it is thirty years since he passed away and there would be few in this audience,

* R.R. Kale Memorial Lecture, delivered on 23 April 1966, and published by GIPE, Poona, 1967.

as among the staff of the Institute, who have any personal knowledge about him. Rao Bahadur Raoji Ramchandra Kale was a distinguished and highly successful lawyer of Satara City. He was also keenly interested in public affairs and actively participated in them. He played a prominent part in the provincial legislature and in the University. He was a Sanskrit scholar, a deeply religious man, and was attracted towards the *Prarthana Samaj*. However, like Ranade, whom he revered greatly, he was averse to breaking off connections with traditional society. In politics, he was a follower of Gokhale both in the insistence on a deep and careful study of problems and in the belief in need of moderation in the expression of opinion. Though living well, he was able to put together a modest fortune, three-quarters of which he gave away, in part during his lifetime and partly by donations and by the creation of a charitable trust at death.

The manner in which he founded this institute exhibits some of his salient characteristics. I was serving as principal of the College of the *Sarvajanik* Education Society at Surat since 1925. I had the option of leaving the college in 1930 and a year earlier made up my mind to do so, because as principal I had little opportunity to engage in research. In the prevailing circumstances I decided to seek an opening in Poona where I could combine teaching with research. When Rao Bahadur Kale learnt of this, he made, without my knowledge, an offer to the Servants of India Society of an endowment which could give me a chance to do what I desired. He did this at a time when he had retired from active legal practice and though it meant giving away immediately a significant part of his capital resources.

The institute was established in June 1930 as a result of the negotiations which followed this initial offer made in June 1929. The President of the Servants of India Society made the suggestion initially that the institute might be named after the founder. However, he felt that naming it after Gokhale, the founder of the Servants of India Society, would be more appropriate and that the institute might more readily attract wider support in this case. Therefore, he quietly substituted the name of Gokhale in the final proposals and his own name was put into brackets as founder. The assistance and co-operation of many have been responsible for the growth of the institute in subsequent decades. However, these could have had no chance to operate but for the imaginative, courageous, and generous initial endowment by the founder. As the greatest single beneficiary of that action I have great pleasure in paying this tribute, on this occasion, to his memory.

It is only proper that I should take this opportunity to express my gratitude to the President and to members of the Servants of India Society for their co-operation and assistance through all these years. In accepting the endowment the Society agreed to house the institute and to give it the use of its library. Though in later years the institute was able to command its own resources for these purposes, the use of the premises and the nucleus of the library have been vital to the growth of the institute. The terms of the endowment created a Board of Management for the institute in which, naturally, the major role was that of the Servants of India Society. It is a pleasure to record that this responsibility has been discharged by the President and connected members of that Society with such great consideration and understanding that the institute has, in fact, functioned during its entire existence as an essentially autonomous academic institute.

II

The subject of my address today is 'District Development Planning'. In terms of the division of the main functions of government there are, in India, three tiers, *viz.*, the Union, the state, and the district. The constitution of the third tier is not uniform in all states. In some states the main unit of self-government is the district, in others it is the block. In Maharashtra, after adoption of the *Zilla Parishad* scheme, the *zilla* (district) authority has been definitely established as the local development planning authority. For a number of reasons this appears to me to be the most appropriate arrangement and for the purpose of this lecture, I shall confine attention to problems of planning where the district authority is in this position.

District development planning, as I consider it, is an integral part of national development planning. In a state in which there exists a constitutional division of functions between a tier of authorities the planning powers are likely to follow this division of functions. However, it is general experience that the actual operation of the division of functions may be greatly modified by the distribution, among various levels and authorities, of the total financial resources of the state and by arrangements connected with this distribution. Moreover, the effective exercise of planning powers is associated with the existence of appropriate organs and the availability of adequate knowledge and efficient agencies for the purpose, in case of each tier in the federal structure. An appreciation of the problems of planning at any level, therefore, requires a detailed study of these and of actual operations.

In terms of the division of powers and functions between the Union and the states, and the actual operation of the planning process, a certain pattern of division of activities and responsibilities had developed in India by the end of the Second Five-Year Plan. In a paper written in 1960, I described this pattern in the following words:

> The fields of action of the centre and of the states are, to a large extent, distinct. The centre builds up and maintains the overall instrumentalities of national economic life such as the credit and the monetary system, the railways and ports. It also acts in relation to the basic requirements of the long-term plan of industrialization, with emphasis on large industry and exploitation of mineral resources. The states are concerned, on the other hand, with acting on the total life of all the people in their charge and on all the diffused, dispersed, small scale units and activities. The centre is concerned with the most generalized features of the national frame and with highly concentrated

action at a few strategic points; the states must affect all areas and localities, all the relevant fields and all units. The centre is concerned with the strategy of the long-term plan and with initiating the crucial movements; the states have to engage themselves in transmitting the forces impelling economic development to all areas and units, and with concretizing for the individual units the fruits of development. The generalized objectives of a state plan are, therefore, making possible, initiating, and encouraging economic development in all activities and sectors, and areas and localities, and protecting the standard of living and improving and ameliorating the situation, social and economic, of all individuals within their territories. The objectives and the constituents of plans of individual sectors and departments must conform to the requirements of these general objectives. In the light of the above, the locality and the individual are placed at the centre of the activities of states, and providing for the universal impact of the developmental process and for a diffusion of its effects becomes their primary aim. (Gadgil 1972: 237–8)

When this was written, the development of district authorities endowed with specific planning powers had yet to take place. However, the objectives and fields of state planning activity, as described in the extract quoted above, may be taken, generally, to apply to the existing situation in relation to district development planning.

Before proceeding to a detailed discussion of the problems of district development planning in India, I would offer a few introductory remarks on some theoretical aspects of the general problem and on experience with the effort in some other countries. It is interesting to note that most of the theoretical work has been done in relation to what may be termed as regional planning.

The newly developed regional science deals with broad aspects of interrelations between the various forms of organized social activity within the context of physical space. Its development is associated chiefly with the theory of location of economic activity, originating in classical economics and greatly elaborated in recent decades. Regional science has progressively attempted to present a spatial framework for social science disciplines, especially economics, through the development of a general theory of location and of space economy. It is, thus, concerned with human social activities distributed over a given territory. It starts with the assumption that such activities are distributed over any region

in certain rhythms and patterns that are neither arbitrary, nor the workings of chance. They result, rather, from the interdependencies that give form to economic space. Spatial patterns will change with shifts in the structure of demand, and of production, in the level of technology and in the social and political organization of the nation. (Friedmann and Alonso 1964: 2)

With the development of the concept of stages of economic growth, regional science has begun to concern itself with the question as to whether there are spatial patterns corresponding to each stage of economic development, and whether there is an optimum strategy for spatial transformation from one stage to the next. In the context of an economy, which is neither directed nor regulated externally and appears to develop in a naturalistic manner, regional science directs attention to the analysis of various forces that appear to determine existing spatial distribution of activity; and in case of change, to the search for originating causes, the reactions and interactions, so as to help in assessing the manner in which any change is brought about and proceeds. All this is attempted in the same way as the analysis of a free market economy. Similar analysis, utilizing historical data, may help in putting forward a theory of economic development in relation to regions. Planning takes the process a step further. In this case it is unnecessary to assume a naturalistic frame and conscious, purposive human effort may be studied in relation to its possible impact on an environment. Regional planning, as such, may take the planning objectives and strategy at the national level for granted, and specially address itself to the specific spatial features emerging in the formulation and operation of a national plan in a particular region. Given any theory of economic development and of pattern of transformation of economy from one stage to another, certain expectations of the formation of agglomerations or of regional imbalances, may be formulated, as a result of such regional analysis. These expectations may be looked upon either as inevitable or logical stages, in the process of development which have to be accepted, or alternatively, as tendencies which could be curbed and regulated in case certain objectives of national plans are desired to be fulfilled. Regional planning, in this context, ceases to look upon the interplay of socio-economic forces within the space economy as working in a naturalistic manner and begins to consider them as capable of being directed and regulated with reference to assumed objectives. Regional analysis then helps the planners to understand operations of forces generated in a given situation or through particular policies, and enables them to visualize the possibilities and limitations of external action and of the framing of objectives of policies.

While a considerable amount of abstract discussion of regional planning and planned development, on lines described above, exists today, detailed attention has so far been paid only to a few specific problems. This has been, largely, due to the fact that complex and elaborate analysis, such as is required in this context, has been attempted only in the highly developed countries. The two major sets of problems of space economy, which these countries confront today, are those connected with the growth of large metropolitan centres and with the existence of patches of depressed economy within a fast growing and affluent society. Most of the detailed work has been done in relation to the planning of, what are called, metropolitan regions. The importance of this is so overwhelming that it is possible for writers to say that while infra-urban space is of primary importance in city planning, regional planning 'focusses attention on supra-urban space' (Friedmann and Alonso 1964: 63). This definition of regional planning as the ordering of human activity in supra-urban space has to be understood against the background of economies in which urban population vastly predominates and most activity is oriented towards city centres.

While concern with regional planning, in the context of metropolitan growth, has been in evidence for many decades, attention to the planning for development of backward regions or depressed areas has been relatively recent. The depression of the thirties first brought into prominence the problem of areas suffering in an especially acute manner from the effects of economic decay or stagnation. Measures to relieve such conditions were widely discussed and studies were undertaken at universities, for example in England, especially in relation to them. However, it is with the post-war vogue of planning that this problem has come to have special importance. In this context, the region is defined as territory which has relatively homogeneous economic characteristics and which appears, to a significant extent, to have been uninfluenced by forces which have brought about growth and diversification of the economy in other parts of the country. Regional analysis is concerned here with a study of the factors making for stagnancy and of the possibilities and means of activization. We, thus, note that the advancement of regional science and, in particular, the use of techniques of regional analysis, so as to render significant assistance in the work of practical planning, are in evidence, chiefly, in the two areas indicated above and that the techniques are not immediately available in relation to the problems that we face in district economic planning.

It may be noted that though district economic planning is concerned with aspects of spatial organization, the district is not a 'region' as the term is usually understood. It is important to emphasize this initial point. The district is essentially a local administrative division and the area divisions of governmental authority or administration do not necessarily, or even usually, coincide with regions defined as contiguous territory sharing common economic characteristics. Economic homogeneity, to the extent that it is present in a district, would be a matter, in part, of accident, and in part, of the fact that the district forms a part of a larger region which may be economically homogeneous. The objectives and reasons for the formation of districts are related to administrative convenience, historical traditions, and other such factors. Obviously physical features and barriers also play some part in determining district boundaries. In India districts, for the most part, are composed of component areas of a sufficient diversity of conditions and interests; and the methods of regional analysis and planning could be appropriately applied only to the relatively homogeneous economic sub-areas in them. It may often happen that a belt of territory in a number of contiguous districts constitutes a homogeneous region while none of the districts are themselves homogeneous. In such a case the development plans of all the districts will have to adopt the appropriate approach for regional development in relation to the particular part of a homogeneous region contained within them. Further, in some districts, the predominance of large urban or metropolitan centres may affect plans of development. In this case, the lessons of metropolitan regional planning will have to be applied. Thus, district development planning presents problems which are comparable with those of planning for the development of a large state with a heterogeneous composition. The problems of planning at the state level are all met in a somewhat simpler form within district development planning; somewhat simpler, because the degree of heterogeneity and complexity in a district would be necessarily less than that in a state.

The above characteristic of district development planning follows from the identification of planning areas with administrative and local self-government areas. Where regional planning is undertaken for a specific homogeneous region, with special characteristics and to attain a particular objective, it is possible to define a region independently and to set up a planning or development authority for it. This could happen with a river valley region, or a metropolitan region or territory defined as backward or depressed and in relation to which special measures are undertaken. In India, we are engaged in planning for the development of the entire country and though the situation and requirements in different areas differ radically from each other, the effort undertaken in each area is a part of the total national planning effort. Moreover, the development planning undertaken in each area has to be equally comprehensive. The total national plan of development, of all activities and classes and all regions, is a multi-objective plan with universal coverage. It follows that the development plan of any area or district, however small, has to be equally comprehensive in the definition of its objectives and the scope of its action. The development attempted must affect all areas within the district and must touch all activities and all classes. This characteristic sharply distinguishes our district development planning from the regional planning undertaken, for regions, formulated, in relation to limited objectives, in an *ad hoc* manner. Inevitably, the areas of local planning in India have to be so constituted that, taken together, they cover the entire area of the country. As local planning has to be undertaken for all areas, it is obvious that the effort should be associated with the administrative and the self-government areas into which the country is already divided. This special aspect of district development planning also makes it desirable and necessary that the planning authority be identified with the local administration or the local self-governing authority. In specific, *ad hoc* regional planning, where the region is specially constituted for a specific purpose, the planning or the development authority may also be specially created or constituted for the limited objective. It is likely in such a case that neither the area nor the functions to be carried out coincide with the area or the functions of any existing authority or administration.

III

Indian planning is highly centralized. Planning, in the sense of attempting formulation of an integrated plan of development, is undertaken only by the Planning Commission at the Centre. Planning thought and information, to the extent these are in evidence, exist only with the Planning Commission, and this body alone is concerned with planning techniques. The central plan is influenced, to some extent, by a perspective plan and there is some discussion at the Planning Commission of desirable strategy, especially in relation to decisions regarding allocations and priorities. However, even the central plan is not built up in an integrated fashion. It results, essentially, from putting together recommendations of a series of working groups or committees concerned with specific subjects or departments. There is little effort at integrating, coordinating, or dovetailing the separate schemes or programmes either at the time of their preparation or later. They are all, more or less, mechanically combined to form the plan and when, as a result of decisions regarding allocation, adjustments have to be made upwards or downwards they are made independently for each separate set of programmes.

The situation at lower levels is much worse. At the state level planning is highly officialized. Non-official leaders or experts are consulted to some extent by the Planning Commission which has set up a large number of panels, committees, etc. No mechanism, through which this may be done, exists in the states, at least in most of them. The Maharashtra Government set up, in 1960, a Consultative Plan Committee. This met twice in the first year and, among other work, set up two sub-committees which produced important reports. No meeting of the Consultative Committee was called after 1961. Planning at the state level is not only highly officialized but is, essentially, a secretariat affair.

In all the major states, there is practically no machinery for planning as such at the state level. The state plans are not made as the result of any wide consultation or efforts at co-ordination. There is no specific definition of the objectives of state planning and no thinking out of a strategy appropriate to it. This follows from the fact that the state plans are prepared, basically, in the same manner as the annual state budget. The departmental proposals in relation to each section and sub-section are formulated in the departments, are put together by the heads of departments, and forwarded to the secretariat. The plan is then prepared, in the sense of being pieced together, in the secretariat. Except for the debate in the legislature, there are no public discussions or consultations of general or specific plan objectives or proposals and no information is available outside as to what is contemplated or proposed. In the secretariat itself, there is neither any attempt to obtain special knowledge or information, nor any personnel specialized in planning techniques.

Moreover, state plans, which are prepared entirely at the departmental and secretariat level, represent, in essence, the reactions of the state government and its officers to the known wishes and proposals of the Planning Commission. The standard Planning Commission schemes or similar departmental schemes, prepared in the states which have obtained the approval of the Planning Commission, are the basic materials from out of which the state and district plans are constituted.

The Second Five-Year Plan contains an entire chapter—Chapter Seven—on District Development Administration. This chapter is concerned, chiefly, with what might be attempted in the future in relation to District Development Administration. Considerable emphasis is placed on the lines on which District Development Councils should be built in the future and on the preparation of village plans. A great deal is written about the establishment of village *Panchayats* and their functions, such as, of land management and the framing of programmes of production. The district development machinery contemplated is that of an *ad hoc* District Development Council and of the development committees constituted for blocks and *talukas*. At this stage, what are now called the Panchayati Raj institutions, had not been universally established at the village level; and though there were, in most states, local self-governing bodies, such as *taluka* or district boards, there was no thought of entrusting these bodies with any aspect of the development planning work. The share of the administrative officers of the district was highlighted in this Plan document, and the responsibility of the collectors, the sub-divisional officers, and the block development officers as leaders was emphasized. In fact, the district administration was described as 'an agency of change towards a new social order' (Planning Commission 1956: 164).

In the Third Five-Year Plan, there is no separate chapter on District Development Administration. The matter is dealt with, in part, in the chapter on Community Development. This deals with the possible effects of the recent establishment of the Panchayati Raj institutions and raises the wider question of the re-organization of the district administration consequent upon the introduction of Panchayati Raj. The emphasis on village production plans is still continued and there appears little appreciation of the existence of grave deficiencies in the machinery for the formulation or implementation of plans at the state and the local level. In fact, as the following quotation will show, the planners were obviously well satisfied with things as they were:

> Large burdens are being placed on planning organizations in the states. States are called upon to interpret national objectives, translate them in terms of the needs, resources

and possibilities open to them, carry the plan to the remotest points and find ways of mobilizing local resources and enthusiasm. Within the limits of its tasks, as conceived thus far, the machinery for planning in the states has served well. (Planning Commission 1961: 289)

The activities of the District Development Councils, set up from the period of the Second Five-Year Plan, were entirely of an advisory nature. These councils were composed mostly of local political leaders who had little special knowledge or expertise in any direction. There was, also, no agency or arrangement for the procurement of local data or for the identification and study of local problems. The councils put together a series of more or less popular demands regarding the construction of irrigation works, roads or the setting up of educational institutions, hospitals, etc. These had no relation to a strategy of long-term planning or to any definition of priorities. The councils put together a list of recommendations which was, usually, fairly comprehensive and large. The preparation of plans by the heads of state departments or by secretariat officials was not likely to be influenced in any significant manner by the recommendations of these councils as no significant ideas, specific constraints, or compulsive recommendations emerged from them.

The situation continues to be similar, at least in Maharashtra, even after the establishment of *Zilla Parishads*. The preparation of the Fourth Five-Year Plan by *Zilla Parishads* was undertaken in most districts on lines which did not differ materially from the operations of the earlier District Development Councils. There was no greater volume of information specially collected or made available to the *Zilla Parishad*, or its sub-committees engaged in planning. Secondly, though the work of planning by the *Zilla Parishads* was more elaborate, in the sense that more attention was paid to the preparation of plans at the block level and to the co-ordination of plan proposals by subjects, its essential character remained unchanged. This was because the district plan was not looked upon as a realistic document which was part of a long-term development plan framed by the *Zilla Parishad* and to be implemented by it. It was, as before, a set of proposals sent up to the State government, or more correctly, to the secretaries, from which the secretariat would put together the plan which the *Zilla Parishad* would, in due course, have to implement. This was emphasized by the fact that no realistic financial limit as to the size of the plan to be prepared by the *Zilla Parishads* was indicated to them. In fact, they were encouraged to prepare plans, of a size very much larger than the most optimistic estimate that could be made, of allocation of resources to the district. Moreover, working groups in the secretariat were preparing departmental plans while the *Zilla Parishads* were engaged in their work and with the continuous pressure for early completion from the Planning Commission it was the secretariat work that really counted.

The working groups, whether in a state secretariat or in the Planning Commission, it should further be noted, operated *ad hoc*, without any clear guide lines and without the help of specially collected data which were critically analysed. As a natural consequence, experience counted for little, no attention was paid even to obvious past failures, and schemes and programmes were carried over from plan to plan with little change or modification. In such a situation, it was futile to expect any attention being paid to variations in a local situation or provision being made for a study of them.

Planning in India, at the lower levels, continues to be, in the main, a matter of putting together standard schemes for each department or each activity, schemes known to be acceptable to the Planning Commission, in such a manner as to attract the largest amount of assistance that the state or the department can obtain from the Centre. It is only fair to add that since 1962, the Planning Commission has begun to pay more attention to problems of district development planning, and a good deal of what I say in this lecture is based upon experience gathered in the course of an effort in this direction, which was sponsored by the Government of Maharashtra, and which received valuable assistance from the Planning Commission.

The almost entire absence of proper planning at the state and district level has imposed a grave handicap on development of Indian rural economy and is reflected in the relatively slow and patchy progress in agriculture, rural industry, and related fields. Problems of planning in agriculture have been discussed by a number of official committees and there has been general emphasis on the need for relating targets and programmes to local circumstances (see Gadgil 1972). This, however, cannot be done *ad hoc* or piecemeal and can only follow appropriate organization of state and district development planning. The situation today is, thus, that where improvement is attainable through programmes involving simple uniform action over a wide area success is achieved; where, however, a close study of particular complex problems is necessary for progress, the problems are either unidentified or are dealt with inadequately.[1]

The reasons for this are two-fold. In the first instance, the administrative machinery is geared to uniform operations over a wide area and not to specialized local work. Secondly, no arrangements are available through which complex, particular problems could be studied closely on the spot. The targets approach of our type of centralized planning accentuates these basic tendencies.

The propositions, made earlier, may be supported by reference to an analysis of the relative successes and failures of the latest intensive district programmes in agriculture. Where, as in the districts of the Punjab, the conditions of agricultural operations were fairly uniform and the overheads and the organizational structure were already available, the progress was striking; where similar conditions did not obtain, the progress has been unimpressive. In a like manner, major schemes of irrigation and power are completed fairly successfully but schemes of minor irrigation, especially those where nature is unfavourable locally, make little progress. Apart from the structure of administrative arrangements and the discouragement of local initiative, the attitude of the government towards programmes of agricultural improvement is also responsible for the phenomenon. Campaigns are still the most important features of these programmes. Inevitably programmes, in a countrywide or state-wide campaign, can only consist of generalized prescriptions which ignore local variations. There is no problem-orientation and no inclination towards evolving a long-term programme based on close study of particular problems. Constant campaigning inhibits the attitudes and dissipates the energy needed for study and long-term action. It also leads to ignoring the total complex of conditions related to the improvement of agriculture. A single item, e.g., fertilizer use, is pushed with no consideration of related technical or financial factors. In an old country, with a relatively intelligent peasantry, it may be assumed that the scope for obvious improvements capable of being brought about easily in existing circumstances is small. Therefore, campaigns or crash programmes, inevitably, give diminishing returns and the next stage requires a changed outlook and altered administrative arrangements.

The approach, through compilation of a plan, by reference to separate standardized departmental schemes, has many other disadvantages also. For example, it leads to an unnecessary proliferation of staff and to its non-integration on the field. This is because the staff proposals are attached to each scheme and are considered separately as for the scheme and its duration. It also results in there being no co-ordination or synchronization of action among various departments or different agencies in the same department. This is responsible for the familiar phenomenon of a number of targets, especially relating to expenditure, being achieved and yet there being an overall failure of the total programme.

There is little difference of opinion in the country relating to the desirability of changing the present system of centralized, departmental planning. However, relatively little thought has so far been given to the positive content and the administrative and organizational implications of local planning or planning from the bottom. The lowest stratum of governmental authorities in India is, in most states, the district. Planning from the bottom has, therefore, to be associated chiefly with the district development planning effort. It is this which vests the subject with great importance and makes it worthwhile to consider, in some detail, the requirements of district development planning and the directions, the quality, and stages of effort implied by it.

IV

Beginning may be made by drawing attention to two primary requirements. The first is the basing of the district plan on knowledge regarding local conditions, and the second is the association of local people with the formulation and implementation of the plan. In a sense, both these aspects are implied in development planning at whatever stage it is undertaken. However, whereas in India, there is some appreciation of the need for obtaining technical and economic knowledge and data, and consulting people before formulating plans at the national level, there is, in practical terms, a complete absence of this at the local level. The gap, in the matter of knowledge and information, is the most glaring at the district level. There are certain series of administrative statistics available, and, depending on the system of land tenure and the method of maintenance of village records, some data are available regarding the distribution of holdings and cropping patterns. Also, some technical information may be available where, previously, surveys, as those relating to minerals, have been conducted. For the rest, technical information is inadequate and relevant economic information is almost totally absent. For example, Centres of Agricultural Research are few in a state and many districts have no such centres with the result that its special problems of agricultural production technique cannot be dealt with, except on the basis of information relating to some distant area which may or may not be relevant, locally.

Planning, in its technical and economic aspect, is closely related to relevant knowledge and information. Unless there is a minimum base of such knowledge and information, a plan of development for an area like the district cannot be built up. Moreover, the minimal base will suffice only for the preliminary effort at planning; as planning extends its coverage and intensifies in depth, the amount and quality of information will have to be progressively increased. An appreciation of the great importance, for local planning, of agencies investigating into local conditions, and collecting information on all aspects of socio-economic life and technical production and other activity, is urgently required for making a proper beginning with district development planning; and provision for continuing extension of investigational and research activity in all the fields at the local level is a necessary concomitant of the continuance and growth of district development planning efforts. As long as detailed local knowledge is not available, to test and question the applicability of standard schemes and to provide the base on which to build alternative proposals, there is no chance of replacing the present approach to planning.

The second aspect, that of local co-operation and participation in formulation and implementation, is equally important. This is so for two reasons. In the first instance, any agencies which are employed for the conduct of research and investigation into varying aspects of the local situation will have to work in close co-operation with different strata in the local population. The success of investigational research effort is closely bound up with an understanding, by the relevant elements in the local population, of the nature of investigation and research undertaken and the objectives to which it was related. Moreover, apart from the limited extent to which technical considerations dictated a certain pattern of the plan and the order of priorities in them, the pattern and the priorities will have to be determined in relation to local choices and opinions. It is true that in a number of directions the margin of such choice would not be wide. The objectives determined, the allocation of funds, the choice of agencies, etc., made at superior levels would impose certain constraints on district planning. Other constraints would be where technical or economic considerations definitely pointed in certain directions. Even though the margin of choice for local decisions might thus, in particular contexts, be small, it is important that within this margin, the choice should be made locally and moreover, that a full understanding of the why and wherefore of the constraints, as described above, and their relevance to local choice are understood by the people concerned.

Another important reason for arousing the interest of local population is that it is only through this that motivation for appropriate formulation and early implementation is created. It is the experience of, for example, regional planning in France, that where unofficial bodies had already worked out plans of regional development of their own, progress had been rapid. The case for local interest and participation at the stage of implementation is obviously overwhelming. Whereas the formulation of a plan may be related to technical knowledge and broader objectives, its implementation on the ground, once formulated, would be impossible without full local understanding and co-operation. This necessary condition further reinforces the need for local participation at the formulation stage. There is no doubt that more intelligence and co-operation in the stage of implementation would be forthcoming if, in the process of formulation itself, the local elements were fully associated with the effort, so that there was widespread appreciation of what was being planned and what the planning was expected to achieve.

Before going on to discuss the implications of the two basic requirements indicated above, consideration has to be given to another preliminary problem. This is that of the lowest area unit of planning. It has been pointed out above that, ordinarily, a district is unlikely to be economically homogeneous and that district development planning must face problems of planning for a mixed or heterogeneous area. It follows that the basic preliminary work, of at least some aspects of the district plan, must be carried out in terms of smaller, homogeneous area units. While this unit should be small and compact, it should also be large enough to serve as a unit of integrated planning. This means that it must embrace within it, the variety of economic activity typical of the particular rural economy and that it must be capable of being treated as an integrated economic unit for purposes of planning. The most common factor of integration at this level of rural economy would be sale and supply activity; and in most parts of India, where there is some commercialization of agriculture, such a unit may be identified as the primary market area. There are many obvious difficulties of definition and demarcation involved in the concept of a market area. It is here put forward, however, not as a theoretical concept but as a practical operative planning device.

While in terms of the existing situation the area unit may be identified as the market area, in terms of development planning it may be looked upon as the lowest area-unit for the integrated provision of socio-economic overheads and services. It is obvious that this approach to the definition of the lowest area-unit does not lead to an immediate ready cut and dried identification. In conceptual terms, the market area has a centre or nucleus, and by reason of specially convenient means of communication or other reasons, it serves a fairly well-defined surrounding area as the primary marketing, sale, and supply centre. In planning for the future, it would be convenient to start with such existing centres and provide, for the surrounding areas, the overheads which must precede development as radiating from the centres. One of the most difficult problems in planning for widespread development is that of providing minimum socio-economic overheads everywhere. The efficient and economic planning of this provision is an important task in the initial stages. For this purpose, it becomes necessary to identify convenient integrated area-units.[2]

This approach clearly rejects the village as the lowest area-unit of planning because it looks upon planning as involving co-ordinated formulation and execution of a number of socio-economic measures and activities for unfolding a given pattern of development. This concept of integrated planning assumes, at each level and in each sector, a strategy and a programme of economic activity in the state and public sectors, combined with a regime of fiscal, monetary, physical, etc., measures of encouragement and inducement, of regulation and prohibition. The plan is integrated in the sense that the effect of the implementation of the plan is expected, according to the implied strategy, to lead to the initiation and cumulation of different types of public and private economic activity, which will bring about development along the prescribed route. The National Plan is supposed to integrate fully the plans of all tiers and authorities in all sectors. At each lower level, i.e., the state and the district, the plan is formulated within the total frame, with given objectives and external data or constraints, derived from the higher level plans. The district is considered here as the lowest area-unit of governmental planning. However, as it is ordinarily too large and heterogeneous, it would be difficult to formulate an integrated plan, directly, for the entire area of the district. Therefore, while some elements of activity and some integrating factors would operate only at the district level, for the bulk of activities in relation to primary production, dispersed industry, rural trading and transport or urban activity oriented towards serving the rural economy, etc., the district has to be divided into convenient areas for formulation of an integrated plan for the lowest level area-unit. And the concept of the mandi area is offered here as the most appropriate for this purpose.

V

It is now necessary to give attention to problems of formulation of a district plan and to its important component elements, the integrating factors, and the constraints and limits within which it has to be put together. Given the assumption that the district plan is not put together as a summation of lists of departmental schemes, and that there is a minimal base of information and knowledge regarding local conditions, we have to begin with an analysis of the main features of an integrated district plan and the procedures or stages by which it could be put together. Subsequently, as long as administration is organized in terms of activities of certain departments, any proposal or plan will have to be translated into terms of departmental schemes for implementation. However, it is one thing to prepare an integrated plan in the first instance, and then transform it into a series of properly co-ordinated departmental schemes, and quite another to start with the preparation of schemes for individual activity and sub-activity of each department and then to put them together as a plan. For the purpose of the formulation of an integrated plan of a district, the stages or aspects that appear appropriate on the basis of some experience are as follows.

The first stage, and an essential one, appears to be that of the preparation of the physico-geographic plan of socio-economic overheads. The preparation of the physico-geographic frame is especially important at the district level. The main business of a district plan is to influence and direct the activities of thousands of small producers. Action, in this regard, has two aspects. Firstly, the provision of those basic services and amenities without which growth and diversification of economic activity will not come about. Secondly, the provision of such incentives, as well as disincentives, as will lead to the development of economic activity in the desired directions. The first requires, very largely, public action in relation to planned provision of utilities and social services. This, in the context of our country, has to be planned in terms of a physico-geographic frame. It includes the provision of communications, which inevitably takes precedence in the initial stages. Most backward regions are characterized by a lack of means of communication. In the ultimate analysis, no area or territory can hope to profit from the economic development of other parts of the country which is not closely integrated with the economic life of the rest. The establishment of a system of communications reaching out to all areas and all locations is thus the first requirement for a plan of development. Other connected, essential requirements are those of water and power and the development of economic organizations such as those of marketing and credit, storage and processing, on the basis of which, economic activity in each region grows to full capacity and becomes diversified. Social services, such as those relating to education and health, are also a vital part of the provision of the socio-economic overheads.

In view of the need to economize and obtain the best results from a given investment, it is necessary to plan carefully, the provision of all these socio-economic overheads. Two requirements of this provision are obvious. In the first instance, the spread must be such as to benefit all areas within the district, and secondly, that the provision of the costlier utilities and services must be arranged from a hierarchy of convenient centres. A third condition may be added to the two. This is that it is highly desirable to follow, in the determination of these centres and the areas served by them, to a large extent, existing patterns of marketing and other economic areas. A physico-geographic plan is thus a plan of communications and of the development of a series of centres at, and from which, certain services and amenities are provided. All of this is obviously, closely connected with the concept of the 'mandi-area' unit discussed above.

Attention may also be drawn at this stage to the possibility of looking at the location of these centres of services and utilities from two different points of view. In the first instance, the centre would essentially be the main centre of marketing and exchange in terms of a small or a large area. Exchange activities, and the provision of the services which have to be most widely spread, would be the normal function of such centres. In terms of planning development it would be necessary to add to these functions, those of furnishing technical assistance or the more modern institutionalized economic services such as of credit, storage, and processing, and of social services such as those relating to education and health. However, from the point of view of a development plan, especially in relation to the growth of non-farm activity, a centre may be thought of as a centre of growth of industrial or other activity which helps to transform the economy of a surrounding region. It is obvious that the concept and the location of a centre of this type would be different from that of the traditional centre. A district plan must provide for the development of well distributed centres of the traditional type for the entire district. The industrial development plan of the district may select some of these centres for intensive development of some types of non-farm activity or find it necessary, for whatever reason, to develop other centres for particular purposes. However, as the two types of centres will have different functions, the utilities and services located in them, and the demarcation of their areas, will follow different principles. Whereas the former will adopt a generalized common approach, the latter will be related to certain specific aims.

The second aspect of an integrated district plan appears to be that concerned with the conservation and development of natural resources. Initially, in a country in which rural economy is so predominant and agriculture employs such a large proportion of the working force, the district plan has to be based on natural resources and concerned with their conservation, exploitation, and development. The conservation and broadening of the base of natural resources is, thus, an essential preliminary step in development planning. Special attention needs to be given to it as large parts of these resources have greatly suffered from neglect in recent decades. Conservation and development of resources of soil, water, and vegetation are extremely important for our agricultural economy. As in the case of agriculture, problems relating to conservation of natural resources arise all over the country but are at the same time highly local; local in the sense firstly, that there is a great variation in the characteristics of resources and the problems of conservation and development presented by them from area to area and secondly, that full conservation and development of all resources, necessarily requires the most detailed local action. A preliminary division of the district into homogeneous economic areas will have to be made for this plan of conservation and development of natural resources and the mandi-area unit may be found convenient for this purpose also.

It is as against the background of the physico-geographic frame of the distribution and placement of socio-economic overheads and services and of the plan for the conservation and development of natural resources that the next aspect of the plan of development comes up for consideration. This aspect deals with production activity. The plan of development of production, agricultural and non-agricultural, is at the centre of the planning process. This aspect of the plan differs in one material aspect from the earlier two. Action in relation to the provision of socio-economic overheads is, largely, action taken by governmental authority or by co-operating groups of persons. The conservation and development of natural resources is also to a large extent either governmental or joint activity of a series of establishments or persons. It is only in an exceptional case like that of construction of wells that an individual, on his own, might take action in regard to the development of natural resources. In relation to the production plan, however, the operations are essentially those of individual agriculturists, artisans, etc. Planning action in this connection is, to a large extent, a matter of providing assistance and incentives to individual producers. Because of this it becomes important in this context to think out carefully, what may be called the objectives and strategy of development.

What is meant by defining objectives is to spell out the particular immediate goals in each field in relation to the previous development and future requirements of the district. For example, at a given level of progress of co-operative activity it may be much more important to look to the functioning of the co-operatives in relation to particular categories, such as tenants or artisans, rather than to pursue the target of universal membership. The concept of strategy may be illustrated by reference to rural industrialization. For example, one may decide to concentrate initial effort on the development of processing in the co-operative sector and on the rehabilitation of traditional artisan industry, because these may not only be immediately important but also because they afford convenient bases for future progress. Or in another context, a programme of providing improved latrines in schools may be adopted for long-term improvement of rural health habits. Choosing a particular set, from among alternative groups of incentives and disincentives, may also be determined by estimates of response and the chain reactions that might be set up; this in a sense is strategy.

Such problems of analysis and estimation will be encountered in each programme in this field. The agricultural production programmes today, give very uneven results, because they do not analyse, and take into account, the local situation. A threefold classification in relation to programmes of agricultural improvement appears basic: (i) improvements which are locally accepted but not yet widespread, (ii) improvements proved to be useful locally but not yet accepted, and (iii) improvements which have to be tried out and established in the local environment. In relation only to (i) is a programme of propaganda and appropriate incentives indicated; in relation to (ii), emphasis must be placed initially on demonstration; and regarding (iii), which is a large class, because of the limited extent of local adaptation effort so far, it is systematic work in local adaptation and adjustment that must precede everything else. Programmes for the development of agricultural and non-agricultural productive activity have to be framed not only to suit local circumstances and conditions but also to suit the requirements of the different classes of producers. The universally present complaint regarding benefits of programmes accruing to the more substantial cultivators flows from lack of differentiation in this regard. Existing programmes have to be specially adapted to, or special programmes framed for the small holders and part-time farmers if these are to profit from the planning effort.

While the emphasis on agricultural production is important, activization of the rural economy requires much greater expansion of the subsidiary primary production and of industrial activity. Intensification of agricultural production activity will meet the employment and development needs of only the middling and substantial cultivators, forming everywhere less than half of the rural families. For the small, effectively part-time cultivators, the landless labourers, rural artisans and others, supplementary and new activities must be found. In part, these would arise from planned programmes of the provision of socio-economic overheads and of the conservation and development of natural resources. In part, they must be found in expansion of the field of non-agricultural primary production, e.g., animal husbandry, fishery, etc. The importance of this has been recently recognized, but no appropriate developments are yet being planned. In this matter, as in plans of industrialization, the technical view dominates the field without reference to the needs of the economic situation. There appears very little awareness that the situation demands the development, for example, of dairy and poultry activities in units and at levels which will be within the competence of, at least, the average, small farmer, if not the landless labourer; and, if necessary, the individual small units must be supported by the requisite network of services and supplies. Finally, the rural economy will begin to move only if industrialization of the countryside is no longer regarded as only a supplementary or side issue but as the main result aimed at by the programme of industrial development.

This naturally leads to a consideration of the immediate problems of non-producers. The provision of socio-economic overheads, the conservation and development of natural resources, and steps to improve and encourage productive activity all benefit those who have a minimum viable base of productive resources. All those who command very inadequate or no productive resources cannot hope to benefit directly from any of these programmes of development planning; and as there is little likelihood of the vast majority belonging to this class obtaining productive resources through measures, say, of redistribution of land, the programme required by them, and for them, is essentially that of the provision of adequate employment. At the same time, the programme of providing employment for non-producers cannot be an additional programme not included in the three aspects of development planning indicated above. The concept of the additional rural works of the Planning Commission is illogical and merely shows up the failure to plan adequately. The contents of a rural works programme cannot be of a type different from those included in the programme of providing socio-economic overheads or of conservation and development of resources or the maintenance of these or of existing works. It is obvious that a rural works programme, which is conceived of as additive, will not be properly integrated with planned programmes and will, to that extent, be wasteful of resources.

The need to provide for adequate local employment through all aspects of development programming thus imposes an additional requirement on the process of plan formulation. This will operate mainly in two directions. Firstly, in relation to the choice and volume of works included in the plan and secondly, as regards their spatial and temporal distribution. The entire programme of additional economic activity directly undertaken by public authorities, together with any expected increase in employment offered by private operators, must generate the total employment required. The size and the degree of labour intensity of planned public activity must be related to this objective; also, as the aggregate employment has to be properly distributed over space and time the distribution, over the area of the district, of planned activity, and its initiation and closure in time, have to be regulated in relation to specific local requirements. Moreover, the generation of additional employment has to be looked at as not being related to a particular year, but as a continuing long-term requirement. The employment requirement should, thus, not only affect the size and shape of the annual plan, but also, deeply influence the perspective and strategy of all planning. The employment aspect of planning thus colours and orients the whole process. It has, also, an integrating effect, because it gives a direction and a measure to large numbers of planning decisions.

In the dovetailing of the plans, there arises also the problem of priorities. Broadly, these have to be determined by scales of valuation and by accepted ideas regarding the route which planned development is likely to take. Conservation might be objectively given high priority, because, logically, the conservation of resources has to precede development. Also, if high value is placed on simultaneous development of all areas, a communication and services programme must be given high priority. The problem becomes more complicated in connection with, what are called, social welfare activities. One may consider a minimum provision of educational and health service for each citizen as an input required for a minimum performance by labour units. From such a point of view, a considerable amount of educational and health expenditure would be treated not as welfare expenditure but as investment expenditure. It is obvious that in this field, a great deal depends on subjective valuations and judgement. However, a limit has to be placed on independent judgement in each local area in such matters. There has to be an accepted framework of overall national objectives and a certain broad valuation must inform all district plans.

The other important integrating factor and constraint is that of financial resources available for the district plan. This is an overall constraint which limits the extent of effort that can be put forward within a period. In a sense, it is this constraint that makes planning meaningful. It provides the frame within which, given local, natural, and human resources and the local interpretation of national objectives, the optimum effort that can be made for the best utilization of the available financial resources has to be defined and determined. The strategy of the plan, as a whole or for the public sector and the determination of priorities and allocations, is made fully with reference to this constraint. In its absence, the district development planning is no more than a compilation of desired schemes and projects which are not necessarily connected together and in which no indication of logical relation or chronological order need be given. With the constraint imposed by the overall financial limit, the interpretation of a district plan means, essentially, the spelling out of the logical relations between various sectoral and departmental plans and the chronological order in which, within all of them together, particular schemes will be initiated and completed.

Reference has to be made, in addition, to a number of calculations of availabilities and balances. A road programme of given size would require certain equipment and trained personnel; the seed multiplication programmes have to be based on a given complement of farms and farmers. In education and health programmes, buildings, equipment, teachers, nurses have to be made available in a given measure for any level of desired performance. In the same way, the total buildings and construction programmes in all sectors together, would be subject to the overall limitation of availability of building materials, e.g., the total output of bricks or the possible allotment of cement. The entire plan, in particular, the socio-economic overheads and the conservation plans, requires labour as an essential input on a large scale. Therefore, the availability of labour would place a limitation on the size of these plans that could be accomplished within any given time. Such calculations in physical terms could serve two purposes; they would indicate limits to possible performance but they could also be taken to present a challenge, so that through, chiefly, better organization, the limits could be stretched.

Better organization is the additional input that could be most readily made available in early stages of planned development. Also, most new programmes of development require, for their success, that attention is paid to the problems of setting up and operating appropriate organizations. In district development planning, two types of organizations, viz., the Panchayati Raj institutions and the co-operatives, would be chiefly utilized. This general approach still leaves unsolved a number of problems. For example, it is general experience that mere provision of a works programme does not, without a special organizational effort, benefit the categories for which it is intended. The organization suggested for this purpose usually takes the form of a labour contract co-operative society. However, the organizational pattern and the functioning of this type in a variety of contexts have yet to be experimentally determined. This is also the situation regarding the major problem of the organization of small holders for agricultural production, for which co-operative farming appears to be the logical solution.

A large variety of other organizational problems are encountered in local planning. Some of these arise out of some aspects of land reforms as for example, the management of forests formerly owned by landlords; some because of a mixture of public and private interest, such as that of the management of a public utility such as a tank which benefits only limited numbers within the community. There are some fields in which new experimental effort requires, mainly, organizational improvisation. This happens with problems relating to, what are called, the weaker sections or with problems of conservation or development of non-arable land in which a number of departments such as forest, revenue, animal husbandry may be interested and where without arousing local interest and co-operation no effective programme could be carried out. Inevitably, problems of organization loom especially large where a departure from the traditional pattern becomes necessary or where the disadvantaged are sought to be benefited. It is thus clear that in the formulation of plans, and more particularly in the plan of implementation, attention has to be paid to indicating carefully the organizations entrusted with operation and co-ordination and, in many fields also to designing and experimenting with new types of organizations for the purpose.

Two aspects of the integration of plans need to be specially stressed. These are, co-ordination and synchronization. Any given objective, such as that of increasing agricultural production, would be related to a large number of schemes and projects and activities of different departments. It would be related to the conservation of land, development of water resources, construction of connecting communications, availability of power, supply of credit both long-term and short-term, institutionalization of marketing, guaranteeing of prices, setting up of co-operative processing units; this is apart from the specific agricultural departmental activities, such as those of supply of seeds, fertilizers, pesticides, introduction of improved practices and implements, the provision of technical assistance and advice, the operation of demonstration and research farms, etc. This small, illustrative list would make clear what is meant by establishing logical relations within the activities of different departments and agencies which are intended in part, or in whole, to subserve one common objective. Given the size of the plan, and the framing of objectives, the extent and nature of each activity and its chronological order would have to be determined in close relation to all the other activities which it supports or by which it is supported. If this aspect of mutual relations is not properly taken into account in the formulation of the plan, there would be, obviously, disproportionate expenditure of energy and financial resources in particular directions, which would be wasteful in so far as for want of necessary support and effort it would not bear fruit. By an integration of district plan is meant, paying close attention to all these aspects of other relations and emphasizing the need to maintain a proper degree of proportionality. Co-ordination and synchronization become especially important for implementation to be effective. The mutually supporting action of different programmes and activities can bear fruit if the activities provided for are not only appropriate and in proportion, but also if in each context, they are in fact undertaken and completed at the appropriate times. Synchronization of implementation of various aspects of programmes is of supreme importance, especially in relation to such objectives as annual agricultural production plans.

It is obvious that to construct such a plan requires much more effort than a plan which merely puts together standard departmental schemes and that if adjustments are required to be made in such a plan, they necessitate much greater thought and labour than would be required in relation to a collection of departmental schemes which can be cut down or pared at will.

VI

The preparation of a district development plan has a number of aspects. As indicated above, the work has to be undertaken chiefly at two levels, the district and the mandi area. While the overall frames, the strategies, and the comprehensive works and schemes have to be planned at the district level, the details of the conservation, production, etc., plans have to be worked for the mandi area. Financial allocations, area-wise and sectoral, have to be finalized at the district level and distribution of schemes and programmes in the light of the employment criterion has also to be carried out here. Organizational problems will, most probably, be common to the entire district, though in some specialized aspects, such as forest and wastelands or animal husbandry, they may be found to have local peculiarities. The work of integration, co-ordination, and synchronization will have to be undertaken appropriately at both levels, though the overall integrative effort will be in relation to the district plan.

The task, at all levels, is twofold. Firstly, there is the work of marshalling all available information, qualitative and quantitative, and judging of requirements, feasibilities, logical priorities, and chronological orders from a technical point of view and, subsequently, given the final judgement regarding programmes and priorities, the work of formulation of an integrated plan taking into consideration all the limitations and constraints. Secondly, there is the work of taking account of differing levels of local competence and knowledge, local attitudes and preferences, and possible local reactions and responses. While the first will be mainly the work of official administrative agencies and official and non-official experts, the second can be achieved only through the association of local leadership with the total enterprise. However, while making this formal distinction, it has to be noted that the ease and the efficiency with which administrators and experts carry out the first, will itself be greatly influenced by the extent of interest they arouse in the local population in relation to it and the co-operation and assistance that they obtain.

Local participation in plan formulation and implementation is secured, essentially, through entrusting a considerable part of district development planning to local authority, i.e., the *Zilla Parishad* in Maharashtra, and in many other states. An initial difference, in the operations regarding the two aspects and agencies, may be noticed. While the work of the administrator and the expert can be made to cover the entire area of planning with more or less equal efficiency, the interest and commitment of local leaders and population may differ widely from field to field.

This is obviously a function of the education of local leadership and of its consciousness of the real meaning of national socio-economic objectives. From the point of view of possible variations in coverage and depth of local interests, it is necessary to recognize the importance of the national frame. Given national objectives and the total scope of the national plan of development, all aspects of it would necessarily be reflected in district planning, even though the local leadership may not be equally interested in all of them. Thus, for example, development of the more backward areas or special relief measures in relation to the weaker sections, may not evoke as much interest in local leadership as, say, the programme of agricultural production or irrigation development. The general compulsions of the national frame would then be useful in relation to the continuance of minimum effort in those directions which do not evoke full local interest. However, in the ultimate analysis, it is necessary to ensure that national objectives are, in fact, fully accepted by local leadership everywhere. This is because no real social transformation can come about through development unless there is full understanding and co-operation from local elements in this regard. Therefore, while in the initial stages, the national frame may serve a useful purpose, the full and meaningful pursuit of national objectives requires an educational effort in relation to local leadership which must be considered as extremely important and essential. In part, therefore, the process of district development planning must be understood as that of communicating, to local leadership and population, aspirations and ideologies with which the national plan is informed. On the other hand, the realism and the effectiveness of the national plan depend, essentially, on an understanding at the national level, of the possibilities and difficulties of local planning.

Most of the discussion has been conducted, so far, in terms of plan formulation. Problems of implementation have been dealt with implicitly. This has happened in two ways. In the first instance, the agencies of plan formulation and plan implementation are, in this context, identical. The various authorities and committees, and non-official associates of the

Zilla Parishad and its administrative set-up will be equally involved in both, the formulation and the implementation of the plan. It is only the outside experts, official and non-official, consulted in plan formulation, who may not be involved in implementation. Secondly, the procedures indicated for the formulation of the details of the plan, and for putting it together in an integrated fashion, have relevance also to implementation. If the operating organizational agencies in each context are carefully thought out and indicated, and proper attention paid to co-ordination and synchronization in formulating the plan and its various component schemes and programmes, analysis for implementation will become easy. Effective implementation requires a clear appreciation, by each operator, of responsibility in relation to every relevant item and the relationship of that item to others. Clear indication of these responsibilities and inter-relationships should be available from the detailed work of plan formulation. Extracting this information, and putting it in appropriate form for communication to the relevant agencies and personnel, is the first step in implementation. When this is done not only actual operations but also constant cross-checking and supervision of their progress would be greatly facilitated. Moreover, the preliminary analysis will help in the concurrent evaluation of the effectiveness of the plan, will bring to the surface any difficulties encountered, any assumption or expectations proved incorrect, and will make possible continuous adaptation and adjustment. It is the great demerit of the existing approach, through standard departmental schemes, that it does not provide for or necessitate this preliminary exercise before implementation.

VII

The exposition of the problem of district development planning, attempted above, has general application, especially in those states in which the district is the main unit of the Panchayati Raj organization. However, there arise in district development planning a number of problems due to the special legal and administrative arrangements of each state. I do not intend to deal with these in any detail. However, the nature and characteristics of these may be briefly indicated by reference to conditions in Maharashtra, of which I have the greatest knowledge.

*Zilla Parishad*s in Maharashtra are endowed by legislation with specific planning powers. However, the proper exercise of these powers has been hampered by a number of factors. The first is finance. The financial resources available to the *Zilla Parishad*s are chiefly in relation to their specific administrative responsibilities, and to individual development programmes or schemes, which have been transferred to them. They have almost no 'free' resources which they could spend on their own. Moreover, all new programmes undertaken by them, or any significant variations in the old, are subject to detailed scrutiny and approval by the heads of relevant departments. It has, in fact, been alleged that the budgetary and administrative control of the secretariat and the departments over the *Zilla Parishads* is more stringent and harassing than over the district administration. Therefore, while *Zilla Parishads* in Maharashtra have been able to spend more money in a few specific directions, they have not been in a position to, and have not been encouraged to, apply their mind to local problems of long-term development planning.

While a number of subjects have been transferred to *Zilla Parishads*, some important aspects of district development planning remain under the direct control of the state government. These are looked after by the residual district administration or by regional or state departmental officers. No arrangements exist at present for effective co-ordination of these aspects with those transferred to the *Zilla Parishad* at the stage of plan formulation or after. The non-transferred subjects in Maharashtra include forests, which are in most districts intimately connected with development of local resources and whose protection and exploitation require close co-operation of the local population.

In considering how the planning apparatus works, attention has to be paid, on the official side, to the secretariat, the state and regional officers of departments, the collector and the residual administration of the district, the chief officer of the *Zilla Parishad* and the staff under him. Even after the recent exercise at devolution, the secretariat continues to be dominant in planning. Its financial and administrative powers seem to have diminished in no measure, and the scrutiny of detail continues as before. Though the *Zilla Parishads* have been given planning officers, and were asked to prepare elaborate documents in relation to the Fourth Five-Year Plan, the state and district plans were, in fact, complied in the secretariat and this work was little affected by the *Zilla Parishad* documents. The role played by the secretariat in finance and overall planning is duplicated by the heads of state departments and their regional officers in relation to details of departmental schemes. The departmental officers—state and regional —have usually considerable expertise and have, in many cases, detailed knowledge of particular localities. This expertise and knowledge are, however, not utilized for local development planning because of, at least, two factors. Firstly, the standard departmental schemes themselves are to a large extent derived from above, i.e., from the Planning Commission and the central ministries, and the state technical officers have rarely subjected them to rigorous scrutiny in relation to particular regional conditions. Therefore, they are not disposed to favour such scrutiny at a lower level and to sanction adjustments. This attitude is reinforced by the feeling of estrangement from the district staff created by the establishment of *Zilla Parishads* and the transfer of the district staff to them. As the district staff is no longer directly controlled by the state department, the higher echelons of officers appear to have lost interest in the work of this staff. This has created a number of problems in the formulation and implementation of district development plans.

It was expected that with the establishment of the *Zilla Parishads*, the collector of the district will lose his importance. This has not happened to any large extent, chiefly because the secretariat and the ministers continue to look upon the collector and his administrative staff as their own special agency. A number of local programmes, such as of famine relief, are still routed chiefly through the collector and this complicates plan formulation and coordination.

Within the official hierarchy itself, one vestige of colonial administration, viz., the IAS, the successor service of the ICS, exerts great influence. The collector of the district and the Chief Officer of the *Zilla Parishad*, both belong to the IAS. In colonial times, British personnel of the highest non-specialized service were naturally put in control of the entire district administration, which in those days was concerned chiefly with collecting revenue and keeping law and order. The central, dominant position of members of the non-specialized service in district administration, continues to this day and has been carried forward to the *Zilla Parishads* which are patterned on the earlier district administration. Consequently, the functioning of the *Zilla Parishad* has come to depend greatly on a single IAS officer, the Chief Officer of the *Zilla Parishad*. The relationship with the non-official part of the organization, on the one hand, and the effective operation and co-ordination of experts and of departmental offices on the other, depend, to a large extent, on the efficiency and disposition of this non-expert officer.

The departmental officers, whose services have been transferred to the *Zilla Parishads*, are of a fairly average quality and are, in many cases, sincere and knowledgeable, especially in relation to local circumstances and problems. However, they suffer from two strong handicaps. In the first instance, they feel cut off from their parent departments and are yet uncertain of the shape the *Zilla Parishad* service will take. Secondly, and more importantly, from the point of view of planning, they still operate within the older tradition which prevents the knowledge and initiative of lower ranks from being meaningfully used. They have been trained and are expected to carry out plans to the letter and not to examine them carefully or to express criticism of them, and they have learnt by experience that it is better to follow instructions blindly rather than to adapt or to make suggestions regarding adjustment to local circumstances.

Finally, the establishment of the *Zilla Parishads* has not yet led to expected rationalization of arrangements of the field staff of the district. There are two sources of confusion. Firstly, the different backgrounds and assignments of the staff, as derived from district local board, revenue and other departments, etc., and secondly, the allotment of particular staff to each new set of schemes. The extent of staffing in the field in most districts of Maharashtra appears liberal. However, the failure to rationalize prevents effective use. Adoption of the integrative approach to district development planning should hasten the process of rationalization in this regard.

The non-official apparatus of the *Zilla Parishads* cannot be divided into well-marked groups for similar consideration. In one part, the problems are organizational, such as those of co-ordinating the work of the subject and the area committees. The adoption of the mandi area, as the lowest area-unit of planning, would require some modifications in existing arrangements regarding area committees and the delegation of powers to them. In another part, the problems relate to the socio-economic composition of local leadership[3] and to the operation of the political party system. Further complication of the latter may result from different parties being in control of different *Zilla Parishads* and of the government of the state. Most of these problems have no direct bearing on district development planning and need not be discussed here.

The relationship of the non-officials with the official hierarchy is also an important factor in the working of *Zilla Parishads*. In this case also, vestiges of the older order remain in the undue importance attached to official position. However, the situation in this regard is undergoing rapid change.

It should be noted that the *Zilla Parishad* experiment is new and that the present is essentially a period of transition. There is nothing in the basic situation which would militate against district development planning of the type discussed in this lecture being undertaken. Today's problems are chiefly those of the changeover from a highly centralized administration to one in which large powers are vested in local self-government authorities. There exists, at present, a widespread distrust of lower authorities and a fear of giving large powers to them among those at all higher levels. Therefore, even when legislative arrangements are changed, administrative practice continues to block real devolution. This is not expected to be a permanent feature. Pressures of circumstances and changing ideas are bound to bring about greater comformity between intention and operation. It is hoped that a proper appreciation of the existing situation will lead to voluntary, deliberate adjustments rather than to *ad hoc* reluctant steps taken under pressure.

VIII

Before concluding, a few observations appear in order regarding the feasibility of the approach suggested above. On a first examination it may appear that the approach requires resources to an extent which could not be expected to be made available and that it also asks for too detailed an operation. A close scrutiny will show that this is not so. In fact, it is experience everywhere that effective rural work is not possible without descending to details and the agricultural production programme envisaged above is, in principle, no different from what is attempted in agricultural extension in any county in the USA. Moreover, as of today, the personnel resources required for the field work sketched above are, for the most part, available on the ground in most districts in India.

There are chiefly two directions in which new inputs will be required. Firstly, local survey and research in all fields. This is a completely neglected area today. In part, the gap can be filled by drawing on the resources of existing academic and training institutions in the district. There are three phases to this work. Firstly, collecting systematic information in relation to each field and identifying problems; secondly, conducting research locally, chiefly in relation to proving, adapting, and adjusting standard prescriptions and solutions in relation to local conditions; thirdly, training local personnel engaged in plan formulation and implementation in specialized aspects of the work in each field. It is true that the existing academic and training institutions are not equipped for this work. However, no insuperable difficulty should arise in making good this deficiency. For example, the staff of the department of economics or commerce in any local college could easily be trained to undertake the preliminary and the later continuous economic surveys; it could also be trained to impart instruction to district staff in appropriate planning techniques. Staffs of local agricultural institutes, polytechnics, public health or medical schools could be utilized in a similar manner. Obviously, existing resources will prove insufficient; more institutions will have to be established and they would have to be properly oriented. However, not only could local institutions play this important role in planning but also their efficiency and competence should greatly increase by this participation. A minimum programme of new institutions is unavoidable. For example, each district must have at least one agricultural research- cum-demonstration centre; but such action is an inevitable concomitant of development itself. As indicated above, the initial survey, etc., is no more than a preliminary step. As local planning becomes more detailed and more effective, it will have to be supported by systematic collection of a greater amount of data and by greater in-depth research in all fields. And with the progress of development planning the resources and competence of local academic and training institutions must also increase.

The second important input required is that of entirely new methods of work and new attitudes towards it. The new attitudes are required chiefly in two directions. Firstly, the adoption of the problem-solving attitude towards all aspects of development planning by all participants in the process; secondly, willingness to trust the judgement and competence of, and delegate authority to, personnel on the lower level on the part of all those on each of the higher levels. The new methods are those required particularly by the adoption of the problem-solving approach. Even if one begins operations, as a matter of convenience, with a standard departmental scheme, this approach requires scrutiny of each of its details in relation to local resources and local circumstances. Defining objectives, translating objectives into programmes of work, and putting programmes in the form of a set of schemes will all require new methods of detailed work, even when one works on the base of the old. Also, the putting together of plans, especially what has been termed above as co-ordination and synchronization, will necessitate evolution of new methods as also a thorough analysis of the plan for implementation.

Effective district development planning will, thus, not require new financial or physical resources in any considerable measure. It will call for a better utilization of old resources, for a reorientation of the existing set-up, and, above all, for new attitudes and a readiness, both to trust more and to delve deeper.

NOTES

1. Preliminary surveys in Wardha District brought to surface a number of local peculiarities that had been previously ignored in all development work. Illustrations may be given from one sector, that of land and water resources development. For example, the problem of a type of waterlogged land common in the district had not been noticed; the potential of utilizing water in streams for winter crops had been ignored; contour bunding in black cotton soils raised a number of problems which had not been tackled. Moreover, a detailed survey of wells in Wardha District revealed that a very large proportion of these were in disuse and that the reasons for disuse varied from area to area (Wardha: District Development Paper I: Irrigation, 1963). These facts were unknown and had not been taken into account in previous plans. As a general rule, even the loaning operation of land development banks for new wells in any district are not today accompanied by a survey of successes and failures in well-digging or of disused wells in any area and do not utilize any information relating to the subject that might be available.

2. In an actual exercise conducted in the Wardha District, it was found that such an area-unit, called in this case for convenience 'the mandi-area unit', usually covered a population of 15 to 20 thousand. The population and area coverage will differ from region to region depending on the intensity of primary production and the density of population. Also, as was the experience in Wardha, while in some cases the centres, and the areas served by them, are fairly easily and clearly identifiable, in other cases, a selection among centres may have to be made and careful demarcation of areas undertaken. This has, then, to be done on the basis not only of the existing situation but also of projected future development.

3. For a discussion of some of these in another context, see Gadgil (1963).

REFERENCES

Friedmann and Alonso (1964) *Regional Development Planning.*

Gadgil, D.R. (1963) 'Socio-economic Factors Underlying Pattern of Leadership', in *International Cooperative Alliance: Co-operative Leadership in South-East Asia.*
——— (1972) *Planning and Economic Policy in India*, 3rd edition.
Planning Commission (1956) *Second Five-Year Plan*, Government of India.
——— (1961) *Third Five-Year Plan*, Government of India.

12

Some Aspects of Development Planning in Kashmir*

The primary requirement for increasing the level of production and of living in Kashmir is extending the scope of continuous operations, both in agriculture and industry. Double cropping is not at present practised, except to a marginal extent, even on irrigated lands. Experiments are being made to take winter wheat and a summer paddy crop on the same land and they are reported to have been successful. However, it appears necessary that much greater research and investigation on suitable varieties with required maturity periods is undertaken and that attention is given also to other suitable winter crops which might produce useful industrial materials. It may be necessary, in this regard, to draw upon and experiment with experiences of countries with similar climate in Asia and Europe. Possibilities of more intensive use of the land surface appear also in relation to a combination of farming and animal husbandry. Some advance is being made in combining sheep farming with orchards and if this is successful it could go a long way towards increasing the income levels of certain classes of farming communities. In relation to farm forestry, it is gratifying to note that already the bulk of Kashmiri farmers grow trees suitable for firewood and domestic timber around their homes and there is a keen appreciation among the people and the Forest Department of the need for increasing wood and timber resources of all kinds for propping up the economy. In this connection, it is necessary to take a long-term view and plan for the future utilization of land and forest resources in a co-ordinated manner. I was told that there is a programme of establishing cross breeds so as to increase milk availability in the valley

* Note circulated to the Planning Commission on 29 October 1969.

very considerably. As this programme proceeds apace, the demand for fodder for the cattle population will grow to a very considerable extent. This will have to be met by (a) putting some land under fodder crops, (b) developing scientifically, and systematically, grass lands and meadows, and (c) drawing upon the resources of the forest for a limited amount of grazing. The evolution of such a programme will require perspective planning and close collaboration on the part of the Departments of Animal Husbandry, Agriculture, and Forest for programmes of controlling erosion, for other measures of conservation and development, and for rationalizing future land use.

Reference may be made, in this connection, to one aspect of forest management. I was told that there are no completely reserved forests in Kashmir and that in all forests local communities have certain rights of grazing cattle or sheep and collecting firewood. It would be useful in this connection to adopt a three-fold classification so that some forests, which are the more valuable and are at a distance from settled communities, should be completely reserved; others which are valuable and subject to regular working plans for regeneration, etc., but are contiguous to settled communities are subject to strictly limited and closely supervised rights in relation to cutting grass and collecting firewood, and thirdly, forests dispersed in settled community areas are largely managed in order to meet the needs of fuel and fodder of the local rural communities. It may be necessary to provide a legal base for these arrangements and, as pointed out above, to provide for joint collaboration of not only the Agricultural, Animal Husbandry, and Forest Departments but also of representatives of local communities in the management of the last category. A point that may be referred to here is regarding the population of goats. Fortunately, the sheep population in Kashmir is dominant and the number of goats is relatively small. However, it may be worthwhile considering whether the goat population cannot be either eliminated or seriously curtailed confining it only to stall-fed goats.

In industry, the main handicaps of the Kashmir economy are its distance from other markets and high costs of importing and exporting materials and commodities. As for quite some time there does not appear likelihood of reducing transport costs materially in real terms, planning of future developments must take account of this factor. It should be noted that though, as a temporary measure in particular contexts, subsidization to reduce transport costs may be felt necessary or desirable such subsidization does not solve the problem either in general terms or for the long-term. The cost of all subsidies ultimately falls on the economy. Development of secondary industry in Kashmir has, thus, to be mainly directed to a consumption goods industry for the local market and for developing export potential in areas in which Kashmir has a special advantage. The transport cost of imports necessarily gives the domestic producer of consumption goods a considerable protection so that in a variety of directions the consumer goods industries should be established. These would obviously be only on the medium or small-scale because of the limited consumer goods market. In relation to industries products of which could be exported the main directions of development appear to be the already established industrial handicrafts in which the value is high in relation to bulk and the transport costs of which can be relatively easily borne by exports. The other is industry based on essentially local materials which are processed or transformed to the largest extent possible within the valley so that the transport costs are the more easily borne. The most obvious basic materials on which future industrial programmes can be based are wool and wood and all other forest products. The possibilities appear large in all these instances but there would have to be careful thinking out of the systematic development at various levels of industrial effort based on these products. I will illustrate what I mean by reference to wool. I was told that pit looms are to a considerable extent still existent in the handloom wool industry of Kashmir. It is important to look at all the processes through which wool has to go after shearing and think of the technique, organization, and labour force appropriate at each stage for different levels of scale and type of product in domestic or local small or medium scale industry. A programme similar to that being evolved in the states in relation to cotton may have to be tried. This is related to preparatory processes, spinning, weaving, and finishing at various stages. For this purpose, it is necessary to conduct research and investigations into the extent to which modern efficient methods can be adopted with the least capital intensity and made applicable to operations either in the household or in small workshops. As in cotton we can think of, say, improved preparatory process at the domestic or workshop level, improved charkhas as well as co-operative spinning mills and improved handlooms and power-looms, and co-operative finishing plants. It should be possible to evolve a similar tier of operations in the wool industry. There is the possibility also of developing a knitting industry on the basis of local wool. It should be emphasized that the various forms of activity at different technological levels indicated above are not necessarily mutually exclusive and that given specialization of products and of areas, all these can subsist together and tap a variety of different markets. Co-ordinated effort on these lines should help in greatly extending employment potential and raising the productivity level of the community. The effort appears to be urgently needed. I was told that surpluses are beginning to accumulate in the hands even of migratory shepherds; these should soon be shown proper avenues of investment.

In view of the transport factor mentioned above, it is vital for the Kashmir Government to see that as far as possible its wool, wood, and other forest products are processed completely within the valley and sent out chiefly in forms of finished commodities. As I have very little technical competence,

I shall not comment on other possibilities of industrial development but confine myself to a few remarks on the artistic handicrafts. These are obviously an extremely important legacy for the Kashmir economy which needs not only to be preserved but developed rapidly to suit modern circumstances of operation and modern types of demand. It appears that in this context there are a very large number of problems which need research and investigation in relation to making the material more suitable or adopting some of the modern techniques for mass production. I may illustrate by reference to two problems to which my attention was drawn during a brief visit to the Industry Design Centre. (i) It is necessary to use seasoned wood for making the joinery etc. perfect, so that articles of furniture do not fall apart and are efficient in use. Seasoned wood, however, is said to be difficult to work upon and not liked by handicrafts men. Here is obviously a technical problem which must be solved in order to extend the market and which ought not to be difficult of solution. (ii) In pottery products the main improvement desired was in the direction of better and more continuous firing at high levels of temperature. This means adaptation, co-operatively, of a low-cost modern kiln. It is reported that experiments in this regard have been made at the Lucknow Institute.

I was told that there was a proposal to build work-sheds for winter for the handicrafts men in which suitable working conditions and temperature would be maintained. It would be important to gather experience in this direction so as to determine the cost-benefits ratio of such an experiment. If it breaks even it could make valuable contribution to raising the productivity and income levels of an important class. It is obvious that much more research input, not only in terms of marketing and design but also in terms of technically improving the quality of the material, the tools, the processes, and the finished products, in all technical and scientific aspects is extremely important. This could provide a large challenge to the local technical institutions and university departments.

Silk is another product in which Kashmir has special advantages and which could, if developed, give considerable employment in both silk-worm rearing and silk industries. It is unfortunate that the output of silk in Kashmir is reported to be on the decline. Research effort has been recently put in improving cocoon production and quality, and appears to have yielded results. However, the basic organization of silk production does not seem to induce increasing numbers to engage themselves in the occupation. It appears necessary to revise the older approach to mulberry plantation and cocoon rearing. In the ultimate, the industry must become a subsidiary occupation of the farming community. For this purpose, farmers must be induced to plant their own mulberry trees to secure the needed supply of mulberry leaves. In view of the general practice of the Kashmiri farmer to plant trees around his house and fields, this should not prove difficult if sufficient technical assistance and an adequate price for the cocoon are offered. One of the difficulties mentioned is that the cocoon rearing season and the season of agriculture coincide. This would indicate that efforts at encouraging sericulture must be made with the small holders whose holdings do not give full employment to the households during the agricultural season and in areas where agriculture is not intensive and irrigated. A selective approach on some such lines has to be evolved, and a programme chalked out, for moving sericulture from its present unsound base and placing it on surer economic footing. This would also require some revision of pricing policy in relation to silk. In view of the special position claimed for Kashmir silk, the great export potential of silk products, and the considerable employment potential for small and unsecure farmers in sericulture, it appears necessary to give immediate and urgent attention to this problem.

In connection with the development of tourist facilities I may draw attention to the importance of eliminating obtrusive military presence from tourist resorts. Our party, on its way from Gulmarg to Khilenmarg, had the unfortunate experience of being stopped by a military sentinel and made to wait till a messenger sent by the Director of Tourism, who accompanied us, was able to obtain clearance from some higher-ups. Obtrusive military presence is likely to create an unpleasant impression and keep away tourists, especially foreigners. I would suggest that before the ambitious Gulmarg development is completed this problem should be solved satisfactorily.

In relation to economic policy, the Kashmir Government appears to be handicapped by some carry-overs from the past regime. It appears necessary to get over these as soon as practicable. The effort has to be made even though the political difficulties in the way are obvious. Older policy in relation to food appears to have been oriented towards favouring the urban population at the cost of the rural. Food was subsidized in the cities at heavy costs to the government and the prices of foodgrains were unduly depressed. Rice production was kept up chiefly because of the subsistence nature of most farming and the legislative prohibition of diverting rice land to other crops. It is understood that during 1968–69 for the first time procurement prices were put on the all-India level. Even so, it is contended that apple-growing is much more profitable than cultivation of rice. As long as very large price disparities prevail, it would not be possible to attain rational distribution of land utilization under crops. It is noticed that in Himachal Pradesh fruit orchards are being planted in hilly areas unsuitable for the cultivation of field crops. A balance between prices, which brings this about in Himachal, must be sought to be attained in Kashmir. However, this would be impossible as long as the policy of heavily subsidizing food to the urban population is continued. For, any increase in the price offered to the cultivator automatically increases the cost of food subsidization. Even today the cost is estimated at about Rs. 6 crores a year. This means that during a five-year plan period the cost of food subsidy could wholly finance a project like the Lower Jhelum Project.

For gradually achieving the objective of abolishing subsidies the extent of responsibility assumed by the state in relation to distribution of food has to be lessened by stages. Ultimately, rationing will be given up and the government will maintain merely a series of fair-price shops, mainly intended to protect vulnerable classes at times of stress. It follows that achieving this will mean revision upwards of foodgrain prices in the fair-price shops system and allowing them gradually to approach the market level. As domestic production increases and enough rice is grown for internal consumption, the element of transport cost in prices would be eliminated. In this connection, the government would have to extend the system of dual prices it has recently introduced so that some categories are charged the adequate economic price while some others are subsidized. It should be possible over the years to achieve this and substantially reduce the present crushing burden of food subsidies on state finances. The main steps required are, increasing considerably the internal production of rice, wheat, and maize so as to attain a balance of internal supply and demand, lessening gradually the present coverage of monopoly procurement and distribution of foodgrains so that a fringe open market comes into being, and if because of increase of internal supply the present element of transport cost in price is eliminated, then try charging the economic price to the bulk of consumers, retaining subsidization only in favour of the really vulnerable.

Consideration of food procurement and subsidy leads naturally to that of finance for agriculture. In this regard, the position was not clear to me. In one district meeting I was told that the government made interest-free advances to agriculturists through co-operative societies on a basis similar to that of crop loan. At another place it was said that these were not production credit loans but rather advances made by the government in relation to later procurement of rice and that these advances were always recovered through sales of rice by the cultivator to the government. This explanation, however, did not appear to cover the sales of fertilizer to cultivators, as these did not appear to have been recovered through rice procurement and sales. Whatever that may be, it is extremely important that the system of agricultural credit be placed on some uniform basis and that it be placed on a business footing. The two possible alternatives in this regard are: (i) a complete scheme of government advances made through official agencies and recovered like payments of revenue; and (ii) a co-operative credit system, as in other states, based on the primary rural societies and a structure of co-operative banks. In this the society would obtain the required additional funds through central co-operative banks which themselves would have to lean upon the Reserve Bank of India. The whole transaction would be, however, a business transaction with no subsidization or remission of interest except in special cases where the government felt it necessary that co-operative societies should make loans to particular categories for particular purposes at lower rates of interest. In this case, the subsidization would be to the co-operative society, through the government paying the difference between the rate of interest normally charged by the co-operative society and the lower rate desired by government. It is obvious that the present mixed system makes for unbusiness-like transactions and makes it impossible for the co-operative system to grow in a healthy manner.

The building-up of a sound co-operative credit system is a condition precedent to proper development of the rural economy. All other types of activity in the co-operative field, such as, marketing and processing are intimately connected with a healthy credit system. There appears considerable scope for a variety of types of marketing and processing societies in a number of products, especially of orchards and animal husbandry. The basic building-up of the primary credit structure and familiarizing farmers with the proper procedures of co-operative business has, in this context, special importance. It may be noted that the possibility of obtaining support for institutional finance from all-India financial agencies is closely linked with the building-up of the primary and district co-operative structure in credit, marketing, and processing. Acceleration of the pace of development planning in rural areas thus depends on the preliminary building-up of this structure.

The emphasis of the Kashmir Government on its power programme appears fully justified. In a variety of directions, of industrial development, of lengthening the period of production, of conserving wood and other resources, increased availability of electrical power holds a crucial place. The major question of future policy in this regard is the management of finances of the Electricity Undertaking. In the long run, generation and distribution of electricity must become economic propositions and total financial operations must come up to standards laid down in this behalf by the Venkataraman Committee. What the operation mix will be, and the relative levels of charges for different purposes, is a matter that will have to be carefully worked out. Unless, however, this is looked at in the proper perspective and the various future stages and steps determined now, the government may get into difficulties of having undertaken a load of subsidization which it will not be able to carry.

I have not been able to understand the full working of the various parts of the irrigation system, and the differentiation in management, rates, construction, and repair responsibility as between the state irrigation system and the zamindari kuhls. However, even here, it is important to insist that future extension of the irrigation system and its continued efficient maintenance depends intimately on the state reimbursing itself adequately for the services that it renders.

During the visit to the Lolak Valley, attention was drawn to the difficulties of obtaining irrigation by villages situated at the tail-end of a zamindari kuhl system. It was reported that this was due to the extra drawing of water by cultivation higher up. With increasing intensification of cultivation this is likely to emerge as a problem in many of these kuhls. Remedies appropriate to such a situation, such as, increasing the total water supply, regulating usage more strictly, or finding alternative sources at the tail-end may have to be thought out. The problem needs to be analysed in advance and charging an economic rate would be one way of economizing in the use of water. I may also draw attention to an observation made recently by a visiting team from the Centre. This was to the effect that the absence of water channels at the field level was coming in the way of the spread of irrigation facilities. If this is related to an absence of legislation which would enable the government to enforce or provide for the construction of channels, this may be remedied.

The field of education presents problems of great difficulty and complexity. In the older regime, all education was free but the facilities available were highly limited. Therefore, the cost to the government was not large or continuously increasing. Since independence, not only has all education been kept completely free but also the government has felt it imperative to open more and more institutions as the demand for them increases. The resulting situation is very peculiar. On the one hand, Kashmir has not as good a showing as many other states in the percentage of literacy or coverage in education of the age group 6 to 11, and it is specially backward in girls' education. On the other hand, the rapidity of the increase of secondary and collegiate educational facilities has been phenomenal. The result of the momentum created by free education has forced the government to increase facilities of secondary and collegiate education.

The problems at the secondary and the higher level are manifold. Firstly, there appears no limit now to the extent of increase in educational expenditure that the government will be forced to make in this direction. Secondly, because the pace in increase in numbers is always larger than the increase in expenditure that the government can undertake, the quality of, and the equipment in, education are reported to be rapidly deteriorating. Thirdly, because the number of matriculates and graduates is increasing at a phenomenal pace and because standards are deteriorating, the situation in relation to both employment and employability is fast worsening. As, at present, the government is the only substantial employer, of what is essentially clerical and white-collar labour, it finds it impossible to offer employment in adequate volume and faces a problem of educated unemployment and its political overtones which is largely a creation of past policy. Another effect that has to be noticed in this context is that the increase in types of skilled labour and technical training is not taking place adequately. The reason for this is clear. In other parts of India a number of school-leavers at various stages find it difficult to continue their education and seek employment opportunities. The presence of these school-leavers leads the government to establish institutions for appropriately training them for modern types of employment. This has resulted in a considerable system of vocational and technical education at the secondary school stage or immediately after. With the ease obtaining in Kashmir for proceeding straight from stage to stage of an ordinary arts or science school and college course, there are no compulsions for seeking other outlets at appropriate earlier stages. Skilled labour recruitment and the recruitment of intermediate technical personnel in other parts of India is largely the effect of the compulsion on large proportions of students to leave school. Given the preference in Indian societies of all types for white-collared jobs, it is natural that as long as the route is clear and made easy, students would flock to high schools and colleges in larger numbers.

While acknowledging the rapid transformation of the educational situation that has been brought about by free education at all levels in the state during the last twenty years, it is necessary to realize that the situation is developing dangerously and that early steps to bring about a change in policy must be taken. The steps needed are obvious enough.

Firstly, the introduction of merit and means tests at all stages above the primary. The provision of seven standards of education to every boy and every girl is a constitutional responsibility. This should be sought to be fulfilled adequately. Above this, the imposition of means and merit tests is both justified and necessary. The one relates to the status and income of the parent and the other, to the ability to profit from further educational opportunities shown by the student. The Government of India is finding it progressively necessary to introduce these elements in scholarships given even to scheduled castes and scheduled tribes. Their introduction in regard to the generality of the population cannot, therefore, be objected to. Together with this should slowly evolve training for skilled and technical personnel, particularly relating to the handicrafts, the wool, the wood, and other promising industries within the state. This is obviously the needed long-term direction. How the minimum transition can begin is essentially a political problem on which I can offer no remarks. It does appear odd, at the same time, that with such large problems in the field of general education, the State Government should undertake substantial expenditure for essentially marginal activities such as the establishment of a public school.

The solution of problems of agricultural and industrial production and development that Kashmir faces could be achieved through proper planning of investment and suitable modification of economic and educational policies. Some aspects have been indicated above. They also seem, however, to require considerable investment in local investigation and particular lines of research. In almost all areas such as field crops, rotations, orchards, animal husbandry, forest management, handicrafts, and resource-based local industry, the problems in Kashmir are somewhat peculiar. Obviously, the peculiar aspects of these problems, to the extent that they are different from the general type in India, are being neglected. It is extremely important that concerted effort is made to fill this gap. It would be necessary, in the first instance, to identify the more important and immediate problems in each context. It would also be necessary to build up appropriate organizations which can lay down the long-term plans for studying and solving these problems. There are already some resources available in the state, at the university level, in technical and basic sciences. These may have to be augmented in some directions, and more particularly, they would have to be organized so as to take up meaningfully the challenges faced by the state's economy.

The work being done by the particular departments of the state in terms of investigation, operation and extension in technical departments appears to be in keen and competent hands. This was the impression that I gathered from what little I saw of such activities as in agriculture, forestry, animal husbandry, and silk-worm rearing. It also appeared, at the same time, as happens in other states, that there was little collaboration and co-ordination in planning activities of the various departments and sometimes, as in the rural industries project at Anantnag, the effort did not seem to have been given proper and definitive orientation. The lack of such co-ordination was fully brought about in a series of discussions I had with the district officers one morning. I suggest that in view of the relatively small size of the state, the government would find it specially fruitful to adopt the approach of integrated district planning in preparing their future plans of development. The Planning Commission is shortly sending out some guidelines in this matter. It may not be necessary in Kashmir to prepare separate plans for each district as such. It would be quite feasible to prepare plans for the three regions—Kashmir, Jammu, and Ladakh—on the pattern of district planning suggested above. I would be glad to depute officers from the Planning Commission to discuss possibilities of this approach if the government decides after study to adopt it.

The last point that I would make in this note is the need to build up local organizations of the co-operative and the Panchayati Raj type. In all states that are considered advanced in India today the contribution in rural development of these types of organizations has been notable. They serve a number of purposes. They can attract additional institutional finance from outside for increasing rural development activity. However, they are everywhere found also, in course of time, to raise very considerable resources from among the local communities and co-operative business organization and, what perhaps is even more important, they contribute leadership and local personnel to man the organization and implementation of local developmental plans. This last makes the formulation of plans at the local level more meaningful and assures their proper implementation. Within my short visit it appeared to me that there was enough of leadership and keenness within the local communities to form a proper base for growth of the super-structure of co-operation, but that this requires to be properly organized and encouraged.

13

Development of Backward Areas*

I have great pleasure in welcoming Chief Ministers to this meeting which has been convened, as directed, to consider one special problem. It may be recalled that the reports of two Working Groups, one on the identification of backward areas, and the other on fiscal and financial incentives for starting industries in backward areas, appointed by the Planning Commission on the suggestion of the Chief Ministers' Committee of the National Development Council (NDC), had been included in the agenda of the last meeting of the NDC held on 19 and 20 April 1969. After a brief discussion of the item it was then decided that the Reports should be considered by the Committee of Chief Ministers of the NDC.

The Planning Commission considered that it would help in arriving at decisions early if discussions on issues arising out of the reports were held with the Reserve Bank, related financial institutions, and certain central ministries before the meeting of the Committee of Chief Ministers. A number of such discussions were, therefore, organized and as a result an approach has been crystallized. This was embodied in a paper presented to the Union Cabinet by the Planning Commission and the Planning Commission has been authorized by the Cabinet to place the approach and the recommendations contained in the Paper for consideration of this Committee of Chief Ministers.

By way of introduction to the discussion, I shall briefly summarize the approach suggested in the Paper.

In relation to the Report of the Working Group for the identification of backward areas, objection is being taken to the identification for special treatment of some states as industrially backward, as proposed by the

* Speech at the meeting of the National Development Council Committee of State Chief Ministers held in New Delhi on 26 September 1969.

Working Group. It is contended that though larger areas or number of districts in some states may be industrially backward than in other states, a number of areas or districts in most states are also industrially backward. Therefore, any policy for giving incentives for development of backward areas, which does not pay any attention to backward areas in states, not defined as a whole to be backward, is likely to leave out of consideration many districts and areas which should receive such consideration. In order to accommodate this point of view, the Planning Commission proposes different lines of action in relation to the various classes of measures that are recommended for accelerating the development of industrially backward areas.

These measures can be divided into three different classes. (i) Concessions offered by financial institutions for financing industries in backward areas. (ii) Concessions, incentives, and positive measures adopted by the government of a state for actively promoting development of industries in backward areas within the state. (iii) Fiscal incentives to be given by the Central Government for industries established in backward areas in pursuance of special programmes in this behalf by governments of states.

It is suggested that measures under (i), namely, concessions given by financial institutions to industries established in backward areas, need not be confined to only a small number of districts. As the concessions are of a general nature, they may be made applicable to all districts which could be considered as being industrially backward. Such a list of districts in all states and Union Territories can be drawn up by using the criteria given by the Committee on identification of backward areas. The Committee recommends two sets of criteria. One for the identification of industrially backward states and Union Territories and the other for the identification of backward districts in industrially advanced states and Union Territories. It would be possible, by making an appropriate combination of these two sets of criteria, to identify backward districts in all states and Union Territories. This exercise could be undertaken by the Reserve Bank and related financial institutions.

In relation to measures to be adopted by the states the problem posed is of an entirely different character. The programme of action required in this instance is not mainly passive, as in identification of districts and areas and the offer of financial concessions or fiscal incentives. In this respect, it is the responsibility of the state government directly to undertake not only a considerable amount of preparatory and promotional work but to build a whole series of socio-economic overheads. The Committee on the identification of backward areas has noted that where there is almost complete lack of necessary infrastructural facilities no useful purpose would be served by extending incentives for industrial development. In relation to such extremely backward areas and districts, initial action has to be taken by the state government for building up infrastructural facilities before active industrial development, through promotional and incentive measures, is contemplated. However, even in areas where certain minimal infrastructural facilities exist further developments in particular directions and locations, so as to actively promote industrial development according to a programme, become necessary. The infrastructural facilities or socio-economic overheads do not include merely communications and supply of power and water but also credit, marketing and storage arrangements, education and health facilities, and a given development of co-operative or other organizations which could actively participate in the process of development. In addition, as the Report of the Working Group on fiscal and financial incentives points out, the state government would have to carry out surveys and feasibility studies, to identify and select growth points, locate entrepreneurs or appropriate organizations like promising co-operatives, and develop industrial estates or industrial areas in which industrial activity can be initiated. All this requires investment of very considerable resources. Apart from the substantial financial resources required for various works and activities, the total promotional effort would have to be placed in charge of carefully selected officers who are enabled to carry the responsibility continuously over a minimum period. It is highly unlikely that the states would be able to initiate such projects simultaneously over a large number of areas. The Committee on the identification of backward areas notes that:

> concentration of organization and administrative machinery by the states in a few districts on a number of short-term and long-term measures required for promotion of industries (e.g., railway siding, housing colony for industrial labour, dispensary or hospital, banking and other facilities), is a pre-requisite for ensuring success. One of the lessons drawn from the working of the industrial development area scheme is also that the progress has been slow in the states which had taken up a relatively larger number of these areas.

From all these points of view, the recommendation of the Committee that each of the states identified as industrially backward should initially concentrate its efforts at specially accelerating industrial development in two districts appears reasonable. In order to meet the contention of the other states, it is also suggested that the states not identified as industrially backward by the Committee should also be allowed to select one backward district in which they undertake special promotional activity.

Apart from the desirability of concentrating attention initially on a small number of districts, the restriction of the number of districts suggested has another relevance. The third class of measures indicated above is that of fiscal assistance by the Central Government to industries included in the special programme of development of backward areas in the states. The Committee on Fiscal and Financial Incentives has made a series of recommendations in this behalf. It is suggested that instead of offering a number of separate incentives, the Central Government should offer one combined measure of assistance and that this should be equal to one-tenth of the capital invested in the newly established industries. This measure of subsidization by the Centre will have to be limited in some manner. Therefore, it will be confined to industries newly established within the district selected as indicated above and fully backed by the programme of development by the state. In relation to recommendations regarding fiscal incentives to be offered by state governments, each state government will have to take a decision. It is, however, suggested that as it is undesirable to have very large variations from state to state in relation to such incentives, there should be an active interchange of ideas between the governments of states, the Ministry of Industrial Development, and the Planning Commission, before the state governments arrive at a final decision regarding their package on incentives.

IV

Problems of Industrial and Agricultural Development

14

Public Interest and Big Business in India*

I am extremely grateful to the authorities of the Nagpur University for honouring me with the invitation to deliver this Convocation address. I experienced some difficulty in choosing the theme for this address. It had to be one on which I had something to say and which would also interest the audience, particularly young University graduates. After some thought I have decided to speak about the aspects of the socio-economic situation in India and the possibilities for the future that they indicate, which affect all citizens and require their attention.

I begin by calling attention to features of the present situation which are causing concern. There appears to be very general agreement among qualified observers that there has been, since Independence, an increase in corruption, and that this is especially in evidence among the highest and most powerful strata in society. It is also widely reported that among large sections of our population, and over wide areas, a sense of frustration and a feeling of disillusionment prevail. The advent of Independence, and the responsibility for self-direction that it threw on the nation, should have made us keenly conscious of social obligations. The changed circumstances should also enthuse and invigorate us in efforts at all-sided improvement and advance. That this has not happened, points to some fundamental defects in the existing situation.

An analysis of the nature and extent of changes that took place at Independence and an examination of new features that have since emerged may help in locating these defects. I shall attempt to do this briefly. For at least a century before the coming of Independence, the leaders of our society were deeply concerned with the low state to which we had fallen

* Address delivered at the 42nd Convocation of the Nagpur University on 20 January 1962.

and the paths and prospects of our regeneration. It was agreed that a number of features of the internal structure of our society, together with the conditions created by foreign rule, were responsible for our depressed state, and that strenuous efforts were necessary in all spheres, social and educational, political and economic, to achieve progress. Leaders in these efforts, whether the effort was general or sectional and covered all aspects or only some, had to exhibit similar qualities. They had to be critical of the people and yet enthuse them and had, for the most part, to work against heavy odds or at least without adequate support. In a number of instances, they incurred the wrath of the government and had to suffer a variety of hardships if they persisted in their chosen paths. Courage, integrity, and, above all, a disregard of immediate self-interest were, in the circumstances, essential and were continuously exhibited in varying degrees by workers in movements of all kinds. Even businessmen incurred some risks when they pressed for the acceptance by the government of economic policy in national interest. All this affected our scales of value and prestige and the moral tone of our society.

The advent of Independence changed the situation in one important respect. The efforts and sacrifices undertaken to overthrow foreign rule were no longer necessary. The large social, economic, educational, and other problems facing the country could not be solved merely by the coming of Independence. However, it was now the authorities of the state that could, and did, take the lead in planning and conducting effort in most directions for their solution.

India attained independence through a peaceful transfer of power. There was, consequently, relatively little change in the form and structure of administration. The most important change was among those who held the reins of political power. Those who had for long fought against the British, replaced the British and their associates. This was natural. There has been much adverse comment on the preference shown by the Indian National Congress to persons who had been sent to jail as political agitators by the British, in the formation of the early ministries before and after Independence. I do not see anything to deride or disapprove in this. During British rule, when future developments were unpredictable, most of those who took a stand that might land them in jail risked a great deal. Jail-going was thus broadly a test of character; and there is everything to be said in favour of using such a test.

What was, however, surprising was that the change of rulers was not accompanied by any large change in the external arrangements connected with the manifestation of political authority. In a colonial regime, the location and style of the residences of rulers, the display of pomp and the security measures taken at public appearances, were all connected with maintaining the sense of separateness—the distance between the ruler and the ruled—and the impression of power. These were, or should be, irrelevant after Independence and yet the new regime has fully maintained the trappings of the old.

Also, the administrative structure remains almost entirely unchanged. The peculiar circumstances of British rule in India led to the development of a structure of administrative services, which combined the rigid separation—characteristic of a caste society, with the careful gradation—characteristic of a class society. The civil service, with a rigid, one-track recruitment-pattern, wielded power at the top. Other services and experts were placed in an inferior position and deliberately excluded from the highest executive positions and from policy-making. The interests of the superior-service personnel, and particularly of the civil services, were important factors in policy and posting decisions. All of this, essential in a colonial regime run by a mainly alien service, remains unchanged today. There has been no change, no thought given to a change, in the structure of the services. Postings at the highest level in government and in the large public sector continue to show that the interests and even convenience of members of the superior administrative service are important determinants of public policy; and, as recent experience has brought home to us, the government attaches much greater importance to maintaining the prestige of high officials than to taking the public into confidence.

A colonial regime is concerned chiefly with the maintenance of power, and welfare aspects of governmental activity cannot receive much attention from it. Consequently, all administrative arrangements, including the provision of public amenities, in such a regime are made to centre around the convenience of officials and of the 'superior classes,' and no particular attention is paid to the needs of the 'lower' classes and the poor. It would, I believe, not be unfair to say that even in this regard the shift since Independence has not been large. For example, the accommodation provided and attention paid to the convenience of first-class passengers and third-class passengers continue to exhibit the same disparity as of old. The difficulties encountered by the poor and those without any backing, in obtaining access to and attention from administrative personnel, remain almost as great as before. The dominance of the VIPs and the rich in all projects and programmes, continues to be a marked feature of the Indian situation. In spite of a very large extension of programmes with an educational and welfare intent the manner and pace of operation of administrative machinery remain substantially unchanged.

These represent important carry-overs from the past. The most important positive change in the total situation brought about after Independence is the programme of planned economic development on which we have embarked. Rapid economic development has become the main national goal, and all pronouncements and proposals are judged by reference to this goal. Inevitably, the structure of the plans of development, and the values implicit in them, has begun to mould the current situation; forces set in motion by them should prove even more powerful in the future. The process and the plan of industrialization lie at the core of the Indian effort at economic development; most aspects of planned effort are oriented towards the long-term plan of the building-up of modern industrial production within the country. In other ways also attention has to be focussed on the process of industrialization and on the modern industry sector. This sector makes the largest and the most intensive use of capital resources. It is the most dynamic sector, and it is in this sector that the largest surpluses emerge. Moreover, as the new and ever-growing urban and industrial sector represents, more than any other, a deliberately-created new socio-economic type, the policies adopted in its creation, and the values explicitly and implicitly incorporated in its shape and structure, must have a powerful impact on society. It may be added that as economic power within this sector is concentrated in a small number of hands the public importance and influence of those occupying the sector is extraordinarily large.

Excepting a limited field reserved for the public sector, industrialization is sought to be brought about through operations of private capitalists. The plan is supposed to determine the objectives and priorities in relation to industrialization, and government policy is directed towards eliminating risks from the appropriate fields and towards enabling private capitalists to procure the needed resources, material and financial. Licensing of industrial establishments selects the limited number of concerns that are allowed to occupy a particular field. Control over foreign trade appropriately shuts off foreign competition; import licensing enables the favoured to obtain initial supplies of capital goods and recurrent supplies of spares and of raw materials. Materials under control are allotted; state financial institutions give finance in a large measure; and where needed, the government itself stands guarantee. Agreements with foreign collaborators are encouraged and approved and these provide a further, many-sided source of strength to Indian capitalists. Wherever the government controls prices, the latter are fixed so as to provide liberal margins to the industrialists, and financial and fiscal policies are shaped to the same end. Direct taxation, we are officially assured, cannot be increased further.

I should like to draw attention to two features of the policy governing industrialization. All growth of modern industry in India since the early twenties has been brought about under a protective regime, major cost of which has been borne by the Indian consumer. In planned industrialization, protection is continued in a variety of ways, and the plan is articulated through selecting particular capitalists for particular fields and enabling them to acquire highly scarce resources of every type. Whatever the financial skill of the capitalist, his success and progress are mainly due to conditions created by state policy and maintained at public cost. Even so, no attempt is made by the government to acquire control, to introduce an element of public ownership, or even to do anything to facilitate such a process in the future. The accumulation of gains and the rapid increase of economic resources and power in particular private hands can thus be described as a deliberate objective of official policy. This view is sustained by other aspects of policy. Almost all government operation is based on the offer of incentives to private capitalists. To give an example, if the government desires that a part of the production of an industry, which it has helped to build up and which it shelters, should be exported, the only way it can think of achieving this end is to afford special incentives for the purpose to producers in the industry. Incentives always mean, in this context, further opportunities, direct or indirect, of adding to the resources under their control.

The second notable feature of existing policy is its declared reliance on capital formation in the private sector. This apparently simple decision becomes a loaded weapon in the present Indian situation. As indicated above, the pace and direction of industrialization and the level of activity are all more or less directly regulated by the government. Therefore, relying on savings of corporations and capitalists means no more than fixing the level of prices and protection at such a level that industrialists are enabled to obtain a large savings margin. Thus, not only are the selected capitalists enabled by government policy to establish themselves in particular sheltered fields but also are their conditions of operation so regulated that they command, over and above a normal profit margin, a large savings potential. The result is that the existing group of capitalists is assured of a monopoly of large expansion opportunities in the future and a continued and increasingly concentrated hold on the industrial economy. There is little wonder that, since these policies became stabilized some three years ago, the stock exchanges of the country are in an almost permanent state of buoyancy.

It might be useful at this stage to examine the usual explanation of the above-mentioned policy embodied in the phrase 'Production before Distribution'. That you can distribute only what you have produced is not truer than that the hen lays the egg. However, equally as the hen itself comes out of the egg, so production cannot be maintained or increased without adequate maintenance in health and well-being of human labour and of natural resources and capital equipment, which is the aim of a proper system of distribution. 'Production before Distribution' is, therefore, no more than a plausible cliche used as a cloak for a policy which its protagonists find it difficult to avow openly. What it conveys, in fact, is that immediate attention should be concentrated on policy which speeds up production, and all other objectives, especially that of distributive justice, should be laid aside. To put it bluntly, it is a plea for allowing concentration of the ownership of means of production and turning a blind eye to the need for improvement of standards of living, with perhaps the added implication that such a policy will be transitional and can, in due time, be reversed. The plea is based on two assumptions. The first is that it is necessary to ignore considerations relating to distribution in order to speed up production, and the second is that after you have speeded up production in this manner up to a given level, you can turn back and set about to repair the damage in the distributive process. Both these assumptions may be challenged. That increasing inequality, or the heavy and continued concentration of the ownership of the means of production in the hands of a few private capitalists, is the only way in which you can speed up production, is far from being universal experience in recent times. It is also very doubtful whether you can continue to concentrate economic and other power in society in the hands of small groups and yet later expect that they will quietly allow you to take it away or even that a state apparatus dominated by such interests will want to reverse current policy.

There are, however, many indications that those who determine policy are apt to disregard social costs in the supposed interests of rapid industrialization. One of the sorriest of these relates to the growth of our metropolitan centres. The Government of Maharashtra has officially represented to the Finance Commission that a large gap exists between the resources available to the state and the minimum outlay required for the existing population of Bombay City. It is also agreed that the condition and the number of pavement dwellers in the city are among the darkest blots on our society. Yet the Government of Maharashtra not only refuses to take steps to stop further growth but at times even allows new obviously undesirable developments by large capitalists.

The dominance of this resurgent group of large capitalists is the most important and significant change in India since Independence. The nature and the extent of this dominance are emphasized when we examine the relations of this class with other important groups. During the British regime the relations of the members of the services with Indian businessmen were moulded by the attitude of the British members of the services. The British civilians traditionally stood aloof from businessmen in general and Indian businessmen in particular. The two classes had little to do with each other, and except in the metropolitan centres, the relations between them were not close; they could not be said to form parts of one stratum anywhere. Also, at that time, the members of the superior services, were among the recipients of highest incomes in India. There were a small number of Indian businessmen with very large fortunes, but, in most parts of the country, business incomes were not high.

This has changed completely during the last two decades. Since the withdrawal of the British, the Indian public officials do not appear to have evolved for themselves any common scale of values or code of conduct. Also, in the meanwhile, the relative levels of income of the highest officials and of Indian businessmen have completely altered. The salaries of civilians in money terms have remained almost unchanged, but their value in real terms has fallen greatly. At the same time, the economic strength and the political influence of Indian businessmen have increased enormously. Most important of all, the range and field of activity of Indian businesses is now so large that they constitute today, overwhelmingly, the most important group of employers of personnel commanding high salaries. As the recent Pay Commission pointed out, the relative positions of government and business, in this regard, had been greatly changed within the short span of eight years between 1948 and 1956. The direction of effort of those who want to get into the top salariat has consequently changed. Their goal is no longer to get into the highest official ranks but into the highest ranks of managers and technicians employed by large Indian and foreign businesses in India. This applies, among others, to the sons and relatives of the highest officials as well as of prominent politicians. The pattern of behaviour of officials on retirement has changed simultaneously. Formerly, they usually sought no employment, almost never with Indian business. Today, the most highly placed officials very readily find highly rewarding positions within business. From the great consideration with which the government treats ex-official employees or associates of business, it would appear that the government also approves of these mutually beneficial arrangements. We have thus arrived at the curious position that most officials who exercise large discretionary powers in relation to the regulation of business might yet look on businessmen as potential employers or patrons of their sons and relatives and even of themselves.

A similar change has come over the position of Indian businessmen vis-à-vis the politicians. An increasingly large proportion of Indian businessmen after 1920 supplied a part of needed resources to political workers, especially to the Indian National Congress. In doing this they ran risks, especially during the earlier periods, and there was hardly ever any element of a quid pro quo in the assistance. The relation changed after these politicians acquired power. But it is the change in the circumstances of the businessmen, sketched above, that made the real difference. The politician out of office and the sons and relatives of politicians look up to businessmen. Above all, the ruling party has deliberately put itself in the position of being a client of businessmen and business corporations by special permissive legislation passed in this behalf. A democracy in which there is an unequal division of incomes is always faced with a difficult problem in relation to the acquisition of funds by political parties, and political thinkers, even in the USA, have advocated the need for ever greater diffusion of the sources of these funds. The situation in this regard in India is, of course, extremely unsatisfactory. The inequality of distribution of incomes is among the largest in the world, and the level of national income is among the lowest. The recent concentration of surpluses in the hands of capitalists and in the corporations they command, gives them an overwhelming dominance as potential sources of political funds. In such a situation the refusal of the ruling party to pass, what might have amounted to, a self-denying ordinance, has certainly worsened the situation politically and ethically.

Businessmen and officials and politicians are, today, the most influential in, at least, urban society. Of the traditional leaders of society, princes, landlords, and the priestly class may be said to have lost overall influence. Some urban professionals like lawyers, who held an especially important position some decades ago, no longer count for much. Moreover, the lawyers, the doctors, the engineers, and other urban professionals depend more and more on the patronage of businessmen, and a large majority of the growing class of technicians and applied scientists trained in India or abroad, have necessarily to look forward, in the main, to employment in modern business.

In former times there existed, in some regions, a discernible difference between political workers and workers in educational, social, and other similar fields and the latter constituted an important social force. Since Independence these appear to be subject to a process of disintegration. A variety of forces work towards this end. Political parties, in the effort to extend their base of operations, have begun to invade these fields. A considerable amount of educational, social, and other work is now undertaken directly by the state, or is heavily subsidized by it. During British times, there was a considerable urge to undertake constructive work in fields neglected by the government, or of types which the government would not, or could not, appreciate. After Independence, this differentiation has largely disappeared and there is consequently a steady movement towards routinizing motivations and conditions of work in all these fields and assimilating them into those of state, or quasi-state, employment.

In view of the great importance that now attaches to the business class, it is necessary to note some important aspects of the structure of business in India and of the operations of businessmen. In terms of the degree of concentration of economic power, Indian business houses can be compared with large corporations in advanced industrial countries. However, the Indian businessman represents an earlier socio-economic type. His roots are still in finance and commerce rather than in industry, and his organization is powerfully influenced by family and community ties. As a result, the public image of him is more that of a speculator and a piratical builder of financial empires than that of a modern innovating producer. Also, the largest agencies and alliances present pictures of family and community combines, for whom, nepotism appears as a natural phenomenon and the industrialization of the country as intended, chiefly, to benefit certain castes and communities.

The Indian businessman happens, at present, to be at a particularly unattractive stage of his development. He was never noted for any highly puritanical or moral qualities such as those exhibited by, say, the Calvinists or the Quakers. He has also not been imbued with that high sense of social and national responsibility which characterized the Japanese businessman in the Meiji era. However, some generations ago he was, at least, frugal and unostentatious. Recently, he has shed these characteristics and is now rapidly adopting the consumption standards of European and American businessmen. As a result, on the large surplus margins that state policy places in their hands, the high consumption standards of owners and managers of modern business constitute a first charge; and expense accounts, air-conditioned restaurants and hotels and night clubs figure as essential lubricants in the progress of Indian industrialization.

If what I have presented is not an untrue account of the leading groups within the urban and industrial life of our country, there should be no surprise at the increase of corruption within the community. The high success of operations of businessmen is guaranteed by government policy, and the guarantees are provided through a large number of regulations and practices framed by politicians and administered by officials. There is an enormous field for discretionary administrative decisions. In such a context, it is, but natural, for agents of administration to desire to share in the gains of business assured through their use of discretion. Where the whole framing of policy so flagrantly benefits a small class at national cost it is idle to talk in moral terms at particular participants in the process. The difficulty is not so much in finding the cause of corruption as in defining clearly what constitutes corruption. There could be such finely graded shades of give-and-take relationships between the various strata and categories—the political party, the politician, the official hierarchy, the businessman and his agents—and such narrowly differentiated types of indirect or direct transactions among them that it would be difficult to isolate and bring home a corruption charge, except in the case of the specially inept. It thus becomes clear why Shri Chintamanrao Deshmukh was unable to proceed far with his crusade against corruption on high.

One important effect of this total situation on other classes in society may be noted. All classes and groups have been encouraged and impelled to make the largest possible demands on the national product. As the state acknowledges the vital need to afford high incentives to the richest, and there is nobody to set an example of self-restraint, no blame can attach to any particular group. In the resulting scramble, those in the strongest positions get away with the largest shares and the weakest suffer the most.

One of the consequences of war-time inflation was the narrowing of various differentials; an opposite trend seems to have set in during the last decade. Whether within various strata in industry, or as between organized and unorganized industry, or between the rural and urban sectors, the differentials are increasing. There is also, similarly, unequal distribution of employment opportunities. All this must lead to a deepening of the sense of frustration over large sections of the disadvantaged and in the regions and economies that remain backward.

It has been claimed that traditionally we have been a contented, even though, a relatively poor, society. This, to the extent that it does not connote mere acquiescence or resignation, is related to the fact that no stigma attached to poverty amongst us. In countries where frontiers are open and opportunities unbounded, it is possible to equate a poor man with a lazy man. In our ancient and crowded land, poverty, flowing either from choice or from compelling, cramping circumstance, was held honourable or, at least, inevitable. Today, with an apparent change in our scale of values, the emergent problem is that of co-existence of the poor with the rich. If affluence is the hallmark of merit, how can the poor co-exist with the rich with self-respect? And if they cannot do this in our basically poor country, the vast majority of us are condemned to a perpetual feeling of frustration. But frustration breeds division and discord. Of what use is the glib talk about national integration if, while the display of wealth and luxury in metropolitan centres increases, the plan produces no visible impact on poverty-stricken regions, on backward classes, and in relation to the unemployed and the houseless? Basic poverty and unequal progress are at the root of most regional and class antagonisms about which we hear so much today.

All that I have said so far raises a highly controversial issue. It has been said that to hold that in a planned Indian society social justice and economic growth could move forward together step by step, is to dream, and that, in fact, rapid economic development in poor countries will remain peculiarly ugly to look at. Acceptance of this contention would, to my mind, be tantamount to acknowledging the inevitability of the ultimate victory of communism. A sensitive American visitor has expressed himself as follows in regard to the conditions in India: 'So every man in India loses his mind within the first three weeks, or manages not to see all the poverty and trouble anymore.' If I were convinced that under the existing set-up there was no alternative to the perpetuation of conditions thus described, I would have no hesitation in advocating its destruction by all means. I do not, however, believe in the invariable association of given attitudes, structures, and operations. For example, among the special features noted about Communist China by most observers are the plain living of her leaders, the absence of wasteful consumption, the focus of administrative arrangements on helping the poor and the backward, and the emphasis on utilizing idle manpower and on the dispersal of industry. I attach importance to all these. It is true that little effective attention is paid to any of them in the Indian plan; but I do not believe that they can be achieved only in a communist regime or only by the communist way.

The main ground for my continued optimism is the belief that the situation I have described has come about, not through deliberate or willing acceptance by our people of a changed scale of values but, through a somewhat special combination of circumstances which may not last. It happens that the values avowed by all political parties are exactly the opposite of those displayed in the developing industrial sector. However, there is another phenomenon to which I attach real weight. In the rural sector, actual economic policies are based on a fundamentally different approach. Tenancy legislation has not been oversensitive regarding property rights, and the widely adopted legislative measures regarding ceilings on land imply a philosophy of distribution and incentives which might well be termed radical. The pattern of policy, even in the rural sphere, is not uniform. For example, our flair, to put it mildly, for impropriety, is exhibited by the excessive price-support granted to producers of sugarcane while the prices of foodgrains are either allowed to fluctuate widely or are deliberately depressed. However, the land reforms of the last decade have definitely established an ideology in the large rural sector, which it should prove impossible to confine to that sector.

Even the most optimistic forecasts regarding possibilities of Indian economic development indicate that, at the end of 25 years, we shall continue to be poor by the world standards of today. In these circumstances, we can look forward to peaceful progress only if we attain a measure of social justice and a relatively egalitarian society at an early date. In circumstances like those of our country, high inequality is explosive not creative. Severe restraint on wasteful consumption through an overall ceiling on incomes, channelling all savings in the modern sector through public agencies, overhauling the structure of administrative services, and the operation of administrative machinery, are among the many reforms that have to be undertaken to achieve rapid and peaceful progress.

These are details. What is fundamental is to recapture the sense of struggle, to realize the magnitude of the task ahead and of the need for discipline and great self-restraint on the part of everybody.

Above all, emphasis has to be placed on co-operative endeavour, on the feeling of sharing by all; and this can be done only if the more fortunately placed and those who aspire to lead set an example. There has been much talk recently of perspective planning. I plead for a beginning to be made with a definition of the moral perspective in the light of which all persons on the threshold of life could be assured of being given opportunities to tackle meaningful tasks directed towards worthwhile ends.

15

Socio-economic Implications of the Existing Institutional Structure in Modern Business in India*

This note discusses briefly the socio-economic implications of the existing structure of the economy and the effects of its operations with special reference to the concept of the mixed economy and the role of private enterprise. Initially it needs to be made clear that the term 'private enterprise' is a comprehensive term including many types of economic activity. At least two distinct types need to be clearly separated in discussing the Indian situation. Firstly, there is private enterprise which may be identified with the type of private operation implicit in all classical economic analysis. In this the number of operators or units of activity in each sphere or field are so numerous and relatively of such size that no single operator could, by his action, affect the market, either for his products or for the resources which he has to acquire in order to produce. Over the major field of Indian economy, a very large number of small operators dispersed over wide regions, are fully in evidence. The constituent elements of agriculture and most primary productive activity in our economy, barring plantations, are small independent units widely dispersed over the country, which cannot, by their own individual operations, affect the working of market forces. The same holds good for the large sphere of traditional cottage industries, and even of small enterprises in the repair and other fields subsidiary to modern industry. In relation to the bulk of activity in

* Memorandum submitted, in April 1955, to the Panel of Economists, Government of India, Planning Commission, and published in *Papers Relating to the Formulation of the Second Five-Year Plan*, Government of India, Planning Commission, New Delhi, 1955, pp. 557–62.

commerce, transport, and most trades and professions, the small man is the typical operator: there has never been any suggestion from any quarter that this large field of private enterprise should be disturbed or included in the public sector. It has often been suggested that in many of these fields the small operating unit is, at present, technically and financially weak and does not, therefore, operate with efficiency in terms of either quality of product or unit cost of production, and the proposal has been made that the handicaps of the small independent operator be removed through co-operative effort of the independent individual units. Such co-operation may be possible in relation to finance, marketing, supply of materials, common technical services, or even in relation to production proper. But such co-operation, even when helped by the state or brought about through its agencies, will essentially leave the unit of production and economic operation as an independent unit. It will not be part of a state-socialistic-apparatus. That the co-operative unit has, and can be made to continue to have, the characteristics of an essentially independent private organization, though influenced by the state, has been agreed to by all. The Khadi Board, in its scheme of self-employment and dispersed economic activity, has recognized the need for the introduction of co-operative units and has included co-operative production in the self-employment category. No dispute between the sphere of private enterprise and the requirements of planned economic development does, therefore, arise in relation to this vast and essentially private and independent sector of the economy.

The dispute arises entirely in the field of, what may be correctly described as, not private enterprise but, monopoly capitalism. The sphere of operation of this is confined to certain restricted, though extremely important, sectors of economic activity within the country. These sectors are modern banking and insurance, large-scale machine industry, modern mining, plantations, foreign trade and internal wholesale trade, and financial operations such as those on the commodity and stock exchanges. The main point to be noticed about this field of economic activity is that, though, in relation to total occupied numbers and total number of economic units and establishments, its constituents are small, they are, by far, the most dominant in political, economic, and social terms in the country today. Secondly, in almost every single field of their operation a degree of concentration of economic resources and power is in evidence. Further, in almost all these spheres the influence of the comparatively restricted number of operators is further increased by trade associations and other devices of common action. A few facts are enumerated here: In the field of banking and insurance, a small number of units, less than a dozen in each case, control the larger part of total activity. In the field of large-scale industry, the bulk of the total field is occupied by a small number of units in a number of newer industries. Even in the older, established, and comparatively more dispersed activities, such as those of cotton textile or sugar manufacture, the number of units is not very large, and the number of units under the control of a small number of entrepreneurs forms a substantial portion of the total. In the field of foreign trade, there has been, as a result of methods of control developed during the last ten years, a large degree of freezing of the situation. The extent to which the whole business of export and import is concentrated in a few hands is not known to the public at large. But the data must be available with the relevant government authorities and it is of extreme and immediate importance that they should be collated and published for public information. It is understood that in this field, even more than in others discussed above, entry is difficult. Whatever precautions may be taken or regulations framed for issuing a small number of licences to new entrants, this field must be considered to be a closed field in which quasi-monopoly rules. There is no real free entry in the field and the operation in it is either a matter of older occupation which means continued privileged position or exercise of patronage by state authorities. Also, by definition, as the number in favour of which such patronage can be exercised as new entrants would be extremely limited, the operation of the new entry regulations can, at the most, amount to a small addition to the privileged class every year. The position is apparently different in internal wholesale trade, in the sense of entry not being formally restricted or closed. But even here, the facts point out to a large degree of concentration in a small number of hands.

The total effect of the existence of monopoly capitalism, in each separate sphere of modern economic activity in India, is further heightened by the device of the managing agency. This distorts the working of the economy in a peculiar manner. Instead of bringing about the ordinary vertical or horizontal extensions and combinations common in other countries, the system of the managing agency has fostered a development which is peculiarly Indian. This is that of concentration, in a small number of units, of power over a large number of disconnected fields of economic activity. The effect of this is that the restrictive influence of the operation of monopoly capitalism in each field is heightened many-fold by bringing together the power in many fields in single agencies. Together with the concentration in the managing agency goes the concentration in terms of regional and communal or social groups. This is an extremely important sociological phenomenon which cannot be ignored in Indian conditions. It cannot be ignored because the total picture that emerges is that of concentration of control over, and patronage resulting from, all modern finance, trade, and industry, in the hands of a comparatively small number of persons concentrated in particular social groups. The diffusion of the benefits of the rise of modern industry and commerce is, thus, severely restricted within the community, and the joint operation of socio-economic and political power makes certain groups so entrenched that social justice is denied and social peace cannot be guaranteed with the continuance of this state of affairs.

The peculiarity of the existing situation is that it cannot be tackled by breaking up monopoly capitalism. This is due, firstly, to the technical consideration. Economies of scale are here so important that the average unit has to be large, and in the total Indian context the number of operating units cannot be numerous. In common with the general trend everywhere capital formation now takes place to a very large extent within the operative business units and is only partly drawn from outside. This strengthens the position of existing units and helps the progress of further concentration. Further, the existence of such measures as price controls, allocation controls, production controls, etc., has made it impossible to think in terms of artificially stimulating competition among units in the field. In fact, all steps taken by the government during the last decade or so have been towards establishing a regime through which all the units in individual fields of modern activity have been drawn close together and have adopted comparatively uniform policies. The result has been that state policy has actively helped the full exploitation by the constituents of the field of modern business of their position as monopoly capitalists. A study of prices of such commodities as cloth or sugar during the post-war period fully exemplifies this.

It has been the experience in all countries, including the USA, that the operation of any policy of governmental regulation or direction, even that of stabilizing measures, tends to slow down the operation of competitive forces within an industry. This effect would be greatly accentuated with the launching of a plan of economic development. The need for closely directing the operation of the private sector would lead to the maintenance of conditions in which, on the one hand, risks would be largely eliminated and there would, on the other hand, be no large gains of, and scope for, a strenuous competitive drive towards expansion. Apart from the operation of the Regulation of Industries Act, the Second Five-Year Plan in India would define to a large extent, the number of new units to be established within the period in each activity and their location. There would thus be little element of free entry in modern manufacturing and mining, and the existing situation regulating entry into foreign trade would continue. In banking and insurance[1] present legal and regulatory systems favour greatly the large-sized concerns. There is a constant trend towards an increase in their importance, and smaller units are being weeded out or seeking amalgamation with one another in order to survive.

Modern industry, more than any other field in the Indian economy, is sheltered, protected, and helped at the cost of the tax-payer and the consumer. Most industrial activity has been protected directly or indirectly, at one time or another, and some of the most important industries have grown up entirely under protection. In the post-war period, apart from avowedly protective duties, the whole system of import restrictions and quotas has guarded the position of domestic industry. The most important activity launched during the war period has been thus protected, and the new ventures established, as in the case of the automobile industry, have been guaranteed a closed market in advance. The largest financial help given by the government has been available to this sector. The operations of the Industrial Finance Corporation, lending Rs 10 crores in five years, have benefited chiefly some of the largest units in this sector; and the government, which perhaps has never yet lent a single rupee free of interest for normal operations in the field of agriculture and small industry, has lent Rs 7.5 crores of rupees free of interest for a long period to a new corporation controlled by the biggest elements in this sector. The government has also, during the post-war period, helped many individual units in the field, by large loans on special terms, because they could not finance themselves on an adequate scale through the private capital market; it has also helped rehabilitation of individual concerns by lending services of government officers. It should be noted that all this help serves strictly private interest, in the sense that the improved positions that are built up in this way are sources of constant and increasing current and capital gains for private owners of the concerns. The current controversy over the compensation to be paid for shares of the Imperial Bank fully illumines the situation. All those concerns whose assets are being constantly protected and improved by public action will, on account of that very factor, demand high compensation from the public treasury in the event their socialization is decided upon.

The last point emphasizes an inevitable concomitant of planned development. Rationally planned development in an under-developed economy necessarily seeks to avoid duplication of effort and to concentrate capital intensive effort in as small a number of units as possible; it seeks, equally naturally, to protect such units as have been built up and to make their operation as free of risk as possible. All this gives the established units a position of advantage which is constantly growing with the development of the economy. These concerns are in a position similar to that of owners of favourably situated sites in an area of rapid urban development. And, given the decision to maintain the units in private hands, nothing can be done either to diminish the advantage of those units or to diffuse their gains.

This inability is due to two reasons. Firstly, it is due to the operation of a rational plan of development. As pointed out above, such a plan must, for reasons of economy and of convenience of direction and regulation, try to eliminate risks and operate through a small number of units. The whole approach of planned development differs radically from that of the highly competitive processes of the model of the free market, especially where units with large resources are concerned. The second reason why you cannot expect the state in India to break up the concentration of units or to exercise power in this sector is apparently the avowed policy of using them for formation of capital in the economy. If these units are to serve as centres of very substantial capital formation, their power and privileges have to be increased, not diminished. Special tax concessions given to new companies, general or selective incentives for ploughing back of capital, etc., are all devices advocated for rapid capital formation. Their result, if successful, is naturally that of helping the growth of total resources in the small number of units in the field.

Having granted the need for capital formation through these private enterprises, maintenance of large inequality in standards of consumption also becomes inevitable. Those in control of the field cannot be expected to form capital in units they control until after their expected consumption standards are satisfied. One of the most striking features of the history of the last fifteen years is the rapid increase in the standards of remuneration and of living of those connected with modern business in India. (The corresponding standards of those connected with modern foreign business in India are even higher.) That any regulatory or taxing devices can significantly affect these standards appears unlikely. After all, these glaringly high standards of remuneration and living are no more than a reflection of relative economic strength. In a large and poor country like India the vast majority of units of operation, whether independent workers or small establishments, operate with extremely slender resources of capital in fields where remuneration is low, conditions are insecure, and profits slender. In contrast, the fortunate few, in possession of the field of modern business, operate with comparatively vast resources and in secure conditions. The case of those engaged in modern business is not entirely exceptional. The position of those in the modern professions and selected services is somewhat similar. Indian society continues to be honeycombed with privilege. The privileged position, social and economic, of the urban intellectual classes is only slowly being undermined. But the attitudes of mind created by the era of privilege have yet to pass and they continue to be exemplified by concepts regarding rates of remuneration as incentives. That the University Grants Commission should consider raising the salaries of university professors as the most potent instrument of improving university teaching is sufficient commentary on current ideology. Entry into the ranks of urban educated classes is now vastly easier as compared with entry into modern business. Therefore, the position, in relation to remuneration and standard of living, among the upper strata of these classes has ceased to be as unique as that in modern business. As a fact, one could say that this movement among the two classes has taken a contrary direction during the last fifteen years. While the privilege and strength of the one class has sensibly diminished—though far from vanished—that of the other has greatly increased, and the trend in the latter case cannot be reversed because of the logic of a plan of development, and the policy regarding formation of capital.

Emphasis has been placed above on capital formation as it is obvious that this can be the only reason for maintaining privileged private enterprise in the modern sector. Some economists have justified high monopolistic gains because of the innovating service of the entrepreneurial class. Such innovation is not required in an economy with a backward technique. The task of the entrepreneurs is not so much to innovate as to adapt and imitate. Moreover, the Indian entrepreneur, whatever his high skill as financier or speculator, has not been specially marked for progress in production technique or high average productive efficiency. Indeed, as the events leading up to the promulgation of the Managing Agency Ordinance, and recent enquiries into management of some groups, have shown, financial acumen has often been associated with low standards of production management. To all this may be added the consideration that the ordinary risks of business have been greatly diminished because of the policy of the government and will be further diminished with the progress of a plan of development.

The whole of this discussion emphasizes the fundamental incompatibility of two aspects of the industrial policy resolution of 1948: one, the formation of capital through modern private enterprise, and two, preventing the concentration of wealth and economic power. If any fiscal or other measures are used to achieve the second objective, the first must be defeated, and the achievement of the first objective must equally inevitably increase concentration. Though no formal enquiry has been conducted into the matter, there appear general indications that concentration has increased, and whether it increases further or not, considerable concentration, together with the entrenched position and power of particular social groups, must be a continued feature of the economic situation as long as private enterprise occupies the strategic position in modern business that it does today.

The alternatives to the existing position are two. Firstly, the steady extension of the public sector so as to embrace more and more of modern business activity within it. Once no great importance is attached to the private capital market, the financial problem presented by such an extension of the public sector presents no great difficulty. The problem of technical personnel or equipment is also not large. The crucial consideration here is that of efficiency of management of business units in the public sector. This is, undoubtedly, a serious and complex issue. However, the whole progress of planned development towards a socialistic pattern depends on its solution, and must be tackled in any case. The second alternative is to regulate operation of the units in the private sector in the same manner as it was done in the UK and the USA during the war. This would lead to the prevention of increase in the concentration of resources and of the exploitation by the units of their quasi-monopolistic position. In such cases, capital formation would be not in private hands but in those of public authorities, and the second alternative can be looked upon partially as the transitional stage to the first.

NOTE

1. This refers to the situation before the nationalization of life insurance in 1956.

16
Notes on Rural Industrialization*

RURAL INDUSTRIALIZATION

This brief note pleads for the adoption of an entirely changed approach to the problem of rural industrialization. The current approach is the result of historical developments. Various Boards, such as the Khadi, the Handicrafts, the Handloom, etc., and other authorities have operated in this field for some years. The Rural Industrialization Committee was established chiefly to co-ordinate and unify the work of these various authorities. Therefore, the work of the Committee has been taken to be coterminous with that of these authorities, and the approach of the Committee and its methods of work have also been appropriately determined. I consider this to be unsatisfactory.

I conceive of rural industrialization to be one of the major economic and social objectives of the plan of economic development. Therefore, it can be achieved only if the entire development plan, in particular, the entire plan of industrialization, is framed so as to attain this objective. No substantial results can be achieved, in the short run, with the present approach and the areas of efforts at rural industrialization; and, in the long run, present trends in policy relating to large industry will inevitably lead to a highly urbanized and capital intensive modern industry and a poor, non-industrial countryside. I assume that the objective of rural industrialization implies industrialization of the country as widely dispersed, on as small a scale, with as high an employment potential, as is compatible with an efficient technique and the requirements of the process of development. Existing

* These notes were submitted to the Rural Industries Planning Committee of the Planning Commission, Government of India. The first was submitted on 20 July 1963; the second on 18 November 1963; and the third on 19 December 1963. Published in *Artha Vijnana*, ,Vol. 6, No. 1, March 1964.

knowledge in regard to planning techniques indicates no easy or quick solutions of this problem. It has, therefore, to be approached tentatively and bit by bit.

Every decision made in relation to the allocation of resources to large industry and to the licensing of industrial establishments shapes, in part, the future pattern of industrialization of the country. The work of the Development Wing is an important factor in determining future arrangements, and recently, policies regarding foreign collaboration and export incentives have also assumed importance in this context. At present it does not appear that any of the above are concerned with the overall objective of rural industrialization. In the circumstances, their activities result in the creation of establishments comparable in size of operations and intensity of capital investment to those of highly industrialized countries. With present availability of external economies, the location pattern of these establishments favours metropolitan areas and large cities. Inevitably, the future pattern of growth of these activities, and activities subsidiary and complementary to them, will also be shaped similarly as regards technique, scale, and location.

Apart from the effects of existing arrangements and practices in the long run, they have important immediate consequences also. The most notable of these is in relation to the availability of materials. Perhaps the most important base for 'rural industrialization', immediately, is the raw material available in rural areas. If this is used up in modern large-scale urban industry, 'rural industrialization' will become well-nigh impossible. This is happening at present, and, to my knowledge, no attention is being paid to the ultimate effects of the steps that are being taken. For example, the molasses and bagasse produced by the sugar industry are planned to be absorbed by modern large-scale industry. I have heard of a proposal for a very large plant for onion dehydration put up with foreign collaboration. In the absence of a clear formulation of overall policy, it is not surprising that this should happen. The obvious step that a technologist would think of is the setting-up of a unit with the most advanced techniques and on the largest possible scale. He will consider alternatives only if policy directives ask him to do so.

There is, I believe, only one case in which an overall policy decision has significantly affected industrial development. This is that of the mill cloth industry, though even here certain loopholes have been created in the name of export incentives. In the cloth industry, the action has been largely negative. This is because the idea of the Common Production Programme accepted since the First Plan has never been seriously followed up. The approach of the Common Production plan has, however, only limited applicability. It applies only to industries where there already exist, side by side, establishments with traditional and modern techniques. Looking to the future, the larger area to be covered will be that of non-traditional products. Hence, arrangements must be made which will lead to the establishment of a modern industry, with appropriate scale and location, in new lines of production also. These arrangements will have to be incorporated in the planning of the total plan of industrialization.

Other requirements of 'rural industrialization' may also be noted. The plan for the spread of facilities is among the most important of these. The attraction of metropolitan centres and large cities is a universal economic phenomenon. Every scheme of dispersed regional development has to take account of this and provide, as liberally as possible, for dispersed transport, water, power, and such other facilities. At present, in India, the older bias in favour of concentrating expenditure on the major routes and centres persists. The plans in this regard have to be recast. But doing this inevitably raises a knotty problem. It is obvious that our scanty resources will permit only of a limited degree of dispersal of facilities. Hence, an interpretation or definition of rural industrialization must be attempted in this context. Rural industrialization must be planned around a series of centres in the countryside. How large or small, how close or dispersed these centres should be, will have to be thought out in relation to ultimate objectives and immediate practicability. This may mean a phased programme which begins with fewer and larger centres but in which provision is made for gradual spreading out.

One of the most vital needs of a plan of rural industrialization is the planning of research activity, especially technological, which could assist the process. The orientation of technological research in advanced industrial countries is necessarily based on the existing situation in them as regards relative availability of capital and labour. Even so, in many of these countries, developments such as automation are creating serious transitional employment difficulties. For us to accept, as we are doing, their technical framework without discrimination or adaptation is to invite very serious trouble. This is not a problem of any particular industry or technique but affects all. The requirement could be met only by reorienting all research activity and all development policy in relation to industrialization.

There is one aspect of research activity to which special attention may be drawn in connection with rural industrialization. It is of developing the scrub, the waste, and the forest lands for production of a variety of materials which could become the base of rural industry. Rural industrialization has to be based, to a large extent, on locally available raw material, and the presently neglected and fast deteriorating non-arable areas appear capable of significantly increasing the supply of such material.

In view of the total Indian situation it is not only desirable but also highly necessary that strenuous attempts be made to build up a dispersed, relatively small-scale but efficient industrial structure in India. This objective, which I take to be rural industrialization, cannot, however, be easily attained. For its attainment requires leaving the path of the line of least resistance—which is currently popular and adopted in India—and making a strenuous effort to guide industrial and economic development. In many aspects of this effort we shall find little guidance elsewhere and must therefore be ready to experiment and make tentative approaches on our own. Success, in this effort, may be attained only if it is comprehensive and earnest. The immediate requirement is, therefore, to recast the whole thinking regarding industrialization,[1] foreign collaboration, transport, and other economic overheads, development, research activity, etc., in the light of the requirement of the objective of rural industrialization.

The definition of rural industrialization has to be appropriately widened, and the immediate programme of the Rural Industrialization Committee must cover many more activities than at present. Some idea of the widened field may be given by enumerating the main directions in which immediate activity should be planned. They appear to be:

1. The traditional village and urban artisan and handicraft industries. Rehabilitation and protection of these can be attempted only on a new, technically and economically sound base together with an operative programme of continuous technical and economic progress in the future.

2. The processing and transformation of agricultural produce, of materials that can be grown on scrub, waste, forest lands, etc., and of other primary production. The attempt here should be to embrace, within an efficient co-operative organization, all existing activity, and, even more importantly, to extend the scope of activity and products by continuous research in techniques and in markets.

3. The rural building and construction activity. This ought to provide an extremely important field for rural industrialization. The larger employment works programmes that are contemplated should provide an important market for a variety of instruments, implements, and other intermediate goods. This market can be catered for by small-scale, dispersed rural industry. Similarly, in this context, attention ought to be paid to improved village layouts and housing, and this again should create an important essential local market.

4. New consumer goods are continuously being introduced in rural areas; there are also many directions in which attempts at standardization of products, particularly in the food industries, could be made. This is a field especially appropriate for rural industrialization.

5. There is considerable current competition between states, and among districts within a state, in relation to the location of units of large industry. The location of a large industrial unit in a particular place can benefit the neighbourhood significantly, only if certain measures are taken. These measures are those required for encouraging the establishment

of small-scale units producing parts and catering for the ancillary and subsidiary requirements of the large unit. Such measures can be taken only if, in the licensing of enterprises, and, in the planning of their future operations, the objective of rural industrialization is constantly paid attention to.

PLANS FOR RURAL INDUSTRIALIZATION

The progress of the work of the Rural Industrialization Committee raises a number of points to which I desire to draw attention in this note. The work of the surveys is over. The reports of the surveys have been prepared and plans of action on the basis of the survey material have either just been completed or are in the process of completion. It is not necessary to say anything regarding the surveys except that they appear to have lacked a definite objective. The result is that the reports of the surveys are like the usual official compilations of data, collected chiefly from official sources and embodying a great deal of programme and target material together with expenditure achievements, but containing nothing that can be considered helpful in evaluation. Because of the lack of definitive objectives, no effort to collect material on any aspect that might have particular interest in the future plans has been made. The reports of the surveys, therefore, are not very promising material from which to start the future plans of industrialization.

What I want to say in this note refers mainly to plans for future action which are in the process of being made. In this regard I would set down a set of propositions: In the first instance, all plans for the future ought to take fully into account the experience in the recent past of related schemes and programmes operating in the area for which future plans are being prepared. To ignore this experience is to court failure. The Khadi Board, the Industries Department, the Co-operative Department, the Small Industries Centres, the Handloom Board have all had a variety of schemes in operation for many years past in most districts of the country. If the new plan of rural industrialization is to do no more than to extend the same types of schemes, perhaps more intensively, this hardly justifies bringing into existence an elaborate organization for the purpose. What I say above applies to schemes for the establishment of new industries as well as to those regarding training, the provision of common facilities, etc. Secondly, a plan for any area prepared by the Rural Industrialization Committee must embody, within itself, a concept of a strategy for industrialization. I use the term 'strategy' to cover a number of aspects: What things are taken up first and why; how, in a programme of action, not only the chronological sequence, but also the possible spatial spread of activities is determined or expected to come about, which parts and elements of these are crucial and to be externally established, and which are considered as necessary consequences or by-products; how are finance, technical know-how, organization, and entrepreneurship linked together in any sphere of activity, and in what manner, and for what reasons, the relations between these would differ from activity to activity; these are the crucial initial problems and they must be thought through to a minimum extent at the very start. These sorts of queries, raised and resolved in relation to various aspects of programmes of industrialization, will determine a possible route of the future process; and the strategy of industrialization consists in acting at important crucial points along the route so that the whole process unfolds itself in due course. The strategy may, in the initial stage, be very crude, highly hypothetical, and speculative. The important point is that no plan of action in an area like this can be logically prepared or can hope to succeed unless there has been some initial thinking on strategy in the above sense.

A third important point is this: It appears to me that the whole set of plans of rural industrialization takes an extremely short-term view of the problem. One of the most fundamental considerations in rural decentralization is that it cannot be effectively achieved without very considerable decentralization of socio-economic overheads. The plans of rural industrialization made at present give no attention whatsoever to whether, in the particular area, the general transport, power, water supply, education, and other facilities are adequate or inadequate, are well spaced or ill-spaced, etc. The result is that the plan of industrialization will help to perpetuate the present, usually unsatisfactory, arrangements. For example, if there are a number of potential important centres which are without proper intercommunication facilities or power and water resources, the plan will bypass them and suggest something at other centres rather than make the initial provision of the proper spread of socio-economic overheads. I do not know whether this comes because of the circumscribed sphere of action and powers of the Rural Industrialization Committee, or a narrow view taken of their functions by those who prepare the plans. Anyway, this feature makes the entire planning process highly defective.

Fourthly, there is an amazing lack of integration and co-ordination within the plan. This appears, largely, to be due to the planners having to operate with schemes of various boards and authorities in the form in which they are at present put. No adjustment or reorientation, etc., for the purpose of making a particular coherent plan, appears to be possible. This is as if one is asked to produce a good out of standard parts which have been fashioned for somewhat different purposes. It appears that even the current Third Five-Year Plan schemes and programmes in the area are treated as unchangeable. The result is that the plan of rural industrialization becomes usually no more than putting in some fresh schemes and programmes in addition to the old ones in any given area. It stands to reason that if a new experimental approach is to be given a chance of success, the whole field of operation in the area must be open to the planner. He must have not only the authority to pick and to choose and to modify, but also to cut out or to scrap, and he must be in a position to co-ordinate all effort over the entire field.

What I have said so far may appear, chiefly, as critical and negative. I would, therefore, add some points by way of constructing an alternative approach. I began with the concept of strategy. Each area-plan should have a strategy which may, and ordinarily should, differ from area to area. Secondly, for building up the main component parts, the total field should be analysed in a significant manner. I consider the following components as the most significant units in relation to which to build:

1. Traditional handicrafts and artisan industries of the area
2. Agricultural processing activity
3. Activity connected with animal husbandry and forest produce
4. Industries related to building and construction activity—present and potential
5. Any core of mechanical industry around which a complex of engineering industries could be thought of
6. Consumer goods industries, in particular, clothing, footwear, and food industries of all kinds

These components would have some representatives in all areas. In particular areas, other specialized components may be added. I think it would be a distinct advantage to try and put together the programme on the basis of a group of activities derived from some such classification as suggested above rather than to think in terms of individual industries and programmes.

There must be a lot of straight thinking done in relation to the very large group of industries included in the first class above. To repeat, in these cases, programmes of training, assistance, and establishment which have repeatedly failed before is deliberately to misuse national resources. The village potter and the village tanner are the most notorious instances of failure. In relation to any particular area, the future programme must be based on a correct evaluation of past performances and realistic prospects of future developments.

The building and construction industries, I should like to link up, specifically, to two aspects of development. The first is the works programme which has been at least notionally established, and the second is the concept of the reconstruction of the villages and of village layouts and rural housing. There is also a need for proper recognition of the large potential that lies in this direction.

In relation to agricultural processing, I would insist that unless specifically proved to the contrary, it should be assumed that all this would be undertaken by the co-operatives. It is surprising to find that programmes of processing in even the Maharashtra area have been unnecessarily left to private enterprises. For the Maharashtra State, I would make a suggestion in this connection. All programmes in the agriculture, animal husbandry and forest produce sectors in all areas in Maharashtra, which the Committee thinks feasible, should be immediately turned over to the Industries Commission of the Maharashtra State Co-operative Bank. I shall see to it that the Commission takes action through its own promotional agencies to begin with the work of organization in all cases.

It is, perhaps, a matter falling within 'strategy' to consider the mutual relations of training, technical assistance, provision of common facilities, and the establishment of industry. The relation may also be likened to the hen and egg conundrum. However, in each particular situation, an appropriate view must be taken of the relation for determining programmes of action. The large failures of previous efforts at training must be taken note of in this context. It does not appear to be advisable to open large centres for training in advance of the establishment of a significant number of units. There is sufficient dispersal of training-facilities now to ensure that the minimum complement required to start initial units could be trained elsewhere and, partly, also recruited from elsewhere. It is only when a certain stage is reached in development that training facilities on the spot should be contemplated. The provision may be elastic enough to enable advancement in case of especially rapid development. Secondly, it is important to remember that a decision taken to locate a large common-facilities centre involves pre-determining a locational pattern and perhaps, in retrospect, giving it a twist. Unless, therefore, there is something in the centrality of location, availability of resources, etc., to suggest overwhelming choice in favour of a particular place, any substantial investment in such things as a common-facilities centre should follow the establishment of some units as a result of other programmes rather than precede them. It may be unkind to suggest this, but one often wonders whether the priority given to large programmes of training, or of common facilities, in advance of the establishment of industries, is not due to the ease with which expenditure can be incurred on these and expenditure targets easily reached in early years. This remark is introduced in order to emphasize the final point that this programme will fail as dismally as its precursors unless it is able, from the beginning, to rise above the mania of target-making and of expenditure performance.

INTERMEDIATE TECHNOLOGY

It is good that the Planning Commission is holding a seminar of technicians connected with intermediate technology. The seminar will presumably consider problems of planning systematic research and co-ordination in this field. It appears to me that before this can be done successfully, it is necessary to be clear as to what is meant by intermediate technology and what place it occupies in the total development plan, especially in relation to the plan of industrialization. The term 'intermediate' denotes a stage somewhere between the 'advanced' and the 'backward'. In India, the 'backward' may be identified with the technology of traditional Indian industry—urban and rural—and the 'advanced', with the technology of the industrially developed countries of the West. The 'intermediate' presumably lies somewhere between the two. A more concrete concept of the intermediate may be obtained if we attempt to understand why the adoption of intermediate technology is considered important in India and how such a technology is expected to evolve or develop.

The need to think in terms of intermediate technology appears to arise primarily from the redundancy of human labour in the country and the inability of the economy to use its labour resources in anything like a full or adequate measure. Important related factors are: a very high proportion of those living in rural areas and engaged in agriculture and other primary occupations, a high rate of increase of population, the generally unfavourable land to man ratio, and the desirability, for better organization of agricultural production, of reducing numbers currently employed in agriculture. All these circumstances call for the creation, on a very large scale, of new non-farm employment opportunities. This can be done on a long-term, stable basis only through the establishment of an industrial base of minimum size and strength. Further, in view of the present distribution of the population and the paucity of capital resources, the industrial complex to be built up has to consist of very large numbers of dispersed establishments capable of creating numerous employment opportunities in relation to capital investment. A subsidiary, but not un-important, consideration is the fate of the large numbers engaged, even today, in traditional small-scale industries—rural and urban. The total situation makes it urgent that the route of development be so planned that significant numbers of these are not rendered unemployed before alternative avenues of employment are opened for them and that, as far as possible, the investment in skills and capital equipment in the traditional industry are utilized in plans of development of industry in the future.

Recent experience gives further support to the analysis of requirements set out above. In the first instance, it has been increasingly emphasized that, in under-developed economies, the transmission of economic forces is very slow and partial. As a result, the creation of a small number of centres of advanced industry in a country fails to have any significant impact on the bulk of the rural masses and areas in the rest of the country and does not initiate a process of transformation which embraces, within any reasonable time-span, the whole of the economy. In addition, it appears that implanting a relatively small element of highly advanced modern business, including industry, within an economy, often leads to the development of a phenomenon often described as a dual economy. This implies the semi-permanent existence of two parallel sectors within the same economy, one characterized by richness of resources, advanced techniques, and economic progress, and the other by poverty, backwardness, and stagnation. Exchange relations between these two spheres would then take on the exploitative character which marked the exchange between industrialized metropolitan countries and their predominantly agricultural dependencies in the colonial era. It may thus happen that the two diverge and become antagonized instead of merging and progressing together.

Everything thus points to the desirability, nay urgency, of initiating widespread industrial development in all regions of the country which will prevent accentuation of dualistic features within the economy and make for concerted and uniform economic progress. This I take to be the justification and purpose of any programme of 'rural industrialization'. It is necessary to set this out because the scientists and the technicians must be made fully aware of what is expected out of the adoption of 'intermediate technology'. Their efforts must be directed towards the selection and development of those procedures and techniques which can serve the given aims.

Does the definition of aims and purposes make possible any generalizations as to the characteristics of intermediate technology? The broadest generalization one can make is about scale. The smallest scale compatible with efficient production is an obvious desideratum, and a significant step in this direction is expected of all intermediate technology. Negatively, intermediate technology would also be expected to keep investment in fixed capital as low as possible; this would be balanced by there being no special emphasis on economy in inputs of labour, especially of those types which are not scarce in under-developed economies. These conditions arise out of the relative paucity of capital, the tendency for fixed capital cost per unit of product to rise with diminution of scale, and the redundancy of labour and its low cost. It is in this context that the problem of use of power may also become important.

Because of undeveloped communications and relatively high transport costs, most situations in which intermediate technology is adopted are characterized by cut-up and limited markets. Production units within these would be protected to some extent from outside competition by the transport costs and by any preferences for local products that they are able to establish. The permissible margin, in costs per unit of product, between advanced and intermediate technology would thus be indicated chiefly by the saving on transport, marketing, etc., costs, any diminution in quality, such as finishing, packing, tolerated by customer in favour of the local product, and by lower labour costs.

Economic development may be defined as the effort to increase the national product, absolute and per capita, by continuously adding to national resources and by making more efficient use of them. An advanced technology is, by definition, one that makes a more efficient use of resources than a backward one. Therefore, economic development is, in a sense, identified with adoption of more and more advanced technology. However, as indicated above, it may neither be possible, nor desirable, to adopt the most advanced technology available in many areas of the economy, and effort has to be made to discover the technology appropriate to a particular field in the context of both the general and the specific economic situation. Where this process of adaptation has to be very widespread and appears likely to persist for a long period of time, it is possible to talk in terms of evolution or development of intermediate technology or research and experimentation in that behalf.

From the point of view of a non-technician, the following approaches to the development of intermediate technology appear to be possible. One approach may be to start with existing techniques in traditional industry and to utilize knowledge of advanced techniques to transform them suitably. Transformation implies retaining some elements in existing equipment, skills, and procedures. If there existed possibilities of a continuous process of transformation so that starting from the traditional technique one could, through continuous change, reach the most advanced technology, the problem would be relatively easy. It would reduce itself to that of choosing, for any industry, for a time and place, a particular position on the continuum as the most suitable. In fact, however, such a situation exists in almost no field, and each important advance in technology renders previous plant and equipment, for the most part, obsolescent. There may, however, exist, limited possibilities of improving traditional technologies so as to keep their operations, at least in part, viable. This process of improvement of traditional technology is extremely important, particularly for that part of the transition in which a holding operation for preventing added technological unemployment appears to be necessary. It is doubtful, however, whether such modification of traditional techniques would be accepted as resulting in intermediate technology.

Another approach would be to start from the end of the most advanced technology and to adapt and adjust so as to meet the requirements of the intermediate. The chief requirements of this, as defined above, are (i) small scale and (ii) change in the proportions of capital and labour inputs; a priori, the process appears to have two prominent components. First is the analysis of the different units and processes in the total plant, equipment, and operations. The analysis would initially aim at determining the extent to which the task of adaptation and adjustment of technique could be undertaken, relatively independently, for separate parts or units. Next, on the basis of a given structure of wage rates and availability of various types of labour, the relative advantages of full or partial adoption of advanced technology for the various parts could be calculated. It is this analysis that would uncover possibilities of maximizing inputs of low-cost labour and of saving on capital. The second component of the process would be the adjustment of the technique and equipment, to the extent they are to be adopted, to a smaller or the smallest scale compatible with efficient and economic production. In some cases, the process would also involve adjustment to special local circumstances such as the type of fuel or power available.

A third, possible approach may be to conduct experimentation and research in a direct effort to establish intermediate technology. However, for this to be fruitfully undertaken, it would be necessary to define, for the scientist and the technician, the limiting economic circumstances. These are, chiefly, the scale of operations aimed at and the relative costs of capital and labour and the scale of their inputs—possible or desirable. Such direct effort at establishing intermediate technology would undoubtedly be conducted against the background of knowledge of advanced technology in the field. However, it could cover a much wider range of possibilities than the effort through the adjustment and adaptation approach.

It should be clear that the establishment, of what is called intermediate technology, is not a once-for-all process. It is related, on the one hand, to current advance in technology and, on the other, to changing economic circumstances, particularly the widening of markets and change in the relative costs and availabilities of labour and capital. Therefore, the evolution and adoption of any type or scale of intermediate technology has to be considered as essentially a transitional stage, though, in the existing situation in India, this transitional stage promises to be fairly long drawn out. The continuous changes in the situation to be visualized, in the future, are mainly: (i) the adoption, in some areas, of fully advanced technology, and (ii) the readjustments in intermediate technology itself, rendered necessary by the total change in the situation, technological and economic.

It follows that any consideration of intermediate technology cannot be conducted in vacuo or by itself; it must be constantly, and meaningfully, related to the total situation. It must be related to technology, both traditional and advanced, to the general economic situation, the plans of development, and to special economic conditions within the particular field of application. If one takes the view that, today, the most important and urgent technological problem confronting India is that of the adaptation of advanced technology to Indian economic circumstances, it is obvious that the bulk of talent and finance in the technological field must be directed towards this effort. The setting-up, or getting-together, of a small number of inadequately staffed and financed units for this purpose is altogether insufficient. The main attention of the personnel on the applied side of National Laboratories, technical institutes, and the large university departments must be concentrated on this work. The advancement of advanced technology in every field is being adequately pursued in the developed countries; the special adaptation and adjustments required in India are not, and are not likely to be, given attention in any other country. They must, therefore, obtain the highest priority in our plans. Intermediate technology should become a national concern and not as at present, a neglected field assigned to a small number of specialists, set apart.

Intermediate technology is closely connected, not only with all technological work in the country but also, perhaps even more closely, with all planning effort. No plan of industrialization, which does not pay the fullest attention to it, can be meaningful. In fact, as pointed out above, the changing circumstances, against whose background intermediate technology has to be evolved, are shaped by the plans. Per contra, realistic planning regarding the route and pace of industrialization must be powerfully influenced by the possibilities and achievements in the direction of intermediate technology. There will be a group of activities, e.g., certain basic industries, capital goods industries, public utilities, etc., in relation to which the adoption of intermediate technology may not be considered. For the rest, the effort must be organized in relation to particular aspects and phases of the plan and the best way of doing this is to organize it not as a distinct separate activity but as part of a plan covering an entire field or aspect. The concept of the Common Production already holds the field. This has not only to be elaborated but also to be made operational. Intermediate technology will obviously find an appropriate place in dynamic common production plans. I would suggest the evolution of a parallel concept of a 'common utilization plan'. By this I mean, taking stock of the total supply of industrial primary and other materials within the country and planning their allocation to various processes of transformation and industrial use. The planning will include, both, the processing of primary products and their later utilization. In relation to intermediate technology, the planning of the total utilization of primary products of agriculture, animal husbandry, forest, etc., whose supplies are available dispersed in rural areas, is especially important. In some of these cases, common utilization plans would be partial counterparts of common production plans, but not in others. The introduction of the concept of common utilization plans is especially important in the case of commodities not touched by common production plans, as for example, bamboo and agave fibre, bagasse and molasses, hides and bones.

The evolution of intermediate technology and a proper definition of its position and function would also be facilitated by planning in relation to a whole group of activities such as building and construction trades. The extent to which the utilization of local materials and local labour can be maximized, while maintaining efficient and economic production through selective adaptation of technological advance, must be established in detail in typical local situations. However, certain broad, common approaches could also be evolved if intensive attention is given by teams of technicians to this widespread and universally important field of economic activity.

As described above, the process of evolving and adopting intermediate technology is a dynamic process which should be the centre of interest of the plan of industrialization of the country. It should claim the attention, in an important way, of the ablest scientists and technicians in the country, and planning in relation to it should be undertaken through integrated planning of whole aspects and fields of industrial development. The effort today is, both, highly inadequate and narrow. The division of jurisdiction in a number of separate Boards, each having different ideas and approaches, has been disastrous. Programmes of action, embodied in rigid schemes, miss the essential dynamics of the situation. The input of scientific and technical talent has been meagre and sectionalized. While, therefore, the move to call together technicians engaged in related effort is welcome, it will bear fruit only if it is the first step in a much more comprehensive and large-scale plan of action.

NOTE

1. Some aspects of the reorientation on the industrial plan, required for this purpose, have been discussed in a note on 'An Approach to Indian Planning', see p. 53.

17

Planning for Agricultural Development in India*

I shall begin with a brief review of the present position of agricultural planning in India. I hold that there is little of, what might properly be called, planning, practised today in this country; and there is less of it in agriculture than in most other areas of economic activity. I also hold that in order to achieve any measure of success in planned, rapid, economic development, an attempt must be made to plan the effort as much as possible, in the domain of agriculture also. My statement regarding the existing absence of planning in Indian agriculture is not intended to suggest that no efforts at development of agriculture, in a variety of directions, are being currently made or that a number of these efforts have not met with success, large or small. Only, I feel it necessary to distinguish carefully between generalized developmental effort and specific planned action.

The concept of a programme for agriculture is old and dates, in some respects, from the time of the famines of the last quarter of the nineteenth century. In their present form, most developmental programmes emerged, chiefly, during the days of the diarchy of the inter-war period. More specifically, one may refer to the monumental report of the Royal Commission on Agriculture as providing an important landmark in their evolution. The next stage was the Grow More Food (GMF) campaign of the war and the post-war periods and it is, I believe, correct to state that, both, in the formulation of the constituent programmes and in the measurement of their results, little change in the procedures evolved in the

* Technical address at the Thirteenth Annual Conference of the Indian Society of Agricultural Statistics held in Poona on 8 January 1960. Published in *Planning and Economic Policy in India*, D.R. Gadgil, GIPE, Poona, 1962, pp. 215–34.

GMF campaign has been made by the adoption of the First or the Second Five-Year Plans.

Two features of the approach evolved in the GMF era, and continued today, are important from the point of view of planning. The first is that the programme is conceived of as consisting of a series of independent developmental activities. ...(pp. 215, 216)

The second feature logically followed from this approach of thinking in terms of the overall effects of nationwide programmes. It was that the targets are first obtained for the country or the state and then broken down notionally for smaller areas. ...(p. 216)

Even for the country as a whole, the targets produced through the putting together of the expected results of a number of programmes of development have little significance. ...(p. 216)

The Planning Commission, when putting forward the Second Five-Year Plan, evidently, realized the limitations of this approach and decided to modify it. The intentions or aspirations of the Planning Commission are indicated by the following extract from the Second Five-Year Plan.

> Despite the uncertainties to which agriculture is necessarily subject, it is important that a more studied effort to introduce a planned approach to agricultural development should be made. The main elements in agricultural planning are:
>
> 1. Planning of land use;
> 2. Determination of targets, both long-term and short-term;
> 3. Linking up of development programmes and Government assistance to production targets and the land use plan, including allocation of fertilizers, etc., according to plan; and
> 4. An appropriate price-policy.
>
> Each district and, in particular, each national extension and community development project area should have a carefully worked out agricultural plan. This should indicate for villages the targets to be aimed at, the broad distribution of land between different uses, and the programme of development. Within the framework of an overall price-policy such as has been outlined in an earlier chapter, such local plans will be valuable steps leading to more careful planning for States and regions and for the country as a whole.

In fact, however, no effect was given to any of the above proposals contained in the Second Five-Year Plan, and the approach and the procedures established in the First Five-Year Plan period, and earlier, continue to be followed till this day. ...(p. 217)

The approach to agricultural planning through framing national schemes of development suffers from two major defects. In the first instance, it fails to provide for the full use of development potentials. Schemes formulated with reference to general or average situations must prove inapplicable or inappropriate, in varying measures, in particular situations. Even more, in special circumstances, the scheme-approach may itself prove wrong, and something not even provided for in the general schemes may have to be attempted. ...(p. 218)

The second, equally important defect of this approach is that it leads to a very low degree of correspondence between expectation and achievement in agricultural planning. ...(p. 218)

A plan, which attempts a co-ordinated development of all sectors of the economy, in all regions and locations, must attain a high degree of specificity. It must not only attempt a full use of the potential, but it must also ensure that the planned development of specific resources in each sector is properly dovetailed with use or consumption in the developmental plans of other sectors. There is, thus, the need for a large degree of correspondence between expectations and achievements in, both, production resource plans and area plans if the developmental process is to move with reasonable smoothness. But this can happen only if the present approach is reversed and the agricultural plan is derived, in the main, through the building up and the putting together of plans originally framed locally rather than through a break-down of programmes and estimates framed at the national level. ...(p. 218)

At the same time, a national plan of economic development is much more than a summation of village plans, and no village plan would itself be possible without the general framework provided by a national plan. Planning has, therefore, been rightly called a two-way process. ...(p. 219)

The two-way process in planning is important in all sectors; however, its need is specially great in the peculiar circumstances of Indian agriculture. Where government directly controls any activity, planning by government is related, in the main, to the efficiency of government administrative machinery. Planning, in the non-government areas, is related to activity on the part of units not under direct control of the government. Such units can be acted upon in a variety of ways by the government. They may be directed, they may be induced, they may be encouraged, or they may be coerced.... In the sphere of agriculture, however, not only are the production units almost all non-governmental, but also mostly small and extremely numerous. Moreover, they are inevitably dispersed over the whole of the area of the country. ... Each family farmer conducts his business separately, and the ultimate results, in terms of total agricultural production, are the added results of the activities of millions of family farmers all over the country. It is their decisions and their actions that have to be influenced; and planning for agriculture necessarily means planning to induce, or influence, this innumerable body of individual, small entrepreneurs to take the decisions and perform the actions that are expected to give the desired results. ...(pp. 219, 220)

In case full utilization of water-resources provided by a work of irrigation is sought early, much more action must be planned and executed than the mere construction of the irrigation work. This planning in advance includes the supply of water to the ultimate user in the field, proposals for the pattern of future land-utilization with rotations of crops and appropriate tested varieties established for use in particular circumstances, the technical training of the cultivator in the adoption of the new programmes, and the supply to him of credit, materials, etc., required for them. It involves also the planning and construction, together with the new works of a system of transportation, of market centres, processing plants, and other equipment, which go with the new crops and production patterns. ... In relation to all future programmes, for example, it appears to me necessary to undertake full planning by joint expertise of engineers, agronomists, economists, and others, of the region that is being commanded by new irrigation works. Such an effort at preparing an optimum plan for use of water and land resources in the region will bring to surface all the problems involved in the developmental process, and the resulting quicker and fuller utilization of new irrigation resources will amply repay the expenditure and effort put in.

Ultimately, the plan for increased agricultural production depends not so much on state action as on action of individual cultivators. State action, in the main, creates possibilities of wider, more intensive or better use of land and other natural resources; realizing these possibilities, in fact, is a matter mostly for action of individual cultivators in the particular areas. Therefore, the basic problem of agricultural planning is the problem of including and directing individual cultivators to act appropriately. ...(p. 224)

I shall now turn to a consideration of the central question as to why it has not yet been found possible to give effect to this approach (plan from bottom upwards) and what appears to be required to give the desire for change a practical shape. This, planning from the bottom, has to be a two-way process and has to take into account, both, the physical equipment, with its limitations, and the human resources, with their dispositions and motivations, of the individual cultivator. ...(p. 224)

I shall consider the requirements of effective planning from bottom in agriculture, for lack of which no progress has been made so far, under two heads: organization, and knowledge. ...(pp. 224, 225)

Effective planning presupposes organization of individual production units. The requirement flows from a number of desiderata, among which the more important are the following: It is highly desirable to eliminate erratic or conflicting patterns of behaviour among producers and to attain some uniformity in their actions and procedures, if goals of planning are to be attained without wastages and lags. Secondly, to the extent that an area of economic activity is occupied by numerous small, weak, and ill-equipped units, coordination of the efforts of all these is necessary to give them economic and technical strength. Finally, when activity in an entire economic field is sought to be guided, it is highly useful to have this done through a relatively small number of organizations of the units in the field.

This not only facilitates the two-way process, but also makes for efficient operation through the cutting-out of considerable external administrative effort and leaving the plans flexible because of the possibility of infernal adjustment. ...(p. 225)

The first step in making agricultural planning possible in India, is to get agricultural producers organized in such a way that they, and their organization, become interested in the objectives of planning, say, increased and efficient production, and are induced to act appropriately. Also, the organization must be such that planning ends could be met without any great exercise of coercive or governmental authority.

I may illustrate possibilities by reference to the details of operations of a co-operative sugar factory. Here is an organization of a number of sugarcane farmers which, by the nature of its business, is vitally interested in securing an adequate supply of sugarcane of good quality from its members. Therefore, the organization attempts to do all it can to ensure a rational spread of sugarcane cultivation and its efficient operation. It becomes profitable for the organization to maintain a staff of agricultural officers, fieldmen, etc., to look after the farming of sugarcane by its members. The organization is interested in seeing that cane is planted at due season, the methods used in planting and subsequent operations are the most efficient, members obtain ample credit and administer adequate dosages of manure and fertilizers, etc., at appropriate times the water-supply with farmers is adequate and evenly maintained, protection is afforded against pests and diseases, the quality of planting sets is maintained and, if possible, improved and so forth. ... Parallel to the organization of its agricultural officers and fieldmen, it sets up committees for small groups of contiguous villages where leading members consult with officers, fieldmen, and members of the board of directors, and express their views regarding the proper functioning of the organization. The assistance of the group committees is available in a variety of ways: for bringing difficulties of members to the notice of officers, for persuading members within the group to adopt innovations, for obtaining co-operation of members in proper alignment of roads, etc. Organization is needed, both, to encourage the adoption of good methods and to discourage uneconomic or unsocial practices. ...(p. 226)

Therefore, the first need in agricultural planning is to organize agriculturist-producers in a co-ordinated and purposive system. The only such organizational device available to us is a many-sided and federal co-operative system. There are already many elements in the existing co-operative organizational structure, which have significance from the point of view of planning. ...(p. 227)

It is, to my mind, a condition precedent of undertaking agricultural planning in India that the scattered agricultural producers be organized into a total integrated co-operative system so that, at each stage of their operations, their extent, direction, and efficiency are within the cognizance of one or another unit of the co-operative system. It is only when this happens that, in the first instance, it will be possible to obtain sufficient information relating to actual operations at various stages of the producers, and next, to influence them effectively. However, as long as any step in the chain is missing, it will be impossible to plan effectively. Apart, therefore, from other reasons for spreading the net of co-operative organization in the country, I put in a plea for the immediate creation of a completely integrated state-sponsored co-operative organization throughout the country as the initial step for making effective planning of agriculture possible. ...(p. 228)

This is a matter in which, however, mere agreement in principle is not enough. What is required is immediate countrywide action. ... From the point of view of agricultural planning, I would emphasize two points in this context. In the first instance, the requisite organization of the small, scattered units could come about only with government initiative and assistance; this is universal experience. Secondly, though the ultimate aim should be a fully integrated co-operative system, considerable latitude for adjustments and improvisations should be left in the transitional stage. The creation of a fully integrated co-operative system will inevitably take time and cannot progress in all areas at the same pace. As the immediate aim is to organize cultivators for participating in planned activity, the substitution of *ad hoc* or looser forms of organization, e.g., farmers' clubs or borrowers' groups for the co-operative society may have to be made to fill the gap temporarily. ... At the higher levels, state-activity will assume greater importance. I would, for example, advocate an immediate incorporation into a state-cum-co-operative system of all mechanical power-driven processing plants operating in connection with all types of field crops. The plants, in future, should all be operated co-operatively, but for immediate acquisition they should first be taken into the public sector and transferred to the co-operative sector in due course. ...(p. 229)

The problem of organization for undertaking agricultural planning from the bottom has two aspects. The first is that of organizing cultivators so as to enable them to participate in planning. The second is the organization of the planning process itself at the lowest levels. ... In my opinion, it would be a mistake to have a village as the lowest planning unit. Even at the lowest level the planning process must be informed by a multi-sided view. In particular, considerations of supply and sale must have weight. Therefore, a unit smaller than what might be called a market area seems inadvisable. ...(p. 230)

The more important question, perhaps, is the structure of planning authority. I should emphasize one point in this connection. It is that the structure should not allow for the membership of elements which are not functionally related to the activities that are being planned. For, when this happens, the door is left open for the entry of political and other considerations, which deflect planning-activity away from its real purpose. ...(p. 230)

The planning authority at the lowest level should be composed of three elements. Firstly, an element representing the local self-government organizations of the area. This is necessary because it is these organizations that will provide, in the main, local socio-economic overheads, which are essential for all planning-effort. They will be responsible for the schools, the road system, local cesses and imposts, for organization of marketing facilities and, in due time, for the administration of town and country planning legislation, including rural housing. The second element should consist of representatives of the expert official technical personnel. The third and the main element should be the representation of co-operatives of all types and at all levels directly connected with the economic life of the particular area. I assume that at this level the interests represented will not only be agriculturists but all others such as artisans, transport agencies, and even labourers, to the extent that labouring interest was separate and had been organized co-operatively within the area.

I suppose that planning authority of the lowest unit will be concerned chiefly with the development of resources within its area and the increase in production of efficiency of all economic units within that area. The data discussed will be the past performance, current operations, and future projections of activities of the varied organizations represented, and the main task will be to dovetail, in a meaningful plan for the area, the operations of the various economic agencies and units as well as the activities of officials and the local self-government authorities. The operation and plan for each village, or for each independent unit, or agent will be derived from this total plan. ...(pp. 230, 231)

I conceive the superstructure of planning as that of the district above the lowest unit, above the district the region, which would mean a relatively homogeneous economic-geographic area within the state, and the state itself. It is important to have a fully operative planning organization at each of these stages. The composition of the planning unit at each of the stages would be similar in principle to the composition indicated for the lowest unit. ... Each planning authority must be endowed with real functions and with appropriate powers. Unless each superior organization allows for the organization below a due measure of devolution and liberty to adjust, it is useless to set up elaborate tiers of such organization. It is only if the federal principle is acted upon in reality that such an organization will have strength. To the extent that the authority for planning is real at the bottom, enthusiasm and spontaneous activity will be generated, if not, a meaningless structure, which merely clogs progress, will emerge. ...(p. 231)

In the field of agriculture, the centre has only a limited role to play. It has to establish appropriate trade and price-policies; it has to indicate broad objectives and general principles, but no more, in the context of land reform, co-operative organization, etc., and it has to maintain an adequate flow of especially imported supplies and regulate their distribution. This is apart from its universal role as general coordinator. It is obvious that the centre has failed in most of these respects. ... There is reason to believe that, in good part, these defects flow from the present organization of planning at the centre. ...(p. 231, 232)

I have left for consideration to the last that requirement of the planning of agriculture, which is of greatest interest to the members of this Society—knowledge, statistical and other. The nature of this knowledge has to be related to the process of planning from the bottom, sketched above. Obviously the data required are detailed local data, and data in the field. ... For effective agricultural planning, it is, I believe, necessary to revert to this older approach of local economic geography. For this, appropriate agricultural statistics, of course, provide the main base. Where agencies for the collection of local data exist, this involves mostly some reorganization and re-shaping; at the same time, where these do not exist, it indicates the need for the proper organization and the setting-up of agencies for collecting local field data in relation, in particular, to extent of availability of natural resources and their use.

There are some requirements of agricultural planning which suggest, in my opinion, a new approach to collection of the relevant agricultural statistics. Today, it would appear that most calculations of requirements of inputs, and of their effects, are based on data of a small number of experimental farms, and perhaps even these, one suspects, have been congealed for some time in conventional yard-sticks. Realistic planning requires that use be made, rather, of actual farm data. ... (pp. 232, 233)

In the field of economics also, systematic collection and collation of data from a variety of sources will have to be attempted. There are a number of problems central to agricultural planning on which there is little relevant knowledge available today. For example, it is admitted that we know almost nothing about the relation between prices and agricultural production in Indian conditions. Similarly, it is not possible to estimate, even for the country as a whole, with any confidence, the marketed surplus of important crops. ... There is, again, the pattern of land-use and of cropping. ... We have yet to make even a beginning with proper research relating to the restraints, limitations, and motivations that fashion the decisions regarding the crop-pattern of individual cultivators. A lot of this effort will be in the nature of case studies. ...(p. 233)

I have tried to place before you a few ideas on planning in agriculture and have tried, briefly, to frame the requirements in relation to statistics flowing out of them. However, on one point I feel sure that the bane of economic policy in this country, in the post-Independence era, has been centralization, and that in the field of statistics the crying need continues to be the strengthening, co-ordinating, and in the new context, proper planning and initiating of the work of primary field agencies. This judgment is founded on a view which I have held for many years and which I put on record in the following words on the eve of the initiation of planning in this country :

> For policy formation you require, not so much the National aggregates, but much more detailed information concerning specific regions and activities and a fairly clear idea of the actual operations of specific parts of the economic system. When you have gathered a fair amount of such specific information the National aggregates may help you to build an overall realistic framework which will give meaning to National Income and Accounts, but so long as the detailed information is not available. National aggregates by themselves would prove of little use for policy formation or for judging of its implications. ...(p. 234)

18

The Problem of Agricultural Labour*

I

This brief note attempts to summarize the main issues raised by the second reference to the Agricultural Labour Committee and indicates some directions in which reorganization of the existing schemes or the launching of the new ones can be examined. In the ultimate analysis, the problem of surplus rural labour is supposed to be solved only by all-sided economic development. The main features of this would be: much greater efficiency of production in agriculture, and the availability of diversified non-agricultural, particularly industrial, employment in such volume as to absorb much larger proportions of the rural population than that absorbed at present in non-agricultural employment. All this has been generally, widely accepted, but its full implications do not appear to have been realized in practice, in planning; in Indian conditions this involves much more than general progress towards industrialization. The existing under-employment in the rural areas, and the rate of growth of population in the country, make it incumbent that early industrialization of the countryside be attempted to as large an extent as possible, and that all plans of industrialization be oriented towards this end. This is necessary to avoid the difficulties and costs of large-scale migrations and to ensure the employment of large numbers at increasing levels of per capita output. In so far as the deliberate adoption or continuance of backward techniques hinders the process of development itself, the only way to reconcile the adoption of advanced techniques with relatively large employment is to adopt the techniques to units of the smallest economic scale and to

* This note was submitted for discussion to the Agricultural Labour Committee of the Plan Consultative Committee of the Maharashtra State in October 1960; published in *Artha Vijnana*, Vol. 3, No. 2, June 1961.

disperse them over the country. The increased costs involved in the small-scale are, in this instance, compensated by the dispersion which reduces costs in relation to movement of goods and the higher overheads involved in operation at large centres of population.

The foregoing has a number of immediate implications for state plans: Firstly, the planning of socio-economic overheads, such as transport, power, water supply, credit, and marketing facilities, so as to make them very widely available. Secondly, undertaking large programmes of conservation and development of natural resources all over the country. This is necessary in order to give some base to the programme of industrialization. Thirdly, the urgent need to do nothing which will make impossible future developments in the direction of dispersed industrialization. One of the most important aspects of immediate action implied in this is that large-scale units of industry, using resources which could become the basis of dispersed industrialization, should not be allowed to be established. The keenness to establish immediately large industrial units in the state may, it is feared, jeopardize future decentralized industrialization. The immediate danger, in this connection, appears to be that of pre-empting existing supplies of molasses, bamboo, etc.

On turning to more direct aspects of the problems, it may be noticed that the agricultural labour class is constituted of diverse elements and in view of the enormity of the problem it would be desirable to deal with problems of each constituent element, if possible, separately. Members of aboriginal tribes, and a number of rural artisan classes, are important elements among agricultural labourers. Increased employment of these classes should, as far as possible, be brought about by special measures. The development of the areas of the aborigines, in relation to both agriculture and forest produce, might, to a large extent, look after the problems of aborigines. In a similar manner rural artisans, as a class, should be provided for through the rehabilitation of their industries. There are, in operation today, a large number of schemes in relation to important rural industries. Unfortunately, they form part of the work of particular commissions and are never properly integrated into general local or state plans. Again, their inclusion in the work of commissions like the Khadi Commission gives programmes in relation to them a turn inappropriate to a plan of general development and makes them largely ineffective. It is, therefore, necessary to consider all these as forming parts of one plan of industrial development. A few, especially important problems may be indicated in this context. From a variety of points of view, the flaying of dead animals, and the tanning of their hides and skins, constitute a difficult but urgent problem crying for an immediate, constructive solution. Its neglect is currently causing loss of considerable national resources. A solution for the problem on a state-wide basis would prevent the loss of these resources and would afford considerable immediate employment and also a broadened base for further industrial production. Two other special artisan problems, which require attention in a similar manner, are the problems of potters and the problems of communities engaged in rope- and basket-making. In all these directions, large-scale experiments and organization of co-operatives of artisans for new types of production, with new methods, are necessary. An important lacuna in most schemes of rehabilitation of artisan industry, at present, is the lack of guaranteed purchase. This is extremely important for obtaining full production early.

All this would still leave unconsidered the bulk of agricultural labour, not associated with any other occupation than agriculture. Before proceeding to deal with this central problem, I may offer some observations on an important characteristic of the data placed before the Committee. This is the difference in proportions of agricultural labour as between west and east Maharashtra. I suggest that this difference is, in the main, due to the historical difference in systems of land tenure. Under the Rayatwari administration of old Bombay State, the land ownership and the cultivating possession of land were both relatively, widely dispersed; under the Malgujari form of tenure, on the other hand, there was a much greater concentration of ownership and cultivating possession. As a result, in west Maharashtra, rural population was dispersed, to a large extent, on small holdings cultivated by the farmer-family itself. The much larger proportion of large holdings in east Maharashtra reduced the production of small family farms; it created, on the other hand, demand for permanent farm-servants on the larger holdings. This appears to be the main explanation for the higher proportions of, both, the agricultural labour and the attached labour in that area. This is relevant to the work of the Committee in so far as it indicates that, even after a measure of land reform, the present disparity in proportions of agricultural labour within the two regions will persist. A ceiling may take off some land from the top holders in the eastern areas; it could, however, not have any effect on the large majority of cultivating holdings and would not redistribute them in the relatively graded manner in which they are, at present, distributed in west Maharashtra. Therefore, while the surplus land afforded by a ceiling may give partial employment in agriculture and as agriculturist to small additional numbers, it is not likely, in any significant manner, to reduce the existing number of agricultural labour families.

To return to the core of the problem of agricultural labour, it may be taken for granted that any increase in the intensity of land-exploitation will not solve, what may be called, the numerical aspect of this problem. Increased intensity is likely, for the major part, to afford large employment, in the first instance, to members of the farm-family; in the second instance, to farm servants employed by it; and thirdly, to casual labour in that area.

Considerable intensification of agriculture in any area will thus result, in the main, in reducing under-employment in that particular area, but will not create substantial employment for new people within it. This connects with another aspect of the problem of agricultural labour: basically the magnitude of the problem has to be measured essentially with reference to the levels of income and standards of living of rural labour in any particular area. All surveys and inquiries reveal that in the areas in which agriculture is intensively developed, agricultural labour not only obtains employment more continuously throughout the year but obtains it at higher rates of wages than elsewhere. Therefore, in such areas, and their immediate environment, the problem of agricultural labour is not as intense as elsewhere.

The Committee could, therefore, begin by paying special attention to the problem in particular areas. One may take for granted that efforts to intensify the development of agriculture will proceed according to plans and these will give some relief in the areas where increased intensity is possible. For the other areas, the problem will have to be tackled in other ways. The main types of regions in Maharashtra, where a special study of the problem has to be made, appear to be as follows: There is, in the first instance, the area of the Konkan and the Maval parts of Desh, where problems are similar. This is a tract agricultural economy of which is based on a single crop of rice during the monsoon, where communications are difficult, and the food grown is hardly sufficient for six months of the year. In many parts of this region, the aboriginal population is in considerable numbers. The dry areas of portions of districts like Ahmednagar, Poona, Satara, and Kolhapur and large parts of Sholapur, with uncertain rainfall and an annual precipitation below 20 inches, constitute the second region. This region, again, is of single-crop economy and specially subject to periodic failures. The other two regions are: Marathawada and Vidarbha. It may be noted that in the first two regions the proportion of landless labour is not large, but their total income and conditions of living are among the worst in the state. In Marathawada and Vidarbha, on the other hand, the proportions of labour are high, but their incomes, especially in Vidarbha, are relatively good.

The solution for the different problems of each region, or each type of region, will have to be elaborated separately. However, the general approach may here be indicated. The approach has to be that of evolving a programme of continuous action, constituent elements of which mutually support each other, and which meets with both short- and long-term requirements. The immediate requirement is to afford, through additional employment, the much-needed additional income to agricultural labour families; but the immediate employment programme must be so framed as to subserve long-term needs. The ultimate need is to industrialize the country-side; however, this can be done only if a wide base of resources is built up for this purpose in the rural areas. Therefore, the employment programme should be directed towards this objective of conserving and developing, as rapidly and intensively as possible, natural resources of each area and region. Everywhere, the immediate step is to frame a diversified programme of public works capable of being sustained over a series of years, undertaken and executed annually, somewhat on the lines of a relief-work programme. This programme should comprehensively embrace all aspects of conservation and development of material resources and formation of social capital, in the countryside. Works in connection with reclamation of lands, contour bunding, afforestation and tree-planting, minor irrigation, road building, public and institutional buildings of all types, will obviously be included in the programme. Special attention may be drawn to the universal need in Maharashtra for taking urgent steps to conserve vegetation and cover and develop intensively fuel and fodder resources. We are, at present, caught in a vicious circle of too many animals which are partly fed on too little pasture, and too little cover giving inadequate resources of fuel and fodder with the result that not only valuable manure is burnt but there is also a progressive and rapid cutting-down of bushes and trees. Large afforestation schemes in the hill areas, and fuel and fodder depot schemes, combined with useful tree and bush planting for each locality in the country, are urgent needs. Though these can later become the responsibility, in the main, of local communities, a considerable amount of initial effort and expenditure has to be made by the state government, in particular, in experimenting with the best ways of dealing with this problem in different circumstances. This must be immediately undertaken and has very considerable employment potentialities. If this is systematically undertaken, not only will the normal, forest wealth and fodder and fuel resources increase but additional wealth can also be created in terms of specially developed pastures, of fibre plants like agave of bamboo, copses, which will, in time, also yield a sound local base for related rural industry. But, so long as the initial effort is not made, the cumulative effects can never become evident.

All this is further connected with an important aspect of development—animal husbandry, including the dairy industry, live-stock rearing, sheep breeding, and wool. The development of pastures, forests, and other non-arable land has to be planned with this in view. In part, animal husbandry can be a whole-time occupation; however, its main function will be that of affording a supplementary source of income and employment to agriculture.

There is another direction in which special effort, with considerable experimentation, is obviously indicated. It is well known that one of the areas in which considerable capital investment is absorbed in the process of development, is housing. In Maharashtra, the problems of proper village layouts and of rural housing reconstruction are extremely important. For the most part, our villages present a dilapidated and straggling appearance, and they are, both, inconvenient and insanitary. The evolution of model layouts and types of rural housing, appropriate to each region, must be systematically attempted; these have to be related, both, to local climatic conditions as well as to the availability of local material. In this direction, there are a number of employment-giving occupations, such as brick-making, tile-making, and lime kilns, the development of which can be encouraged. In this connection also, the practical implementation of what is often theoretically put forward, viz., the use of local woods for construction purposes, may be emphasized. Efforts, in the past, by the Forest Department have been reported, but practical development, in terms of the choice of trees and tree-planting and actual use in construction, seems to be non-evident.

I have deliberately made this concise statement of my views on the problem, in broad and comprehensive terms, because, in my opinion, the prevailing approach of looking at the problem in a piecemeal and isolated manner, as exemplified by the latest circular of the Planning Commission, is very wrong. Agricultural under-employment and the low standards of living of agricultural labour are among the most important manifestations of under-development, and the plans of development must be judged by the ultimate test of how they affect these phenomena. Therefore, I should insist that it is the total orientation of planning-effort, as indicated above, that must be pressed for. If this is accepted, the immediate steps that I would suggest for concrete action are as follows:

1. Examination of the total State Plan to see in what respects it takes into account, and gives importance to, the objective of rapid industrialization of the rural areas, and what elements in the Plan are likely to hinder progress in this direction.

2. Examination of current plans of transport, power, water supply, credit, marketing, education, public health, etc., from the point of view of creating, in a widespread manner, conditions favourable for decentralized industrialization.

3. Examination of plans of conservation and development of natural resources, especially in relation to land surface not under arable agriculture, and of plans for re-organization of village industry, of animal husbandry, and of rural construction industries, from the point of view of widening the base of rural industrialization.

4. Examination of existing, total public expenditure programmes in particular areas with a view to judging how far they can be arranged in time and space so as to provide maximum employment of the relief type to agricultural labour in the areas.

5. Examination of the volume of existing public expenditure programmes in relation to each major geographical division of every district, and of the volume of potential employment created by them, for judging the gap that has to be filled by re-allocation and re-organization of plan expenditure, if adequate additional employment is to be given to agricultural labour.

19

Price Policy for Foodgrains

*Its Implications**

It would be useful to begin by considering how it is supposed that the market in foodgrains works. The main motivating factor in keeping in operation private trade in foodgrains would be the prospect of making a profitable living out of the trade. But the social justification for the system is that it enables supplies to be distributed continuously and evenly in time and space and to bring about some equilibrium between changing demand and changing supply. In passing a judgment on the operations of the private trader, in this context, it is necessary to remember that the chief way in which he can perform this social function is by varying prices and supplies, at given locations and at given time, in consonance with his judgment of variations of demand and of supply. The trading system operates through the convergence of the effects of judgments of innumerable traders belonging to various strata at various locations and at different times. There is no provision in the trading system for taking an overall view or distinguishing between, what may be called, the long and the short run. All decisions are essentially immediate or short-run decisions of individuals taken against the background of their own expectations, short or long. To blame traders, therefore, because they raise prices on becoming aware of scarce supplies, is wrong-headed.

* Originally published in *The Economic Weekly*, Vol. XVI, No. 39, 26 September 1964, pp. 1561–8.

THE MARKET PROCESS

The market process of determining or making prices does not only reflect, in a static manner, existing relations of stocks to demand but also, and more importantly, it points to desired corrections in supply over time and space. The pricing process serves to initiate the corrections by indicating the extra margins to be earned through undertaking them. The continuous variations in prices, and the reactions of individuals to them, constitute the essentials of the price equilibrium system. When prices are fixed through the actions of the state, or a trade group, the price variations which act as signals for variations in demand and supply are done away with. Consequently, the authority which attempts to fix prices must also provide a substitute mechanism for equating supply with demand. In the absence of such provision, constant and cumulative excesses in either direction may come about.

IMPLICATIONS OF SHORTAGE

This simplified account of the pricing process says nothing about its equitable operation, which depends, essentially, on the distribution of incomes in society. In a monetized market, the demand which is not backed by purchasing power in money has no operative significance. Therefore, when shortages occur, supply will flow to areas where demand is concentrated and is backed by relatively high money income and the poorer regions which are difficult to access will be faced with a physical lack of supply. Also, moving prices high enough to cut down sharply the consumption of the poorest is the only manner in which the market mechanism can meet a situation of prolonged shortage. As pointed out above, there is no device within the trading system by which the system itself could do anything about such a situation. Moreover, if by any device, it was able to hold prices at levels lower than the equilibrium level this would create a problem of excess demand which could be met only by some scheme of authoritarian and regulated distribution. The foodgrains market in India is marked by high seasonality of supply, distances and difficulties relating to transport and storages and inelastic demand. In such a market temporary acute shortages may carry prices to very high levels at which they may tend to stick in even a mildly inflationary situation.

It follows that in a country which is attempting to force the pace of development, there may always be an element of unsatisfied demand because of the increased rate of income generation and the trader may be able to take advantage of this situation. However, in such a context, it is not the traders who are to blame, but rather the government which itself creates conditions under which traders can make extra profits and then does nothing to prevent traders from making that profit.

ACTION AT TWO LEVELS

I suppose that the new policy will not be based on any unreal assumptions and that there will be no expectation that the average trader will refrain from acting so as to make a high profit when he can do so legitimately, or even illegitimately, if there is little fear of being found out. In these circumstances, the new policy will have to give due attention to the effects on the operation of the market mechanism, of the fixation of prices. A note will have to be taken of these effects for planning action at two levels. Firstly, in the short run, maintenance of fixed prices over, say, a year involves maintaining fluctuations in them within a narrow margin in spite of variations in intensity of demand from place to place and day to day. This can be done only if the government or the corporation or its agents have enough supplies at their disposal to deploy suitably between places and to carry, spread adequately over the year. This requirement points to the futility of the belief that an authority can maintain fixed prices without acquiring control over ample stocks at harvest.

The fixation of prices at a given level has also significance for the longer term equilibrium between demand and supply. It is likely that government policy will favour a level of prices for consumers at which the demand will be in excess of the total available supply. This may happen for either the supply of foodgrains as a whole and even more probably for the supply of a particular foodgrain. In such contingencies action, in the direction of some regulated distribution of stocks, will have to be undertaken. This may vary from full rationing to controlled distribution, according to households, of limited quantities through fair price shops. The need for such action may arise, even though the level of fixed prices is not especially low, because of failures of expected supply during a particular period or at some places. Maintenance of fixed prices over time needs, thus, to be backed by reserve powers for requisitioning and for bringing about controlled distribution. The above further emphasizes the need for the abolition of zoning. Economic management with a small margin is possible only if the area of operations is the largest possible.

ZONES MUST GO

On the basis of this summary analysis more specific observations might be attempted. The fixation of prices of rice, if it is to have any meaning, will have to be done, both, comprehensively and elaborately, and it will have to be related to the objectives of total food policy vis-à-vis the cultivators on the one hand and the consumer on the other. The price for the cultivator can be a floor price; it can be a support price or it can be a standard purchase price. I assume that the government's intentions are no longer confined to maintaining a low floor to rice prices. 'Support prices,' in the sense of highly favourable prices, may be ruled out in view of the total situation. I take it, therefore, that the prices that are sought to be fixed are standard purchase prices, that is, prices at which the cultivator will find it profitable to sell, and yet on the basis of which the retail prices to the consumer will not be pushed very high. The fixation of such standard prices involves a large number of detailed practical problems. Only the important ones can be referred to here.

It is assumed that progress will be made towards the abolition of zones. The abolition of zones would mean that a movement is set on foot towards equalization of prices in India. The abolition of zones by themselves would not immediately, or by itself, bring about such equalization. In the context of the new food policy, it would be important for the government to define, very carefully, the extent of the operations allowed to the private trader. Will everybody be free to do trading as they like or will only the holders of licences be able to purchase and sell foodgrains? Will the holders of particular types of licences be confined in their operations to particular grains, particular locations or regions, or particular stages of wholesale or retail trading etc.? Will a licence to purchase and sell mean, also, a licence to undertake the movement of foodgrains to any distance? In this context, it appears logical to suggest that even with the abolition of zones, movement by rail, and possibly, also by coastal shipping, of foodgrains should be denied to private trade. There are a number of reasons which can be adduced in justification of this measure. In the new situation, the government must have the ability to control the upsetting effects of sudden fluctuations in demand and supply and the specially strong attraction of metropolitan centres; the control of movement by rail and coastal shipping would be very valuable in this context.

FIXING PRICES

Though such restriction will prevent very large movements of foodgrains over long distances it will not entirely counteract the equalizing effects on prices of the abolition of zones. Road movements within states would continue. These would be largely over short distances in bordering areas, but would serve as a check. In the circumstances, sharp differences in prices fixed by the neighbouring states would no longer be allowable. Such sharp differences have always given rise to smuggling. One of the main aims of price fixation should now be rationalization of the levels of prices in the various states so that there is a gradual transition from the low to the high price states.

The task of the fixation of prices, immediately this year, cannot be tackled on the basis of any objective criteria or elaborate enquiries. The only relevant data are data of ruling, immediate prices and especially of ruling harvest prices during the last two harvests. When such data are mapped out, the artificial influence of the existence of zones will first have to be allowed for and judgment must then be made regarding the manner in which from the main surplus low price areas movements will radiate so that the differentiation in prices fixed has concrete relation to availability of local supplies and costs of movements from surplus areas. Another immediate judgment which will have to be made, in a somewhat arbitrary fashion, is the general level of fixation of the price for the cultivator. This is related to two aspects of policy. One is the evaluation of the element of incentive to sell and to produce more largely next year, that it is supposed necessary to incorporate in the price. The second is the level at which a price that is generous or fair for the cultivator is yet not too high as the base on which the retail price level for the consumer is determined. Some attention must be paid to the agency of purchase to make clear the connection between the two.

A curious phrase has been used recently in this context. It has been said that the agents of the government will buy in competition with the trader. Whatever this may mean, it seems to ignore the handicaps under which an agent of government, buying in competition with the trader, acts. A mere announcement of a standard purchase price which is fair to the cultivator will not necessarily suffice for obtaining for the proposed corporation adequate supplies of foodgrains, as long as the private trader acts alongside of the corporation without any restriction or check. The ability of the private trader to do well in foodgrains depends on his capacity to purchase as large quantities of foodgrains as possible from cultivators at harvest. The private trader will, therefore, do all he can to obtain supplies from cultivators and if his new rival, the corporation, is offering a given price the trader will necessarily offer a slightly higher price to obtain his usual supplies and induce the usual suppliers to sell to him. If the corporation is limited in its activity, to a given level of prices, the trader can, by offering a somewhat higher price, divert all supplies away from the corporation. If the corporation, however, offers a higher price to counteract the efforts of the trader, the trader, in turn, will necessarily try to outbid. In this way will begin the movement of prices upward, which is said usually to result from the intrusion of the government, or its agency, in trade at harvest.

The objective of getting control over supplies at harvest being paramount for the trader, he would naturally keep on raising his bid as far as praticable. The only limitation on the increase of the offer of price by a trader would be the level at which he can expect to sell at retail or to intermediaries who sell ultimately at retail later in the season. Given two conditions, that there is shortage (and this, in relative terms, will always be there) and that all supplies are in the hands of the traders (and this condition is always fulfilled substantially a few months after harvest unless the government or the co-operatives have bought up a very large part of the crop), there is practically no limit, as has been demonstrated this year, to the extent of the possible increase in prices at retail. Therefore, the trader can safely offer continuously higher prices as against a corporation in order to put himself into a position to profit from the shortages that begin to be felt after harvest. Thus, the mere fixation of purchase prices, and the setting up of a corporation to make purchases at fixed prices, would merely push up the level of purchase prices but will not obtain for the government, the supplies necessary to give effect to its policies. For doing this the major needed additional requirement is the fixation of prices of sales at retail.

FUTILITY OF FIXING PROFIT

It is an important objective of government policy to make foodgrains at fair prices available to the consumer. The determination of prices fair to the consumer is, therefore, essential for the fulfilment of government policy and the guarantee of fair prices and keeping watch over their maintenance can be done best by direct announcement of retail prices. The determination of margins of traders has often been attempted in the past in the place of specifically determined prices at retail. However, the determination of a set of margins applied to a fluctuating base yields indeterminate retail prices. When numerous traders are making purchases at various times, the sale prices charged by them, calculated as a per cent over their prices of purchase can be known only after detailed calculations. In the circumstances, persistent infringement of regulations in this behalf can only be proved on highly detailed enquiry. Furthermore, there exist many stages of intermediate trading between purchase from the producer and retail sale to the consumer. The determination of detailed margins at various stages and the identification of a transaction as having taken place at a given stage are again matters which depend on close examination of records, identification of particular transactions, and elaborate calculations. It is obvious that any system of regulation of a trade, as far-flung and large in volume and in number of transactions as that of foodgrains, which involves continuous elaborate enquiry for proper supervision and checking must be found unworkable. This has been amply proved by experience during the last decade.

DETAILS OF PRICE FIXATION

If there are to be any sets of fixed prices announced by the government, these should be only at two levels. Those of (i) purchase from the cultivator defined as of purchase either in the village or of purchase at some primary market, and of (ii) retail sale to the consumer, defined for particular areas and locations. The difference between the purchase price and the retail price will have to be determined in relation to some calculations of the margins. This margin, apart from the commission and handling, etc., charges, will include an average allowance for transport costs. The total fixation of the elaborate price schedules at the two levels will have to be done in two stages. The Government of India should determine the broad levels of purchase prices and retail prices. On the assumption that there will be no zones, the Government of India should also determine the permissible margin of difference between the levels of purchase prices as between state and state. The determination of the level of retail prices involves calculations regarding margins at various stages of intermediate trading and an averaging of handling and transport costs.

On the basis of the broad levels or ranges of prices indicated by the Government of India, each state should be asked to work out the detailed notification regarding purchase and retail prices. For price fixation to be effective, these notifications will have to be elaborate. The purchase price notifications will have to have as their base each district or producing region for a given crop. In the light of the level indicated by the Government of India and the permissible inter-state margins, the state will define for each district or region, the fixed purchase price for each sort or kind of foodgrain and for each recognised quality and grade within it.

Price fixation, to be effective, must be meaningfully related to specific varieties or sorts and their quality. There has to be a detailed description attached to each fixed price and there has to be provision made for determining gradation of produce and for checking the grades in course of supervision of trade later. It is the experience that without detailed specification and price description, and in the absence of grading arrangements, price fixation can be easily reduced to a farce by the trader. The difference, as between different varieties or sorts, or as between different qualities, would, to begin with, embody traditional judgment and market indicators in the recent past. In later years a dynamic policy, in relation to them, can be adopted. The same is true of difference in prices in the levels, as between different production districts or regions. It is important that the State Notification should cover the entire region of the state and should take account of every production region or area, however small. It does not, however, appear necessary that, at least initially, all sorts or varieties must be covered. The most highly priced varieties which are, clearly, separately identifiable, may well be left out of regulation. The chief safeguards in this behalf are to see that the varieties brought under regulation cover, say, 80 per cent of total production and to ensure that evasion is not made too easy through the varieties that are left out.

RETAIL PRICES

The fixation of prices at retail will have to be equally elaborate, in the sense that a retail price must be indicated for each variety and quality for which there has been a fixation of a purchase price. The base for the fixation of prices at retail would have to be the main consuming areas so that, in accordance with the general directive of the Government of India, the prices at retail, in relation to specific sorts and qualities, will be notified as for each important city or town area. Care will have to be taken to see that the announcement of retail price covers all locations, i.e., where in a district, only for a few important towns or municipal areas separate retail prices have been determined, there should be a schedule of prices at retail for the rest of the district, including all its rural parts. The extent to which a price schedule is elaborated will depend on the government of the state and will be related, necessarily, to the arrangements for distribution of the foodgrains made by the government of that state.

The above appears to be the minimum necessary elaboration for the attainment of a fixed set of foodgrains' prices. Within this framework it should be possible for a corporation or for co-operatives within the states to obtain a fair supply of foodgrains from the open market. The operation of the trader will now be limited by the maximum prices obtainable at retail and he will not be able to push up purchase prices beyond a certain level. If the corporation and the co-operatives are able to operate at relatively small margins, they should be in a position to obtain a fair share of the supplies offered by the cultivator. Two requirements appear essential in respect of purchase arrangements. The first is the provision of arrangements to purchase and to store at a large number of points all over the country. The extent to which the purchase price will be effective will depend on the extent to which the alternative purchaser to the trader operates within or near the location of the cultivator. Therefore, a set of dispersed purchase points at which the corporation or the co-operative is equipped to grade, weigh, and store produce and pay for it, or make advances on it, must be maintained. The minimum number of such points for satisfactory administration would seem to be between 40 to 50 per district. It is conceivable that a newly-established corporation at the all-India level will be able to provide this number of purchasing points throughout the country, without seeking co-operation of either the state authorities or the co-operative system in each state. In the long run also it appears neither possible nor desirable for an all-India corporation to act in the various markets, on its own, without using local agencies. There is already such a large measure of organizational effort and storage capacity built up through state and co-operative systems of management of agricultural produce, that it would be an act of national waste to try and raise alongside these, a third system of a new all-India corporation.

LIMITS OF ALL-INDIA CORPORATION

It is likely that the all-India corporation is, at this stage, thought of as operating in only a few surplus districts and not affecting all areas in various states. A rice corporation, for example, may be conceived of as acting only within a small number of districts in some surplus states and not acting at all in any district in some states. To be content with such a concept of operation is, however, to misconceive the whole issue. Fixation of prices has no meaning except as being operative all over the country. It has been indicated above, that fixation of purchase prices all over the country would have no meaning except as accompanied by fixation of retail prices. Any attempt at the maintenance or enforcement of prices at retail would be entirely dependent on deployment of sufficient stock through a system such as that of fair price shops. For this being done, the purchase and sale operations must be on a significant scale within each state. An all-India foodgrains corporation has thus meaning only as the apex of a system of which there are constituent operational parts within each state. It is a matter for practical choice whether these operational parts are themselves independent state systems, or act as agents, within the state, of the corporation.

There is another reason why only limited operation by an all-India corporation will prove to be inadequate and fruitless. A major task before the corporation will be the adjustment of supplies as between the deficit and surplus states. This is an essential job which the contemplated corporation must take on itself. The movement of surplus away from surplus states, and meeting the needs of a deficit state, is a task that can be kept within manageable proportions only if fairly uniform systems of purchase and distribution are operative within each state. If they are not so operative, difficulties will arise in both connections. If there are no systematic purchases planned in districts of the surplus state, and if there is no fixation of prices at retail, the operations of the trader within the surplus state cannot be put under control and the corporation will find it difficult to make its purchases, except at constantly increasing prices. On the other hand, if there are no planned systems of purchase and sale within the deficit states, the deficit states could, at any time, find themselves in a crisis and would be making constantly increasing demands on the centre for supplies. All this is part of the experience since the days of zonal planning. The abolition of zones will put a pressure on the surplus states to have a system of food management of their own. The regulation of retail prices in deficit states will also give some protection to them in their operation. However, if the basic operative state systems are not built up, the activities of an all-India rice corporation will mean no more than some addition in respect of rice to the activities in respect of wheat which the Government of India indulges in on the basis of PL-480 supplies. The rice corporation's action will be much less effective than that of PL-480 supplies as it does not increase the net supply but acts with supplies obtained from within. As has been the experience in case of PL-480 supplies release, even of large quantities of these supplies, does not, at all times, succeed in restraining high rises in prices. Obviously, thus, the activities of a corporation, if undertaken in a circumscribed manner, will make no contribution to the fixation of prices and to the maintenance of fixed prices over time.

CO-ORDINATION

When zones are abolished it will also become necessary to see that the systems of operation, and levels of prices fixed by the states, have correspondence with each other even apart from the operations of an all-India corporation. For example, even if jowar is not handled by any all-India corporation the prices and trading in jowar in contiguous states, say, Madhya Pradesh and Maharashtra, cannot be too disparate. The level of purchase price for jowar in Maharashtra will have to be determined, both, with relation to purchase and retail prices in Madhya Pradesh and the level of possible retail prices in Maharashtra in relation to, say, price of atta. This illustration will make clear how, with a comprehensive view of state systems co-ordinated by an all-India body, the working of each, in detail, will be restrained and put within a meaningful framework.

The basic propositions on which my exposition is based are as follows. No prices can be fixed and maintained at the fixed level by any authority without the help of trading operations, both of purchase and of sale. It is possible to operate a system merely of floor prices with only purchase arrangements. To limit the price to a fixed level, or within a narrow margin, only purchase arrangements will not suffice. The control of cotton prices operates with a very wide margin—a low floor and a high ceiling. Even so, the government is seen to be much more powerless when the ceiling is pierced than when the floor is reached. Experience of the last ten years has consistently and repeatedly proved the ineffectiveness of announced prices, legal regulation of margins, or of official threats in the absence of the ability to act in the concrete. Licensing of traders and the calling in of returns is also of little use. Licensing, by itself, affords no check and the returns are never subject to scrutiny or compiled or collated in a manner that could give assistance in administration. They cannot be made the basis on which the location of stocks or the movements of foodgrains can be kept under close or constant enough surveillance, even if scrutiny and compilation are made much more prompt and elaborate. The control of margins is ineffective because checking involves detailed enquiry and firm identification of transactions at both ends. Regulation of price through defined margins is, for the same reasons, inconvenient and harassing for the honest trader.

PRICES, PURCHASE, AND SALE

The simplest, effective approach to definition of the price structure is by prescribing the two end limits, viz., the purchase price paid to producer and the retail price charged to consumer, and taking the minimum necessary action for their maintenance. The two aspects of this action, purchase and sale, are mutually related. Without a proper purchase organization the maintenance of the purchase price cannot be ensured, also, without adequate purchases the supply need to maintain the retail price could not become available. On the other hand, it is only the ability to guarantee that retail price does not increase above a given level that gives firm basis to the operations of institutional purchasers in the open market; and keeping the prices of foodgrains at a reasonable level is an even more primary and urgent objective of socio-economic policy than ensuring high prices to cultivators.

The task to be attempted is detailed and countrywide. In terms of any proper definition of national priorities the aboriginal and other populations of inaccessible areas have as high a claim on and as much need of protective action by the state as the labouring classes of big cities. The rural economy of all areas, secure, insecure, deficit, surplus, stands in need of the boost given by good prices for the producer. An all-India corporation acting in a small number of surplus districts in a few states cannot fulfil, by itself, these requirements. It can do so only if it is the apex of a system operating comprehensively in each state. It has also to be realized that unless all states, deficit or surplus, are induced to adopt certain minimum policy objectives and action measures there will be failure in the long run. The case for such conjoint and co-ordinated action is overwhelming if the aim of national policy is not only that of getting over a short-term crisis but also of building up a permanent system which will lead to the most rational and economical management of internal supplies and will progressively decrease our dependence on imports of foodgrains.

TWO LEVELS OF ACTION

The total task has to be divided clearly into two; action at the all-India and that at the states' level. Each of these has elements of, both, price fixation and of purchase and sale operations. The all-India organisation should preferably handle together all foodgrains and pulses which enter into the trade between states to any significant extent. It would have the monopoly of inter-state movements by rail or coastal shipping. It should not aim to create an independent organization in all respects, another empire. This will be wasteful of scarce national resources and will lead to difficulties in co-ordinating and rationalizing policies and action. It should act through existing organizations in states and other territories and also use available public facilities such as those of warehousing and storage to the maximum extent possible. If such an all-India corporation is set up it should be entrusted with the handling of all imported supplies of foodgrains. Such a corporation will sell to and purchase from only the accredited agencies within a state except in areas where such agencies cannot be set up or where their performance is inadequate. It follows that there must come into existence in each state, systems of management of foodgrain supplies which will purchase and sell foodgrains grown within the state, receive imported supplies for distribution within the state and receive surplus supplies from other states or send out surplus supplies of own state produce, from and to, either, the all-India corporation or the other state systems. The state systems could be either departmental or managed by a state corporation operating with the help of the co-operatives.

The fixation of prices will also be done in two stages. The first stage is that of fixation of basic levels of (a) purchase prices from cultivators, and (b) retail prices charged to the consumer, for all important foodgrains and the permissible margins in both price levels as between state and state. This must be done for the country as a whole. The second stage is that of elaborate price notifications for each regulated sort and quality of purchase prices of a foodgrain for each production region and of retail prices for each area or location together with all the descriptive detail necessary for effective implementation. The determination of fixed prices, in both stages, this year, will necessarily be quick and *ad hoc*, largely based on past experience and limited by estimates of practical effective immediate action. In future years, if the system gets properly built up, the basis of action could be made more sure and the price fixation begin to be used as a dynamic instrument of policy. Apart from an operative corporation or a price-fixing commission, the system will necessarily require high level co-ordination of state and central policies in relation to foodgrains.

20

Economic Aspects of Irrigation Water Management*

The problems of the proper development of irrigation systems are among the most difficult and among those which have not so far been dealt with very satisfactorily in this country. The development of an irrigation system is far from being an engineering problem, in the main. We have a large array of situations in this country in which large irrigation systems are being developed. They vary from densely populated and considerably developed areas, like those of Uttar Pradesh and Bihar, to the semi-desert areas of Rajasthan. Whether in the one or the other, the development of an irrigation system involves, basically, the task of planning and creating the infrastructure required for the utilization of the added water supply in irrigated agriculture and transferring the technology and capital required for the transformation in agricultural practice. It is a total task which has to be viewed in an integrated fashion. Some of the problems of under-utilization of irrigation works that we face today have stemmed from our failure in planning and programming for the proper development of our irrigation systems. I presume that the Symposium on Irrigation Water Management will not be concerned with these problems of development and that its discussions will be in the context of an appropriately already developed irrigation system. I felt it necessary to say this by way of introduction because a number of problems of irrigation water management in actual situations today arise out of inappropriate development measures in the past.

I shall now go on to draw your attention to a few aspects of irrigation water management. I shall, for obvious reasons, deal mainly with economic

* Inaugural Address, Central Board of Irrigation and Power, 40th Annual Session, Symposia, New Delhi, 23 November 1967.

and financial aspects of the subject. I shall, in doing so, draw largely on the Report of the Maharashtra Irrigation Commission of 1960. This is because the most intensive study that I made of these problems was during the period of my membership of the Commission and because most of my own ideas on the subject have been incorporated in that report.

Before discussing management, there is need to be clear as to the aims of management. Unless we are fully aware of the objectives which management is supposed to attain or achieve, it will not be possible to define properly the principles and practice of good management. It may appear to some that the question I am raising is superfluous and that the objectives of irrigation water management should be obvious to all. In order to emphasize the need to define clearly the objectives, I would draw your attention to the manner in which these objectives have been changing over past decades. The Irrigation Commission of the first decade of this century paid considerable attention to the distinction between productive and protective irrigation works. In laying down criteria for undertaking irrigation works and in formulating the principles of the management of such works, this distinction played a great part. However, over the subsequent decades, the distinction has almost completely lost its importance. With the steady commercialization of agriculture, the concept of a protective irrigation work has fallen into the background and the productive aspect of irrigation works, which were initially constructed entirely as protective works, has progressively attained prominence. The protective concept was appropriate to a static and self-sufficient agricultural economy. In a dynamic economy, it is no longer relevant and could not survive. However, the elimination of the protective concept meant, at the same time, a considerable change in the original design of utilization of water and a change, inevitably, in the principles of irrigation water management as related to the protective systems. One has only to look at the transformation of the century-old Mutha Canals System to realize the full measure of the change. As originally designed, this system, with head-works less than 10 miles above Poona, had under command a region of nearly 40 miles below Poona. In the course of decades, the transformation was such that in 1961 the entire water supply was absorbed by the growing needs of Poona city and by the intensive vegetable, fruit, and sugar-cane agriculture between Poona and the headworks and for a distance of less than 10 miles below Poona. Irrigation channels for over 30 miles were left dry and the whole of this area, which is the most liable to famine and required protection most, was deprived of the water supply originally meant essentially for it. The same truncating effect was observed, because of the establishment of sugar factories, near the headworks of both the Godavari and the Pravara systems. Therefore, when considering problems of irrigation water management it is important to project yourself into the future and to see what sort of requirements you are going to fulfil and how you are going to be sure that the investment made originally for given objectives is not seriously deflected from them during the course of time.

Apart from a change in objectives of irrigation water management which might come about by transformation of agriculture, as has occurred during the past decades, there are other problems that have to be faced in determining the aims of irrigation water management. The basic conflict, in this context, is that between intensity of use and dispersal of benefits. There are certain regions in which this conflict may not arise because the supply of water is both plentiful and cheap, so that all areas that are under the command of a given work can fully find their needs met. In other cases, however, where conditions are not so favourable, the problem has to be squarely faced. The problem, in one of its aspects, is met with even in the allocation of national resources for purposes of development of irrigation systems. It appears obvious to say that investment in irrigation should be so directed as to yield the maximum overall benefit; and a number of times, the concept of maximum overall benefit is supposed to be identifiable with maximum production in physical terms, especially of an immediately scarce commodity like food. However, this apparently obvious statement has to face many questions. For example, how do you evaluate the physical production increase in a particular region, or in the hands of a particular category of persons, in terms of benefits to the national economy? Here, the old dilemma of concentration and intensity versus dispersal of benefits to very much larger numbers, and to many regions, which is faced in all plans of development comes to the fore in a sharp manner. This is not the place to go into the pros and cons of this controversial issue. I draw your attention to them merely in order to highlight the nature of problems involved in determining the aims of irrigation water management. For, the issues have to be faced not only at the national level but also at the level of the management of a single individual irrigation system.

The Maharashtra Irrigation Commission thought it necessary on this account to determine initially the basic aim of the future development and management of the various irrigation systems in the state. The Commission found that the bulk of the cultivable area in Maharashtra was destined to remain under dry farming conditions, relieved in the main only by small areas of well irrigation wherever underground resources permitted of this. At the same time, it was also observed that farmers located in the irrigated areas, particularly where perennial cash crops could be grown, became far more prosperous than those outside such areas and that these canal-irrigated areas and their environs virtually became pockets of all-round prosperity. The Commission, therefore, recommended that in each river basin irrigation facilities should be spread over as much of the region as possible, thereby permitting the development of pockets of prosperity all along the river course. The recommendation of the Commission regarding the dispersal of irrigation benefits over the widest possible area of each river basin was thus based on a view of the total management of the water resources of the state; and the Commission warned that unless the dispersal of irrigation facilities, various aspects of which the Commission had examined in detail and framed recommendations about, was deliberately and properly planned in advance and the plan adhered to implemented fully, lopsided development would result on the new irrigation works as it had already been on the old.

It is interesting to note how with this clear definition of the basic objective the Commission was led, in the especially difficult circumstances of Maharashtra, to recommend very elaborate systems of management for full economic use of highly scarce water resources. The exploitation of underground water supply, in combination with surface water, has recently become recognized as an important management requirement in all parts of India. Even in regions where supply of water in canal systems is plentiful and the underground water level favourable, the exploitation of underground water supplies through tube wells, etc., is expected to lead not only to a more intensive use of water over a much larger area but also to help in preventing such evils as waterlogging. The Maharashtra Commission had, however, to go much beyond treating underground water supply as merely additional or supplementary. Maharashtra has a substratum homogeneous rock of great depth which makes practically all dependable sources of underground water very much a matter of chance. At the same time, it has been found that the underground water table in the command of the canals gets considerably enriched. This has been established by experience though the nature of surcharging of water underground table by seepage from canals is not fully known. The Maharashtra Irrigation Commission found it necessary, in the circumstances, to recommend the adoption, in the future, of a lift-cum-flow irrigation system in the working of canals. The basic idea was that the underground water from the enriched sub-soil in the canal command should be utilized for supplementing irrigation by flow from the canal, thus increasing total area irrigated from the limited surface water resources. After discussing several alternative suggestions put forward for working out a system for this purpose, the Commission recommended one of these; this was that canal water should be supplied to perennial crops at alternative rotations, the other rotations being taken up by wells which the irrigators are encouraged or compelled to construct. It was thought that in such an arrangement the canal will run continuously but the different distributaries will run at alternate rotations. The continuous running of the canal would keep the underground water table sufficiently high throughout the period, enabling well irrigation to be done.

To my knowledge, the recommendations regarding the lift-cum-flow system in the area under command of canals have not yet been adopted by the Maharashtra Government. I can see that there would be difficulties in the adoption of this system and that, both, administrators of irrigation systems and the existing groups of beneficiaries under these might oppose such adoption. However, I feel that in the ultimate analysis, if you adopt the objectives for irrigation water management accepted by the Maharashtra Irrigation Commission, there is no real alternative to the adoption of some such system for full dispersal of the benefit of water resources.

May I refer to some other aspects of irrigation water management which were considered by the Maharashtra Irrigation Commission and which have economic overtones? The first relates to the arrangements according to which water is supplied to cultivators for different crops and in different seasons. Here, again, it appears that some regions in India do not find it necessary to concern themselves in any detail with such problems. This may be because either the water supply is ample and adequate for lands under command throughout the year or because there is no diversity in the cropping pattern. However, I feel that in most areas such especially favourable conditions may not last forever and that in most irrigation systems it would be necessary to evolve some detailed arrangements for supply of water. The question is likely to assume special importance when the need for raising the revenue income from irrigation systems becomes urgent. It is obvious that a schedule of water charges which has been linked to the quality of the crop raised, and the time and duration of supply, is likely to be more productive of revenue than a uniform rate over the whole year. A cultivator who obtains water supply for a more costly and more intensively cultivated crop is in a position to, and would be willing to, pay a correspondingly higher price for the supply of water for raising the crop. In the same way, water supplied during a season when there is general scarcity of the commodity could be made to fetch a higher price. It is obvious that elaborating or refining the system of charging in this manner would mean evolving a detailed arrangement for the supply of water to different crops at different times. This involves, obviously, greater control over the distribution of water and implicitly, also, over the operations of the cultivator.

This elaboration may be necessary from other points of view also which have significance in irrigation water management. Within a system, in which the total supply of water is much less than the potential demand from irrigators under command, irrigation water management faces a number of problems. The problem of distributing water so as to benefit as large numbers as possible has been referred to above. However, there are other problems such as those of keeping a balance between perennial crops, consuming water on a large scale, and the other largely seasonal crops, the need for controlling areas under certain crops for preventing water-logging, etc., the need to encourage utilization of water during periods when the supply is especially plentiful and, in particular situations, the need to encourage the adoption of social crop patterns such as those in which foodgrains predominate.

When, within an irrigation system, water supply is apt to vary between one year and another, irrigation water management is faced with the additional problem of a proper balance between long-term and short-term contracts. The need to encourage cultivators to make investments in costly, capital-intensive, perennial crops so as to obtain maximum production and financial returns has to be balanced against the possibility of a shortfall in supply in particular years. In Maharashtra, all these sets of conditions have led to the elaboration of the Block System—in the initial development of which, that eminent engineer-statesman, Shri M. Vishweshwarya, played a great part. I feel that even though, as at present, in many areas, such elaborations and refinements may appear superfluous, the need to adopt them in some measure would arise everywhere in time.

At the same time, an elaborate system of management through blocks may have the defect of rigidifying the crop pattern of irrigators, especially of those under long-term agreement for supply of water. It is highly desirable that such rigidity should be avoided. This can be done to some extent by not making the long-term contract too long. However, even within such a period as the six-year period, flexibility should be available and it would, therefore, be necessary to define the crop patterns of blocks rather in terms of generalized categories of crop than in terms of individual crops. The Maharashtra Irrigation Commission made a number of specific recommendations in this direction. I am not sure that they have been given effect to. I am particularly reminded of this problem at this juncture and venture to bring it to the notice of the Symposium because I have lately heard complaints from some progressive farmers in Maharashtra that their efforts at experimenting with a number of combinations of crops during a year, made possible by the recent emergence of the hybrid varieties, have been obstructed by operation of the present block system.

Finally, I may refer to one aspect of irrigation water management which has socio-political as well as economic overtones. This is the problem of the local management of the distribution of water and of the repairs and maintenance of distribution channels. In this context, I shall permit myself to indulge in a generalization. The transition from an authoritarian colonial regime to a federal democratic one involves large changes in administrative practice and in the attitude of the administrators, and these changes we have been slow to recognize, and slower to put into practice. I am convinced that in the ultimate analysis, efficiency and appropriate local administration require active participation of the local community, whether the administration pertains to education or irrigation or to forest or health. In all contexts it has been found that of recent years the efficiency and authority of the local government officials have been undermined but local responsibility has not increased correspondingly. That local administration can be both efficient and honest I have no doubt at all. While I was Chairman of a sugar co-operative factory, our factory administration was able to obtain from the state government the work, on an agency basis, of distributing water during summer months not only to members of our co-operative but also to all irrigators within the area of the villages falling within the jurisdiction of the co-operative. We were able to show that administration by the co-operative sugar factory, of this scheme of distribution, raised fewer complaints than formerly and was able to distribute a given supply of water over a larger area. I am free to confess that a later Chairman of the same factory told me of strains that could arise in the operation of the factory itself through taking on such burden of irrigation management. I cite my experience, therefore, not as suggesting a particular direction in which devolution of management should come about but merely to point to the fact that devolution can be successfully experimented with. I realise that conditions in our country vary greatly from region to region and that even within an area the changing human factor may lead to differing levels of efficiency of management. At the same time, I am convinced that the ultimate solution to our problems of local management can be found only by persistently experimenting with local devolution in all contexts in which it appears to have the least chance of success.

To sum up, it is seen that irrigation water management has to take into consideration a large number of socio-economic objectives such as a proper distribution of benefits, the conservation and optimum use of water and land resources, obtaining the maximum financial return from the irrigation systems, encouraging the adoption of the most profitable crop patterns compatible with conservation aims, and making for the participation of the local community in management.

21

Problems Relating to Land Reform*

As I visualize it, this Conference is called upon to consider problems relating to land reform at two levels. Firstly, it is necessary to look into the follow-up of policies regarding land reform adopted many years ago. In this respect, it is recognized that there are still significant gaps in legislation and that implementation is unsatisfactory in many respects. A frank discussion as to the difficulties encountered, particularly in implementation, should prove extremely valuable for future progress.

Apart from following our policies initiated many years ago, it would be useful for the Conference to consider land reforms and related questions from the point of view of recent developments and in relation to problems that are likely to emerge in the future. I propose to deal chiefly with these problems in my introductory remarks. The most important recent development to be considered is the impending breakthrough in agriculture. In the context of this possible technological transformation two important problems emerge for consideration in this Conference. In the first instance, what is the extent to which actual cultivators of land have such precarious or unprofitable tenure in relation to their holdings that they could not be thought of as putting themselves to any special trouble and expenditure for adopting improvements in practices or increasing inputs? This is the large area where the many gaps in legislation and implementation assume importance. The tenant may feel insecure because of provisions regarding resumption of land; whole categories or classes, e.g., share-croppers, may not be recognized in law or given adequate protection. Records may be out-of-date or so highly defective that advantages of legal provisions cannot flow to those in whose behalf they are supposed to have been enacted.

* Speech on 28 November 1969, at the Conference of Chief Ministers on Land Reform.

In relation to this aspect of the question, I would offer only one comment. The prospect of the green revolution vests with great importance and urgency, the need to close gaps in implementation and legislation. This is because the green revolution, wherever it is impending, adds very considerably to the incentives to superior holders to resume land or deny the benefit of legislation temporarily or permanently to existing actual cultivators. It is in this context of the aggravation of an already difficult situation that governments of states have to look at this problem. For, while on the one hand the incentive to superior holders held out by the technological revolution becomes large and tempting, by the same token the impending deprivation of the prospect, of all possible improvement of their own conditions as those who are deprived or denied their proper cultivating rights would see it, would rankle all the more. Both ways, therefore, the situation would be pushed towards one of acute conflict. This is the case of acting urgently to implement the accepted policies. It is necessary, in this context, to draw pointed attention to some grave problems that administrative implementation of land reforms face in India. It has been pointed that administrative structures deriving from colonial times have a juridical bias and are apt to implement measures of even socio-economic reform in a rigidly administrative and legalistic manner. The results of such administration are usually unsatisfactory. This is because of the unequal terms on which the existing vested interests, and the weaker classes in whose favour legislation is passed, are placed in relation to such matters as knowledge of administrative forms and capacity to produce legally satisfactory evidence. In many countries, this bias is sought to be corrected through associating representatives of beneficiaries with various stages of implementation. It is for consideration to what extent this approach could be adopted in India.

In this context, it is necessary to appreciate the importance of local opinion and the structure of local society in the implementation of land reforms. At present these factors are not everywhere favourable to proper implementation and how to get over handicaps imposed by the nature of administrative machinery and the structure of local society becomes an acute problem. It might have been expected that a movement like that of Gramdan might show the way to building up favourable public opinion and an appropriate organization for flexible management of land problems. This has not yet happened. The other possible agencies who could provide the corrective are groups of social workers or party cadres. None of these are seen to be effective on any large scale. The problems posed above are especially acute in the more depressed areas and the tribal areas and nowhere is there a satisfactory solution in sight. This aspect of land reform implementation has to be thought about much more widely, and in greater depth, than has been usual so far.

The other aspect of the problem is the need to take action on a much broader front than that of closing gaps in legislation and implementing land reform adequately. One of the main justifications for giving security against eviction or enhancement of rent to the actual cultivator has been the incentive afforded to him for greater investment and harder work. Productivity of land per acre with tenants was expected to go up following effective implementation of land reforms. Though there are obvious gaps in our performance in this regard, it cannot be denied that during the last two decades very large numbers of erstwhile tenant farmers have become either owners of land or have attained a secure status as tenant. At the same time, no large increase in per acre productivity of small farmers in this class has been recorded.

This does not, however, imply that land reform was unnecessary. It merely indicates that though for increasing productivity land reform was necessary it was, by itself, not sufficient. Or rather that land reform must in this context be more broadly interpreted so as to include all those institutional and organizational changes and programmes which would enable the small farmer class to participate fully in the technological transformation of agriculture. Such broader interpretation of the scope of land reforms is now being increasingly accepted in international discussions. A large number of developmental policies and programmes are intended to implement land reforms in this wider sense. Special attention may be drawn to a programme in the Central sector of the Fourth Five-Year Plan regarding setting up small-farmer agencies to look after the problems of small farmers in a co-ordinated manner and to enable the potentially viable amongst them to invest in development, increase inputs, improve practices so as to put their economy on a firm basis. The setting up of the agencies for the small-farmer and devising their operational planes have emphasized the role of local organizations, particularly, the *Zilla Parishad*s and the co-operatives, in the implementation of this aspect of land reform.

The small-farmer agency project with its emphasis on the potentially viable farmer brings to the fore another problem which is urgent. This is that of the cultivators who are not even potentially viable and the large class of agricultural labourers. An examination of this problem would reveal that the existing approach to the organization of the unit of agricultural production may prove increasingly inadequate in the future. The basis of the older approach to land reform was that through proper implementation of land reform and the development of agriculture a soundly based agrarian economy would be established. This approach proved relevant upto the class of middling peasant and with special effort it may hold good in relation to the class of the potentially viable small farmer. With the recent improvements in technology of agriculture it would also be possible to establish viable farming on rather smaller holdings than before. However, this still leaves out the problems of the very small farmers in irrigated or secure areas and the small farmers in non-irrigated or the unsecure areas. In short, the problem of, what may be called, the uneconomic holders, still remains. This constitutes a very large section of cultivators and together with landless labourers forms the most substantial class of rural families in most regions of the country.

In part, the problems of this class are problems of planned development, increased employment, and diversification of the economy. However, in part they also belong, properly speaking, to land reform. For, they are problems that can be tackled only by measures which make it possible for the areas in cultivating possession of the uneconomic holders to be brought together in some way so that each unit of production is sufficiently large for being exported with improved methods and larger inputs. This is a problem to which sporadic attention has been given in the past. At one time, the formation of co-operative farming societies was an important plank in official policy. If this move had succeeded it might have afforded a solution in a large part. However, the co-operative farming experiment did not prove, in most cases, a striking success and the concept as a whole was not enthusiastically pursued by any government or any section of the population. From the long-term point of view it is inadvisable to neglect this problem and it is necessary to start at least an active debate in relation to it immediately. As I view it, the solution must be found in the direction of some way of pooling together lands which are in cultivating possession of uneconomic holders. A primary obstacle in doing this as at present is that the holdings of the small and uneconomic holders are not necessarily contiguous and are scattered all over the area of a village. A preliminary step for future reorganization would be to pay attention to this aspect in measures of consolidation so that in the post-consolidation lay-out of fields the holdings of the smaller men are placed in reasonable contiguity. Attention may be drawn to steps taken in Egypt to consolidate the lay-out of fields or lay out fields in new settlements in such a manner that, whoever the owner might be, a uniform crop pattern is adopted for a series of contiguous fields. With the control through irrigation available in Egypt such an approach is easy to adopt in that country. However, there does not appear any insuperable obstacle to paying attention in our consolidation efforts to the consideration noted above.

Reference to difficulties in the organization of production effort of uneconomic holders raises for consideration another aspect of the existing programme of land reform. This is the programme of distribution of waste or surplus land to certain categories and classes and establishing, in effect, a number of new cultivating families. In implementing this policy both the aspects discussed above must be taken account of. On the one hand, it will have to be seen that, as far as possible, units of cultivation newly created are potentially viable and that adequate policy measures in relation to credit, supply, marketing, etc., are being taken so that the potentially viable families become, in fact, viable within a short time. The other aspect emerges to the extent where the new cultivating holdings either because of their size or physical characteristics are not even potentially viable. In this case, pooling of land for production would either have to be initially insisted on, or the manner of immediate creation of new holdings and distribution of land provided for future pooling arrangements. It is necessary to draw pointed attention to this aspect. Otherwise we shall be adding to the size of an intractable problem that we have already on hand.

Finally, attention may be drawn to another aspect of emergent land policy. It is obvious that with the growth of urbanization and of industrial economy there would be considerable movement of populations in future decades. These movements may involve to a large extent rural families, some of whom may be cultivating families. Therefore, there may be considerable need for adjustment in the extent and composition of holdings. This raises the problem of possibility of including an element of flexibility in land tenure arrangements. As at present, we are steadily moving towards a relatively rigid frame. Once the effect of the ceiling has been worked out and resumption of land becomes insignificant and as legislation to prevent new fragments or sub-division of holding below a level is adopted and consolidation is carried out distribution of land would become fairly fixed in terms of size and composition of holdings and cultivating families. For a variety of reasons leasing in and leasing out are, at present, being discouraged. As time passes, this may lead to difficulties because of non-flexibility. This is type of a dilemma which land reform policy in India has continuously faced in the past. Where alienation has been discouraged to prevent exploitation, the problem of the drying up of credit has had to be met. We may soon reach a stage where large numbers of uneconomic holders may move out of agricultural activity but may not want, at least for the time being, to give up rights in relation to holdings. It is more likely than not that the cultivator who leases in from the small holder may be a big man who is contiguous. As at present, land reform legislation does not pay attention to such a possibility because of the large danger of abuse of any permissive leasing in or leasing out provisions. The problem could be relatively easily solved in relation to the uneconomic holder if his land forms, in fact, part of a pool.

These introductory remarks are intended to make clear the central position of land reforms in the planning of development of rural society. They also bring out how the definition of land reforms, and of policies governing it, have to be related to successive stages of such development.

V

Income Policy

22

Existing Differentials in Salaries and Wages and Their Relation to a Socialistic Pattern*

The problem of differentials of wages and salary scales together with the related question of incentives is of vital importance in an economic plan intended to lead society towards a socialistic pattern. In case complete equality of opportunity and complete mobility and freedom of entry already existed, differentials in payments would, it is generally agreed, be determined by: (i) costs of waiting and training; (ii) compensation for special hardships in relation to nature of work, location, conditions of work, etc., and (iii) payment for specially scarce abilities. If attention is concentrated on the first two, it is likely that under the hypothetical conditions the differentials would move within a very narrow range. As the educability of the individual in modern economics has been found to be fairly high, with equality of opportunity, the return to costs of waiting and training would not cause large differentials in the more progressive and richer societies, especially as a larger part of these costs would also tend to be borne by the public exchequer.

In fact, of course, the differentials in India today are very large. The existing situation regarding variations in wages and salaries in India can be attributed, in the main, to pre-existing inequalities in the distribution of wealth and income which the current system of payments and remunerations perhaps further continues to aggravate and certainly does little or nothing to reduce. The existing system of differentials is, thus, of little relevance to the future socialistic arrangements, except to indicate

* Memorandum submitted to the Panel of Economists, Government of India Planning Commission, in December 1956.

or measure the extent and direction of corrections that might become necessary.

Before proceeding further with the consideration of the internal situation, we may examine some influences of external factors on payments of salaries, etc., in India. The scales of salaries of higher officials in India had been completely dominated by British scales and the influence persists in spite of the rise in prices during war, and because of the inadequacy of the recommendations of the Salaries Commission. In recent years foreign companies operating in India have been recruiting Indians in large numbers as officers under pressure from the government. This has introduced a new disturbing element in the situation. The scales offered by these companies to the Indian recruits are completely out of line even with the prevailing standards of pay in government, or private Indian business. These payments are presumably justified on the grounds of parity with payments that have to be offered to the non-Indian officers of these companies. Thus an external factor, which in the past determined the scale of salaries of higher officials in India, is now operating towards setting up standards equally irrelevant and equally extravagant in the business sector. Another possible external factor is the scales of remuneration of the new and expanding international organizations. The scales of payment offered by these international organizations are, of course, very much higher than anything contemplated by business or government in India today, and even a cursory glance at the extent of the disparities is enough to prove that no attempt could be made to settle even the highest scales in India *vis-à-vis* the practice of international authorities. At the same time, it cannot be gainsaid that posts in these international organizations have offered alternative employment to some Indians.

The influence of external standards has to be judged from effects in the other directions also. The expectations of the rich in general, especially those of big businessmen, are, mostly, powerfully influenced by the pattern of consumption by the rich in other countries, particularly those of Western Europe and North America. And these expectations set a standard of net income against which all personal tax measures and all proposals, such as that of a ceiling on incomes, are examined by those who virtually rule the private sector in modern Indian industry and trade. The influence of the same factor is also seen in, for example, standards, or targets of standards, of hotel accommodation and amenities in railway and other travel that are beginning to be accepted in India. Even the continually expanding provision of internal air travel may be considered directly or indirectly the result of hopes of tourist traffic or the supposed expectations of foreigners. It is a matter to be very seriously considered whether the presumed advantage flowing from, say, tourist traffic may not be counterbalanced by the possible misdirection of national resource utilization through the setting up of unreal standards in this manner. All this seems to emphasize the need to eliminate, as far as possible, the influence of external factors on our expected as well as actual standards of consumption in all directions.

The restrictions already existing on movements of capital make it unnecessary to consider returns to capital in India in the international context, i.e., from the point of view of a rate of return having to look to prevention of migration of capital from India to other places where it could obtain higher returns. In terms of labour employment, migration possibilities are almost non-existent. That the world is far from being an international community is underlined by the fact that for our labour, and even for our small trader, opportunities in economic activity abroad are contracting rather than expanding. Perhaps, the one exception where there is a link to employment abroad is that mentioned above of the employment offered by international organizations.

The statement that the existing set of differentials in India is the result of historical forces, and of the highly stratified structure of our society, may be illustrated by drawing attention to a number of features of the current situation. The first of these is the success of the war-time efforts to train raw recruits from rural areas in semi-skilled and skilled work in machine shops, etc. This success indicates how in terms of modern technology a large reservoir of labour can always be drawn upon, provided an opportunity and a minimum training are given.

The same phenomenon is strikingly brought out by the rapidly growing numbers of the educated unemployed, particularly in urban areas. This growth is the result not of a shrinkage of demand for the services of the educated urban classes but of a rapid and continuing increase of the numbers within the class. This increase may be said to be due to two forces: firstly, the pressure on an increasing number of strata in rural society to find employment for the younger generation in non-rural occupations, and secondly, the growth of opportunities, in many rural areas, for obtaining the urban type of education. The educational opportunities, newly created in the rural areas, are availed of for obtaining, what are considered to be, the qualifications for securing employment. With existing disparities in standards of payment, and opportunities of remunerative employment in urban and rural areas, the possibility of obtaining clerical, etc., employment in towns holds very great attraction to the bulk of the rural population which has access to educational opportunities. As far as one can see, with even a modest programme of educational development in rural areas, the numbers of those who will take to all kinds of training—specialized or non-specialized—with hopes of obtaining non-rural employment must continuously increase at a rapid pace. To this will be added the numbers from among those urban classes to whom educational facilities have become newly accessible.

Those who are in cultivating possession of land, in any capacity, hold on to cultivation of land tenaciously, and this happens also in the ranks of traditional hand-industry until it ceases to provide even the barest subsistence. These classes, i.e., the cultivators and the artisans, suffer from varying degrees of underemployment; overt unemployment is not strikingly present in their ranks. In rural areas it is the casual agricultural labouring class, to which additions are presumably being made continuously from the ranks of cultivators and artisans, that suffers most from unemployment. But whether it is from classes that suffer from unemployment or from those that suffer from underemployment, all those who can escape from the depressed rural sector strive to do so, and the only general avenue for such escape in the Indian situation is the attainment of a minimum standard of education, general or technical. It is an entirely wrong view of the situation to explain existing difficulties as arising out of the defects of the educational structure. The prevalence of non-specialized general educational institutions reflects the non-diversified nature of occupational opportunities in the Indian economy. This is made clear by the fact that where the number of any type of technically trained personnel is increased rapidly over the existing level it tends to suffer from unemployment to an extent even greater than that from which the general educated class suffers; it is also emphasized by the significant numbers of those with technical training seeking and being found in jobs where their special training is not required. The last is an illustration of disguised unemployment or 'underemployment' as defined by Mrs Robinson.

One of the most important illustrations of the influence of the stratification of the existing socio-economic structure in India is non-continuity in the scale of emoluments obtained by the employed. This is particularly noticeable in the employment of the educated urban classes. In the employment market there is a small number of highly privileged positions to which are attached especially high emoluments. Those who occupy these or have entry to these usually possess certain advantages of background or connections. In particular cases, such as that of recruitment by competitive public examinations, the entry may be said to be comparatively open. That, in fact, the entry by examination is far from being completely open can be discovered from any careful analysis of the successful entrants each year. This will show high concentration of fairly small groups in Indian society. Granting, however, that at least with reference to these groups, members of which have the predominant chance of being recruited to the services, the tests may keep the field fairly open, the element of non-continuity is brought out by the great disparity in the prospects and performances of those who are selected as a result of the tests and those others who are just not selected. The levels of remuneration in every direction obtained by those who are just not selected are ordinarily very much below the average of those who are selected or just selected. The service recruitment is a good illustration of the total situation as it contains no element, as in the returns of business, of individual risk or venture. To the bulk of those who attempt to enter public services through competitive examinations there is only a comparatively narrow range of possible openings. Recruitment to the better-paid jobs in private industry and commerce is confined for the most part to the small group of communities that own and operate modern business in India. This phenomenon of non-continuity, i.e., of an absence of gradually descending scales of remuneration in important classes of employment, not only throws light on the existing situation but also makes clear how it is possible, in this field, to maintain payments for a restricted group at an artificially high level.

The problem of salary or wage differentials is usually considered in two different parts, one relating to the range of differentials within an occupation and the other relating to differentials between different occupations or strata. Before proceeding to offer observations on these two aspects, I may draw attention to an important feature of the context in which this question is being considered. This is that of a planned economy. In a *laissez faire* economy it might be possible to take the view that whatever the range and character of differentials, they were the result of an open market pricing process, and because this was so, no interference with them was justified. Having given the extent of limitation and modification of the pricing mechanism involved in planning for development in India, the open market pricing explanation is no longer relevant. Differentials in a planned or even the so-called mixed economy will have to be justified either on the ground that they are required for the proper functioning or smooth operation of the economy and the plan or on the ground that they are justified in the light of some ethical or other non-economic value accepted by society. Therefore, in dealing with the problem it is necessary, first, to consider the two aspects in relation to the functioning of the economy and then go on to consider the overall influence of non-economic considerations.

Within an occupation the differentials would depend on variations in, what may be generally termed, skill; they might also depend on location. With progress of a process of development the locational and regional differences should diminish. This would be the result of a number of different factors. In the first instance, the process of development should diminish the measure of variation in economic conditions and standards of living. With no artificial barriers in the economy and with mobility increasing and costs of movement declining, inter-regional differences should become less. Also, presumably, the plan of development will be especially devoted towards improving conditions in backward regions and among backward classes. The whole emphasis of the world's concern with the plight of under-developed economies is on the undesirability of maintaining wide, and widening, differences among different constituents in world society. Obviously, the under-developed economies which count upon help from outside richer countries must, as part of their initial programme, bring about greater equality in standards of living, etc., within their own areas. Large differentials among various degrees of skill, etc., are usually associated with lack of opportunity. The differentials, as between the unskilled and the comparatively skilled in the same occupation, are relatively much larger in the under-developed than in the advanced economies. Among the advanced countries themselves, it has been observed that the progress of collective bargaining and of national wage agreements leads to progressive diminution of the range of locational or regional differentials and also of the comparative skill differentials, within an occupation. The total effect of the various forces acting on the Indian situation since 1939 has also been in the same direction. The enforcement of minimum-wage legislation in the important, unorganized industries and in the more organized part of agricultural activity, and the adoption of standardized wages in the organized sector of industry, banking, etc., would result in diminishing and rationalizing the differentials within individual occupations.

The main problem, in this context, to be faced by a planned economy is likely to be connected with methods of payment; this will be that of the possibility and pace of the adoption of a system of piece-rate wages. The advantage of this system from the point of view, both, of incentive payments and of adjustment of payment to productive effort is obvious. With proper safeguards against abuse provided by regulatory devices, it should be possible to extend with advantage the piece-rate system without opposition in large areas of economic activity.

The problem of the range of differentials, as between different strata and different occupations, is much more important for the subject under discussion than that of differentials within an occupation or grade. Its consideration has to begin with an abstract statement of the governing factors. As existing conditions are the result of socio-economic stratification, the radical modification of which must be an important part of the programme of any society progressing deliberately towards a socialistic pattern, they cannot serve as guides in determination of the framework of future arrangements. They will, of course, have to be taken as the starting points of the process of transition. Theoretically, apart from the facts of a given historical situation or of stratification, there are only a small number of factors which may be said to determine differentials between occupations. These appear to be: (i) investments to be made in making an entry into the occupation and the uncertainties in relation to returns to be faced in it; (ii) pleasantness or unpleasantness of the occupation and of conditions of work in it; and (iii) payment to scarce ability. In a dynamic situation, to these may be added the factor of special incentives or disincentives to adjust supply to demand and also perhaps special individual incentive payments to call forth the optimum production effort on the part of individuals.

One of these, (ii), may be supposed not to lead to very large differentials though a full allowance for it may change the existing scheme of differentials radically. In a society approaching a socialistic pattern, (i) also would have only a limited effect. In such a society, education, including the expenses of waiting during the period of education, would be largely socially borne and the uncertainties would tend to be progressively reduced. As investment and production are planned, there would be no special costs of entry. As regards adjustments between demand and supply of labour, a society developing according to a plan would have so many other instruments available for making the appropriate adjustments in labour supply, that it should not find it necessary to use differential wages as an important device for this purpose. Therefore, in the society of the future, the range of variations in level of rates of payments and of earnings should be comparatively small in virtue of all factors other than those relating to payments to individuals as incentives for productive effort and as return to scarce ability. The two are almost identical in a socialistic society. For, in such a society the holders of scarce ability will not be in the position of monopolists in an otherwise competitive market; they will not be able to dictate their own terms. However, the socialistic society may fear that they will not put forth their best effort and may hence be forced to offer them specially high incentive payments.

It is not the concern of this note to discuss the various forms of individual incentives that may be possible or necessary in planned economic development. The large body of knowledge in the field of operation of incentives and of industrial psychology can be drawn upon to determine appropriate individual and group incentives that may be needed and used in particular circumstances. All these forms of incentives are concerned, in the main, with methods of remuneration. For the larger part of the field they do not affect, in an important way, the differentials in the range of earnings. I am also not concerned in this note with the problems of the checks, the controls, and the monetary and the non-monetary incentives that may be required for the proper functioning of large autonomous corporations. Having granted that the size and gains of private business would be limited, the highest level of earnings would be indicated by the payments that are held to be necessary to afford the proper incentives to high public functionaries. In determining the level of the highest range, we are thus concerned with a comparatively small number of administrators, executives, and intellectuals in society. We assume that the standard of comfort appropriate to the putting forth of arduous and responsible effort could be maintained without very high differential payments.

A deliberate effort to improve the standard of living of the most disadvantaged would bring about a movement of closing in the differentials among the lower strata. This will be helped materially, so far as the differentials between the manual labour and non-manual labour classes are concerned, by the spread of educational facilities and other factors noted above. The closing in of the differentials from the top, however, cannot come about except by deliberate effort. This effort in the context of private business will depend on effectiveness of the steps taken in relation to the concentration of economic wealth and power in private hands and the policy in relation to the formation of capital. As regards payments of salaries in the public and also in the private sphere, the effort is related, in the main, to ideas about, appropriate standards of living and about the needed incentives.

The last is a problem that derives special importance from the report that in the communist countries, especially Russia, very high incentive payments are made to certain classes of individuals and from the conclusion derived therefrom that these are necessary for operating a planned economy. The conclusion obviously presupposes a social philosophy and a view of human psychology. It may be emphasized that the psychology which is relevant here is only that of the elite. We have argued above that the range of relative differences necessary to afford appropriate incentives to the large bulk of people will not lead to very large differentials if the total range, as dictated by the requirements of the elite, is in itself not wide.

As during British rule, the decisive consideration in determining this range will be the requirement of those who wield economic and political power; and this will depend, in the existing context, on the philosophical and psychological make-up of this group or class. Is there anything in the Indian tradition that should lead to the Russian model being followed in this regard and heavy reliance being placed on the material incentives offered to the people at the top? It has been indicated above that, because of the wide disparity in national incomes, the standards of living in the richer countries set up models before the rich in the poorest countries, which are completely out of relation to the levels of incomes in these countries. In terms of requirements, which to them could be psychologically very important, the elite in poor countries could well consider the standards of the rich countries essential for themselves. This is a matter which can be settled in terms, only, of attitudes and judgments. The two main questions that emerge in this context appear to be about: (i) the motivations of those in power, and (ii) the accepted code of values in society. To a large extent the two are interrelated. If there is a certain set of professed values in society, the leaders of a society to be accepted as such voluntarily must show that their actions and attitudes are influenced, at least to some extent, by these values; this means that the motivation of the leaders must bear some apparent relation to the values they profess and preach as leaders of the society. In terms of traditional Indian values, and in the light of the special, recent emphasis on certain aspects of them, it is obvious that a large range of differentiation and high economic incentive payments in favour of the elite are not only not required but are also to be positively avoided. The whole set of values associated with democratic functioning of quasi-autonomous, small groups and with decentralization of political and economic power makes it necessary that the leaders, the top executives, and the administrators must have standards of consumption which do not mark them off sharply from the tiers below. In fact, in this context, and in a poor country where the leaders have constantly to preach the need for abstinence from wasteful consumption, a comparatively moderate standard of consumption for leaders may have a high moral and incentive value for society as a whole. At least high incentive payments, would, in such a society have adverse effects through their reactions on public psychology. Also, there is nothing in the Indian tradition, or in the existing Indian situation, to show that socially valuable or highly responsible intellectual effort has been called forth only, or chiefly, by high incentive payments.

People become accustomed to high standards of living very quickly and begin soon to consider as minimum what they had previously thought unattainable; undoubtedly, the last few decades have greatly enhanced the expectations of our middle and richer classes. This trend can yet be stopped and reversed with comparative ease, if the need for doing so is realized. In the Indian tradition, comparative poverty has not been associated with either lack of character or ability. On the contrary, persons who have deliberately avoided acquiring wealth, have always commanded, and perhaps still command, considerable influence in our society. Acceptance of a moderate standard of living by our elite, therefore, seems to be almost a necessary condition precedent, at least in the initial stages of planned economic development.

There might be no opposition to a general theoretical acceptance of the ideas put forth above. It is highly doubtful whether they would be equally acceptable and enforceable if worked out in specific detail. The problem may be said to have two aspects. Firstly, with regard to scales of emoluments in the public and the semi-public services, and secondly, payments in private industry. The dispute relating to payments to employees of banks has recently drawn attention to the public importance of the highest scales of salaries having some relation to levels of payments of the lower staff. However, barring some occasional action in relation to salaries of top executives in some nationalized institutions, little has so far been done in the matter. Even more important is the fact that there has been no systematic thinking on the subject, and no thought or action appears to have been contemplated or even deemed necessary.

The problem may be illustrated with reference to action by the University Grants Commission about the scales of salaries of university teachers. This particular episode illustrates many peculiarities of the Indian situation. In the first instance, teachers employed by universities are, relatively, about the best paid among teachers in India. If, therefore, monies were available for improving conditions of work or living of any class of teachers, university teachers should have been the last to be thought of. It is true that in some universities salaries of professors, etc., are at a lower level than in others; but then, in those universities, the salaries of other classes of teachers are also correspondingly low. The first point to be noted in connection with this move is that in India, in any scheme of development or public expenditure, the top executives and administrators not only get prior consideration, but also absorb disproportionately large amounts. The University Grants Commission has not expounded the reasons for its proposals. At one time it was suggested that the low salaries of university professors contributed to student-indiscipline. However, whether it is student-indiscipline, or standards of teaching and education, it would obviously pay to concentrate attention on the ranks of lecturers, etc., in colleges rather than on the relatively well-paid teachers in university departments.

The original scheme of subsidization of salaries by the University Grants Commission was confined to two grades of university teachers. It has subsequently been extended conditionally to college teachers. This raises the second point as to whether there has been any previous thought on the implied problem of the best utilization of available finance. Raising the salaries of existing incumbents or raising existing grades must be related to some objective which is supposed to have priority over possible advantages of new schemes of development, employment, or expansion. It must also have some relation to a framework of comparative payments within the occupation, and the relation of these payments to those outside.

The proposals of the University Grants Commission appear to be modelled on the recommendations of the Radhakrishnan Commission. The only argument put forward by this Commission, in support of the scales recommended by it, is that 'there is no reason why they (universities salaries) should not compare favourably with those of provincial services'. The scale of salaries recommended by the Radhakrishnan Commission for professors is Rs 900–50–1350, and it is interesting that the Commission itself notes the following facts: 'In Indian money the average salary of a professor in the USA is Rs 1,750 a month, the maximum salary (fixed only in Columbia) Rs 4,000 a month, and that of professor in the premier universities of the United Kingdom about Rs 1,750 a month.' The Commission, while noting the scales in the USA and the UK, does not feel called upon to comment on the close approximation of the scales recommended by it to the salaries of professors in countries so very much richer than India. If the Commission had cared to note the scales in countries nearer our own level of poverty or wealth, it would have found them very illuminating. For example, it may be noted that the salaries of professors in Japan, whose per capita income is roughly three times that of India, do not usually exceed Rs 700 per month. A comparison of the relative salaries of primary teachers, secondary teachers, and university teachers in India with those in other countries would similarly emphasize that the so-called low levels of existing salaries in universities and colleges in India are, in fact, now low relatively to our national economic circumstances.

Another point to note in the proposals of the University Grants Commission is that, even in its revised proposals, the raising of the salaries of college teachers is contingent on a very substantial part of the extra cost being borne by the governments of states. Because of this it will most probably happen that in the large majority of states, and certainly in all the poorer states, the proposals in relation to college lecturers, etc., will not be implemented, and only the university professors, etc., will obtain substantial increase in their salaries. It may be that in view of the sphere of direct responsibility of the University Grants Commission, it is justified in making the proposals it has made. However, on an overall view of the matter, the developments are hardly in consonance with planning for economic development. If a purely sectional view of the matter is taken it might be possible to argue in favour of the Commission's proposal even for raising salaries of university professors. The Commission, it could be said, is primarily interested in keeping up standards of university education, and an important course of action for achieving this is ensuring the quality of recruits to the profession of university teachers by way of providing attractive posts at the top. However, such a sectional view, especially at a time when an overall scarcity of trained personnel is impending, can only lead to chaos.

The moral of all this appears fairly clear. In any system, working like the present Indian system, there is little likelihood of any rationalization of the emoluments of the highest paid. There will always be shallow professions of moving towards equality and occasional action under pressure of public opinion in relation to a few posts at the top. For the rest, instead of any revision downwards, as more monies become available through development plans to various departments, there will be a multiplication of highly paid jobs and a levelling upwards of the scales obtained by those in the relatively less well-paid departments. This process of levelling upwards will most powerfully affect the upper grades in the central and the all-India services. The lower grades and the services of the state governments and of local authorities will feel the influence in a lesser and lesser degree. This is so for obvious reasons: The largest surpluses are with the centre; improvements in the highest grades involve small numbers and are thus not too costly; and also, members of these are closest to those who wield political and economic power and make policy decisions. The only period during which this trend was reversed was that of the inflationary rise of prices. During this period the operation of the system of dearness allowance brought somewhat closer than before the distance between the highest and the lowest. The Central Pay Commission had the opportunity of erecting an entirely new and rational framework. However, that body failed to do this, and developments since then have brought about no rationalization. India continues to have, therefore, one of the most non-equalitarian systems of payments to higher public officials. On a realistic view of the matter, no correction of this, except perhaps through another bout of inflation, appears immediately possible.

To the situation in the public sphere has recently been added another complicating and worsening factor of the salaries paid to their officers by the large corporations and managing agencies, especially the foreign companies, in the sphere of private industry. These are now the highest-paid jobs open to sons of the elite. Apart from the many consequences of the presence of a large section of well-connected young men as employees of private foreign companies, the direct influence of the salary-scales paid to these on recruitment and of salaries of public officials is itself bound to be important. This is not the place to consider whether the government will directly attempt to regulate these salary scales or not. It is, however, relevant to observe that all these payments come out of the total Indian national product, and the planned development of the country, with all the regulations on activity and burdens on the consumer that it involves, is largely responsible for maintaining the conditions under which they are earned. Whether the economic activity is in the private or public sector, whether it is conducted by indigenous or foreign operators, and whether the emoluments received are in the nature of salaries, wages, or profits, the absolute and relative heights of all incomes received out of the national pool are the concern of the government and the planning authority. And whether the payments are imposed, prescribed, permitted, or merely tolerated they must be taken as parts of the plan. Therefore, whether through appropriate tax policy or through direct regulation, all salaries as well as high entrepreneurial incomes must be set at appropriate levels.

Attention may be drawn to another type of complication in the existing situation. This arises through the progressive regulation of wages, especially in organized industry. It is well known that the standardized or other regulated wages in organized industry are usually set at levels which are notably above current levels. The phenomenon of non-continuity noticed above in the case of salaries of high government officials is noticed in this case also, and employees in some types of organized industry find themselves in a privileged position. Similar and sometimes even greater anomalies are caused by some minimum-wage regulations. Especially when these affect payment in rural areas, as, for example, in case of plantation labour or labour in sugar factories, the difference in the regulated and non-regulated wages is seen to be very large. These facts are set out here not to call into question the trend in policy relating to regulation of wages. That policy is one of the important operative factors in levelling up incomes in the community. The anomalies that are created in giving effect to it merely underline the gravity of the employment situation in the country and the extremely low levels of current standards of living, particularly in the rural areas. The minimum at which tribunals or other bodies can bring themselves to set the level of remuneration to unskilled general labour is yet far above that of actual earnings of very large numbers in our towns and countryside. This further emphasizes the fact that a grossly disproportionate share of the national dividend is appropriated by those who wield political and economic power, and by the classes from whom the state and the social leaders are drawn. The disproportion is all the more striking in view of the social philosophy they profess and their continuous preaching of self-denial and abstinence to others.

From the point of view of immediate policy decisions, the following points appear to emerge from what has been discussed in the preceding paragraphs: (i) One of the major aims of the Plan should be to raise the standard of living in the poorest areas and of the most disadvantaged classes through appropriate plans of development and employment. (ii) The minimum-wage legislation should be enforced in the unorganized sector of industry and in the organized sector of agriculture over as large an area as possible. (iii) In the organized sectors of industry collective bargaining and standardization of rates of remuneration be actively encouraged. (iv) Continuous and systematic attempts to be made to rationalize progressively scales of salaries and other types of remuneration paid to top executives, administrators, and intellectuals in all official and semi-official employment. One of the main objectives of the rationalizing process should be to see that, by the end of the plan-period, the range of differentials between the highest and the lowest scale of official payments should not be wider than that obtaining in the UK. Attempt should be made to narrow the variations between payments by various official departments and agencies and payments by various strata of governmental authority—central, state, and local. (v) Standards of remuneration and earnings at the higher levels in private modern business should be amenable to public regulation. (vi) The standards of convenience, amenities, etc., afforded by public services and agencies should not be set at levels current in the rich countries but should be evolved in appropriate relation to the size of our national product and the level of general well-being in our society.

23

Ex-colonial and New Income Differentials in India*

Under the British rule the levels of salaries paid to British personnel in the government, and to all Europeans in private business, were relatively very high. Also, the spread between the lowest and the highest salaries paid by the Indian Government was much greater than in other countries. In the 1920s the relation was no less than 1:133 in India, as compared with 1:32 in the UK and only 1:14 in Germany and Japan. As long as the highest categories of employment were monopolized by the British, this had no relevance for the standards of living of Indians. However, when at last Indians began to be recruited to those higher categories, British and Indians employed in the same service shared the same salary level. Thus, a tiny minority of Indians now received salaries which were related to standards obtaining in rich countries.

It might have been expected that this discrepancy would disappear after Independence. But this has not been the case. The government undertook no salary-scale reform, even though all British personnel had left. To some extent, war-time inflation and frequent cost-of-living allowances for junior staff had a mitigating effect. Even so, extremes in government salaries remain greater in India than in most countries of the world.

Even more important than these disparities in official salary levels are those that exist today in the private business sector. Here, we see the influence of foreign concerns operating in India or Indian concerns operating with foreign participation. Foreign concerns have been under pressure from the government to employ increasingly larger proportions of Indians. In Indian concerns with foreign participation, foreign technicians

* Originally published in *Co-Existence*, Vol. I, No. 1, May 1964, pp. 74–6.

and managers play important roles, at least in the initial years. In either case, Indians and foreigners are employed on similar jobs and parity of salaries is usually maintained. But this has been to set the standards of payment to Indian personnel at levels which are determined by those of richer foreign countries. Salaries paid to foreign technicians and others are of a level required to attract them to serve in foreign, and usually less congenial, surroundings. But these salaries paid by companies employing foreigners, in turn, influence those of the highest managerial and technical personnel in the purely Indian companies, and also to some extent the salaries paid by industrial organizations in the public sector.

Since Independence, certain controls have prevented disparities in salaries in government service from increasing. By contrast, business expansion has been rapid, and as the number of lucrative posts has increased, so salaries have moved higher. The situation was examined by the Commission on Emoluments and Conditions of Service of Central Government Employees, 1957–59.

The following extract from the Commission's report strikingly portrays the position in 1956–57:

'The disparity ratio between the highest salaries and the lowest wages in the private sector is also far higher than in the Central Government sector, and has, moreover, increased considerably since 1948–49. The table below brings this out:

	Category	1948–49	1956–57
		Income per annum in Rs.	
I.	Total emoluments of an unskilled worker:		
	(a) Cotton Textiles, Bombay	999	1,185
	(b) Jute Textiles, W. Bengal	702	806
II.	Average post-tax salary income of the highest salary earners	77,250	286,929
III.	Disparity ratio II : I (a)	77	242
	II : I (b)	110	356

...And we should invite attention to the fact that we are all through this chapter referring to incomes of purely salary earners in the private sector; earnings in the other forms at the top levels of that sector are higher' (Report pp. 82–4).

If anything, the situation today is worse than that of five years ago. The picture presented above may be somewhat exaggerated through the selection, for purposes of comparison, of the very highest salaries. However, there is no doubt that the number of high-salaried posts in private business is increasing rapidly, and that the gap is widening between the industrial wage earners and the highest-paid managerial personnel.

The salaries paid by international organizations have a similar influence on levels or remuneration of the highest qualified technical and other personnel in India. The tendency is accentuated because of the possibility, albeit limited, for members of these categories to go abroad to accept positions in more affluent countries.

Thus, at the lower level, the labour market in India is overstocked, with avenues of emigration barred, and resulting remuneration very low. Yet, at top levels the supply is very limited due to high costs of training and limited entry, while the international economy determines standards of payment.

Other elements to be taken into account are the standards of living and the expectations of businessmen as a class. Top Indian businessmen in collaborating with foreign business find themselves paying high managerial salaries, and they have come to expect that their own remuneration will be correspondingly high. They are influenced by frequent contacts with foreigners and by visits abroad. As a result, the standard of living of such businessmen in India tends to approximate the standard of living of their opposite numbers in the affluent countries. These factors in turn affect standards, both, in private life and in the public sector, such as are represented in entertainment, luxury restaurant and hotel accommodation, travel arrangements, and other public amenities.

Of the many possible implications, two may, perhaps, be mentioned here. First, high salaries direct current resources towards consumption, and capital is invested in the production of luxury goods: a situation which might ordinarily be considered highly inappropriate in the case of poorer countries. Second, and even more important, is what may be called the exhibition of conspicuous injustice in distribution. On the assumption that social cohesion and solidarity are important pre-requisites of successful democratic planning for the development of poorer countries, this exhibition of distributive injustice must be considered a most adverse factor.

24

The Stabilization of Agricultural Incomes*

I

The problem of stabilization of agricultural incomes has always been considered extremely important in India and it has always been recognized that the liability to fluctuations of the income of agriculturists was one of the main causes of the distresses and difficulties of agricultural classes in India. In ancient times, the fluctuations were essentially connected with the character of the seasons; the famine was an extreme manifestation of the evil. The monetization and commercialization of agriculture added the new factor of variation in prices from year to year. The development of markets for agricultural produce and the remarkable improvement in transportation facilities which accompanied monetization and commercialization relieved, to a large extent, the extreme evil effects of local failure of seasons. The famine, instead of being a period when supply of food for man and cattle was grossly inadequate, became one in which employment of all resources was interrupted and the real income of the village population fell to a very low level.

Today, fluctuations of agricultural incomes result, both, from variations in the physical output of agriculture from year to year and from variations in the prices obtained for quantities of agricultural produce sold. It is not possible to make any definite statement regarding mutual relations between the volume of physical production in agriculture, the marketed surplus of agriculturists, and the prices received for agricultural products. Also, we have little data showing the combined effects of all these variations on any set or groups of families from year to year. Apart from the older *annewari*, the data in relation to variations of physical output are usually available as

* Submitted to the Seminar on Economic Planning held in Delhi in April 1962.

a result of estimates or enquiries for particular crops in large regions or in single villages. Even here, except where enquiries have been conducted into the same set of farmers for successive years, the data do not indicate the effect of the variations in relation to individual families. Moreover, crop-cutting, and such other data referring to variations in yield of crops can be made the basis of the measurement of variations in the fortunes of the agriculturists of a region, only in the case of single-crop regions. Where more than one crop is grown by most farmers, difficulty is experienced in reasoning out from the data relating to crop-yields. No doubt, if crop-yield data or estimates are available for the major crops of a region, some combined index of average variations in physical yield might be based on these.

For the data in relation to price fluctuations, the chief source is the officially collected prices of agricultural products. The most relevant price-series is that of wholesale prices. However, these prices do not necessarily represent prices received by farmers, and the efforts to obtain reliable information relating to harvest prices or the prices received by farmers have not proved very successful. Quotations of wholesale prices in particular months from year to year may be considered to give a fairly good indication of the variation in the range of farm-prices received on the average by farmers. No doubt, decisions of farmers relating to sale of given quantities in particular months may be influenced by ruling levels of prices and by expectations in relation to them. However, the practice or possibility of taking such decisions deliberately might be predicated in relation, only, to a small proportion of farmers; for the vast majority, a fairly rigid pattern of sales-behaviour may be assumed. Almost no data are available regarding variations in the proportions of the total crop marketed by individual farmers or groups of farmers from year to year. This variable would, however, appear to be important, chiefly in the case of foodgrains. In the group of fibres or oilseeds and other commercial crops like tobacco, *gur,* etc., the farmer is known to sell the vast bulk of his crop. Fluctuations, if any, in this regard would relate rather to the timing of sales than to the proportion of output sold.

The combined effect of all these fluctuations on the incomes of agriculturists is difficult to estimate on the basis of the separate sets of data. The only source of information on fluctuations of agricultural incomes of families could thus be the enquiries into farm management or farm business. It is particularly difficult to generalize on the basis of price and production series because the proportion of produce sold is known to vary as between farmers with varying sizes of business, and the incidence of effects of variations in production or prices from year to year on different-sized farmers would be far from being the same. Direct surveys of farm business could be used to estimate fluctuations in agricultural incomes over the years only when comparable results of enquiries are available for successive years. This is so only in a few, dispersed instances.

In the absence of adequate data one has to reason, partly in the abstract, and partly by reference to general experience. Indian experience in the past, as well as in recent times, has emphasized the role of fluctuations in the economic situation of the agriculturist. What might be called the state of under-development equilibrium is the result of severe fluctuations in agricultural incomes operating in conjunction with a highly exploitative moneylender-trader system. The small surpluses emerging in Indian agriculture, have been insufficient in the past because of the cost imposed by fluctuations. The system has attained a sort of equilibrium with the moneylender-trader system making up the deficiency of resources during the adverse years and mopping up all the surpluses during good years, thus leaving the cultivator in a permanent state of poverty and dependence. It was only the long period of favourable terms of trade during the war and post-war years and the contemporary inflationary rises in prices which increased the money receipts of cultivators and lowered the real burden of past debts, that radically and quasi-permanently improved the position of agriculturists in India. Even so, the improvement came about only in restricted regions and only for certain types of cultivators or certain strata of them. The general transformation of the forties provided the background against which new programmes of co-operative credit and other developmental efforts could succeed. But the unevenness of the incident of success of these programmes itself underlines the continued difficulties in the other parts of the economy. So that, even today, the state of under-development equilibrium persists in all the more backward regions and the more subsistent types of economies or for uneconomic holders in the commercialized regions. The problem of the last category, where solved, has been solved not owing to any improvement in agricultural incomes but owing to increase in non-farm receipts. All this amounts to saying that current fluctuation in incomes of agriculturists in India are so large that deficiencies in adverse years have to be made up by borrowing, and for many classes of agriculturists, this borrowing is high and its costs very heavy.

II

It is not necessary, in this context, to discuss elaborately the general problem of stabilization of agricultural incomes. The various measures and programmes advocated and adopted towards this end in many countries of the world have received full examination in recent years. A recent (1960) publication of the FAO, containing reports by two expert international groups, on problems of agricultural price stabilization and support policies, gives an excellent account of these and a balanced evaluation. All that need be attempted here, is to group together suitably the various measures suggested and to pass them under rapid review.

One group of such measures is concerned with agricultural production. It seeks to make production more secure or to increase it. Important measures in this group are: projects for increasing and assuring water supply; long-term schemes of land improvement, and of improvement in the supply of crucial production requisites such as fertilizers; establishment of improved methods through education, technical assistance, etc.; and improved organization of fields such as through consolidation, and of farms as through co-operative farming. All of these are undertaken as independent parts of plans of development; and while they help to stabilize agricultural incomes, no special orientation is, or needs to be, given to them because of this effect. The following points need, however, to be noted in relation to this group of measures under present conditions in India. Firstly, the emphasis on production has led to almost exclusive attention being given to irrigated and intensive agriculture. It has to be realized that, over extensive areas within the country, secure water-supply may be unobtainable, at least for many years. The problem of stabilization of agricultural production in such areas requires urgent attention. This can be done only by intensive research into methods of dry farming, by appropriate plans of land utilization, and by evolving other similar measures for these regions. In relation to the area under insecure dry-farming this effort does not, today, appear to receive adequate attention. Another point which deserves notice is the close connection of the programme of distribution of supplies, especially fertilizers, with the structure of relative prices. For such a programme to succeed in relation to particular crops, it must be operated in conjunction with an appropriate price-policy and not against the established price-relations. The price factor also plays an important part in the popularity and success of all improvements, on private account, which require substantial investment of resources. The improvements will be undertaken only if the receipts from increased yields, etc., justify the investment and the risk.

A second group of measures may be said to aim at improvement of the business organization of the farmer. These measures include programmes of credit reorganization, improvement of marketing-facilities or organizations, provision of crop and livestock insurance, etc. Though they might involve state initiative and some element of subsidy in the early stages, they have to be treated essentially as self-sustaining business-propositions. Because of this characteristic, they have a close connection with price stability. Unstable prices provide an ideal setting for the operation of speculators; stability of prices, on the other hand, makes easy the establishment and operation of such institutional arrangements as farmers' co-operative marketing societies. This is also true in many ways in relation to co-operative credit.

Organization of co-operative credit has played an important part in recent Indian plans of agricultural development. To the extent this effort has succeeded, it has prevented the resurgence and dominance of the moneylender-trader system in the post-war period. However, success in this matter has not been uniform. There are, in particular, two large areas which require urgent attention. Over extensive regions in many states, co-operative organization has yet failed to strike root. This raises an acute, immediate problem. Can anything be done to supply effectively the credit needs of expanding production in these regions during the period, which will necessarily be taken for building up an efficient and viable co-operative structure? Empty debates over theory and forms of co-operative organization have unfortunately diverted attention from this real problem.

The second, important class not covered by existing co-operative effort is that of low-income farmers in all regions. Their problem has received much attention in recent years and the usual remedy suggested is that of giving guarantees and making extra funds available to co-operative credit societies to enable them to assist members of this class. For example, the Third Five-Year Plan suggests outright contributions to the funds of co-operative societies to enable them to provide 'adequate credit on the basis of their production requirement and repaying capacity' to 'marginal and sub-marginal cultivators, landless tenants, etc.' (p. 203). The formulation in the Plan and similar formulations elsewhere in this context fail to take notice of a crucial fact that whatever their production requirements—a concept difficult to concretize—the 'repaying capacity' of the classes under reference is low and that its actuarial value over the years is made very low because of the wide range of fluctuations to which it is exposed. If they are not to be continuously subsidized, the only way to make them creditworthy is to reorganize the base of their production structure and to eliminate fluctuations. If they are helped in this way, the co-operative credit structure can take care of them even without any extra funds or guarantees; in the absence of reorganization and stabilization, even ample guarantee and funds are not going to help. In the whole range of measures available, in this context, stabilization of prices is a measure that could be made effective within the shortest time and would have a larger impact on the situation than any other measure would have.

Even with some stabilization of prices of agricultural products, fluctuations in incomes of agriculturists, induced by variations in physical output, would continue to be large in all insecure tracts. In view of the small margin at the command of the majority of farmers, the deficit created by a significant fall in physical output could be bridged only by increased borrowings. That is, the role of balancing the economy, played by the moneylender-trader agency in the past, will have to be continued by some other agency—at less cost and more purposefully and constructively—in the future. This problem does not appear to have attracted attention earlier because in the analysis of the operation of moneylender-traders it had not to be, and was not, separately demarcated or treated. At the same time, the extent of financing by institutional agencies such as government or the co-operatives was, for the most part, very low and these agencies did not, and could not, play the balancing role over any long period of time. In the circumstances, the problem did not figure in the discussion on co-operative policy. It is only in recent years, with experiments in the direction of fully adequate short-term credit being undertaken, such as in the crop-loan system, that the magnitude and importance of the problem are being realized. The problem is referred to, for example, in the report of the Crop Loan Evaluation Committee of the Bombay State Co-operative Bank (1958, Part I, p. 83).

However, the problem requires a much fuller study and a much greater elaboration of institutional practice for adequate treatment. The main problem is that of dealing with overdues of short-term and other credit caused by a large or small failure of the seasons. This involves providing for the spread of the year's repayments over subsequent years, and at the same time, continuing supply of the minimum needed credit for efficient operation of the next year's business. This is a delicate balancing operation, and the dangers of over-adjustment either way are obvious. On the one hand, an illiberal view could mean, either, severe curtailment of production or driving the farmer to other credit agencies, or both. On the other hand, an over-generous policy could create reluctance to repay even when able, and lead to accumulation of loans and overdues so large that extensive writing-off and ultimate liquidation might have to be faced. This dilemma, created by the liability to fluctuation in physical production in the less secure tracts, further emphasizes the urgency of removing the other important source of fluctuations through stabilization of prices.

Another set of measures attempts to stabilize incomes through direct payments or subsidies. These measures take a variety of forms, such as tax concessions, subsidies, direct or through lowered prices of materials or services, or direct cash payments such as those called 'deficiency income payments'. Some of these measures may be connected with other objectives such as those of encouraging particular improvements. However, to the extent that they are intended to stabilize incomes significantly, direct payments or subsidies are likely to prove extremely onerous in cost.

Finally, there is the group of measures which aim at influencing prices. Among these measures we may distinguish between those which operate through regulation of supply and those which operate directly on prices. Ordinarily, planned development is incompatible with measures which restrict outputs or supplies. However, measures adopted with other ends in view may have such restrictive effects.

The severe regulation of imports to save foreign-exchange resources results in restricting imports of certain agricultural products and creating a sheltered internal market for them. It is necessary to see that this does not result in the diversion of land to inferior uses. Control over exports is said to be connected with conserving internal supplies and regulating the internal price-level. They appear to have had some peculiar results. There is obvious need of a better articulation of policy in this regard and of bringing it in proper relation with a policy of stabilization of internal prices.

One aspect of export policy, which is very important from the point of view of overall stabilization of agricultural incomes, is diversification of agricultural exports in order to stabilize the terms of trade and obtain, if possible, progressively more favourable terms. Unfortunately, almost no attention has been paid to this subject. Analysis of trends of the post-war period reveals substantial differences in movements of terms of trade in relation to different groups of agricultural products entering into international trade. Broadly, foodgrains and the main types of older exports such as cotton, sugar, and oilseeds have fared worse than the majority of products of plantation and horticulture. In India, the bulk of the acreage under newly irrigated lands continues to be placed under sugarcane, cotton, and oilseeds. In view of our geographical situation in relation to the Asian and some African markets, a planned attempt to encourage the production and export of a variety of garden crops is obviously indicated. General considerations also point to continuing advantage, in the future, of a diversified garden crop economy over staple field-crops. No doubt, any significant transition would require conscious, planned, and assisted effort for both production and export, in the early stages. There is every reason to believe that such effort is necessary and that it will pay in the long run.

This rapid survey of the other types of measures indicates the central place of measures which directly attempt stabilization of prices of agricultural products in any programme of stabilization of agricultural incomes in India. Stabilization is itself important for a variety of other programmes such as those of building up a co-operative structure, or implementation of many aspects of the programme in relation to agricultural production. Stabilization of prices of agricultural products must thus be accepted as the main plank in plans of development of agriculture and the welfare of rural society.

The foregoing might be supplemented by a few observations on some features of the overall conditions under which a policy of stabilization of agricultural prices has to be framed and operated in India. Firstly, Indian plans of development are at a stage in which great importance attaches to an increase in the efficiency of methods of production and to a rapid increase in the volume of total agricultural production within the country.

Secondly, agricultural production provides, in the main, food for the population, and an important base for industrialization. In both contexts, especially the former, the market is highly price-sensitive. Therefore, it is of the utmost importance to see that prices charged to consumers of agricultural products do not soar high. The market, even for foodgrains within the country, is not likely to reach a point of saturation early; but this fact itself emphasizes the importance of the price factor. The reduction of the margin between producers and consumers prices, through eliminating instability and other devices, therefore, becomes an essential aspect of policy. Next, there are limitations imposed by the relation to the level of international prices. In respect of imports this has an important bearing on foodgrain production and policy. High prices of imported foodgrains make it desirable to undertake special investment and expenditure in order to be free from the need to import foodgrains. In relation to prices of exportable agricultural products, policy considerations that appear to be important are as follows: There is no justification for artificially making the terms of trade unfavourable to agriculturists through a restriction of exports so as to make available internal supplies to the trader and the industrialist at low prices. There might be a justification for regulating exports to adjust them to international market-conditions for exported products. In this case, however, the regulatory mechanism must be, as in other conditions, an Export Board which would be able to pool gains over the years and to route all of them back, directly or indirectly, for the benefit of the agriculturist. The maintenance of an internal, stabilized structure of relative prices would also involve insulation of the internal market, and exercise of some control over exports and the prices received by producers for them. This does not, however, justify arrangements which route extra gains to the trader and the industrialist.

A few observations on prices of sugar and sugarcane may underline some issues involved. The guarantee of a stable and highly favourable price to an important section of producers of sugarcane has helped to keep up prices of, both, sugar and *gur* and brought about a rapid increase in the production of sugarcane. The guaranteed price of sugarcane has, however, been fixed at a level which puts it out of proper relation with internal prices of other agricultural products, and international prices of sugar and sugarcane. The result has been an extra and undesirable diversion of areas to sugarcane, windfall gains to sugar manufacturers, an internal price which unduly checks consumption of sugar, the need to export which can be fulfilled only at the cost of the general tax-payer and a worsening internal situation in relation to supply and costs of sugar and sugarcane for which no automatic correction is available.

Finally, it is vital that the measures adopted for implementing any policy of stabilization of agricultural prices in India must be self-financing, i.e., they must not involve, in the long run, any net burden on government finances.

All this means that while the stabilization of prices of agriculture products is of utmost importance and urgency, the limits within which the policy has to be framed are fairly rigid and narrow. Essentially it must be a policy of stabilization, not of support. The stabilization must be strictly an operation over the year with room for adjustment in absolute and relative prices from year to year. The stabilization operations, internal and external, must be manager by public authorities. The present system of taking policy decision separately in respect of a small number of individual commodities and of implementing policy through manipulation of export quotas or operations of associations of traders or industrialists, is unsatisfactory in every way.

III

The purpose of this note was chiefly to bring out the crucial role of the measures for stabilization of prices, and the limits within which they have to operate. It is not intended here to discuss details of that policy: A committee of representative public men made detailed and specific recommendations on important aspects of it, in the early phase of the Second-Plan period (Report of the Foodgrains Enquiry Committee, 1957, Chapters VI and VII). An influential team of American experts made categorical and detailed recommendations regarding it towards the end of the Second-Plan period (Ford Foundation Team Report 1959, Chapter I). I wrote a note on some practical aspects of the problem which was circulated to the Economists Panel in October 1960.[1] It is not the details that cause anxiety but the rooted inability of the government to take a decision in this matter.

Government inaction in the matter is particularly inexplicable, after the formulations in the Third Five-Year Plan. The stabilization of agricultural incomes finds no mention in it. However, price policy is discussed in a number of places in the Plan. 'An agricultural price policy which is both fair to the urban consumer and fully safeguards the farmer's interest' is mentioned in connection with the problem of the widening gap between rural and non-rural incomes (p. 17). The Plan has an entire chapter (Chapter VII) on price-policy. The consideration of policy for the Third Plan in this chapter starts with the following observation:

'It must be stressed that price-policy has to be viewed as one aspect of overall economic policy; the question is not merely what can or ought to be done in respect of particular prices.' (p. 125)

The chapter concludes as follows:

> The plan provides for adequate increases in the output of essential commodities to permit reasonable increase in essential consumption. The primary task is to achieve these targets. Deficiencies in this respect can be overcome only with difficulty. Fiscal and

monetary policies have continually to be orientated towards restraint in consumption and maximization of savings. The role of direct regulation and controls is essentially to correct imbalance in selected sectors and, for this purpose, buffer stocks and market operations are vital. These operations have to be directed towards keeping price fluctuations in respect of food-grains and other basic essentials within defined maximum and minimum limits. Price rigidity is incompatible with development and some prices cannot but rise. The object must be to regulate within defined limits the prices of basic essentials. Price regulation involves action at various points. The necessary incentives to larger production have to be preserved. It is, therefore, envisaged that Government would set up and promote the necessary co-operative and State agencies for purchase and sale of food-grains at appropriate stages so as to strengthen its power to influence the course of prices and to prevent anti-social activities like hoarding and profiteering from getting the upper hand. (Chapter VII, para 31, pp. 131–2)

This refers chiefly to prices of foodgrains. In the chapter on agricultural production (Chapter XIX), there is a much wider and more specific definition of policy in relation to prices of agricultural products:

For achieving the high targets of agricultural production set for the Third Plan, it is important that growers should have full confidence that the additional effort and investment which are called for will yield adequate return. Changes in the prices and production of fibres during the last few years show that wide fluctuations in prices affect the growers' capacity to make sustained efforts for increasing production. The fall in prices of jute in 1958 affected production in subsequent years. The assurance of minimum remunerative prices for important cereals and cash crops like cotton, oilseeds and jute over the period of the Plan will provide the necessary incentives for increasing production, thus adding to the effectiveness of the various development programmes provided for in the Third Plan. With this object in view, decisions regarding the prices at which Government should buy and sell, should be taken sufficiently in advance of the sowing season. Where floor and ceiling prices are fixed, they should be related to the requirements of production, and the range between the minimum and maximum prices should not be too wide. (Chapter XIX, para 49, p. 323)

It will be realized that all these policy formulations, taken together, imply a large country-wide network of co-operative and state agencies, which will handle appropriately the purchase and sale of foodgrains and of all the more important cash-crops. They also involve fixation for various crops of levels of minimum and maximum prices which can operate meaningfully in relation to each individual crop and are also mutually related appropriately. This amounts to socialization of trade in agricultural products and the maintenance of a relative structure of prices. It is these features of policy which the reports of previous committees and other discussions have emphasized. At the same time, this is very different from the actual sporadic, piecemeal, and hesitant action which has characterized and continues to characterize official policy all these years.

The main problem today is, therefore, that of inducing government, as a whole, to activate and implement policies to which prominent members of it have subscribed through the document called the 'Third Five-Year Plan'. It is difficult for an outsider to indicate reasons for the long and persistent government inaction in this matter. I should venture, however, to point to two possible sets of considerations. Firstly, the reluctance of all governments to undertake any commitments in relation to prices and distribution of agricultural products, especially, foodgrains, may be connected with the experience of the war and post-war period and the risk of incurring unpopularity involved in such measures. Secondly, the inability of government to act may be connected with the basic requirement of all such policy, viz., the socialization of the trade in agricultural products. Such socialization would endanger the entrenched position of the rural moneylender-trader class which is not only the most numerous class of private entrepreneurs in the country, but also the class from which Indian capitalism basically derives and on which, perhaps, it heavily depends even today. I am not in a position to suggest how the government can be steered past these two obstacles.

NOTE

1. Note on 'Price Policy'. Published in *Planning and Economic Policy in India*, D.R. Gadgil, GIPE, Poona, 1972, pp. 247–59.

VI

Issues in Co-operation and Economic Development

25

A Note on Co-operative Farming

ENVIRONMENT

In studying an experiment in progress like that of co-operative farming in China, it is necessary to take account of all the components in the situation in judging of reasons of success or failure. I feel that enough attention is not usually paid to the influence of environment on the success of a programme. In evaluating success of co-operative farming on a nation-wide scale it is necessary to note two environmental aspects in particular. There is, firstly, what I might call the climate of opinion; this includes attitudes on the part of the public or of particular sections of it and of the government; and this determines effectiveness of declared governmental policy. During the British regime the co-operatives were treated merely as one element in a total *laissez faire* economy. Today, even though the avowed policy is changed, the attitudes are materially what they were during the British regime. In view of the great disparity in strength between the individual units in the agricultural economy, the fact that the attitudes have not changed is extremely important. It is well known that in the 'regulated markets' of Bombay State a large part of legal provisions are not observed even in the letter and that the government has found it impossible to enforce their observance. This has happened in all cases because of the enormous strength of the trading community and their resistance to all practices which would result in weakening their hold. The progress of, for example, marketing co-operative societies is everywhere impeded by deliberate action, overt or secret, taken by trading interests. Nowhere is the government, its officials, or members of the public seen to treat such action on the part of private traders as unsocial. Practices which are undoubtedly unfair are openly indulged without fear of any kind of public displeasure or disfavour of the government. We had bitter experience of this even in the establishment and licensing of co-operative sugar factories. A society in which the rich and the privileged classes are not afraid of openly exercising all their influence and power in favour of attaining their private interests, and against the rise of new forms such as the co-operative, cannot possibly expect the new forms to flourish and to spread quickly. Unless the strong and the rich begin to feel that the exercise of power in their own private interests will be reckoned as unsocial, rapid co-operative development must be despaired of. A corollary of this exercise of their power by the rich traders, etc., is seen in the attitude of officials at all levels. Whether in the licensing and the operation of ration shops during the war period or in the working of productive and marketing co-operative enterprises later, the favouring of private organizations, directly and indirectly, by the bulk of officials at all levels and the consequent handicap to co-operatives are within the experience of all workers.

Another aspect of the total environment is equally important. This is the operation of the economic system, with particular reference to prices and markets. In any economy where market conditions and prices are liable to rapid and large fluctuations, the speculator and the large trader have obvious advantages. Individual small producers or small producer organizations operate under a handicap in such conditions. On the contrary, where prices and market conditions are kept comparatively stable, the co-operative endeavour of small men has much larger chances of success. This has been the experience, in war and other times, of control of all types of economic activity. Consumer shops were not difficult to manage during the war period. Because, apart from a minimum efficiency and honesty, they did not require on the part of individual shops, the assumption of large risks; the comparative failure of co-operative trading in cloth, when faced with large fluctuations in the open market, emphasizes the same lesson. In the sphere of small scale industry it has been pointed out that continuously increased and efficient production could be assured only if a guarantee of demand at minimum market prices is forthcoming. In all spheres of co-operative producer organizations, especially where the individual producer is small and the total co-operative unit is not in a position to assume large risks, success would be possible on a large scale only when the markets are comparatively stable. It is presumed that in China with very considerable state trading and regulation, farm co-operatives do not face widely fluctuating markets. Stability in markets and prices affects not only conditions of sale of the finished product but also conditions of purchase of materials, etc. When the cost-price structures and relations are comparatively stable the producer and his organization can devote all attention to the efficient organization of production. In the alternative state of circumstances, production activity is at a handicap, and the trader and the speculator naturally flourish.

ORGANIZATION AND OPERATION

When a co-operative farming society is set up it faces the initial problem of the acquisition of land and equipment. In terms of organization the first problem, therefore, is that of the inducements offered for joining co-operatives with one's land and equipment. There might be some compulsion or quasi-compulsion; that is, some persons or classes find it necessary to join co-operatives if they are to remain in farming or in cultivating possession of the whole or part of their lands. The compulsion exercised through law or through administration policy in relation to joining co-operatives must play a large part in their rapid formation. Secondly, inducements must be held out especially to the smaller cultivators. These may not obtain certain concessions, privileges, or assistance except through co-operative farms. If the concessions, privileges, and assistances are so routed, and are seen to be immediately beneficial, they would act as powerful inducements to join co-operative farming, particularly if individual farms, large or small, find it difficult to continue their business.

In the organization and operation of the co-operatives, difficulties are likely to arise in relation to the conduct of business and the distribution of the product. Initially, it is important to ascertain the area of discretion allowed to, and the extent of responsibilities thrown on, the primary co-operative, as also the extent of assistance afforded to it. Without a certain minimum of resources in terms of land, livestock, and equipment a co-operative farming society is not likely to succeed. What are the steps taken to ensure that this minimum is always achieved; does the government guarantee the minimum of land resources and does it ensure supply of the minimum of capital resources and what are the means of ensuring that government targets or government guarantees in this regard are, in fact, fulfilled.

Next, there is the question of the conduct of operations through the year, viz., planning and utilization, determining the techniques and executing the annual plan. Here, obviously, the requirements are both in terms of technical and administrative ability. How is the technical guidance provided, are crop plans made on some uniform prescribed pattern, what are the agencies of supply of improved seeds, implements, etc., and who gives the needed training in new methods. The enquiry has to concern itself with, at least, two aspects; one is the organization for making available, trained personnel for administrative establishments, for example, managers and accountants and the technical personnel needed for planning and improvement. The other is the procedure by which it is ensured that each co-operative will adopt a plan which is of a minimum level of technical competence and that the plan will be executed with minimum efficiency. The evolution of standard plans and adoption of uniform procedures for operation may, for example, be one approach.

Similar considerations apply to the pattern of distribution; whether any rents are paid for land and if so how are they determined; what is the manner in which the labour programme is drawn up; how is the produce or other income shared; how are the various relative valuations made. All these are problems in relation to which standard procedures and norms for a set of uniform conditions can be evolved; if they are so evolved and enforced, a considerable proportion of the difficulties currently faced in the day to day administration of many co-operatives would vanish. For, it is the exercise of discretion and arriving at decisions in relation to problems such as these which is the source of a number of quarrels and discontents.

In this connection the standard procedure followed for arriving at all decisions deserves to be studied. With us the ordinary procedure of a *Panch* Committee means considerable dilatoriness, and a certain amount of inevitable log-rolling, where important interests within the society are involved. It would be important to observe if these are avoided in the Chinese pattern and, if so, how. To what extent does the general body, if any, exercise real control; how is the day-to-day executive authority exercised, and what are the sanctions which make for the smooth running of the daily operations. Do outside experts, state officials, or party members play an important part in solving or eliminating the problems of organization, administration, and operation that are encountered in India? If so, are their positions built into the legal and administrative structure or is it due only to general conventions and understanding? It is likely that with a largely controlled and regulated economy, problems of disposal of the product such as marketing, processing, etc., are not as important in China as in India. Even so, some technical and administrative problems must emerge in this sphere even in China.

Problems which have been raised above in relation to the organization and operation of the primary society will be matched by similar problems in the total structure of co-operative organizations. Here, the most important aspects to study would be the hierarchical structure of co-operative bodies, the element of federalization, if any, in the structure and the extent of discretion at each level, compared with the extent of authority exercised from above. The relationship of the co-operative structure with the machinery of government at all levels, the routing of government directives if any, or the communication, formally or informally, of implications of state policy for co-operative operation need to be made clear. Also, the extent to which these relations are lubricated by financial and technical assistance rendered by governmental machinery needs to be looked into. Here, the training of personnel, the supply of personnel, and the filling of the key positions in the co-operative structure, with either state servants or party personnel, all these must be clarified for gaining a real insight into the operation of the societies.

Lastly, I would draw attention to the problems of replication. It has been our experience in India that an initial successful experiment is quickly copied nearby in similar environments. The slowness of our progress is due, largely, to the fact that we have no plan of deliberate experimentation fully backed by social approval and state assistance and, further, that we have no means whereby successful experiments are studied and reproduced later over larger and larger areas. The process of replication involves isolation of important elements in successful experiments in the structural and operational model; and it is the simplification that has to be reproduced, with necessary adaptation to circumstances, over all regions. A study must be made of both these processes. Firstly, that of incorporation of a simplified model of the essential elements in a successful experiment and, secondly, the procedures, the administration, the agency, the assistance, and the propaganda, that are needed for successful replication in a variety of co-operatives on a large scale. It is only when this has been done that it would be possible to say whether the Chinese experience has something that we can immediately put to use or not.

26

Co-operation and the Transformation of Economic Society*

I propose to confine what I say relating to the concept of the Co-operative Commonwealth to conditions arid possibilities in India of the near future. The review so far has indicated that while co-operative activity does not cover all aspects of economic life and has limited significance in most highly industrialized societies, it could assume great importance in under-developed economies. In these economies, in agriculture and other primary production and in small industry and transport, the co-operative way is not only available but is eminently suitable. This is also true of co-operation among consumers; consumers are, again, ordinarily small and weak units. Obviously such co-operative activity will acquire strength only when the consumer is keen on making small economies in relation to his purchases and when he is ready to accept common standardized commodities for this purpose. ... (pp. 56, 57)

The importance of co-operation, to a society which is poor and in which weak economic units are overwhelmingly large in number, cannot be overestimated. However, in many of such societies, for co-operation to succeed, it is necessary that it should be initiated and nursed by external effort and that co-operative activity should always be supported by appropriate government policy in relation to economic security and economic progress. Not only is the number of economic units vary large in under-developed

* The Brij Narain Memorial Lectures were delivered by Gadgil in 1959 at the Punjab University. The three lectures delivered, related to (i) origin and spread of co-operative activity, (ii) government-sponsored co-operation, and (iii) co-operation and the transformation of economic society. This article covers the second half of the third lecture, published in *Writings and Speeches of Prof. D.R. Gadgil on Co-operation*, GIPE, Poona, 1975, pp. 56–71.

countries, but there exists in them great disparity in strength between the weak and the strong, between urban and rural sectors, between those based on modern techniques and the units using old techniques, and between those operating on a small scale and the large-scale modern business. ... (p. 57)

Moreover, in countries engaged in development planning, there are two particular reasons why co-operative organizations should be encouraged to spread widely. Planning, in the ultimate analysis, can be effective only through action of each individual unit of activity in the economy; so that unless the planned target and the pattern of behaviour called forth by plan-requirements are communicated effectively to each individual, dispersed unit, the success of the plan cannot be guaranteed. This involves the creation of organizations which can act as intermediaries in the two-way process of communicating planning decisions down to units and communicating reactions of the units to the planning authorities. ... It is only when these producers get organized in a co-operative structure of their own that one can expect both to learn more of their wishes, their capacities, and their potentialities and to be able to communicate and interpret to them the overall decisions to get proper implementations of the plans from them. ... (pp. 57, 58)

Secondly, co-operative organizations could be relied on not only to implement the plans more effectively but also to carry them out with greater scrupulousness, care, and honesty. Co-operative organizations particularly when there is an element of government sponsorship in their initiation, are amenable to public direction, and are subject, invariably, to public audit. Also, policy decisions, even in their internal affairs, are taken, by and large, in an open manner. ...(p. 58)

These considerations amount to a powerful plea for the active sponsoring and spread of co-operative activity, not only among the bulk of farmers and artisans but also among every type of dispersed economic activity, as in fishing and in forestry, in quarrying and in transport, in public works and in construction. Indeed, such a policy may be thought of in our situation as the most effective manner in which, not only more effective performance is guaranteed, but also, social security and welfare is provided for. ...(p. 58)

Even so, all this falls far short of the image conjured by the term Co-operative Commonwealth and I now turn my attention to the final task of defining the wider interpretation of the term. ...(p. 58)

In the early stages of the growth of all communist economies that came into being after 1918, resort was taken, on a large scale, to setting up co-operative organizations. And though, in most developed, communist systems, co-operative organizations appear no longer important, in the Yugoslav system, in particular, the co-operative form appears to have gained an important and permanent place. In this context, it becomes necessary to bring together a number of strands, from thinking and action in diverse co-operative manifestations, for obtaining an idea of the essentials of the structure of a Co-operative Commonwealth. The wider interpretation of the concept of Co-operative Commonwealth has to draw upon all sources, viz., the aspirations and motivations of co-operative idealists from the days of Owen to those of the Kibbutz, the principles incorporated in co-operative practice, and the diverse forms of organization that co-operation has taken in many countries and for, different purposes. The attempted synthesis has also to take a note of the fact that it is the structure and basis of a new or transformed society that is being considered and not the operation of a sheltered area within a capitalistic or socialistic society. Inevitably, in considering the question in the Indian context, both, experience of recent developments in India and traditional values of Indian society, will have to be given due weight. ...(pp. 59, 60)

In relation to the structure of productive organization or economic organization in general, the emphasis of co-operation would be on operating, as far as possible, through small independent units. These units would co-operate together for achieving economies of scale and for other mutually beneficial activities. The co-operative could take a variety of forms and its extent and coverage would differ from group to group. It may, for example, be held advantageous for groups of uneconomic farmers to advance as far as joint farming in the direction of co-operation, while the viable farmers might be content only with co-operative credit, supply, and processing activity. Whatever that may be, co-operation would emphasize dispersal and decentralization of activity and would put the small independent enterprise and the primary co-operative unit at the centre of the economic picture. This is consistent with the origins and continued motivation of co-operative activity as being concerned with the protection and strengthening of the small and the weak. ...(p. 60)

On the operational side, co-operation would be distinguished by the view it takes in relation to incentives. Belief in co-operation implies accepting the possibility of the established fact that men are not guided in their work solely by hopes of material gain, that they recognize the importance of group and social obligations and are ready to accept voluntarily limitations on expectations and rewards and to exhibit restraints in behaviour patterns in pursuit of economic gains, that non-economic incentives such as social recognition and opportunities for social work are of value in motivating them, and that efficiency and sound business are compatible with a regime of deliberately limited economic incentives. Another important operative aspect of co-operation is its deliberate divorce of control from ownership. This is related, in part, to the attitude of co-operation towards incentives; it is also related to the belief that control of economic activity arising out of concentrated power and in pursuit of private gain has serious disadvantages, and that control of operations which are connected only in part with hopes of such gain can both be efficient and socially beneficial. ...(pp. 60, 61)

Other aspects of co-operative values may be brought out through reference to the universally accepted concepts of equality and democracy. Though not insisting on any rigid or mechanical formula relating to equality, co-operation, with its insistence on small units, with its anti-monopolistic attitude and its philosophy of control, obviously favours great diffusion of ownership of resources, and where such diffusion of ownership is not possible, will insist on the diffusion of power. Because of its attitude towards economic incentives and emphasis on fair sharing, it would obviously favour a relative equality in distributive shares. In particular, co-operation discourages high rewards associated with the ownership of capital. It looks for savings being formed through deliberate, joint social effort rather than through offer of high incentive rewards to individual savers. While not advocating the abolition of property, it would, therefore, insist on keeping its share of the national product at as low a level as possible. Further, believing as it does, in the power of non-economic incentives and the individual's sense of social obligations, its scale of remuneration to individual effort could not exhibit wide differentials. Above all, its emphasis on educational and cultural values, and on the responsibility of the social group for not only protecting but grading up the quality of individual members, would also make for an egalitarian outlook, though it is obvious that equality in this case is achieved not as a condition precedent but as a result of the practice of co-operation. ...(p. 61)

Co-operation is essentially democratic. Its philosophy of control and its principle of open membership indicate that the co-operative order will be an economic democracy in which privilege in any form will not be countenanced. ... Co-operation is thus against concentration of control not only in the sense of concentration in the hands of a few individuals or a small group, but also in the sense of concentration at a point or in a stratum in a structure. Co-operation stands for a diffusion of power through the whole structure through its insistence on what is best called 'federalism'. The autonomy of the primary and intermediate groups is carefully guarded, though minimum requisite power is always available to the central organization and the top strata. ...(pp. 61, 62)

The acceptance of co-operation also involves the idea of fair sharing of gains through mutual adjustment and understanding. The possibility and actuality of independent co-operative organizations of all kinds of economic interests make possible a meaningful articulation of the points of view of different groups and avoid the facile assumption that often leads to the identification of national interest with a particular view and requires that other groups' points of view should not be pressed. On the other hand, co-operation, while accepting thus openly the possible conflicts of interest of groups, regions, etc., must by its very nature, make arrangements for a peaceful settlement of all possible differences of opinions and their reconciliation. ...(p. 62)

In relation to the attitude towards the state, widely, differing views have been expressed. It has, for example, been suggested that state-sponsored co-operation is no co-operation at all. ... With a state which pursues programmes of planned economic development and which avows full faith in co-operative values, no sense of antagonism need be entertained. In fact, the state can, if properly oriented, be considered responsible for impregnating co-operative values in spheres in which actual co-operative organizations may not be established. This is the only way in which a completely Co-operative Commonwealth can be brought into existence and can be made to function. Voluntarism, in such a context, would mean not keeping away from the state and its organizations, or refusing state aid for co-operative effort in appropriate contexts, but insisting on relying on own, individual and mutual co-operative effort to the largest extent possible. Where needed, especially in view of the backwardness in techniques and organizations and the paucity of resources, state help should be fully availed of; but this should, however, be only to the extent that is required and is beneficial and only for the necessary period. ...(p. 62)

It could be said that co-operation differs from socialism in not laying the same emphasis on public ownership of means of production. Where the ownership of means of production can be highly diffused, or where it can be placed into the hands of co-operative groups of small independent units of operators, it would be so retained in a co-operative order. However, in view of the anti-monopoly attitude of co-operation and its insistence on divorcing control from ownership, co-operation would favour the placing of, at least, the control of large-scale oligopolistic undertakings, chiefly in the hands of public authority. ... Because of its insistence on decentralization, on small units, on federalism, and on voluntary effort co-operation would obviously favour a much less than overwhelming role for the state. The basic difference of co-operation from capitalism and capitalistic society would seem to lie in the insistence of co-operation on taking a moral view of economic activity. Co-operation insists on incorporating the concepts of justice and of social obligations into the structure of economic society and recognizing moral values as being a non-separable part of the operation of economic life and activity. In doing this, its whole attitude towards incentives, controls, ownership, etc., is marked out sharply from that of capitalism. ...(pp. 63, 64)

It is important to note, in the first instance, that belief in competition is no longer based on any acknowledgement of its efficacy in working. It is increasingly recognized that in economies even like that of the US the competitive system as such does not appear to work. ...(p. 65) Even economic theory is no longer prepared to hold that the prices of factors such as rates of wages or of interest or of profits are determined as prices in the ordinary competitive market. ...(p. 65) From the side of social psychology, it is being more and more firmly established that the working of a social group improves greatly under a general co-operative situation as compared with that in a competitive situation. ...(p. 65) Even in its early, days the concept of competition as the main force in operating an economy was held suspect. Mandeville's famous formulation 'private vices, public virtues' underscored the basic difficulty. Even apart from the ethical angle, the possibility of a mass of uncoordinated, autonomous entities operating naturally in such a manner as to produce beneficial social results always strained the imagination, and some kind of invisible hand had always to be postulated. ...(p. 66)

Though the theoretical status and the proved, operational efficiency of competition are no longer rated high, its hold on the imagination of Western societies appears to be yet great. It is reported, in particular, to have a very powerful hold on American society. In all activities and manifestations, in business and in academics, in behaviour patterns in production as well as in consumption, American society is supposed to be largely governed by competitive psychology. During the post-war years this has been apparently reinforced by certain extraneous considerations. The need to maintain that capitalist society was efficient and to avow a social philosophy which was diametrically opposed to that of communism greatly and, evidently, artificially increased the prestige of a system of thought which had suffered considerable setbacks earlier during the depression. ...(p. 66)

We are, of course, concerned here, primarily, with ruling concepts in Indian society. There is considerable difficulty in talking or writing about the working of Indian society. This flows largely from the lack of homogeneity both in its composition and its thinking. In particular, it is difficult to identify a set of value systems as attributable to Indian society as a whole. A society which has been stratified into castes, with particular attitudes and values associated especially with particular castes, cannot be described as holding a uniform set of values. To the extent the caste hierarchy was dominated by the Brahmin and Kshatriya elements, the value systems of these two might, in some measure, be said to represent the value system of Indian society; but even this would not be a correct statement in so far as the large financial and trading elements were never fully identified with the highest castes. The imposition of foreign rule for long periods also made for a considerable degree of confusion in this regard. Developments of the last 150 years have further complicated the situation, chiefly, through influence of Western values. Even so, it cannot be said that capitalism, or the competitive psychology, has had general acceptance or is rated highly in India today. At the same time, such indigenous efforts as have been made to create a new or revised system of values in relation to modern socio-economic life have hardly succeeded. The efforts of Mahatma Gandhi and Vinoba have been directed so entirely towards the more austere and self-sufficient aspects of economic life that they lose relevance in relation to the continuing modern problems. In particular, in relation to industrialism and modern large business, which present everywhere the most intractable problems, there is very little except by way of general retrogression that these philosophers have to offer. There is, however, one strong strain in most current trends; this is a suspicion of state activity. The '*Sarvodaya*' attitude towards the state has given support, indirectly, to the plea for non-regulation, which modern business in India has been only too ready to adopt. The great fear of bureaucratization entertained, not unjustifiably, by the Indian socialists has led to the same result. In a word, the present situation, both in relation to leaders of society and intellectuals and the masses of the people, is one chiefly of confusion and, particularly, in relation to state activity, one of ambivalence. In these circumstances, modern business has found it very easy, especially during the last decade, to lay emphasis on free enterprise and virtues of competition in a way which would ordinarily be held as surprising. ...(pp. 66, 67)

In reality, the Indian economic system is even further away from the competitive model than the American or the Western European. The Indian economic system is more riddled with inequality, privileges, and monopolistic, entrenched positions, than any other. The normal difficulties of obtaining diffusion of the gains of development and progress encountered in a non-integrated backward society are intensified in India with its system of hierarchical castes and communities. This leads to a concentration of modern business in the hands of a few communities and to continuous growth of their gains and their power, leading to a serious imbalance within society. Also, in the operation of the Indian competitive system, unrestrained, uninhibited, competitive behaviour is more nakedly evident than anywhere else. In strict logic, a competitive system, whether looked on as a game or a war, must lead men to resort to all methods and practices which can be adopted without inviting immediate retribution or correction. It has been claimed that in societies like the American, tendencies towards unrestrained behaviour on the part of entrepreneurs have been modified through increasing acceptance of social restraints by later generations of industrialists. The economic history of India, on the other hand, exhibits the continuous rise in importance of business communities who have set up successively lower and lower standards in this regard. In short, the operation of competitive business in India cannot today be considered as being ethically, or socially, an attractive phenomenon; economically it is of doubtful competence. ...(p. 67)

The real danger of prevalence of the present situation is the general corruption that it breeds within the body politic. There is little doubt that the power of modern business is responsible to a large extent for corruption amongst politicians, amongst officials, and amongst professionals and intellectuals, and that urban society in India, in particular, is, through these influences. in a highly corrupt state. The real danger of this development lies in the explosive situation that it builds up. With great emphasis on development expenditure, opportunities of gain arising from which are limited to certain classes and communities, the economic and political power of these grow apace and when their corrupting influence is recognized more and more by the people, social leaders lose more and more of their moral influence on the masses or the lower middle classes. These, if they do not experience any elevation of their circumstances, must begin to question the very basis of the system and of the order. Such a situation may lead to a revolution if sufficiently strong leadership is found, otherwise to mere chaos. ...(pp. 67, 68)

There is no reason why we should adopt the principles of the so-called liberal economy and competitive capitalism. They have never been incorporated in our traditional values and, whatever their relevance to Western society, they are highly unsuited to our present circumstances. It is no longer even held that for attaining efficiency or technological progress a competitive society is alone effective. The progress made by the communistic societies under entirely different structures belies any claim in this regard. In a society in which resources are unbounded and a frontier always open, the evil effects of a competitive psychology or attitude may not appear on the surface. However, where resources and opportunities, as related to numbers of persons, are extremely limited and there exists a great deal of stratification and privilege with mutual suspicion and distrust, it is highly dangerous to encourage the spirit of competition and rivalry. In a crowded society with highly restricted opportunities, the development of society as a whole requires the most careful mutual adjustment, constant reiteration of the need for co-operation, and a stern discouragement of unsocial selfish behaviour of anyone at the expense of another. For this, if for no other reason, the philosophy of co-operation alone appears appropriate to present-day India. ...(p. 68)

It remains to indicate briefly what I consider to be the immediate practical implications of the acceptance of co-operation. I do not give any weight, in this context, to the current avowal of socialistic aims, as obviously neither in the sphere of production nor in that of distribution do these appear to affect practice. Socialistic views are also widely held in the country, in combination with the *Sarvodaya* philosophy. Co-operation has many values in common with this philosophy. They, however, seem to differ in two important respects. The first is the much greater concern of co-operation with rapid economic development as an important objective and with practical business; the second is the emphasis of co-operation on organizational effort. In fact, it might well be said that co-operation is essentially a philosophy or ideology of organization. It indicates a special way of organizing economic activity so as to make it both efficient and beneficent. *Sarvodaya,* on the other hand, apparently distrusts all organizational effort and is, therefore, inevitably unable to tackle practical problems. Results of *Sarvodaya* effort, thus, remain marginal or almost non-existent, though *Sarvodaya* philosophy has evidently a wide vogue. ... (pp. 68, 69)

The actual, mixed economy of today is neither socialistic nor infused with ideals of *Sarvodaya,* but grossly capitalistic. In terms of practical policy, acceptance of co-operation will mean, in the first instance, a full implementation of the programme of sponsoring and establishing co-operative activity in all spheres where it is appropriate. Today, a co-operative programme is accepted in the abstract. In fact, however, governmental policy does not fully implement it. It is well known, for example, that in the entire field of marketing and processing of agricultural produce, the activities of private-traders are, in a large number of instances, deliberately directed against the establishment of co-operative effort. Even when such obstructive efforts of private agencies are expressed through bodies like the Regulated Market Committees, the state has taken no preventive action. It has been, for many years, pointed out that the transfer of processing activity from traders to co-operatives is crucial not only to co-operative development, but also to such policy objectives as stabilization of prices. Such a transfer from established processors to new co-operatives, however, requires many-sided, simultaneous governmental effort. This has been completely lacking. In fact, there is reason to believe that the effort has been deliberately sidetracked. Obviously, with the acceptance of co-operation, all this will change. Co-operatives will, it is expected, be also accepted more and more as agencies in all kinds of public operations. If properly co-ordinated and articulated, this will get over many of the difficulties of detailed local operation by corporations in the public sector. ...(p. 69)

As within the public sector, the acceptance of co-operation, apart from the use of co-operatives as agencies in diverse contexts, will chiefly affect systems of payment and incentives. As at present, the public sector seems to be unable to evolve within itself an appropriate system for this purpose. It is necessary for the poor economies planning development to evolve such a system. To describe the problem briefly, whereas at the lower ranges of activity, the labour market in India is highly overstocked and remuneration to labour is low, at the highest range, the labour market is linked with the international economy and has its operation and standards influenced by those of the most affluent countries. The reconciliation of the conflicting situations presents a problem, which will be insoluble unless there is a wide and voluntary acceptance, at the highest levels, of self-imposed restraints as required by the total capacity of the national economy. However, there can be no general acceptance of the attitudes that this calls for, unless the whole philosophy of incentives and of market pricing of services, valid under capitalism, is thrown overboard. ...(pp. 69, 70)

The large majority of the constituents of the private sector are small-scale. All these could be brought within the co-operative sector itself. As pointed out above, doing this, however, appears difficult in relation to the very large units in modern, organized business, which usually take the form of large public corporations. These large private business corporations and their executives are today, in India, the chief exponents and the major influence making for the acceptance of ideas and practices appropriate to competitive capitalism. In spite of the obvious historical origin of their possessions and fortunes in state and social support and in quasi-monopolistic exploitation, they oppose all, even mild, moves in the direction of egalitarianism with cries of expropriation and talk of incentives needed by them either for continuing productive effort or for channelling it in particular lines and the standards of living and of remuneration appropriate to themselves. Acceptance of co-operation will involve a categorical rejection of all such claims. In a Co-operative Commonwealth, rights of property will be acknowledged only in so far as their exercise can be beneficent. Wherever there is danger of concentration of power so that it is possible for a few to behave in an unsocial manner a correction must be provided. Therefore, even if some concentration of ownership is tolerated, control must be divorced from ownership. It becomes necessary, from this point of view, to treat all corporations above a certain size or controlling productive resources of a given magnitude or holding any strategic positions in the economy as corporations informed with public interest. Such corporations must have open procedures and public accounting systems. ...(p. 70)

In this context, it is necessary to refer to the growing importance, in India, of government financial institutions such as the Industrial Finance and other similar Corporations, the State Bank, the LIC, etc. Through all these organizations acting together, a considerable measure of public financial interest has already been created in most large Indian corporations. This devolves an important responsibility on the government, one side of which was emphasized by the Mundhra affair. When we look at it from the point of view of a co-operative philosophy, it appears necessary that the government should exercise its financial power and participation, in order to obtain effective control over the total modern corporative sphere. The least it could do in this matter is to insist on open above-board public accounting and audit systems, and the ability to detect promptly and to prevent all unsocial activities on the part of owners, directors, and managers of these corporations. ...(pp. 70, 71)

Finally, in the administrative and political sphere, co-operation will be seen to be very closely linked with federalism. An unfortunate tendency, observable during recent decades, is the waning of the importance of federalism. Possibly, this is directly due to the rise of communism. A fight with communism has given rise to a centralizing tendency in democracy, which pushes greatly into the background the older federalist trends. Centralization leads, essentially, to authoritarianism and to bureaucratization and ultimately to non-democratic practices and attitudes. Co-operation, by insisting on the actual operation, as far as possible in the economic sphere, with the local, primary, small-scale scattered units, reinforces the federal political ideology in the strongest possible terms. It, thus, not only seeks to establish economic democracy but is also an essential factor in the working of political democracy. ...(p. 71)

I should reiterate my belief that the Indian situation, political and economic, requires today, a categorical rejection of competitive philosophy and psychology and the assertion of a belief in co-operation. Such an act of assertion, followed by the implementation of a programme of concrete logical action, is alone likely to lead us out of our present situation. ...(p. 71)

27

The Pravara Sahakari Sakhar Karkhana

*An Interpretative Account**

The successful establishment and operation of the Pravara Sahakari Sakhar Karkhana may be said to have initiated a trend in co-operative developments in India which has already led to important results. It was chiefly because of the early success of the venture that the Government of Bombay adopted in 1954 the policy of confining, in the future, the licensing of all new sugar manufacturing establishments to co-operatives. This had, in turn, an effect on policies of other states and of the Planning Commission. The development of sugar co-operatives in Maharashtra has subsequently, followed closely, the lines established at Pravaranagar. During the 1961–2 season, sugar co-operatives in Maharashtra produced 2,33,000 tons of sugar of the approximate value of Rs 26,16,00,000. There is very large scope for further expansion of the industry in this state and it may be safely predicted that most of the future expansion in sugar industry in the South will take place through co-operatives. Moreover, the sugar co-operatives in Maharashtra have already shown considerable willingness and capacity to move into other lines of economic activity and may be expected to be active leaders of many-sided economic development in their areas. It would, therefore, be no exaggeration to claim that they represent the most significant development in India since Independence in the progress towards a Co-operative Commonwealth.

The Pravara Karkhana took a long time in being formed. The idea was canvassed in the early forties by officers of the Bombay State Co-operative Bank and local co-operative leaders. It was publicly discussed and

* Written on the occasion of the visit of Pandit Jawaharlal Nehru to the Karkhana on 15 May 1961.

sponsored for the first time at a conference of irrigators held at Shrirampur in December 1945. After this the scheme took concrete shape, the area of operations (of about 40 villages with a population of more than 50,000) was defined, and advance share subscriptions began to be collected. Progress was slow, largely because of procedural difficulties and the need to convince a number of authorities, and the Society was registered only at the end of the year 1948. Immediately after registration, however, the tide turned, and the conjuncture of circumstances became favourable. The Government of Bombay, through its Co-operation and Finance Minister Shri V.L. Mehta, took, for these times, the novel and important decision of subscribing Rs 6 lakhs to the share capital of the Karkhana and the Industrial Finance Corporation took a sympathetic view in giving it a loan of Rs 20 lakhs. The Karkhana was also lucky in obtaining a small but new Skoda plant. Within a year of registration, financial arrangements had been completed, the site determined, lands purchased, and the order for machinery placed. Within another year, the machinery had arrived at the site and had been erected without the help of foreign erectors and the first bag of sugar had been produced.

The Karkhana began in a small way. In the first year of production (1950–1) the number of members was less than 500 and the area under sugarcane held by them was less than 800 acres. The average acreage of sugarcane per member was only about 1.6 acres. Almost all members were small farmers; some had yet to undertake planting of sugarcane. Only a small number of members were substantial farmers with 20 acres or more of their farm area under sugarcane. However, the base was sound. Most of the members were men who had paid advance share money at considerable inconvenience to themselves when the prospects were uncertain and the prevalent mood everywhere was of scepticism regarding the 'over-ambitious' project. They had been prompted to come together by a number of motives. There was the prospect of stability of the price of sugar as against the wide fluctuations in prices of *gur*. There was hope of obtaining additional supplies of canal water from the government. Above all, however, there was the urge to prove that the indigenous farmers of the area, though now reduced in importance, could still, through mutual co-operation, make good and obtain the full benefits of irrigation which, hitherto, had accrued to capitalists and some classes of immigrant farmers. It was this last, more than the mere economic incentives, which welded the membership into a cohesive whole and to which the leaders appealed.

The cohesion and the loyalty to the organization were to be put to a severe test before the factory went into production. In the season 1950–1, the prices of *gur* soared high and it became greatly remunerative to convert sugarcane into *gur*. The first bag of sugar in the new factory was produced only on 31 December 1950 and at the beginning of the *gur* season, i.e., in

October–November, it was uncertain when production would begin. Even so, not a single member proved disloyal; all waited, some at considerable sacrifice, for sugar production to start and to have their cane converted into sugar by the new factory. They had their reward; on account of a turn of government policy, the prices of sugar obtained by the new factory in 1950–1 were very high and it was possible to pay a fully remunerative price to members during the very first season.

Once the factory went into production the record was one of almost continuous progress. The farmer members, by their vision and tenacity, had brought into existence a central organization and as this grew in resources and strength it proved fully its utility to the farmer community. This is evident in the record of services rendered by the factory and expansion in activity resulting from it. However, even before the cumulative effects of the existence of the Karkhana began to appear, a difficult season underscored the changed situation in a dramatic manner. The year 1952–3 was a year in which west Maharashtra experienced conditions of a severe drought. The large majority of members of the Pravara Karkhana did not obtain supply of water from government canals and grew their cane on wells. The drought affected the supply of water in the wells and cane crops began to suffer severely. The existence of the Karkhana saved the situation for members. The Karkhana, through its agricultural staff, explored all avenues of expanding and conserving the water supply and promptly extended financial assistance to individual members to enable them to take appropriate steps. Without this concerted and multi-sided action not only would the cane crops have been almost ruined but also individual farmers would have had to contract debts which would have handicapped them for years to come. The Karkhana, during this year, also went out of its way to crush the precarious sugarcane crop of even small non-member farmers and thus demonstrated its value to the community at large.

It is necessary to note that the co-operative, being a mutuality, the interests of the organization and of its members are identical and that by helping the business of members the co-operative helps itself. This can be illustrated in a variety of ways through the development of operation of the Pravara Karkhana. It is of the utmost importance for the sugar factory to obtain a regular supply of freshly cut and mature cane throughout the crushing season. The requirement induced the Karkhana to take upon itself arrangements for cutting of cane and its transport from the fields to the factory from the very first year. The arrangement involved the employment of hundreds of bullock carts and teams of workers and also looking after the entire road system of the area of the factory. The road system had to be such that a bullock cart could travel safely and fairly expeditiously from any sugarcane field in any of the villages in the area of the Karkhana to the factory and to the extent that public authorities did not construct or maintain the roads the Karkhana had to do this itself. The road mileage maintained by the Karkhana today covers 140. The harvesting of the cane crop had to be arranged in a systematic manner so that the flow of cane was even and of optimum quality. This meant ranking each individual field under sugarcane and to do this the factory had to have full information regarding the crop in each field of each member, such as, the sort, the date of planting, and the progress of later operations. This information could be gathered only through a staff of fieldmen working under Agricultural Officers, all of whom were in close touch with individual members and their fields.

Above all, the Karkhana was interested in the quality and quantity of the cane crushed. The growing of cane has two aspects: resources and technique. If the cultivator does not command adequate resources at appropriate times his crop is bound to suffer. It is, essentially, the chronic inadequacy of resources of the peasant that has brought about and still maintains what may be termed the 'under-development equilibrium' in Indian agriculture. Low level, high cost borrowings have ever kept our agriculturists at the mercy of the moneylender–trader and have never allowed him to command any surplus or make the best use of his land. The Pravara Karkhana broke this vicious circle by giving from the beginning all the credit required by any member for raising his crop. As far as possible, this credit was encouraged to be utilized for purchase of ground-nut cake, etc., through co-operative purchase and sale organizations and its use was noticed and recorded by the agricultural field staff. The short-term loan was soon extended to cover such requirements as oil for the engine, workshop repairs, etc. In 1951–2 the Karkhana also instituted a special fund, called the Development Fund, to which allocation was made from profits. This was used to extend intermediate-term loans to members for purposes such as purchase of oil engines, improvement of lands, deepening of wells, etc.

While the lack of resources, especially, resources of working capital, could easily be made up for, the improvement of technique was a laborious and long-term process. The bye-laws of the Karkhana vest in the Board of Management powers to give directives to members in regard to the cultivation of cane. However, the coercive powers have never been used and all improvement is attempted to be brought about through persuasion, demonstration, and encouragement. The chief agency of this effort is the staff of agricultural officers and fieldmen of the Karkhana and the Group Committees provide the forum for discussion. The coverage of effort in this matter is very wide. It embraces improvement of the quality of cane through multiplication and supply of planting sets, improvement of manurial practices, standardization of field operations, individual and group use of insecticides and pesticides, etc. With the passage of time, the Karkhana attempted ever wider and fuller activity in this sphere. The latest extension has been in the direction of a soil survey of the area of operations and the Karkhana laboratory has been equipped for soil analysis so that cultivating and manurial practices might be adapted to the requirements of each field. The Karkhana itself maintains a number of tractors which are hired to members for ploughing and other field operations and the Karkhana Workshop undertakes, on a preferential basis, repair work, such as for oil engines, for members. The Karkhana has also paid, in recent years, attention to limiting the area under sugarcane that members plant under individual wells.

A Producers' Co-operative is, essentially, a joint venture of actual producers and the hallmark of a co-operative is, or should be, that it helps especially the weak to become strong through co-operative action. In the structure and operation of the Pravara Karkhana close attention has been paid, from the beginning, to the fulfilment of these requirements. In framing the constitution of the Pravara Karkhana, care was taken to emphasize the producer aspect. Though provision was made in the bye-laws for admission, for specific purposes, of other types of members, the admission of these was to be exceptional and power was vested, in the main, in the representatives of producers. Another important feature was that each producer member was required to buy shares in a fixed proportion to the number of acres of sugarcane grown by him. This made his contribution to share capital correspond to the service the factory performed for him and made him interested in supplying cane to the Karkhana. This was apart from the bye-law which compelled each producer member to offer all the cane grown by him to the Karkhana.

The Pravara Karkhana, it has been indicated above, was predominantly a co-operative of small farmers. Deliberate efforts were made in later administration to see that this feature was retained. An elaborate set of conventions was built up in relation to the transfer of shares to see that no increase took place in the concentration of share-holding. Small farmers were given special treatment in such matters as grant of intermediate term loans or concessions in the payment of share money. Two major decisions further benefited small farmers in a special way. The insistent demand by the Karkhana that its members should be given a larger share in canal water supply, at the time of the six-yearly revision, led to a somewhat peculiar response from the government. This was, an offer of 100 acres of canal water to the Karkhana itself. As the Karkhana was not interested in conducting cultivation on its own account, the Board of Management unanimously decided to distribute this water right to members holding three or less shares, whose lands were appropriately situated, but who had less than two acres under sugarcane.

The Karkhana was in a position to extend privilege of membership to new entrants when order was placed for the larger capacity plant. The total number of shares for which applications were received at this time was, however, much larger than the additional shares to be sold. In allotting these shares priority was given to applications of the very small farmers and these were allotted shares in full. Also, a block of these shares was especially reserved for subsequent allocation to very small farmers and these were helped by special financial concessions to acquire the shares over the years. It may be noted in the context that as no new shares are likely to be issued, except in case of further expansion, and as transfers to non-members and among members are subject to a number of limitations, change of ownership of shares now takes place, chiefly, through partition or succession and this leads, in the vast majority of cases, to a further fragmentation of ownership of shares.

A co-operative is primarily a business organization and its success has to be judged largely by performance in this context. There are a number of tests of such success. Two such tests are financial strength and expansion of activity. The showing of the Pravara Karkhana is good in both these respects.

The Karkhana has not only met its dues promptly and regularly but was also able to repay the Industrial Finance Corporation loans some years in advance; so that, within less than ten years of the erection of the first factory, the Karkhana did not owe any long-term loans and its much enlarged block, of the value of more than Rs one crore, is free today of any encumbrances. The first plant of the Karkhana was of much less than 500 tons capacity; and within two seasons, it became clear that expansion of capacity would soon have to be undertaken. Therefore, when the government announced, in 1954, that it would permit the licensing of new factories and imports of plants, decision was taken to replace the original plant by one of 1200 tons capacity. It was possible to think of this step because, since the first season, the Karkhana had followed a conservative policy in relation to allocations to depreciation, reserve, and other funds. Moreover, the members showed great readiness to contribute to the capital needed through compulsory deposits out of the amounts receivable by them for the price of sugarcane supplied by them. Even the new large plant erected in 1956 has been found inadequate to meet the needs of members and efforts are being made, for some time past, to obtain permission from the government to expand the plant.

Another aspect of financial success is the return made to shareholders. Limit is laid by law to the dividend that can be paid to shareholders by a co-operative society. The more important criterion in a sugar co-operative is, therefore, the price paid for the sugarcane supplied by members. It has been possible for the Karkhana to pay, over the years of its working, a price, in cash, to the members which compared favourably with the minimum prices announced by the government. It has, in many years, also included in the price, substantial amount for compulsory deposits placed by members with the Karkhana to augment its capital resources and to be ultimately converted into share subscriptions. That the price paid by the Karkhana to members has been attractive and remunerative may be judged from the steady extension of the acreage under cane brought about by members. The number of members has increased nearly three-fold during the last ten years while the acreage under sugarcane, of members, has increased more than six-fold. The average holding of a member, of sugarcane, has thus about doubled. Other indications of the improvement in the financial positions of members are their readiness to contribute to educational activity, to the small savings campaign, and towards capital for new co-operative activities.

The co-operative may be described, properly, as an example of economic democracy in working. The Pravara Karkhana exhibits, in practice, the essential features of an economic democracy. The general body of a co-operative is its supreme authority. Though the membership of the Karkhana is now somewhat too large for effective functioning of the general body, the annual meetings are still lively and provide the forum on which criticism of the management is freely voiced. And the general bodies in the early years virtually took or sanctioned all the important decisions. As a matter of historical record, the general body which considered the question of extension of the plant in 1954 proved overwhelmingly important. Opinion on the question of extension was divided. Fears were expressed regarding the risks of a large plant and of the extra financial commitment; there was, also, a strong prejudice against admitting to membership benefits the many cultivators, large and small, who had kept aloof earlier when the experiment was unproven. The majority appeared against expansion and the leadership overwhelmingly against it. And it was only because a plea for large hearted co-operative behaviour, following our true traditions, obtained a ready and sympathetic response from the mass of the members at the general meeting that the right decision was taken.

The management of the Karkhana vests in the Board of Management. A majority of members of this is formed of elected representatives of the producer members. It is a measure of the feeling of diffidence felt in the initial stages that reservation of seats in the Board was provided for, in the bye-laws, in favour of the larger farmers. This was, however, soon done away with and the principle of one member one vote adopted fully in all respects. Other members are representatives of the government, of the Registrar, Co-operative Societies, and of the co-operative financing authority. The Industrial Finance Corporation had powers to nominate two members until its loan was repaid. The Board works largely through sub-committees whose membership is almost entirely confined to the representatives of producer members. It has been found useful to evolve a supplementary organization to help the Board in detailed management. This is that of group committees. For constituting these, the total area of the operation of the factory has been divided into five groups, and a committee of six to seven members formed for each group. The main functions of the group committees are to help in the programme of cutting and transport of sugarcane, including the aligning and maintenance of roads. Where occasion has arisen, they have also been asked to assist in the distribution of canal water. The group committees are useful for explaining to the members the decisions of the Board and also act as a general sounding board for member opinion; they are constantly making recommendations to the Board of Management on all matters connected with the working of the Karkhana. Often mass meetings of members within the group are held to discuss specific questions and a few times in the year all the group committees meet together jointly. It should be noted that most of these developments were the result of gradual adaptation to meet needs as they arose; they appear to have evolved into a satisfactory system of devolution of authority and of inter-communication between the members and the Board.

The Managing Director, a full time salaried official, is the executive head. He is in charge of the Karkhana and all the staff work under his authority. The structure of the technical, supervisory, and labouring staff of the Karkhana differs in no way from that of other sugar manufacturers. However, in some ways the problems of management and of relation with staff are different. Members of the board of a co-operative cannot be expected to be as familiar with business management in its manifold aspects as members of boards of private concerns. With the passage of time, a number of members of co-operative boards are acquiring familiarity with intricacies of the business; however, some difference is bound to persist. Also, the Board being an authority selected by local members, problems, partly similar to those of management in a local authority, arise in this case. The local knowledge and influence of members of the Board is a compensating factor on the other side. It cannot be said that the relations of co-operative boards with the Managing Director, and the staff of officers, have yet been settled into a satisfactory pattern. In the Pravara Karkhana the relations have, on the whole, been satisfactory and changes among heads of departments have been infrequent.

In regard to relations with labour also, there is no distinctive pattern. Labour unions exist and disputes arise. In the Pravara Karkhana the relations with leaders of unions have been cordial and disputes are settled amicably through negotiations. The important point for consideration here is the possibility of associating labour with management and ultimately offering labour partnership in the co-operative. The Pravara Karkhana makes special allotments of shares to labourers or members of staff who undertake cultivation within the area of the factory. However, advantage of such membership can be taken by only very small numbers. The Board of the Karkhana has accepted the principle of association of representatives of labour with management. The Federation of Co-operative Sugar Factories in the state has also done this in its deposition to the Sugar Wage Board. It remains true, however, that little progress has yet been made in this direction.

How does one measure the total achievement? An attempt may be made to indicate it in both quantitative and qualitative terms. Firstly as to the Karkhana itself. Whereas, just before production of sugar began, the contribution to funds of members amounted to a little over Rs 6 lakhs, ten years later, owned funds of the Karkhana amounted to over Rs 120 lakhs. These were all owned by members as during the last year even the share capital held by the government has been refunded. To these may be added Rs 30 lakhs of deposits, of members, with the Karkhana towards later share subscriptions, making a total of Rs 1.5 crores, all of which may be properly attributed to the establishment and working of the Karkhana. The size of the Karkhana as a producing unit is indicated by the value of the sugar produced which exceeded in value Rs 2.5 crores this year. The Karkhana directly employs over 900 persons throughout the year and for nearly six months each year it affords work to 1200 carts, each cart representing a unit of at least two bullocks and a team of three persons. The latter are recruited chiefly from the neighbouring dry *talukas* where agriculture affords employment only during the rainy season.

All this relates only directly to the Karkhana. A much wider picture is presented if we take into account the expansion in activities of producer members which has been made possible by the Karkhana. Agriculture in the area has virtually been transformed. In 1950, the tract still showed signs of the effects of the depression of the thirties. The fall in *gur* prices during this period had ruined many cultivators with the result that they had lost their claims to canal water. Large stretches of even good quality land remained uncultivated, water logging was common, there was little cultivation of cash crops, and the cultivator was still indebted and at the mercy of moneylender–traders. The picture has wholly changed today. Sugarcane production dominates the area, irrigated cotton has begun to make headway, and because of the improved tillage and manuring the production of cereal crops has greatly increased. In qualitative terms, whereas in 1950 the total acreage under sugarcane in the area was about 1200, of which less than 800 acres were with members of the Karkhana, in 1960, the acreage under sugarcane exceeded 5000 acres, almost all of which was with members. This expansion of sugarcane acreage itself required large investment of capital. Moreover, in the Pravara Karkhana area, because of the non-availability of canal water, the extension of sugarcane acreage necessitated investments in wells and engines and pumps. In 1950 the number of wells recorded was 288 and the oil engines installed numbered only 32, the corresponding figures for 1960 were: wells 1531, oil engines 1005. The enormous capital formation represented by this expansion can again be safely said to be a direct result of the working of the Karkhana.

These are indicators of fixed capital investment. The expansion of working capital is indicated by the operation of co-operative credit societies in the area. In 1949–50, these societies had 1121 members and their loaning operations amounted to Rs 3.9 lakhs; in 1960–1, the number of members had risen to 4359 and the loaning operations to Rs 37 lakhs. It need not be emphasized that the employment opportunities created have, with the expansion of industry and agriculture, greatly increased, as has the total volume of all economic activity.

On the general welfare side, the most important quantitative indicator available is that of educational facilities. In 1950, the area was not fully covered with primary schools and there were no secondary schools within it. Today every village has a primary school and there are five high schools with 700 pupils in them. The Karkhana has spent nearly Rs 5 lakhs on capital expenditure on educational facilities and the high schools have been established because of the voluntary educational contribution of Rs 4 per ton of sugarcane crushed, made by producer members of the Karkhana.

The quantitative indicators are impressive. However, in the long run, and in the wider context, the lessons provided and hopes infused through the operations and results of this experiment are even more important. Before concluding, brief attention may be paid to these. The success of the Karkhana underlines the importance of the emergence of the surplus and of the fertilization effect of the ploughing in of surplus within the rural community. In the poor, insecure areas no surplus is available. In the secured but exploited areas the surplus is drained away by the moneylender–trader and by the urban sector of which he is agent and representative. Therefore, development cannot proceed beyond a point. Security, favourable terms of trade, a surplus, and leaving the surplus to fructify within the rural community, all these are necessary for a steady development process, which has cumulative effects, to get started. It is this which the first decade of the Pravara Karkhana illustrates; it is this which points to the compelling necessity of keeping the marketing and processing of agricultural products within the rural community. Unfortunately, it is also this whose importance has, so far, almost completely eluded the attention of policy-makers at the centre and in the Planning Commission.

The second lesson is the great importance and utility of a central, cohesive institution and the multiplicative effects of its activity. Our rural society is today characterized by the decay of old institutions and the failure of new ones to arise. Therefore, the society is disorganized and leaderless in the sense of having no stable organization to take a comprehensive view and to step in at times of need. Reference has been made above to the service performed by the Karkhana during the drought of 1952–3. The Pravara Karkhana is, strictly speaking, an organization of a relatively small number of sugarcane farmers. Even so it has been able to function in a number of cases, such as of epidemics, as the rallying point in the area and it has provided leadership in all economic matters. What has been called the multiplicative effect may be illustrated by reference to two cases. The first is that of the reorganization of the co-operative credit structure in the area. It has been pointed out above that the Karkhana began by giving liberal crop loans to its members. In a sense, this was unorthodox, because giving crop loans is properly the function of a co-operative credit society. However, at that time, the co-operative credit structure in the area was weak and its coverage limited and hence the Karkhana's action could be justified. It could not, at the same time, be a permanent arrangement. And as the apex co-operative bank insisted on the business being gradually handed over to the credit societies, and as members of the Karkhana were apprehensive of results of transfer, the Karkhana had to take active interest in the strength and proper functioning of the credit societies. As a result every important village is, today, served by a credit society and the total structure is both strong and efficient. The second case is that of distribution of canal water. One of the relative failures of the Karkhana, so far, has been in the matter of obtaining additional supply of government canal water for members. In recent years it has, however, succeeded in obtaining a given supply of the water during summer months. This was, however, offered in bulk and only if the Karkhana made arrangements for distribution. This was a challenge which the Karkhana accepted and by calling upon group committees and creating *ad hoc* local organizations carried out the distribution successfully. The success was complete in so far as the Karkhana agency proved more efficient than the government agency; and in following years the government was willing to let the Karkhana undertake the *ad hoc* distribution even for non-members of the Karkhana. Incidentally, however, the Karkhana had proved the feasibility of voluntary distribution of water by irrigation groups about which a lot had been talked but no concrete experimentation undertaken.

The Pravara Karkhana experience further emphasizes the practicability of efficient work in a decentralized system, especially in matters of agricultural development, and the importance of a proper line of communications. It also holds a warning against any rigid system. For some activities the most appropriate organization has been found to be that for one village, for others for five, for still others for forty. Wherever deliberate attempt is made to suit the organization or agency to the work in hand, and there is widespread understanding about the means and the objectives, the chances of success are considerable; and any failures can always be reckoned as providing data for the next experimentation.

Lastly, the total experience appears to suggest that it pays first to work deliberately and cautiously with a pilot or a model and only afterwards to attempt rapid multiplication. In effect, the Pravara Karkhana proved a pilot project. Though it started with some especially favourable circumstances, the pattern of organization and operation evolved in it was capable of being widely copied in Maharashtra. In this, perhaps, lies the key to the rapid spread of the sugar co-operatives in Maharashtra.

The claim to attention, of the Pravara Karkhana, rests ultimately not so much on the solid results already achieved and the fully rounded and healthy co-operative structure raised but on the fact that the work was done in and by a rural community, which enjoyed no special advantages in regard to economic well being or education but, which had the urge to prove itself and did this on the strength of native grit and good sense and sound leadership.

APPENDIX

Pravara Sahakari Sakhar Karkhana, Pravaranagar

Trend in sugar production

Year	*Sugarcane crushed (Tons)*	*No. of sugar bags produced*	*Average recovery*
1950–1	33,055	37,501	11.49
1951–2	64,705	69,526	10.86
1952–3	60,310	64,362	11.49
1953–4	71,098	80,994	10.79
1954–5	84,530	92,531	11.06
1955–6	1,36,811	1,37,828	10.00
1956–7	1,74,990	1,90,712	11.05
1957–8	2,08,091	2 20,702	10.67
1958–9	1,59,728	1,79,774	11.30
1959-60	2,08,701	2,33,797	11.31
1960–1	2,12,587	2,46,377	11.60

Progress made by the members in deepening wells and in purchase of oil engines

Year	*No. of wells*	*No. of engines*
1950–1	288	32
1951–2	326	67
1952–3	401	164
1953–4	457	192
1954–5	466	200
1955–6	1000	470
1956–7	1145	595
1957–8	1232	751
1958–9	1514	906
1959-60	1514	906
1960–1	1531	1005

Membership of the Karkhana

Class of Member	*1951*	*1955*	*1961*
Producer Members	477	567	1478
Ordinary Members	13	22	21
Total	490	589	1499

Classification of producer members as on 30-4-1961		
1.	No. of members holding shares for one acre	685
2.	No. of members holding shares for two acres	357
3.	No. of members holding shares for three acres	143
4.	No. of members holding shares for four to ten acres	242
5.	No. of members holding shares for eleven to twenty acres	43
6.	No. of members holding shares for twenty-one to twenty-four acres	5
7.	No. of members holding shares for twenty-five acres	3
	Total	1478

28

Prospective Development in Co-operative Finance*

A number of issues of policy are emerging in co-operative developments in India. One of these is the problem arising out of the concept of the crop loan and its definition and implementation. It should be noted that the crop loan emerged as a device which could take co-operative credit a step beyond the stage which it had reached previously. At this earlier stage, whether explicitly related to the value of owned land or not, the credit of a cultivator depended largely on his real assets and the loan was made for a twelve-month period and was renewable. There was no explicit linking of the loan or its size to the purpose of utilization; also, fairly severe limits on loans to individuals, and to societies as a whole, were laid down. The result, almost universally, was that in no case could the credit extended by co-operative societies to an individual member serve his needs fully. The co-operative credit system could not, in the circumstances, hope to replace, even theoretically, the moneylender-trader system.

CROP LOAN SYSTEM

The crop loan sought to transform the situation in two directions. First, by shifting the emphasis from real property to the crop as security, it brought in even pure tenants as potential borrowers, and secondly, by relating the size of the loan to the requirements of business, it emphasized productive purpose. Incidentally, it did away with the older, highly restrictive limits on credits to individuals and societies. The new basis, however, resulted in an exclusive emphasis on the requirements of production credit and benefited most those classes and groups whose requirements of this type of credit were relatively large. Therefore, in considering the operation of the existing

* Originally published in *Maharashtra Co-operative Quarterly*, January 1964.

crop loan system, it is necessary to distinguish between defects which are inherent in it and those that are incidental to the operation of the system and are remediable.

In relation to the latter type, the main problems are of ensuring that the loan is used for the purpose for which it is granted, and that repayment is assured at the time of, or soon after, the disposal of the crop on which the loan is secured. The system of giving a large part of the loan in kind is part of the design to ensure proper utilization. Theoretically, it should not matter if a cultivator uses any part of the total resources available to him for either production or consumption needs as long as both are satisfied. The objection to the entire loan being given in cash lies in the danger of insufficient resources being utilized in production, through diversion to non-production needs. The successful formulation of a system of division, in cash and in kind, of crop loans, assumes the possibility of isolating items of production inputs which are universally required and whose normal level could be generalized and incorporated into a system. It further raises the problem of ensuring timely supply from reliable sources. The cash and kind division also leads to the concept of instalment. This is itself another device to secure proper utilization. However, the division of a loan into cash and kind components, which are themselves given in instalments, implies a close adaptation of the division and instalments to requirements of cultivation and an efficient operation of the administrative loaning and supply system. Thus the crop loan system, whatever its originating impulse, becomes, with proper development, an elaborate system which goes far in the direction of supervised credit.

On the side of repayments, the crop loan implies establishment of congruence between maturity and disposal of crop and the recovery of the corresponding part of the loan. As the charge is on the crop, the repayment has to be closely linked with disposal of the crop. Where such linkage is possible within the overall co-operative system, the crop loan system can work fairly successfully. Where this is not so, there should at least be a logical insistence on repayment of an appropriate part of the loan at a time not too distant from the time of the disposal of the crop on the security of which such loan was extended.

Logically, a developed crop loan system thus involves a full analysis of the credit requirements of a cultivator according to crops, times, and types; an appropriate administration of the cash and kind supply and recovery through sales or immediately after. If such a system can be administered in the required detail, it would also make available data needed for its proper structuring and also data needed for continuous agricultural and operational improvements.

It has to be realized, in fact, that even in the case of the co-operative sugar factories, where all the conditions needed are satisfied, neither is the system operated in detail nor are the data collected, analysed, or utilized as required or desired. The main initial contribution of the crop loan system has been that of loosening the fetters of the older structure and enabling co-operatives to meet, more fully, the credit needs of the cultivators. In actual administration of the system, for the most part, the total borrowings continue to be treated as one lump sum, with little pretence at providing supply only when needed. On the other hand, the recovery, instead of being tied to each crop and its disposal, is expected on the average at the end of the agricultural year.

This should not lead one to ignore the very real advance in the functioning of co-operative credit brought about by the acceptance of the concept of the crop loan. An essential objective and stage in co-operative progress is the replacement of the moneylender-trader system. An effective inroad in the field occupied by that system was made possible through the crop loan idea. This enabled fairly adequate credit being given to large groups, such as substantial farmers of commercial crops, and this made a dent in the moneylender-trader system, of a size and quality which was otherwise unimaginable.

INADEQUACY OF THE SYSTEM

This partial initial success of the crop loan system has itself brought into the forefront a large number of complex problems. The numerous defects pointed out in the operation of the crop loan system all derive from insufficient progress in its logical implementation.

The implementation requires that a fuller understanding of the implications of the crop loan system must be achieved among all connected with the co-operative credit system, viz., among borrowers as well as among those who direct and conduct operations of financing agencies at all levels. Even more importantly, it requires considerable enlargement and improvement of the staff of the financing agencies. The required collection and field scrutiny of information, the preparation of elaborate individual loan papers, the administration of loans and their recovery at appropriate periods would not be possible without this step being taken. This conclusion raises two important issues: (i) whether the considerably increased expenditure on staff is financially and otherwise possible for co-operative financing agencies at all levels and in all tracts, and (ii) whether in the future development of the co-operative credit system the administrative tasks resulting from such elaboration could or should all be sustained by the co-operative financing agencies alone. Before dealing with these issues, it may be useful to turn to problems outside the strict application of the crop loan system.

The report of the Committee of Direction of the Rural Credit Survey of the Reserve Bank of India, on which the present policies are largely based, did not adequately deal with a set of questions. In the main, these are the problems of subsistence and uneconomic farmers, the problem of consumption loans, and the problem of the co-operatively backward states. An important finding of the Rural Credit Survey was that the larger and the more intensively developed the agricultural production activity of the cultivator, the larger, proportionately, was his need for production credit. The crop loan system could, on this account, meet more or less fully the needs of the more substantial cultivators in most areas where important commercial crops were grown. This class of cultivators had, usually, some resources of their own and the crop loan limit for them, worked out on a generous enough scale to satisfy all normal credit needs. The manner in which the share-holding contributions by cultivators to a number of processing factories in Maharashtra were met through crop loans indicates the extent of the margin which, on an average, was made available through crop loan limits to substantial cultivators. On the other hand, the smaller cultivator and the cultivators who grew the less costly crops, because of soil or climatic conditions, did not equally benefit from the crop loan system. This was because production credit needs played a relatively small part in their total requirements of credit.

CREDITWORTHY AND NON-CREDITWORTHY FARMERS

The Rural Credit Survey Committee also ignored the distinction between the creditworthy and non-creditworthy farmers which had been drawn by the Agricultural Finance Sub-Committee of 1945. In doing this, the Rural Credit Survey was following the example set by the Bombay State Co-operative Bank in its policy resolution of 1948. The distinction between the creditworthy and the non-creditworthy made by the earlier Committee is, no doubt, important; but it has significance only if concurrently a programme of rehabilitation of the non-creditworthy is devised and implemented by the state. In the absence of such action, the distinction loses meaning because the co-operative credit organizations, themselves, are in no position to undertake a rehabilitation programme or to give special assistance. The Board of the Bombay State Co-operative Bank was faced with this problem in 1948 when it came to define the amount of loan to be advanced under the crop loan system to various classes of cultivators. In doing this through linking the quantum of the loan to the acreage under crops, the Board decided not to exclude any farmer, however small. This was because the definition of a class of farmers below a certain level of holding, etc., as non-creditworthy would only have resulted in denying all credit to very large numbers of small holders. This would obviously have been unfair and contrary to co-operative developments so far. Therefore, no differentiation was made in the application of the crop loan system among the various types of cultivators by size of holding or business.

Of course, the crop loan system itself led to wide variations in the amounts of crop loan to which an individual farmer was entitled. The small holder got a loan which was related only to the small number of acres of his crop acreage, and if he grew only cereal and pulse crops, the amount of the crop loan to which he was entitled was small indeed. It was presumably argued that this small loan even the uneconomic farmer would be able to repay. The natural consequence of this arrangement, to which, however, not sufficient attention was given, was that the credit obtained by these classes of cultivators was very inadequate. For requirements of credit other than those for agricultural production, the crop loan system made no provision; therefore, this system, however elaborately or properly administered, could not deal adequately with the credit problem of these classes of cultivators. The Rural Credit Survey did pay some attention to consumption aspects, but the recommendations that it made, viz., that of practices modelled on the Chit Fund were obviously not likely to meet the needs of the small farming community. It should, therefore, not be a matter of surprise that the present policies are found to be inadequate to deal with, what have been termed, the weaker sections of the community.

The Crop Loan Evaluation Committee of the Bombay State Co-operative Bank tried to get over, in part, the difficulty by expressly including expenditure on subsistence of the farm family during the off-season as a part of the overall crop loan limit. This was tantamount to broadening the concept of the crop loan and almost to changing its character. It can be argued that if a farm family incurred cash outlay to feed itself during the off-season, this was as essential to growing the crop as any production expenditure. Moreover, if this necessary outlay led the family to contract debt from another credit agency, the operation of the crop loan system was put in danger. However, the acceptance of such reasoning meant adopting a view of the crop loan which related the loan to the broader requirements of the farm family rather than to the direct production credit required by the crop. Another problem raised by this procedure was that of the relation between the loan and the proceeds obtained through sale of crops. As long as the crop was strictly limited to the direct inputs required for growing the crop, the presumption was that the total value of the crop would be normally much higher than the crop loan limit. Once other expenditures such as those on subsistence of the family are counted in, the assumption can no longer be regarded as generally valid.

CONSUMPTION NEEDS OF FARMERS

If the co-operative structure is to serve fully the small or uneconomic farmer class and to liberate it from the moneylender-trader system, it must make credit available for all the production and consumption needs of the farm family. However, if this is done, the security and repayment base of the crop loan system become non-applicable; for example, it is highly unlikely that the proceeds of sale of farm produce by the small farmer will cover his total requirements of credit. However, it is equally true that no alternative base is readily available, at least not one that can be put in a generalized form. The difficulties are obvious. The small or uneconomic farmer, almost by definition, is not only an agriculturist producer but also obtains income from a variety of other sources. Neither supply nor recovery of the loan is, in this case, related to the comparatively simple calculations regarding type of crop grown and its returns, which can be put into average generalized forms. The problem would be less difficult if the other resources of income could also, in some way or another, be linked with the operation of the co-operative organizations. If the supplementary income sources were, for example, livestock or artisan industry, a separate assessment of requirements and possibilities of repayments could be made for each activity and combined together. (This would, of course, require detailed individual assessment and programming.) Where the other source of income is wage income or remittance, its definition and evaluation become much more difficult. The financial problem of the weaker sections of the rural community then becomes, in large part, the problem of consumption finance of the wage earning class. As defined above, it is also the problem of production finance of miscellaneous activities about which no generalized procedure can be formulated. It is thus not only fraught with more risk but requires for administration a much more detailed and individualistic approach. In a sense, therefore, developments required for this purpose are in the same direction of supervised individual credit. Ultimately, the only development that can help substantially in this matter is a more close-knit organization of the weaker sections themselves, such as of the small farmers in types of co-operative farming or co-operative bullock or labour sharing units and of wage earners in labour contract societies, etc. The only sure way of helping weaker sections of the community is trying to spread the network of co-operative production and labour activity among them.

Even apart from the special needs of the small farmer, the problem of consumption credit needs now to be tackled explicitly by all financing agencies. It may be recognized that the only base for such credit is that of actual or potential savings. No system can be built in rural India on expectation of voluntary savings. However, it may be noted that, it is now a general practice for co-operative financing organizations to make regular deductions for contributions to capital. On the analogy of these, in addition to or in part replacement of these, compulsory non-withdrawable deposits could be created. A certain measure of consumption credit could be given on the ultimate security of such deposits. Such a device is necessary, even for the more substantial farmers, for the period for which a farmer is not entitled to draw on production credit lines. This does not mean that the emphasis on production needs or objectives is forgotten or lessened, but that it is recognized that a credit system which claims to be universal must provide within itself for all needs in a systematic manner.

PROBLEM OF OVERDUES

Attention may be paid, at this stage, to the problem of overdues which is engaging greater and greater attention in recent years. There are two aspects of this question which need to be considered. In relation to the crop loan system, there is the problem of the failure of the crop. This problem—it has become clear during the last ten years—is of serious dimensions in parts of Maharashtra. In a number of districts, crops have failed in certain areas in successive years. With such failure, full recovery of loans becomes difficult. It is inevitable that the greater the progress made by co-operatives towards supplying adequate finance, the greater will be the extent of non-repayment in the event of failure of a crop. As yet, no procedures have been fully established to deal with this question. It is necessary to elaborate these procedures and to arrange, both, for proper enquiry and prompt extension of relief in the event of a significantly serious failure of any crop. The better such a system of relief is, the more insistent can be the demand for fullest repayment in normal circumstances.

A question which has never yet been considered in this context is the possibility of a measure of relief extending beyond postponement of repayment. Co-operative banks and societies are expected to look especially after the weaker among their members. At present, co-operative banks give rebate to good customers and this is right. They yet do not give any rebate in interest to those who are visited with failure of crops in successive years. It would at least serve as a valuable gesture if it was possible to do something in this direction in the more serious cases. The risk fund necessary to give more substantial relief in the worst cases, to which the Rural Credit Survey Committee referred, needs also to be set up.

The other point that needs consideration in connection with current overdues is the concept of complete repayment at a point of time with reference to which overdues are defined. It was, no doubt, necessary in the earlier stages of the development of the Co-operative Movement to guarantee that at an appropriate time in the year the cultivator worked off his loan completely. It is proper also that the practice of fictitious repayments and early renewal is discouraged. However, when the co-operative becomes the only source of finance for a farm family and when the total loan operations become large, the question may be raised as to whether it is proper to expect that an account will be completely cleared at one particular point in the year. It is necessary, in this context, to look realistically at receipts and expenditure flowing in the economy of the individual cultivator. If during the production season the borrowings and the production outlay of the cultivator are increasing, at the end of the production season he has not only the repayment but the accumulated consumption expenditure needs to meet. It is well known how consumption outlays in rural India go up in the post-harvest seasons. If the co-operative system, in fact, fully finances the cultivators, the outlays on consumption needs, which he has in part to meet out of the proceeds of sales of crops, are a feature for which some allowance must also be made. Suppose, for example, that in a fully elaborate system of supervised credit allowance is made for a certain outlay on important consumption items by the farmer in addition to his requirements for different production purposes, it would then happen that at no time in the year would his account ever be brought to zero. The banking account of a company with continuous production operations is never expected to be fully repaid at any one point of time. A good banker watches the accounts to see that they are active in an appropriate manner and that in the slack season, if there is one, outstandings are brought down fairly low. There is, however, no insistence on complete clearing of debts in the renewable limits. When progress is made in the direction of giving full credit and covering consumption needs together with production needs, a revised view of the definition of overdues may have to be taken. The present formula of complete repayment leads to the need of artificial adjustments in many cases and, therefore, a more satisfactory index of the behaviour of accounts may have to be established. This, again, is something which indicates the need for a greater elaboration of administration of credit in the direction of supervised individual credit.

It will be evident from the above that I do not take an alarmist view of the increase in the volume of credit and do not agree with the position that it is necessary to withdraw from the crop loan concept. Current developments may have some undesirable features but they are basically in the right directions. At the same time, they present a challenge and it can be met only by thinking out, carefully in advance, the principles and procedures of future action. As set out above, the main requirements are a fully elaborate implementation of the crop loan system and a comprehensive definition of co-operative credit which will take account of all needs of all classes. It has, further, been indicated that these developments are possible only if a much more detailed administration and supervision of credit, reaching down to the individual family, is provided. Experiments with some variations on the crop loan theme are being currently made in some districts of Maharashtra. These relate, chiefly, to an increase or decrease of the crop loan limit in individual cases to bring about a closer linking of co-operative credit with marketing. This, together with increase in the number of processing units, may help better performance. There is also the possibility, in some areas in Maharashtra, particularly in the areas of co-operative sugar factories, not only to elaborate the working of the crop loan system but also to watch closely its effects on production and to use it as an incentive to greater productive effort. However, all this experimentation has scope, chiefly, in areas of intensive cultivation of commercial crops and will not help to solve the problems of the uneconomic farmers and of the predominantly foodgrain areas. Moreover, in these latter contexts and areas the resources of the financing agencies, both the primary societies and the District Central Banks, are among the lowest.

SUPERVISED CREDIT

An appreciation of this situation raises the issue of the extent to which financial agencies can, and may be expected to, act by themselves in further elaboration and experimentation. The development of a detailed system of supervised, individual credit has significance not only for financial operations but also for the entire process of development planning. Therefore, all agencies must help in an appropriate manner in the process. In this context, beginnings have been made in Maharashtra in two directions: first, in the joint planning and implementation of annual targets by the Co-operative Department and the co-operative banks; second, attempts are being made to co-ordinate fully the work of the co-operative central banks and the co-operative land development banks. But the work must go much further. It must take in all developmental agencies in the field at the block and the district levels. Theoretically, something of this sort is presumably being attempted in the package district plans. In practice, very little has been accomplished anywhere. The view still appears in general that making a large loan is a developmental activity, while recovery is a purely financial one. Unless this attitude is changed, and the total operations of the financial system are looked upon as integral to the development plan and a shared responsibility of all, no further progress appears possible. Also, it is only in this manner that the personnel required for the working of an elaborate system of supervised credit could be made available.

All the above assumes a certain minimum development of the co-operative structure. Admittedly, this is non-existent in a number of states in India. The problem of future developments in these states must be considered, at least initially, somewhat apart from the programme sketched above. It must be considered a serious lacuna in the post-Rural Credit Survey programme, and perhaps of the RCC recommendations themselves, that this problem was not separately tackled. The main difficulty in this context is the great weakness of the primaries. Therefore, a beginning has to be made with building the structure, so to say, from the top. The situation has, so far, led merely to the perpetuation of the control of co-operatives at all levels by the state and its officials. A breakthrough requires conceptualization of an alternative practicable approach. I have not sufficient knowledge of conditions in these states to think through this problem. However, I shall put forward an idea merely to illustrate what I mean by an alternative approach. It may, for example, be taken for granted that it is impossible at this stage to build up directly co-operative primaries in sufficient numbers. In this case, the District Central Bank may be taken as the initial operative unit on the building up of which energies are concentrated. The main and vital requirement is that this should be attempted to be directly built as a genuine co-operative organization. And it should be the main task of this organization to promote, supervise, and direct the operations of primaries so that they grow up in time as genuine co-operative organizations. In the transition stage, as happened in all states formerly, the central bank could deal even with individual cultivators in the absence of a proper primary structure. A good deal of improvisation and unorthodoxy may be permitted, provided a genuine co-operative nucleus is created and it works in the direction of proliferation of its activities. Without some such operational approach and concept, the present stalemate in many states appears likely to continue indefinitely.

Finally, some observations may be made in relation to the role of the Reserve Bank in future developments. The Reserve Bank has been an active agent in promoting the development of co-operative organizations during the last decade. It has done this according to a set pattern and through its inspecting mechanism and the terms and conditions of its financial assistance. The success achieved has been remarkable, but it appears as if the limit of advance, according to this pattern, through these means, has been almost reached. Those who shape co-operative policy of the Reserve Bank have to address themselves to two sets of questions. First, what is the new orientation of policy to be? This has to be decided jointly by non-official co-operative opinion and the authorities, viz., the Governments of the Union and States and the Reserve Bank. The present note has been chiefly concerned with problems of future policy.

The second issue, which must be determined mainly by the Reserve Bank itself, relates to the change in the approach and methods of the Bank. On this, only some general observations can be usefully made. First, it appears clear that it is no longer appropriate to adopt and operate a uniform all-India policy. Possibly, adoption of some aspects of even the earlier programme, e.g., the large-sized society, was too generalized. Henceforth, different programmes of action must be evoked for different states in accordance with their existing condition, and the history of the last decade. This will be possible only with a changed approach on the part of the Reserve Bank and its officials. Today, the co-operative organization and governments of states study the terms and conditions of loan, assistance, etc., of the Reserve Bank only for achieving the greatest formal compliance so as to obtain the largest measure of assistance. The Reserve Bank is able to do little, even if it is fully aware of the frequent large differences between the reality and the facade. The situation can be met only if there is real understanding between the Bank and the non-official co-operators and the governments of the states. No doubt a general framework of policy, and of generally applicable terms and conditions of financial assistance, will have to be retained. But with this broad frame, programmes of immediate action for each individual state or region will have to be formulated and for implementing these, appropriate short-term adjustments in the general scheme will have to be offered or allowed in individual cases. Reserve Bank officials must have informal contacts with, and intimate knowledge of, those in charge of co-operative organizations and must be able to function in an informal advisory capacity.

29

Reflections on a Co-operative Social Order*

I consider it a privilege to have been invited on this occasion. It is the completion of the first year since the passing away of Shri Vaikunthbhai and to have to deliver a lecture in his memory was an assignment which I could not possibly refuse. I am deliberately not going to say anything about Shri Vaikunthbhai, nor is it very easy for a person like me to talk about him. It is also not necessary because I take it that the majority here was well acquainted with him personally and with his work. His has been a substantial and valuable contribution in Indian socio-economic thinking and practice. I believe with him that the co-operative way holds out promise of development, in relation to concrete achievements in the modern world and the reconstruction of modern society, on lines of much greater conformity with our traditions and thinking than any other. Vaikunthbhai's life was, for the greater part, spent in establishing co-operative organizations in what might be called an essentially hostile environment and therefore, his pioneering work did not appear to lead to the building up of as many solid edifices as could result from the work of his successors who build on the foundations laid down by him. The work was nevertheless extremely valuable. Moreover, apart from being an able practical banker and co-operative worker, Vaikunthbhai, whom I always considered as essentially an intellectual, was interested continuously in theoretical formulations about co-operation, among other things. He was greatly attracted by the idea of an essentially egalitarian decentralized society and the two main planks of his practical work and theoretical thinking were, on the one hand co-operation and on the other village industries. These, from the point of view of the structure of an

* *Bombay Gandhi Smarak Nidhi*, Vaikunth L. Mehta Memorial Lecture, Bombay, 3 November 1965.

essentially egalitarian modern society, merge together. It is because of this, and because of the interest that Vaikunthbhai developed, notably in the later years of his life, in thinking about the co-operative order generally, the co-operative economy as a whole (I think he has one article on the 'Co-operative Socialist Commonwealth'), because of this, that I thought that this would be the appropriate occasion on which I could place before you some ideas on the Co-operative Social Order.

You will find, from the way in which I have formulated the subject of my lecture, that I have not obviously thought it all out, that I am not fully prepared for it. It is a rather difficult subject. What I am going to do today is to place before you some essentially fragmented thinking on what I consider to be the main areas in relation to which we must go more deeply into these problems of construction of the Co-operative Social Order. You will note that there has been relatively little writing or thinking, even in other countries, on this broad area. That is because, most co-operative workers and most people who wrote about co-operation were exercised about practical and theoretical problems of co-operative organizations operating in an order which was not essentially co-operative. If you take any, beginning right from Rochdale pioneers or even earlier, say, the socialist experimenters whom Marx derided as utopian, if you take any from these, to the later, more practical workers, they are all concerned with how, in what manner and on what principles, with what discipline, you could build an individual co-operative organization, or a chain of co-operative organizations, which could help particular sections of the society, the weaker sections or, let us say, the more disorganized sections in society, to hold their own and to derive somewhat larger benefit from the prevailing order than they could by acting by themselves as discrete individuals. So most of the problems discussed, or practical problems sought to be solved, were problems of how co-operative organizations could establish themselves, how co-operative organizations could best operate, and so forth. For the larger part, this was in what we now call a capitalist society. In recent decades, there have been similar instances of operations of co-operative organizations in what is, essentially, a socialist or a communist society. If you take co-operatives operating in the Russian centralized economy, they are also operating in an environment which is alien, a communistic environment, just as those in America and Europe operate in an essentially capitalistic environment. Therefore, you will find that the thinking is not about a co-operative order but about co-operative organizations, or a co-operative sector at the most, in an order which is other than co-operative. This, in my opinion, is the essential reason, why relatively little thought has so far been given to a co-operative order and to its establishment.

The resulting gap I want to indicate today by dealing with three subjects, in a sense, quite different, but which have, from a broad perspective, many common features. I shall begin with the problem of the structure and organization of a co-operative economic society. How would you think of this, what are the problems that arise in its construction, this is not being thought out even in theoretical terms. There is a great deal of talk today in India about a co-operative order. We are thinking, at least in terms of a rural economy which may become basically very largely co-operative and we have to foresee as to what will happen, or what should happen, if this transformation comes about. If you will look at the history of co-operative structures in various countries, you will find that according to the peculiar favourable conjuncture of circumstances in each country, a certain form was given to the structure. Yet nowhere do we find thinking about the logical ordering of a co-operative society or about the concept of a whole structure which is co-operative. This is because, say in the UK where it first grew, you will find a predominantly consumers' activity with very little of industrial or agricultural co-operation. In Ireland, and some of the Scandinavian countries like Denmark, you will have an agricultural processing, marketing, and a rural consumers' movement but very little in the industrial sector. Perhaps in Japan, we have the most comprehensive co-operativization of the rural economy today than in almost any other country in the world. But here again, there is no thinking about a co-operative order as such. The co-operative rural economy thinks of itself, essentially, as a subordinate partner in a broad, generally aggressive, capitalistic society. We have the example of Israel where a larger part of the economy, you may say, is presumably in the co-operative sector. I say presumably, because the co-operative organization in Israel is essentially a counterpart of the Histadrut, i.e., essentially a counterpart of the workers' movement in Israel. It is not co-operation built from bottom to the top, but a counterpart or representative of the trade union movement, in the co-operative sector.

I should like to make my point clear by raising some problems as we face them today in India in building up a logical structure. In building a logical co-operative structure, what are the elements with which one works, the elementary principles? This, you will see, is an extremely ticklish problem, because you have to extract from the history of co-operation, from the writing and thinking on co-operation, what appear to one to be the more essential things and leave out what appear to be the more adventitious, historically accidental, and so forth. In this search I think it is appropriate to begin with considering co-operation as a device, a measure, means, or instrument which is offered to the weak and the disorganized in the society to strengthen themselves. I consider the co-operative way as, essentially, the way which offers to the smaller, the weaker, the dispersed units in society, the means by which they can come together, organize themselves appropriately in relation to what you may call two important features of the modern economy. As a matter of fact, you may even say that they are one but I personally think that they can analytically be divided into two, viz., technology and scale. The smaller units fail, in an advancing technology and an industrializing society, to maintain their independent existence, largely because of the pressure of the efficiency of large scale operation and the technologically advanced operation. If you consider co-operation as an endeavour to retain the values of the existence of small units and yet obtain for the small units advantages of modern technology and working on a larger-scale, you might get a clue as to what the principles of a co-operative order are or ought to be. You can, on the basis of such an approach, visualize the possibility of an entire order in which the varying units and their organizations find a proper place.

Here, unfortunately, I have not the time to argue the whole process out. The result, as I see it, is that of a co-operative structure in which the basic primary unit may be a multi-purpose or multi-sided unit, that is, a unit with a variety of economic activities, but in which, because of the essential requirement of getting advantage of the technology and the scale at the higher stages of the structure, a functional division has to appear. So that you can think of a multi-purpose village society combining certain amount of credit, marketing, and possibly a few other miscellaneous activities even a consumers' store. But as you rise upwards, you get a functional differentiation between the marketing, the credit, the processing, and all the productive trading, transport, etc., activities. I insist in this manner on the unity and reality of the primary and the functional specialization of higher tiers because without some concepts like these, you cannot build up a logical structure, or avoid problems relating to genuineness or conflict of jurisdiction.

Let me illustrate with the help of one or two examples. Take the example of English Wholesale Co-operatives which run dairies or manufacture cloth and leather goods. A dairy that is owned by the English Wholesale Co-operatives is, essentially, something that is operated, so to say, from outside the organization. In this case you find that the workers, or the farmers, or the animal husbandry-men are as subservient as they are in the capitalist order. Basically, the co-operative is a mutuality, or should be a mutuality, in which the small elements come together in order to serve themselves in relation to a specific need, service, production, trading whatever it is, on their own. Granted this, the character of the co-operative enterprise is not obtained by being owned by another co-operative organization but by being owned by a number of individual members or member units, for whom the co-operative serves a meaningful mutual purpose. Looked at in that way, it will be clear why I consider the Israel experiment as not essentially co-operative. As a matter of fact, there are a number of writers who call this sector of the economy in Israel, labour economy and not co-operative economy, because over it, the labouring class in Israel, wields economic control. The labouring class in the economy, having control over certain organizations, is different from their being under co-operative in structure. For example, the Israel co-operatives run one of the biggest construction organizations, a building and works organization taking very large scale contracts all over the place, but the structure of this organization, including the status of the labour, is not different from any other type, say, the capitalist type, and has no specific co-operative features. Therefore, you have to give considerable attention to the manner in which you build up the structure of the co-operative economy. You can think of a primary society which is small-scale and limited in its geographical area and can thus well serve a variety of needs in a small location, may be multi-purpose. Higher tiers in the structure have to specialize functionally. Adoption of this approach enables one to deal with a large number of problems that we are continuously facing. For example, we are facing a problem as to whether the sugar co-operative factories should distribute fertilizers to their members, or whether a consumers' co-operative should receive finance by itself by way of attracting deposits. These problems begin to become clearer, if you think in terms of the functional specialization which is required to get full advantages of scale and technology.

Or take the other problems, for example, those of producers' organizations; how does one organize production right from agriculture to industry, how does the co-operative form spread to higher levels. Here again I would insist that it is direct interest and the mutuality that is important. You will then find that you cannot just call anything co-operative by merely organizing a few people and having model bye-laws. It must essentially pass the test of mutuality, and if it has to pass the test of mutuality then we, necessarily, get a tier of organizations. For example, you may take, let us say, groundnut producers; you start with the oil expeller as the primary processing society. Now if you are thinking in terms of industrialization based on oil this has to be organized on the basis of those primaries. Then it is these primaries that become the owners and operators of a more complicated industry that is raised for the utilization of their products. Some of this type may in turn come together to form an industrial organization at a still higher level. I am citing this as an illustration and not drawing in the more familiar example of the banking or marketing structure, because I want to emphasize how I think the co-operative order is differently structured and how it will operate in a different manner.

Inevitably, one can also see that this approach imposes certain limitations. It is very difficult with this approach to get public utility concerns within the co-operative order and it becomes very difficult to organize a large extractive industry co-operatively in which there is no possibility of separate ownership of small units. So that you have to live with the idea that though the co-operative order can cover large numbers and the bulk of the working population in various kinds of activity, it has to co-exist with a public utility sphere and some type of corporative sector.

The other set of problems in the field of structure and organization, problems which are extremely difficult to deal with, relate to labour. The co-operative organizations emerge as mutualities from one or the other side of economic activity either of producers or say, consumers. But whether you base your organization structure on the base of producers' or consumers' co-operation, the workers in these organizations are, for the most part, left out and the problem of labour participation is not tackled. The position is somewhat different where labourers or artisans themselves come together to form a co-operative. But this by itself does not eliminate the problem, as is underlined by the practice of the more meticulous among the co-operative artisan societies of Israel, of having a rule by which the hiring of outside labour is disallowed. This is justified because an artisans' co-operative is, essentially, a workers' co-operative of which every worker in it must be a member. If you hire workers, how do you maintain its co-operative character; since basically in a co-operative the essential aspect of membership is not contribution towards capital but participation in the mutual business of the co-operative. In a consumer store this last is evidenced by dealing with the stores, in a producers' processing co-operative by bringing raw product for processing, in a workers' co-operative by working. Logically therefore, in the last, at least, no worker can remain a non-member without affecting the co-operative character of the organization.

But in the other organizations, such as of consumers or producers, where labour is employed on a large scale, the problem remains. In a society of producers in, say, a sugar co-operative factory or a large-scale consumers' store, how do you get the workers to be members? After all, by no definition can you show that these labourers are not participants in the work of the mutuality. And if they are participants in the work, how can the structure of the mutuality be adjusted to allow for their membership? This problem has not yet been solved anywhere except, in a sense, in Yugoslavia. The Yugoslav solution is, of course, a heroic solution which is not open to be copied everywhere. The Yugoslav economy, as of today, was constructed in its present shape by a complete and sweeping measure of nationalization; everything was nationalized and then every nationalized industry was, so to say, turned over to the workers. The problem we face is different; it is that of labourers' participation in a co-operative which has been formed initially as producers' or consumers', etc., organization. We have the problem of how to reconcile the interests, which may in part conflict, of the two elements.

This leads me to another problem. I have mentioned in the first category or structure and organization the vital problem of division of the product: how does the total product get divided, how is the surplus to be divided, what, if any, are the relevant co-operative principles, or are there any principles at all? Some of these problems are emerging even today, for example, when today governments as in Maharashtra, control the whole series of operations in food as of buying from producers, distribution through co-operative wholesale societies, and selling through consumer stores. Here you have a whole series of operations in which you have, so to stay, no guide from the outside market price at all. The prices that the producer gets for his rice or jowar are prices fixed by the state and the prices which the consumer pays are also fixed by the state. How should these prices be fixed and how is the product divided are decisions which must be independently taken. I suggest that the only clue, you have here in the absence of a 'competitive' market (and as I will immediately explain to you 'competitive' marketing in the ordinary sense, becomes almost non-existent in the co-operative order) is that of a national incomes policy. This is essentially a social and a national decision. It is a decision regarding what you think is the appropriate level of living of various classes. Because, ultimately, this is what determines the distributive pattern. If comprehensive decisions are made regarding nil prices of food and other goods and you derive there from prices that the producer and the labourers get; this is really the overall task of determining the relative structure of prices and the implied distribution of the product. Remember that in a large number of European countries today, the prices of agricultural products are, in fact, determined by conferences round the table in which you get farmers' union's representatives on the one hand and the state's representatives representing the consumers on the other hand, fixing the whole set of prices. So that for a whole category of people, the whole of the peasant order, so to say, the producer price level is, in fact, arbitrarily fixed. So far, I have said something about a couple of important aspects of the co-operative organization and structure. Much more detailed, elaborate thinking, exploring things much deeper, is required if you are to think of building a co-operative order, because in it a large number of specific problems will arise regarding individual products, sectoral prices, etc., which we must be ready to tackle.

The second set of problems are more important. The second set of problems that I have mentioned are the problems of operation of the economy. If you have a co-operative economy, how does a co-operative economy operate, how is it guided, how is it regulated? Obviously, this is an important question. With the recent background of the so called liberal economy, one is apt to think of regulation of an economy as something artificial. Actually, what has been exceptional in human history is this: this episode of a few decades, not even of a full century, in which two things, viz., automatism and rationality were equated in theory and in which it was contended (it was not established) that forces of the market automatically decide everything. So that there is no need for regulation; because all decisions, short-term or long-term, the immediate prices or the long-term investment programmes are all decided and determined by the prices that are established through the action of large numbers of persons operating independently of each other in the market economy as a whole. Now, one has to forget this episode, because as the so-called 'free economies' operate today, each of them is heavily regulated. Not only are they heavily regulated but in the larger and the more advanced economies prices are administered in most of the crucial sectors and the whole of the labour market is largely managed, is in fact, oligopolistic. Large blocks of personnel are offered together as labour supply, so to say, in the market and not individuals coming and competing with each other. And the ability to withdraw or supply whole blocks of labour on the market is linked with the ability to paralyse the whole economy. So that as result of consequent bargaining, you have an arbitrary division of product on an extremely large scale. You thus face problems of regulating economy in the sense of determining the division of the product ultimately by arbitration. I am using the word arbitration deliberately because in an economy dominated by employers' associations and labour unions on a large-scale independent arbitration is, has to be, accepted as the regulator and the regulation is needed for guiding the economy or keeping it on an even keel.

Moreover, since immediately after the depression and now even in advanced countries policy markets and economists are informed by growth consciousness, therefore, maintaining a certain rate of growth becomes an imperative and it acts as an integrating force in national policy measures. And once you get concerned with development and growth and think of regulating and guiding development and growth, obviously the automatism and the free market analysis or model go to pieces.

The co-operative economy is by definition neither an autonomous, nor a free market economy. Its emphasis is on organizing all activities for mutual advantage at a series of levels right from the primary level group in a ladder to the highest possible level. Such organization requires a great deal of fore-thinking of the problems, thinking not only in terms of static state, but in terms of growth. You could call, in a sense, all the older stratified economies static, co-operative economies and by co-operative economy I mean something different from a non-competitive economy. If you take, for example, the old Indian economy, you will find that it was essentially an economy having a static co-operative structure. There was a division of labour, there was a division of product, there was a given technique and co-operation between the various strata in that technique. All these were pre-determined and it was supposed that the annual cycle of seasons repeated itself over generations. It was a static order but it was a completely co-operative order. It was co-operative in the sense that its successful operation depended upon the co-operation along fixed lines of the various elements involved and no departure from the pattern through competitive behaviour was expected or allowed. The presence of the element of coercion or the amount of force exercised I am not going to discuss. Because all hierarchical systems may be said a work under coercion of those at the top. It may be that it is power that maintains the co-operative pattern; even so the operation of the structure is essentially co-operative. The order was static as most hierarchical orders must be static; because hierarchy itself implies a certain amount of, so to say, stable stratification in terms of status and rank. Therefore hierarchy is conceptually static. It would, I suppose, be correct to say that as a matter of fact the Smithian justification for *laissez faire* was essentially based on the contention that a hierarchical order was not only a static order but also a stagnant order. All that Smith has to say about guilds, etc., is so much of an indictment against the old hierarchical order. Thus the eruption of the free market economy or liberal economy in the modern world was, so to say, needed for freeing the older economies from the hierarchical order ; or to put the other way round, this came about because the effects of the advance in scientific and technical thought in Europe could no longer be contained within the older hierarchical socio-economic order.

Looking upon the *laissez faire* period as an essentially transitional period we now perceive a return to economies in which the co-operative element again begins to dominate. However, these co-operative economies are no longer static and hierarchical. One must, therefore, pay attention to basic characteristics of modern co-operative orders.

I suggest that the modern co-operative order must be essentially a planned order. However, to the extent that it is a co-operative order, it is different from the centralized planning order. The structure and operation of centralized planned economy are not to be identified with that of the co-operative economy. If what I have suggested about the special characteristics of the structure of the co-operative economy is correct, the co-operative economy will be able to modify the operation of a centralized plan, exactly in those respects in which centralized planning is supposed to be most defective, i.e., in respect of dispersal of authority and in respect of the ability to take account of local circumstances. These are the two important aspects in which centralized planning is usually blamed.

It might be noted that, in recent years, a large number of people do not describe the capitalist economy as a capitalistic economy but as an economy of decentralized decision making. That is the term that is often used nowadays. I suggest that it is possible for the co-operative economy to become really an economy of decentralized decision making, where decentralized decision making is yet significantly allied to the planning process. In my opinion the planning process is a two-way process. It is a process which takes note of local circumstances, local possibilities, and local capacities and takes note also of the overall possibilities of the economy and overall objectives of the economy. Now this two-way process of conveying overall aims to the locality and conveying local knowledge, knowledge of local possibilities to the centre is significantly possible in an integrated manner only in the co-operative order. Because, as I emphasize, the co-operative order has at its base the primary which is essentially a local and neighbourhood unit and it has at appropriate stages for each function to be performed at the upper level a higher-tier federal authority. It is such a co-operative order that can lend itself to decentralized planning.

It is important to note that you can project the possibility of the co-operative order functioning in this manner only if an important requirement is fulfilled. It is that the political authority, which in the modern state is overwhelmingly important, considers its function mainly that of maintaining the basic legalistic structures and incorporating the accepted values and philosophy of the people into broad economic policy decisions and regulatory systems and then to leave the economic order as largely an autonomous order. This is slightly outside my subject. But I think this is a needed logical approach. The modern state, about which all kinds of terms such as 'a leviathan' are used, is possible of being reformed in its operation only by introducing an element of autonomy of various sectors including the autonomy of the co-operative order within the general political framework afforded by the political state. If such a concept is accepted by the State Planning authority then, you can get a great many of the benefits of decentralization associated with the advantages and values of broad centralized decisions and plans.

I have left myself only a little time to give some thought to the last of the areas, which in some ways is actually the most important area, in which I have divided my subject. In this I am thinking of the difference between the attitude appropriate to and the spirit that should inform the co-operative order. So far I have been talking basically in economic terms, terms of economic operation, forces of the economy or of the economic structure. This is merely the external aspect. In my opinion, when thinking in terms of the Co-operative Social Order and the co-operative economy, the essential difference is that, it is, so to say, an explicitly a moral economy and an economy which explicitly accepts certain ethical principles. I say explicitly ethical, because I do not conceive of any social order which disregards ethical principles. But there are certain societies which may pretend that they have no moral aims or that their values and objectives do not necessarily go along any ethical principles. In my opinion the co-operative order is an ethical order and it has certain values. Its most important values are the values derived from the earlier formulation I gave, which is respect and concern for the small, the weak, dispersed unit which is essentially a concern for the majority of the people.

In a broad retrospect, one may consider that the competitive idea and the co-operative idea have, so to say, co-existed all the times. They co-exist in the sense that even the earliest social unit, the independent family (barring the example of Robinson Crusoe or an entirely self-sufficient single family) is essentially a highly co-operative group. With external groups, it may be considered to be competitive but internally it is necessarily co-operative. It may be that the general spread of moral ideas, in practice, is, so to say, a history of the extent to which the field of co-operation had covered larger and larger societies from the larger family groups to the tribal group or village; and within the group to a large extent, especially where status and ranks were well-defined, co-operative behaviour had a very definite place and competitiveness was largely suppressed. Because of a certain conjuncture of circumstances, in the modern European context, the competitive idea came to the fore and became very important. I suggest that even though the competitive idea, in some of the modern forms, may have yielded beneficial results for mankind in the recent past, it is now becoming more and more of a danger and a threat. It is extremely important to remember that your basic attitude in life covers really the entire field of your existence and of your operations. If the basic attitudes encouraged are essentially competitive and consequently aggressive, you cannot expect an individual in a society to exhibit the competitive and aggressive spirit only in some respects and become entirely co-operative in other respects. This thought, in my opinion, needs today the most careful consideration. This is, for the world as a whole, an extremely important and critical juncture, in which the problem of basic attitudes is of fundamental importance. If you are thinking in terms of societies, of nations co-operating together, then the basic attitudes of peoples have to be in conformity with this aim all over the world and the task of shaping it has to be undertaken at the ground level; for, it is only in this manner that you can transform society. Let me illustrate with a lowly example. Look at the working of sugar factories in India. You have a problem here of improving the sugarcane, quality and yield, and one of our modern prescriptions is to relate the price of sugarcane to its quality. If you relate the price to quality, it is suggested that automatically sugarcane quality and yields will improve. This has been tried in some states by private factories though there are difficulties in the way of connecting the price with the cane output of each individual. In co-operative sugar factories, we think it more appropriate to relate quality to the average price paid to member. Because we consider that the sugar factory has to bear the responsibility of the improvement of quality of sugarcane of all members. And this it does as a programme; so that it appoints technicians, it has to incur expenses for giving seeds, pesticide, etc., and to improve the strains of sugarcane. Of course, even in pursuing this programme the sugar factories benefit themselves ultimately and may be said to have a profit motive. But the point is that the programme really brings up the average of the whole membership of the society and only this can do it. Because when you fix the price for quality of the individual supplier you are taking it for granted that everybody is in a position to improve by himself; that he is in a position to get credit when wanted, to get pesticide when wanted and that he has the requisite knowledge and information. In fact, this is not so. It is only the better and the more resourceful that have these and the higher price operates in the direction of giving them more resources and giving relatively less to those in the lower order. Now I consider that the essence of the co-operative order is this concern with the improvement of the average of the whole society, the levelling up of all and not doing it indirectly but doing it directly and explicitly as a social responsibility.

There has been a great contribution made by the competitive spirit in terms of innovation and efficiency of the modern technical order. However, I would suggest that because of historical developments competition today has lost this value. Innovation and efficiency are now being built into the structure of industrial operations. Co-operative research on the large scale predominates and efficiency can be so objectively measured that it is no longer necessary for the producer to suffer losses in order to know himself or to make known to the public that he is less efficient than others. Therefore the very large price that has to be incurred for operating through the competitive process need no longer be paid. Innovation and efficiency can take care of themselves. On the other hand, I am appalled at and greatly concerned with the perspective unfolded by unchecked continuation of aggressiveness and competitiveness in the modern world with advancing modern technology. In the old world there were only a few million people living in very large space. The independent groups could be hostile towards each other and the natural reaction of heaving bricks at strangers could operate without really very much great immediate loss to the world and the humanity as a whole. But today with the small world in which we live and the advancing technology, overwhelmingly the most important and immediate programme appears to me that of curbing the competitive and aggressive spirit and of replacing it essentially by the co-operative spirit. It is in this respect that I think that we have the opportunity of fundamental contribution by way of experimentation on a larger and larger scale and establishment practically, in sector after sector of something approaching a co-operative order, co-operative economy. Moreover, in attempting this we will have an opportunity of realizing in a practical manner some of the values that we have cherished for centuries.

30

Role of Co-operation in Planned Development*

May I first thank the authorities of the ICA for having invited me to deliver an address on this occasion? May I, in the second instance, assure the audience that I am not going to deliver anything like an address. I realize that everybody has been here for more than one and a quarter hours already, and has listened to a considerable disquisition on the Co-operative Movement. It would be unfair on my part if I abuse the invitation that has been extended to me and proceed to inflict another address on this very distinguished and patient audience. The course that I shall therefore take is a sort of a tabloid of what might be called an address, i.e., an attempt at making summary points that could perhaps be elaborated in a lengthier address. The subject I was asked to talk about is 'Co-operation and National Development'. It is a very vast area, and in a way, I am not competent to speak on any but a limited field within that area, and that field I would define as the field of the role of co-operation as an instrument or agency, in planned national development in under-developed countries. In this regard I would necessarily draw almost entirely upon the Indian experience. I plead guilty in not having any real and intimate knowledge of co-operative development and operations in other countries.

You will see that the basic question that arises when you consider co-operative organization—as an agency or instrument of planned

* Address delivered on the occasion of the 48th International Co-operative Day, observed by The International Co-operative Alliance, Regional Office and Education Centre for South-East Asia, New Delhi, 4 July 1970.

development—is two-fold: (a) Why should governments want to use co-operative organizations as an agency? (b) Why should co-operators wish to allow themselves to be used as an agency?

It is from these two points of view that one has to look at this question. I take it that one can answer the first part in roughly the following manner. Planned development—especially in a country which is under-developed having a dispersed rural population and small-scale production units—is faced with the very important problem of organizing the small producers, the small customers, and the dispersed households so as to raise the scale of their activities to serve as an agency through which planning objectives, operations, and information are passed on to the people on the one hand, and on the other, to communicate the reactions of the population to the Plan. It is extremely important to have such intermediary organizations and it is quite obvious that in an under-developed country, a successful Co-operative Movement and organizations of the co-operative type serve this purpose ideally and are therefore naturally preferred by governments.

The preference of co-operators has not always been distinctly expressed. I remember—in the early forties, for example, before Independence, there was a lot of talk about planning, and keen debates among co-operative leaders in India as to whether co-operators should offer their organizations as agencies or instruments for planned development operations. The basic objection was quite clear. It was that you gave up your voluntary character if you became with whatever safeguards an instrument of governmental policy. In a number of respects the purely voluntary character of the Co-operative Movement was necessarily lost. For example, take membership. If you were an agent or instrument of government policy then you could not arbitrarily limit entrance to certain people. Again, if you said that you are going to supply credit to all creditworthy agriculturists, then once you accepted that obligation, all those who were included in the definition of creditworthy agriculturists had to be admitted, and consequently there was a specific limitation to your discretion in admitting members. There are a considerable number of modifications of the older co-operative type of pattern of the Co-operative Movement. In the under-developed areas, where the new co-operatives are struggling, you have to ensure certain government assistance and certain privileges may have to be extended. However, with these privileges you must accept certain obligations. Therefore, if you accept obligations and assistance, you, necessarily, also accept supervision up to a point, because government has the responsibility to see that the purpose for which it uses the co-operatives is properly fulfilled. A variety of modifications of the structure therefore become necessary. As I said, in the early days—I am talking about the early forties—there was quite a considerable difference of opinion in India as to whether co-operators should offer themselves as agencies in this effort. But with the advent of

Independence and planning this was forgotten; it was brushed aside. New leaders came in with a definite stand on this. I remember that the first step we took, for example in the then State of Bombay, was the re-organization, of the credit movement, and of the entire banking structure in order to fulfil the government obligation. As a result of a committee report, the government offered certain privileges and assistance if the Co-operative Movement undertook to finance all creditworthy agriculturists and this involved a fair amount of re-organization which was alien to co-operative principles, but was a re-organization which we accepted not as arising out of any immediate problem of the Co-operative Movement but as arising out of the acceptance of the obligation to subserve the government aim. In this I identify the government aim as a popular aim or a highly desirable aim. Now this is a basic question. I think Chaudhary Brahm Perkash's concern is quite right. You do become a part of the organization. After all, there are different ways of looking at any society which is alive and growing, and which keeps on growing, and in which changes are peacefully brought about. One way of looking at it is, that the society is so rotten—rotten to the core, that nothing except a revolution can save it.

Now, as far as I can see, co-operators have never been revolutionaries and they never could be revolutionaries because they are always running a business organization, so that whether you are a co-operator in the USA or a co-operator in the USSR, you are working within a framework. It is an establishment—a different kind of an establishment, I suppose if you are working in Mao's China, where you are also working within an establishment, you are working within certain constraints which the society has accepted. There are a number of other forces which you can employ for bringing about radical changes, but co-operative business can hardly operate in this way. Therefore, I am quite sympathetic to the concern a live radical like Chaudhary Brahm Perkash may feel towards what happens to co-operatives. However, what happens to co-operatives is that they operate within a frame. The frame changes. They work in a changed frame. Now, a number of problems arise once you think in terms of some reconciliation between these points of view. That is, once you think that the co-operators have accepted their role as an agency or instrument of national development.

I draw your attention only to two or three aspects of this problem. One is the aspect of coverage and of continuity. You are wanting to be an instrument of national policy. Now, government is naturally desirous that its policy be effective for the whole of the country. If co-operation is still basically voluntary, in the sense that the establishment of co-operative societies and their operations is largely in the hands of non-official leadership, it cannot just be made to order. Then a problem arises regarding this coverage. You cannot be sure that it will be uniformly effective throughout the country, and this is a problem that we in India are facing in the field of credit.

Some 15 years ago, as a result of a government policy based on a report of a committee, a certain re-organization of the credit movement and the credit and banking structure was attempted. The experience has been that while this has succeeded remarkably in two or three states, and as the Chairman remarked, in some states we are hopeful about it, in other states, if you are realistic, you will quite clearly admit—that the experiment has failed. If this happens, then it is quite obvious that the state has to investigate, where the co-operative has failed, that some agency must be appointed. It is difficult for the co-operators to accept this view. They refuse to accept the facts of the case. They still continue to be hopeful that they will be chosen as an agency. If they fail, government cannot just sit back. So this coverage is an extremely important point. So is the point of continuity. If you undertake to supply a continuous service, then the efficiency of operation of the co-operative instrument must be maintained through all time. There are more difficulties. Take, for example, the public sector. In the public sector, the government can guarantee establishment of agencies, branches, and sub-offices and can guarantee continuity up to a point. In the co-operative sector, this becomes more difficult. On the other hand, it is quite obvious that motivationally the co-operative sector is far superior to the public sector so that an efficiently working co-operative is far superior to a public sector undertaking. On the other hand, can co-operatives guarantee to function efficiently at all times and in all places? These are some of the problems of acting as an agent, but an even larger problem which I merely touch here is that of getting co-operatives to work as a system.

What I have said already will indicate to you that I am not satisfied with a patchwork of co-operatives, individual co-operatives here and there, co-operatives in a few regions or only in one sector. If you are looking at co-operation as an instrument of national development, a patchwork sporadically and randomly distributed is not of much help in national policy.

What you want in a national policy is really an organized system of co-operative organizations. Even in the rural economy, unless the problems of credit, of marketing, or production, and of processing are welded together and some link established with the consumer co-operatives in the urban area, you do not really get a strong co-operative structure which can be an efficient instrument of national policy. Now, this is an extremely important point which has not yet been fully appreciated by the Indian co-operative leadership. You find, therefore, that the various sectoral organizations, even if they are strong, make very little effort to organize themselves into a system, and unless they do, we will not really be able to make an impact that will be accepted by the public and the government as an ideal instrument of this policy. Finally, you get back to the old question, the question as to whether it is really worth our while as co-operators to accept this role. You will see that it is a very difficult and delicate question to answer. As I said, it is quite obvious that you lose your power in certain ways. You restrain your liberties in some ways, you accept certain obligations, you accept the supervision of outside authority. You do all this.

Why do you do this at all? Because you feel that in the under-developed conditions of your country, acceptance of these restraints will help you to make progress in co-operative organizations all over the area much more quickly and you will be able to achieve a more satisfactory build-up of the co-operatives than you would if you were left only in the purely voluntary state. Because the difficulties ahead are so great, you accept this alternative. Now, it is anybody's judgment as to whether given these alternatives, you can achieve the objective. I believe there are some states in India which can prove that the decisions that some of us took 15 or 20 years ago to accept government assistance and to accept the character of a government agency were not wrong. Equally, there are other states which seem to prove that it has not helped. Now whether, in those areas where it has not helped it is because the basic conditions are unfavourable or whether it is because of some other reasons is a matter which I cannot really talk about. I would not be dogmatic. I would not even go so far as to say that, though this is a decision in which I was personally involved, that it was always right or the right answer. I would say that this is a matter for judgment.

You have to see what the basic co-operative values are and you have to decide whether these basic co-operative values have been realized, whether they have been fully realized or whether only to some extent, and also whether you would have been possibly worse off, with your whole state of organization weaker, more disjointed, and the co-operative spirit less in evidence than if you had acted otherwise. This is a large question on which history may give a judgment which is more authoritative than the sort of biased judgments that we who have been involved in the process can give today.

VII

Socio-economic Development in New States

31

Social Change and Liberal Democracy in New States*

The problem on which I desire to set down a few observations relates to the transition in the new states, from the existing social organization to a new one, which will be more conducive to the working of a liberal democracy. It is not necessary to describe in full the existing social situation in any particular country or region. It will be sufficient to point to the main relevant features. In what follows, discussion centres round the situation in India. Attempt is, however, made to place it on as generalized a level as possible; so that it may, at least in part, have relevance to the situation in other regions such as, for example, South East Asia or the Middle East.

The most important characteristic of the Indian social situation is the dominance of caste. The caste system places groups in society in a predetermined, relatively ranking order, and one's position in the caste structure is determined by birth. Theoretically, not only social status but also economic occupation was supposed to be determined by caste. However, occupational determination was, perhaps, never rigid, and during recent times this has been confined to preventing entry of members of some groups to some pursuits. Today, the direct effect of caste in this regard may be considered to be negligible. However, the historical importance of the factor in shaping the existing economic situation should not be minimized. This varies from region to region in India. In the Maharashtra region, the

* Paper submitted to the Seminar on 'Representative Government and Public Liberties in the New States', held under the auspices of the Congress for Cultural Freedom in association with the School of Political Sciences, Pantios, Athens, at Rhodes in October 1958, and published in *Artha Vijnana*, Vol. I, No. 3, September 1959, pp. 177–86.

results of a number of field enquiries indicate close correspondence of the ranking in terms of (i) caste hierarchy, (ii) income levels, and (iii) educational attainments of the three groups of urban, professional, priestly, and trading castes; of the peasant and artisan castes; and of the depressed, untouchable, low occupational, and rural labour group. In talking of the social situation created by the caste structure, it is necessary to bear in mind these lasting historical effects. They remain even where social ranking is no longer regarded, or where entry to any occupation or vocation becomes conceptually free.

Within the general framework of caste society, each group, caste, or subcaste was relatively self-regulated. There was overall determination of the ranking of the groups and of the behaviour of members of different groups towards each other. But within the group, social control was exercised by the group itself. This permitted the existence, side by side, of an immense variety of practices relating to dress, food and drink habits, religious worship, marriage customs, etc. Within the group, at least theoretically, conformity to the group pattern of conduct and behaviour was rigidly enforced, but within the society as a whole, great diversity from group to group was considered natural.

Side by side of the numerically overwhelmingly important Hindus, there are a number of other sections of the populace, distinguished from the Hindus chiefly on grounds of religious faith or worship. Some of these, like the Jains, Sikhs, or Lingayats, represent indigenous developments; others like the Muslims and the Christians may be said to exist because of influences coming from outside the country. However, in a varying degree, the social structure of all these has been affected by the concept of caste. Some of these, especially those of Indian origin, have close connection with Hindu society; others keep apart. However, even the latter are divided into a number of communities or groups which are largely self-regulated.

The whole structure was not completely immobile or rigid. There was always some movement, e.g., movement of individuals from one group into another, changes in ranking, emergence of new groups or, disappearance of old ones, and entry of new elements into society. But all these were slow, chiefly marginal, and no formal or avowed arrangements were made for them. Moreover, there was little assimilation; the entry of fresh elements usually resulted in the creation of new groups. It has been claimed that these slow and informal procedures allowed for admission of new elements without bringing about a sudden large change in their living or outlook and that the resulting tolerance of diversity proved of great value. It is equally necessary to emphasize that the process also prevented any close integration or the emergence of any feeling of identity within members of different groups. Thus, in a state or region, the society which functions as a political or economic unit is socially made up of a number of large sections based on religious, ethnic, linguistic, etc., differences, in each of which there are graded groups. The degree of social cohesion in such a society is necessarily limited and there is at least as much emphasis on difference and diversity as on sameness or common features.

In discussing the process of transition it is necessary to remember that the primary group, the caste or the community, in this type of social organization is an extended kinship group. It is usually within the group that marriage is possible or permissible and that all one's blood relations are found. It is within this group that close economic co-operation has been traditionally fostered and such social security and welfare elements as exist have been provided. The continued hold of the group is, therefore, extremely strong; it shapes current behaviour, as is evidenced by the universal complaints relating to nepotism and communal feeling. Some modern developments have helped to strengthen this hold. For example, the importance of credit and finance in economic life, and of elections and voting behaviour in political life, have led to general attempts at exploitation of the old ties, though, usually, on a somewhat widened basis.

Reorganization of social grouping involves, in the first instance, the rejection, in ideological terms, of the hierarchical, birth, and status basis of present arrangements. This, by itself, is a difficult enough task, especially in relation to the frank acceptance of claims to equality of those lower than oneself in the hierarchical scale. A change in ideology is merely the precursor of a change in fact. The latter is a slow and difficult process which usually involves a change in marriage customs and habits also. As long as the older marriage customs continue, all that can be expected is a wider interpretation of the community so as to include many sub-castes or closely related communities. It will only be when the practice of young persons choosing their marriage partners on their own prevails that the new family and kinship groupings may come to have no necessary connection with the old caste and community structures. However, this would itself impose a new limitation: that marriages would be limited to the group of habitual social intercourse of any set of young persons. And whether, in fact, the old community ties will be effectively dissolved will depend on the composition of these groups. If there exists educational, cultural, and economic stratification in society and this is closely related to the older caste and community groupings, the change in marriage customs will not result in making the new basis of social groupings much more wide or open than before. Or, to put it in alternative terms, the extent to which the latter happens will depend on the extent of mobility in economic and educational terms in society, on the extent to which opportunities are widely diffused and economic and cultural equality, in fact, obtain.

The process assumed in the above paragraph, however limited its actual operation and effect, is itself dependent on the emergence of the concept of a regional or national cultural society. On the ideological plane this has been largely achieved, chiefly as a result of the nationalistic political sentiment.

In the smaller and less complex states, the intelligentsia has successfully popularized the idea of a large cultural society based on common history and languages; elsewhere, as in India and Pakistan, within a wider cultural framework, the idea of large regional societies has emerged and has been accepted. It is important to recognize, in this process, the role of political feeling or sentiment. It is the growth of this, essentially in its democratic form, that has served to undermine the prestige of old hierarchical structures and that can potentially build up a feeling of social solidarity transcending the old ties of caste and community. Political sentiment, attached to the concept of an emergent territorial society, has, therefore, a great part to play in the coming social revolution.

What part would or could be played by the location, village or city, in the concept of the regional cultural society? So far, units smaller than the state or the region do not seem to have been important in the flowering of political sentiment. That is, however, no reason why in the actual working of a political democracy they should not prove important. The village has been the primary unit of political organization in a large number of traditional societies and has often evoked some emotional attachment. It is possible to make use of this fact in operating a democratic political society, provided the socio-economic structure of the village itself becomes democratic, and provided the state vests the primary unit with some element of autonomy. In traditional rural society, political and economic power rested in the hands of a limited number of groups, and the actual rural leadership could only notionally be supposed to represent and look after the interests of others. Socio-economic structures of the countryside prove more resistant to change than those in towns and cities, with the result that, today, the older neglected or oppressed elements feel usually more safe in urban areas than in the villages. This places some limitation on relying upon village leadership and autonomy as important elements in democratic working. At the same time, it is of the utmost importance that the politico-economic organization of rural areas should receive every consideration and due weight. This is because the rural-urban imbalance in the newer states is extremely pronounced.

The causes of this imbalance are not far to seek. The urban areas are the seats of most modern economic and political activity, and they are the initial recipients of the impact of the external forces which are pressing on traditional society. To an unusual degree, political and economic power has been concentrated in the rapidly growing city and metropolitan areas, irrespective of the extent or pace of modernization or industrialization. Consideration of the social and political organization and life of urban areas, thus, becomes vested with particular importance. At the outset, an important difference as between the European and Asian developments may be indicated. Terms such as 'civic spirit' derive special meaning from the history of the Greek city-states and the quasi-independent medieval European cities. There is little comparable to this in Asian history. In Asia, the village might often be largely self-regulated and autonomous. The city on the other hand, was almost invariably administered directly by officers of the political state. Its composition would be heterogeneous and the characteristic of the larger society—that of being constituted of a number of independent social groups loosely held together—would be fully exhibited in the towns, much more so than in the villages. The element of autonomy, if any, would be reflected only within certain types of closed trade or craft organizations. Therefore, in terms of socio-political sentiment, the city has little historical contribution to make.

The prospects for the future, in this regard, may be best discussed in the light of current experience in the West. The experience is difficult to summarize. There is, however, a very large body of opinion which insists on the disintegrative effect of the large cities, the lost individual in them, and on the feelings of alienation and insecurity. Studies which emphasize the continued importance of kinship groups in large cities appear, further, to emphasize that the cities ordinarily fail to provide an alternative basis of social cohesion. In this connection, the findings of a study of the moral integration of American cities appear particularly instructive. These are that low moral integration, which may be interpreted as relative lack of civic spirit, is associated very significantly with heterogeneity and mobility.

Heterogeneity and mobility are characteristics which are particularly marked in the growing large cities of the under-developed areas of the world. Heterogeneity is a function, as already indicated, of the structure of these societies. Heterogeneity can diminish only to the extent that the process of integration, discussed above, gains momentum. At present, however, there are no pressures at work in these societies such as operate, for example, on a fresh immigrant into the USA, for adoption of a common pattern. Heterogeneity in the growing cities becomes marked because of the attraction that the city has for all kinds of elements from all regions within its economic pull. The rapid rate of growth of these cities in recent times has invited considerable attention. The rapid growth is due to high concentration of new types of economic activity in the cities and to great disparities in opportunities of employment and levels of earnings in these cities and the rest of the economy. Consequently, in these cities, the feelings of alienation and insecurity among the mass of the people are bound to be highly pronounced. This would be all the more so because the immigrants have previously been members of close-knit groups and because the conditions of housing in the cities make family life well-nigh impossible for very large numbers. It is, thus, highly unrealistic to talk of the emergence of a civic spirit as a factor in the working of these new democracies, at least in relation to the mass of population in the cities.

How is the conception of national unity related to the smooth working of democracy in the new states and to the maintenance of public liberties? It seems often to be taken for granted that, firstly, because a political state exists, people within it will be or, at least, ought to be imbued with a sense of national unity, and secondly, that talking about national unity is in some way closely associated with a concern for the welfare of the whole society. Both these assumptions appear questionable. If the new states had come into existence as a result of a deliberate, free choice of all concerned (after a kind of universal plebiscite offering a number of alternatives), the first assumption might have some validity. In fact, nothing of this sort has happened. It is, therefore, not possible to say today that the boundaries of all states are coterminous with those of single national cultural societies. The whole of Korea is usually conceded to be one national cultural society; it is, today, divided into two obviously artificial units. How would the concept of national unity be expected to operate in this context? Malaya is currently undertaking a large experiment in the creation of a new regional society. A priori statements regarding national unity have little relevance to its case. Most outsiders may be ready ordinarily to accept the idea of Indonesian national unity. However, one can imagine situations in which quite a number of them might argue plausibly that, say, Java and Sumatra did not form parts of one nation. Till the eve of the partition of India, most outsiders did not recognize any force in the case for Pakistan. There are, perhaps, few groups of peoples in Asia more emotionally attached to their linguistic and cultural traditions than the Bengalis. And yet, a political separation of Hindu from Muslim Bengal could not be avoided. How is the present situation in Ceylon to be described? What is the connotation, in this context, of the boundaries which divide states in the Arab world? And quite obviously the formation of political areas in Africa was determined, for the most part, more by the opportunities open to colonial powers in the 19th century than to anything else.

Where the state, in fact, embraces a national cultural society and evokes feeling of attachment from the people, this should help the working of democratic forms. But where this is not so, appeal to claims of national unity is not likely to prove useful, and may, indeed, be dangerous. Attention may be drawn specifically to two types of situations. The first relates to the problem of the re-formation of states. Rigidity of the situation, in the face of a keen desire on the part of peoples to re-form states by amalgamation, division, etc., has been a fruitful source of international friction. The rigidity is due, to a large extent, to a widely held prejudice in favour of the *status quo* and the whipping up of emotional feelings. In the circumstances, it appears wise to refrain from doing anything which would prevent or obstruct a dispassionate re-examination of the boundaries of states.

Even more important, perhaps, than this is a feature of the internal situation. Most new states are heterogeneous in their social composition, and where they are large, contain territories or regional societies which are not completely integrated. In this context, it is necessary to examine carefully, the use of the slogan of national unity. It is, of course, possible naively to assume that ruling groups in a state are genuinely and solely concerned with the welfare of the whole society. But, in case one feels that this condition is not likely to be always satisfied, it has to be conceded that the cry of 'national unity in danger' might be raised to distract attention from either harsh and undue centralization or differential treatment of ethnical, religious, regional, etc., minorities. Historically, nationalism and national feeling have proved sources of great intolerance. The only remedy against this is to deny any exclusive claim on behalf of the national group and to insist on the principle of concentric loyalties. This leads to a proper recognition, on the one hand, of loyalty to groups or sub-groups within the state or nation and, on the other hand, of the concept of wider units extending up to world government.

In the absence of such a moderation of the claim of national sentiment, it is likely to be an instrument of destruction of internal liberties. The attainment of national unity should be considered a challenge to the leaders and rulers of the new states. It has to be achieved and cannot be taken for granted.

We thus return to the central problem of social transition. Existing societies in the new states exhibit very considerable vestiges of a hierarchical structure; they contain elements which, though partaking in the ordinary economic and administrative structures, have yet not been accepted within the broader central society, and also contain elements which have either been plainly treated as external for all purposes or have been so dispossessed and discriminated against that they could have no feeling of identity with the rest. The problem is of moving on to a situation where a minimum degree of integration and of cohesiveness within society will have been achieved. If this is done, civic spirit and national unity will be exhibited in ample measure; if not, search after them will prove futile.

The maintenance of some sort of equilibrium, while successfully accomplishing the transition, will require great sympathy, tact, and patience on all sides. However, on the ruling and dominant groups, the transition will make much greater demands. They will have to show readiness to shed, with good grace, positions of prestige, privilege, and advantage in all directions social, political, and economic—positions which they have come to hold through the operation of the traditional structure. If the transition is successfully and peacefully effected through action of the existing ruling groups themselves, democracy will be strengthened and no liberties will be endangered.

What are the impending dangers in the process of transition? The situation in this regard differs greatly from country to country. The major common problems concern the behaviour of groups holding, in the main, political and economic power. In part, these represent vestiges of the older order and, in part, they are growths arising out of modern developments. The vestiges belong to aristocratic, priestly, etc., classes, and are usually based on concentration of property in land; the new growths are related chiefly to the rise of modern business. It is generally agreed that the state must take an active part in breaking the power of the older groups. The removal of social privilege or disability, and the attainment of political equality are acknowledged objectives of state action. Even in the economic field, action against older elements is welcomed, as evidenced by the universal interest shown in land reform programmes. However, when it comes to corrective or preventive action in relation to similar phenomena connected with modern business, there appears not only lack of understanding but also concerted and strong opposition which is supported, evidently, by important elements from among the older democracies.

The extent of economic inequality in the new states is greater, usually much greater, than in other parts in the world. Because of the peculiar structure of society, the direct and major benefits flowing from the possession and control of modern productive resources and activity are restricted to a small number of groups in this society. As economic development takes place and modern business grows, the wealth and power of these groups tend to be progressively increased. On the other hand, with the disintegration of traditional society the older types of security and protective measures lose their operative force, and more individuals in rural society and urban artisan, etc., classes are dispossessed and cut adrift. Within the cities, the concentration of wealth and power is glaring and naked, and the proletarian mass grows apace in number. As between the country and city, opportunities and standards differ widely.

In this situation, without vigorous social action the economic or the social problems cannot even begin to be solved. However, the groups that possess power and wealth are against any such social action. They welcome and, in fact, deliberately bring about regimes of protection, subsidies, export and import control, etc., which give them a sheltered position within the internal market. They are anxious that public outlay on economic overheads in relation to transport, energy, and other systems be undertaken on a large scale. But they do not desire that the area of public trading or industrial activities be increased, or that concentration of economic power be curbed through appropriate regulatory regimes, or that any significant social security or welfare programmes be undertaken; they would not accord high priority to large expenditure on mass education.

Significantly, this opposition often takes the form of a cry for 'economic liberty', for scope for individual initiative, and freedom for private enterprise. To the 'liberal' intellectual, drawn from the groups in which economic power is concentrated in India, even such action as procurement and distribution of food in face of shortages or state encouragement of the co-operative efforts of small and poor producers appear as precursors of authoritarianism; and he talks of 'production before distribution', whatever the phrase may mean.

The private enterprise, on whose behalf the cry is raised, belongs, in the main, to the category whose position and practices would be clearly labelled as monopolistic in other countries. Even so, the cry is fully taken up by many forces in the Western world. The international organizations betray a marked bias in favour of these interests when any loan, etc., programmes are considered. The activities of the large international combines and joint investment groups inevitably result in strengthening the position of their counterparts in these new states; and even the intellectuals from abroad preach to the peoples of these states on the merits of hastening slowly and the dangers and difficulties of over-egalitarianism.

Domestic interests take full advantage of this climate of foreign opinion and put forward—it is unknown with what justification—the plea of foreign disapproval for not pushing ahead with 'extreme policies'. One has heard the whisper go round that there should be no talk of even partial 'socialization' of wholesale trade in foodgrains, or that it was undesirable to press forward with the programme of creating an essential nation-wide State Bank, because 'the Americans do not like these things'.

It is contended that in the older democracies, two elements effectively moderate the influence of pressure groups. Firstly, because of overlapping membership, no group ever comes close to having the characteristics of a class; and secondly, the more powerful organized groups, those having privileged access to government, recognize the existence of unorganized or potential interest groups and pay some attention to their interests. In the new states, neither of these safeguards works. Because of the structure of these societies, economic development leads to the groups previously in control of economic and financial activity acquiring the characteristics of a class and, at least so far, modern big business in these states has not shown itself enlightened enough not to abuse its privileged access to government.

The supposed conflict of equality and liberty is false. Egalitarianism, in the context of these countries, is a highly relative term. Nobody can or does contemplate a programme that will bring about in these countries, in the near future, the degree of equality that exists, in fact, today in, say, the United Kingdom or Japan. The programme called 'socialistic' includes little which is not accepted in principle and practised in, say, the United States under the anti-cyclical or social security measures and nothing which is not part of accepted government policy in the United Kingdom. It usually includes some enlargement of the public sector, so that basic, major investments are properly made and their fruits conserved for economic development and social progress; and aims at maintenance of stability, stopping further increase in the concentration of power and wealth, making a beginning with the humbler forms of social security, encouraging decentralization, strengthening co-operatives, and making a beginning in the building of an open national educational system. Unless such a programme is rapidly pushed ahead, there is little hope of a peaceful social transition. In face of the concentrated and growing strength of big business in these countries, the only possible countervailing force is action by the state.

It has been argued that democratic forms have meaning only when there exists in society a basic minimum national level in education and when conditions of economic security and living are such that men do not have to worry about their survival. If this is agreed to, urgent implementation of the so-called 'egalitarian' programme in the new states is no more than an essential condition for the functioning of democracy and the preservation of public liberties.

32

Economic Challenges on World Scale*

I have been asked to talk about the challenges facing the world community in the economic sphere, especially those that are likely to affect the peaceful progress of the world. This is a large assignment and my address will be brief. I, therefore, select for treatment, only two major issues. I shall also treat these issues from the point of view with which I am familiar, that of a large, poor, under-developed country—India.

The first issue with which I deal is that of poverty. It is well-known that a small number of nations in the world are advanced industrially and enjoy a standard of living that entitles them to be called affluent. At the other extreme are countries with very large populations, where a large proportion of the inhabitants are poor and live in want. Among these are included countries with very large populations, such as China, India, Indonesia, and Pakistan.

The existing situation is the culmination of a trend that started some centuries ago. This was initiated by the leap forward in knowledge, particularly in science and technology, that took place in some Western European communities. It led to the spread of European peoples over the world, in many parts of which colonies were established following extinction of the original inhabitants and in many others, especially the older settled countries, Western dominance—political and economic—was established in various degrees. This resulted in bringing the economies of the countries of other continents into close connection with European countries and in giving a special direction to political, economic, and social developments in these countries. Western colonialism has recently

* Talk given at the 18th International Congress of Women's International League for Peace and Freedom, New Delhi, 28 December 1970.

declined, and most peoples in Asia and Africa now enjoy independence. However, their present situation is powerfully influenced by the historical period of European dominance. Because of this, they have been integrated to a varying degree in the stream of modern history and have accepted, in varying measures, ideas and products originating in the West. However, their progress has not been uniform on all fronts and, as a result, they exhibit a lack of balance in many respects. Attention may be drawn to a particular aspect of this situation. Recent rapid progress in public hygiene and medicine has upset, within a short period, the previous balance of births and deaths, and most of the under-developed countries find themselves with a very rapidly growing population. At the same time, their system of production remains much as before. Most of these countries still depend largely on primary production and have been unable to make any progress in industrialization, chiefly because of continued colonial rule. Thus, whereas a balance between birth and death was achieved in the Western world over a series of decades in which progress in medicine and hygiene went side by side with progress in industrialization and urbanization, the situation in the under-developed countries is very different. These have to cope with the results of a very high rate of growth of population while their economies are still backward. Backwardness makes it difficult to cope with the problems of bringing down the high birth-rate, and the rapid progress in population, in its turn, creates difficulties in the pace of industrialization of the economy.

The division of the world into poor and rich, the advanced and the backward, is no doubt an old problem. The evolution of its modern version has also taken place over the centuries. However, it could be said that the concern with the problem is something that is new. During colonial rule it was taken for granted that economies of dependent countries should be fashioned as complementary to the economies of those governing them; that economic policies should be directed so as to redound to the benefit of the governing European peoples was almost unchallenged, even in theory. It is chiefly after the end of the colonial era, at the end of the Second World War, that the problem, as it is being visualized today, may be said to have emerged.

A number of factors have contributed to considerable attention being given to this problem in recent times. In the first instance, this has been due to the clash and competition of ideologies. Planned progress of the USSR under communist rule appeared to indicate that economic progress could be accelerated according to a plan in under-developed economies and it began to be claimed that the path chalked by Russia was suitable for other under-developed countries, such as those of Asia, Africa, and Latin America. Poverty and development thus became involved in the clash between ideologies. It was obvious that in the face of claims made by the USSR, countries of the capitalist world had to place a viable alternative before the developing countries. Competition was thus begun for the allegiance of, what was called, the third world. Each side had to demonstrate that its methods and prescriptions could accelerate progress in the under-developed countries, the capitalist countries having in the process accepted planning in a mild form as among their own permissible concepts.

The present situation is also due, in part, to the great change brought about by the technical revolution in the last quarter of a century. The most impressive way of stating the results of this technical revolution is that of saying that the world has significantly shrunk in size. Whether in terms of physical movement of men and goods or in the range of weapons and armaments or in terms of the transmission of concepts and ideologies, an almost revolutionary change seems to have taken place during the last quarter of a century. It is now difficult for even large and powerful nations to suggest that they could live in isolation. It follows that most countries, especially those who aspire to the leadership of the world, have to give attention to problems of areas from which possible dangers can arise to their positions. The problem of poverty and lack of development of a large part of the world is perhaps the biggest of such problems. It is natural, therefore, for leaders of the world, and for international organizations, to give increasing attention to world poverty.

Lastly, the cumulative effect of rapid growth of advanced economies has further intensified the problem. The measure of difference between the rich and the poor, even in the colonial 19th century, was relatively small as compared with differences today. Also, this differentiation between the rich and the poor appears to be progressively increasing. It is clear that during the last three decades, the progress of the gross national product of a number of advanced countries has been phenomenal and that, as a result, the distance between them and the under-developed countries has greatly increased, especially in absolute terms. This may be brought out by the following figures of relevant per capita incomes of, say, Japan and India. The per capita incomes of Japan and India in 1953 expressed in US dollars at current prices were 183 and 59, respectively. The per capita incomes of the two countries in 1967 expressed in US dollars at current prices were 921 and 75. Calculations available at constant prices show that between 1951 and 1964 the per capita income of Japan increased at the rate of 8.1 per cent per annum, the corresponding rate for India being only 1.8.

The concern with the problem of poverty, which has recently grown, has led to some action on the international plane. Since the end of the Second World War, economic co-operation among countries has reached a much higher level than ever before. The establishment of the UN and the IMF were among the first steps. The Marshal Plan was a notable attempt at rehabilitation of economies by international action. After the success of this plan had been assured, attention turned to problems of continents other than Europe. International organizations, whose number continues to grow, designed a number of programmes to help what were called the under-developed countries, and a number of advanced nations gave aid on bilateral terms also. The scope as well as extent of action has continuously extended. It no longer aims chiefly at relief of distress, as in previous times, but has meant support to long-term efforts of individual countries to develop their economies. In a small number of cases, these efforts have proved remarkably successful. For the larger part, however, the results have not been striking. A number of factors have been held responsible for the relatively slow response in the developing economies. It has been said that this is due, in part, to the inadequate quantum of the aid and also to a number of conditions tied to the aid, which make it very much less effective than it should be. The developing countries are now well represented in international organizations and have been conferring together to draw up targets and programmes for quanta of aid and types of other assistance which they would like the advanced countries to accept. For example, a target of 1 per cent of the GNP given as aid to developing countries has been set before the richer nations, for being attained during the next few years. Demand such as of united aid, or a number of tariff preferences, has been made and progress is being made slowly in some directions.

It yet remains true that the gravity of the problem of poverty of the under-developed countries has not been materially lessened during the last two decades. The growth of population has been an important factor in keeping the rate of increase of per capita income low, and the basic difficulty of the poor countries, *viz.,* poverty, which means a paucity of resources in all directions, has rendered rapid advance difficult. External aid not only has been inadequate or not on sufficiently liberal terms but also has often been given for military and other ends which deflect the attention of countries as well as valuable resources from economic development. For a proper understanding of the problem of poverty of the under-developed countries it is necessary, in addition, to take a view of their internal difficulties.

Modern times are characterized by a continuously increasing pace of the development of techniques of production. The changes brought about by the industrial revolution have been followed by progress in technology which has attained an amazing pace within the last few decades. This continuous change in the techniques of production has led to the evolution of a structure of socio-economic organizations adapted to the new technical situation. Recently, the pace of the change has been so considerable that it appears to have taxed the capacity to adapt of even the advanced industrial countries. As has been indicated earlier, during colonial rule in the under-developed countries there had been selective introduction of Western innovations and ideas. Also, in most countries under colonial rule, the rule had the effect of disintegrating the older socio-political structure. The societies were thus rendered both less resistant and less adaptive than they had been before.

Further, the post-industrial revolution era in the advanced industrial countries has been the era through which nation-states have been formed. The nation-state type now dominates the world, in practice as well as in theory, and the more successful of these nation-states are those that exhibit qualities of homogeneity and cohesiveness, discipline and aggressiveness. Modernizing the economy and making planned progress in under-developed countries involve not only the building up of the appropriate structure of socio-economic institutions but also the transformation of these countries into something like nation-states.

The qualities required of a nation-state or a modern developing country are usually absent in the under-developed areas of the world. This is fully exemplified by the case of India. Modern India was not, except under colonial rule, a single unit of administration of political organization. It has characteristics of a continent, is divided into many linguistic regions, and has people of different faiths and ethnic groups living at widely separated levels of development of culture. The older organization of Indian society provided for a general loose frame in which groups and communities could live at peace with others but with no compulsive movement towards integration with them. In such a society, an immigrant group could settle and live and prosper in peace for centuries together, without losing its identity or merging with the general community. In such context the term 'general community' had little significance. The society was a complex of specific communities or groups living in well-understood traditional relations with each other. Cohesion was strong within each group but there was little emphasis on the identity or cohesiveness of society as a whole. Such an organization, though well adapted to the needs of earlier times and making for survival, is obviously not suitable in modern conditions.

In this context, it may be useful to recall Dr Myrdal's statement regarding Asian states being 'soft'. The criticism of Dr Myrdal is perfectly valid, in the sense that it is true that Asian states are unable to take firm, resolute, disciplined action in given directions even when leaders are convinced that such action is appropriate. This phenomenon has to be connected with characteristics which Asian states derive from the composition and structure of their societies. Imposition of discipline and resolute action imply a degree of cohesiveness and readiness among different social groups and strata to identify themselves with the general social good, and this is lacking in these societies. It has been indicated by keen observers that democracy as it functions in India is too free. This again is related to the inability of anybody to enforce discipline. In a loosely organized society with numerous separate groupings and divided loyalties, attempts to impose rigour or discipline may lead, it is feared, to disintegration.

The older societies which were tolerant and hospitable and possibly because of the virtue of non-cohesiveness were non-aggressive today prove anachronistic. They have to be replaced by cohesive nation-states which are disciplined and in which enthusiasm for working towards common ends can be built up. They must acquire the attributes of dynamism and efficiency. These are extremely important in planned economic development. Planning requires common acceptance of distant goals and ends, considerable agreement as to methods and procedures, the will and determination to work strenuously and persistently for planned objectives along pre-settled routes, efficient action by the state apparatus, and the ability in a poor country, to impose sacrifices and hardships on the people, or of the people to do this for themselves so as to achieve a distant end.

The difficult progress that the under-developed countries have to make is, thus, not only along the economic route but also along the socio-political. They have to undertake a transformation of their social organization, create new bonds of cohesion and loyalty, and have also to accept new values in the process. It should be remembered that the European peoples who are in the vanguard have themselves made these adjustments over centuries under favourable circumstances. The anciently settled under-developed countries are, on the other hand, faced with the problem of moving from one era into another within a matter of decades and to do this in circumstances which are highly unfavourable.

It may be doubted whether this compulsive trend towards making the potentially aggressive type of nation-state universal, is in the real long-term interests of the world. While dynamism and efficiency are no doubt desirable and beneficial, it is equally necessary for world peace that states, in framing their programmes and policies, are not unduly influenced by considerations of short-term self-interest. However, in this matter of transformation the under-developed countries appear to have little choice. For progress, for sheer survival, they have to change many of their ways and have to follow, at least immediately, the trail blazed by the advanced countries. With a compact, heavily interacting international community, the range of choice open to an individual people, particularly in a weak and poor country, is very narrow. The large, desirable changes regarding fundamental values and the operation of national and international organizations can come about only with wide acceptance, especially among the dominant nations.

It is clear that progress towards the eradication of poverty in under-developed countries, is unlikely to be rapid. Change is bound to be slow, internally and externally. In the meantime, with further technological advance, the inequalities between the poor and the rich countries are bound to grow and international relations will be subject to greater strains.

This will happen particularly so long as competing groups of states, divided by ideology or interest, perforce fish in the troubled waters of the 'third world'.

Many features of the existing situation are due to the recent, rapid advance of technology. It is also in the further advance of technology that hope for the elimination of poverty lies. Attaining a balanced population and making it possible for the much larger population to derive adequate sustenance from exploitation of available natural resources can both flow only out of further advance in science and technology. At the same time, a number of directions in which it is making progress at present are such as to lead to considerable dangers for the world as a whole in the future. But ill-directed advance is fraught with perils for the world. Therefore, the possibility of properly regulating and directing future progress of technology is extremely important, not only to solve the problem of poverty of nations but also for world peace.

At present it cannot be said that technological progress is well-directed or, in fact, directed or regulated, in any manner, externally and as a whole. In the absence of such direction a number of acute problems have come to surface. The advance of armaments and nuclear technology is the most important of these. Here is a direction in which fundamental scientific discoveries were followed up intensively to serve the purpose of war. It then became evident that rapid advance of nuclear technology in the service of war would endanger the very existence of mankind. As a result, those possessing nuclear technology made some attempts to limit its spread. After a number of years a non-proliferation treaty was produced, which has yet to obtain universal acceptance. The experience gained in the attempt to limit the spread of nuclear weapons has revealed clearly the difficulties of a piecemeal approach to such subjects as disarmament and universal peace. It is also shown how it is difficult to limit the spread of scientific and technological knowledge, except on the basis of universal consent. It has been pointed out, for example, that countries which are in a position to exploit atomic energy for peaceful purposes could, without a great deal of difficulty, make the transition to nuclear weapons. Therefore, unless the well-nigh impossible step of laying an embargo on the spread of atomic technology for peaceful purposes is taken, no real guarantee against an eventual proliferation of nuclear weapons can be maintained. Defence and security are of prime importance to all nations and with competing groups of nation-states, it becomes difficult to eliminate the armaments race. The only effective way of securing a peaceful future is thus obtaining the consent of all nations to pursuing technological advance in peaceful directions and not further perfecting offensive and defensive weapons.

Another direction in which the dangers of technological advance have been strikingly brought to surface is in the effects of technological development on human environment. Economists have for long distinguished between individual cost and social cost. In a given framework of law and administration an individual may find it possible to pursue certain activities which redound to his own benefit but which, in the long run, may be socially harmful. After the industrial revolution, the blight of smoke from factory chimnies came to be recognized as a social cost which was not, ordinarily, successfully brought home to the individual owner of the factory. With the rapid scientific and technological advance in recent years, man's ability to affect the environment through his activities has become so considerable that the problems posed by it can be tackled only at the national or the international level. In this case again it is the ability to regulate technological advance that appears as the crucial issue. The total effects flowing out of a particular set of scientific discoveries or technological innovations have to be worked out in advance not only in the totality of the physico-social environment but also for the very long-term. The ability to prevent the use of particular items in the technological advance which do not pass the totality of the environment and long-term tests now assumes great importance for the future of mankind.

The possibility of directing technological advance need not be viewed only from the point of view of preventing harmful effects. The direction could be positive for goals especially desired. This could be illustrated from requirements of the under-developed countries. As of today, the under-developed countries find that their special needs do not prove of relevance to applied scientific and technological work undertaken in the advanced countries. Where, therefore, they are likely to suffer from such advance, they are unable to protect themselves. An example of this is the progress of synthetics and their effect on the farming communities producing natural products in the under-developed countries. Through the last hundred years, the under-developed countries suffered passively the harmful effects of the development of synthetics on their economies. Today, some of them undertake scientific work themselves, in order to protect their position. However, even when this happens, the position remains highly unequal. In production of synthetic substitutes for natural products like rubber or jute, the capacity of large corporations interested in the development of synthetics to undertake expenditure on research and development is very much larger and more carefully and intensively directed than the capacity of the farming communities and governments interested in the natural production of jute and rubber. Moreover, distribution of research and development expenditure could make natural production much more efficient and less costly than before and any necessary transition that farmers in a region have to make, more smooth and less harmful.

Another example would be of the development of technology that is appropriate to the requirements of the under-developed countries. Many economists have pointed out that relative prices of capital and labour and their relative availabilities are very different as between advanced industrial countries and the under-developed countries. However, the dominant and advancing industrial technology has been evolved in the economic conditions of the richer, highly industrialized nations and many aspects of this technology are inappropriate in the present situation of the developing countries. The developing countries could, with the same resources, do much better if, in a number of directions, a technology more adapted to their needs had been evolved. The money and talent required for such attempts are, however, not available. This is because the capitalists or technologists of the advanced countries are not interested in the problem or, perhaps, even aware of it. On the other hand, the limited scientific and technological resources of the developing countries are all used up in borrowing technology from the advanced countries and establishing it in their own economies. Only a small part of the resources spent in research and development in the advanced countries give ample global returns if spent in this direction. However, this cannot obviously happen until an overall direction to technological advance can be given, looking at the problem as of global welfare.

Technological advance is no longer a matter of individual effort or accidental results. Today, its ends are deliberately set out and pursued with elaborate equipment by teams of scientists backed by enormous resources. But the direction given is governed by the interests of the entity undertaking and financing technological development. In the main, research and development are undertaken either by nations or by large corporations conducting economic activity on a national or international scale. The dominant interests of nation-states have been defence and security. The dominant interest of the corporations is profit gained out of the production and sale of commodities and services. The view taken by each entity is necessarily limited by its own narrow and relatively short-term interests. It is obvious that if the present state of affairs continues, the adverse effects of technological advance are likely to become more apparent than its beneficial effects in the future. Not only for the elimination of poverty of the under-developed countries but also for securing peace and prosperity of the world as a whole, it is vital to be able to regulate the direction and pace of future technological advance, to limit it in given directions, and to encourage it in special ways and for special objectives.

The gravest economic challenge facing the world today is that of the conditions of want in which large proportions of the populations of the majority of countries of the world live. Solution of this problem requires resolute internal action by these countries, generous external assistance given with sympathy and understanding, and appropriate technological progress. It is clear that progress in all these directions, especially the latter two, would be made only with the prevention of war and with the institution of international law and broadly based political, social, and economic co-operation among the peoples of the world. All this would happen if and when the co-operative idea gains ascendancy over the competitive and when the co-operative pattern of behaviour is inculcated in peoples through their systems of education and through the operations of their socio-economic institutions.

VIII

Social and Economic Thinking of Gadgil

An Appraisal

33

Planning and Economic Policy in India*

A.I. LEVKOVSKY

A deep preoccupation with the fate of the country runs through the work of D.R. Gadgil. With the advent of Indian Independence the social life of the country changed to a great extent. Definite progress is visible in the economic construction, in various cultures, and in other spheres. But together with these, there are a number of urgent problems of the country which are undecided since long. It is not by chance that Prof. Gadgil is disturbed by some marked tendencies in the socio-economic attitude. There is great originality in this book and more than that is the forcefulness of this work. Gadgil in his work introduces to us in depth many burning problems of socio-economic life of the contemporary Indian society. The significance of the book by Gadgil lies in its analysis of the socio-economic measures which are directed towards the overcoming of the economic backwardness of the country and the poverty of the masses. The construction of the book is original. It is constructed from different, so to say, social and economic stories. They are connected with and supplemented by each other, though, initially they have seen the light separately; as articles in press, or as memoranda presented at the official instance.

Gadgil is the Head of a very well-known socio-political research institute of contemporary India—Gokhale Institute of Politics and Economics —in the city of Poona. Gadgil wrote a number of books and hundreds of articles. Headed by him, the Institute, with its individual specialists,

* Introductory article (abridged version) to the Russian translation published in 1963 of D.R. Gadgil, *Planning and Economic Policy in India*, published in 1962, GIPE, Poona.

published dozens of fundamental works on various problems of the socio-economic and political life of the Indian society—in the colonial period as well as after the attainment of independence. The Institute has attained wide fame not only in India but also beyond its borders. It is connected with many big social organizations of the country and some of the specialists take part in the activity of the governmental committees, and also show definite influence on the economic and political set up of the country. Gadgil himself is in the Panel of Economists of the Planning Commission, planning economic development of the country. Thus, we are speaking about a big scientist economist, head of a school with a long and big tradition, showing influences not only in science but also in the social life of India (especially of Maharashtra State).

The main theme of the book is the analysis of the many facets of such important events in the life of Indian people, as the struggle for economic independence. The work contains valuable data and consideration of the ways of construction of individual national economy, shows the obstacles present, and the failures and successes in advancement to the stated goal. Gadgil speaks about the heterogeneous class structure of the Indian society and analyzes the changes occurring in the positions of various classes. He comes to the conclusion that after the attainment of independence in India the big bourgeoisie became particularly stronger, to the share of whom fell the largest gain from economic development. Examining the position of the working class Gadgil notes the difference in the material position of their separate groups, the real wages of the factory workers in the period 1951 to 1957 increased but after that deteriorated and in 1960 reached the 1951 level. As for artisans and workers in the small workshops and cottage industries and agricultural labourers, their real income in these years decreased nearly by 10 per cent. The author pays great attention to the problem of growing unemployment in cities and villages and to the deterioration in living conditions in cities which is due partly to the influx of the unemployed from the rural areas.

Economic development of India has reached a stage when rapid industrialization proves to be the urgent problem of the day, when it is understood by all classes and strata of Indian society that through it alone lies the road to the achievement of economic independence. The important speciality of planning in India lies in the fact that planning is subjected to a significant extent to the solution of the problem of industrialization. As for India where planning at present is all the more developed as compared to other non-socialist countries, not only its successes but at the same time its limits are clearly visible. Firstly, the sphere of its operations is narrow. It belongs to, first of all, the state sector and to the relatively thin, though very important, stratum of developed national capitalistic enterprise. The great bulk of the petty capitalistic economy (particularly in agricultural sector) remains outside the sphere of its influence. The financial base is extremely unstable and limited. This planning does not embrace important objects; prices, wages, and movement of labour force. It adopts itself to the anarchic laws of capitalism, reflects them, and does not accommodate them as asserted by bourgeois sociology, towards the achievement of the 'common good'. Planning carries with it a bourgeois class character.

Cognitive significance of the book of D.R. Gadgil lies in the fact that it shows many sides of the mechanism of capitalistic planning in practice. The critical approach of the author himself permits him to note a number of contradictory appearances, deficiencies, and even defects of capitalistic planning in under-developed countries, and not of planning in general. D.R. Gadgil while analyzing a number of important economic processes, as a matter of fact, starts from 'perpetuity' of capitalism as the natural form of production, but at the same time he comes forward for its serious reformation. What tendencies are reflected by this will be demonstrated below. Here it suffices to note that such self-contradictory stand of the author compels him to devote special attention to the economic policy and planning as the important means of achieving desired aim from his view point. And the radicalism of the proposed measures often do not fit into the framework of the capitalist means of production. This reflects the fact that the author himself is, definitely, at cross roads.

The data given in the book and the conclusion about the First Five-Year Plan, the detailed analysis of the course of fulfilment of the Second Five-Year Plan (1956-61) and the consideration given to the principles and character of the working of the Third Five-Year Plan (which went into operation in April 1961) offer, by all means, immense interest to the Soviet readers. Original observations and inferences of the author on this issue grow stronger by an analysis of the contemporary economic policy of India (in which attention is concentrated on criticism thereof). As for concrete examples, the divergence—which often takes place between word (official declarations and proclaimed aims) and deed (practical work of the bureaucrats) is shown and the class orientation of the economic policy is demonstrated, serving according to the assertion of the author, the interest of the big bourgeoisie.

In our opinion, the originality of the book lies not only in the fact that the whole work penetrates literally into the problem of the inter-relations of the sectors, but also in its very evaluation of and approach to the structure of the sectors and their roles. Consequently, as distinguished from orthodox bourgeois sociologists and economists, D.R. Gadgil consistently divides the private capitalist sector into two parts, big business and small enterprises. This division has significant meaning because the representatives of big capital try to depict the private sector as a unified one and to represent their own interests as the programme of the entire nation. The rapid growth of the economic power of the national big bourgeoisie is one of the results of the development of India after her Independence. In 1958, less than 1 per cent of the shareholders of all companies accounted for 46 per cent of their total paid up capital (Nigam and Chaudhari 1960: 14–15). Besides utilizing such specific forms as the system of managing agency, Indian big capital also utilizes other organizational forms for expanding their business.

It is necessary to mention also about the strengthening mutual ties, since the second half of the fifties—between Indian and foreign monopolies, towards collaboration and appearance of new forms of connection between them. As a result, the interests of a considerable section of the big national bourgeoisie and overseas financiers became closely interlaced. The big bourgeoisie, the most integrated and organized on an all-India scale, does everything so as to prevent the consolidation of other layers of the bourgeoisie. Besides that, the specific dual character of the lower and middle groups of national bourgeoisie permits the latter to split these layers and draw over to their own side, their separate sections, over more or less prolonged period. The entire complicated complex of phenomena, which emerged out of the peculiarities of the development of capitalism in India—the existence of small, middle, and big capitalist enterprises and their uneven growth as well as a number of other circumstances—have brought quite an original combination of development of capitalism wide and deep. Attention should be drawn also to this that D.R. Gadgil is not simply critical but also clearly opposed towards the big business. Certainly, he explains fairly thoroughly the meaning of 'monopolistic bourgeoisie', having included in it the entire big and even a part of middle bourgeoisie.

D.R. Gadgil rightly considers that for the overcoming of economic difficulties and for accelerating the development of the country, it is necessary that the state sector should have embraced those branches and spheres of business in which now function the big capitalist enterprises. He is decidedly in favour of transferring the internal trade in grain and the entire foreign trade to state authority. He considers that, in the petty-commodity sector, it is necessary to develop a Co-operative Movement as an important instrument of solving the agrarian problem. Certainly, as in the case of planning, what he talks about is not socialist, but capitalistic co-operation. However, in the programme given by D.R. Gadgil, it is characterized by distinct bourgeois democratic features.

At the same time, he puts forward a programme of reconstructing the organs of planning. It envisages their determined democratization to the detriment of the top stratum of the bureaucracy. In this way, presently the programme of social economic measures in this and that form is put forward or supported by the small and middle bourgeoisie and by a number of influential fractions in bourgeois parties, in the first instance, by the leftist Congressites. The author straightforwardly points out towards the danger from the side of the Rightist behind whom stands, as the author himself says, the big capital. He decidedly stands against any shift to the 'right' in economic policy. The suggested programme contains a number of points concerning with those complex socio-economic measures which must be carried out by a state of national democracy to translate them into reality. However, the realization of the possibilities connected with these, demands a number of conditions, not noted in D.R. Gadgil's book. Finally, the translation of this work of the renowned Indian scientist permits us to peep more penetratingly into the essence of the complicated and conflicting phenomena emerging out of contemporary India, as well as to have a better understanding of the life of our friendly Indian people.

REFERENCE

Nigam, R. and N. Chaudhari (1960) *The Corporate Sector in India*, New Delhi.

34
Gadgil and the Economics of Indian Democracy*

S.A. DANGE

AN INTRODUCTION

On this day, one month ago, D.R. Gadgil died on his way to Poona. The autocrats of Delhi could not stomach this intellectual crusader against monopoly capitalism in the planning chief's chair. He had to resign. He was returning to his institute when he got a heart attack in the train and died on the way. His wife was with him.

I came to know Gadgil in 1936 when, after my release from a long imprisonment, I went to Poona to take some rest and also work on my history project. In that connection I used to visit the Servants of India Society Library. I was introduced there to the company of Gadgil, Vaze, and others by N.M. Joshi.

Gadgil used to deliver talks in the society on the subject of economics which I sometimes attended. But mostly I used to meet him at the afternoon tea-table. The lectures struck me as being rather unusual in their logic. But Gadgil, after building the premises of the theme, would many a time drop the inevitable and unavoidable conclusion and sidetrack it into many other variants. If he struck to the unavoidable conclusion, he would be arriving at a line nearer to scientific socialism than bourgeois economics.

When I would confront him at the tea-table with this view and ask him what prevented him from crossing that line, he would fold his hands in the

* Abridged version of the booklet entitled *Gadgil and the Economics of Indian Democracy*, People's Publishing House, Bombay, 3 June 1971.

characteristic Marathi way, saying, 'I am comfortable where I am. Crossing the line is for people like you. It is not for me.'

And yet he was not an idle thinker. He used to participate in movements affecting the peasant interests, land questions, co-operative development, linguistic reorganization of states, and so on. He would argue fearlessly and furiously. But he had decided for himself not to join any 'active politics.'

We had an opportunity to sit together again in 1937, when he was appointed a member of the Bombay Textile Inquiry Committee. The textile workers, under the leadership of the Bombay *Girni Kamgar* Union, were agitating for increase in wages, which had been cut during the depression of 1930s to the extent of over 25 per cent. The mill owners pleaded that they were still making losses and could pay nothing. In my evidence before the committee, I pressed for a thorough scrutiny of the finances of the mills, which I said, were hiding their profits.

Gadgil took up the question. To his surprise, he found that the mills were showing fraudulent losses by manipulating speculative transactions in cotton. Gadgil scrutinized the financial dealings of every mill and showed that the mill industry had made profits enough to restore the wage-cut. It was due to his efforts that the committee, presided over by Jairamdas Daulatram, gave us an increase of 25 per cent. The mill owners' representative on the committee could not dislodge Gadgil from his position. And it was mainly due to his deep study that the other members also saw the justice of our demands.

Gadgil was well known as an economist and educationist. But the real Gadgil is never taught to students nor is he properly represented before the people.

His writings have not drawn 'political notice' from political parties and young revolutionary thinkers of Indian economy because many a time he used a very deceptive garb of abstruse terms to convey his real ideas. But when he was forced to speak out his mind on the question of planning and reshaping of the Indian economy, he could not hide his real soul, though he tried much.

He could not then avoid talking straightaway against monopoly capitalism, the need for class outlook, the necessity of a party of social revolution, the bureaucracy and monopoly capital as the main enemy of growth and true democracy. He then did not hesitate to expose the ruling classes and their robbery of the people and national economy in all its nakedness. The student, the peasant, the unemployed, the intelligentsia and all had their sufferings traced to that fountainhead of poison that is monopoly capital and the powers that served it. In spite of his style, the burning fire of his wrath and the heavy blows of his intellectual hammer and sarcasm came out fully in his notes to the Planning Commission.

He had no certainty that he would be heard. But he still wanted to try. And hence he agreed to head the Planning Commission. But monopoly capital throttled his voice as he had predicted.

I thought of summarizing Gadgil's notes in this booklet for many reasons. But I know I have not been able to do justice to the task fully and cover his writings and study Gadgil in evolution. I have concentrated attention on the last and final phase of his thinking.

MONOPOLY CAPITAL—THE KING PIN

Gadgil was what we call a bourgeois economist to begin with. But historical experience changed him. He then refused to hold, like the official vulgar economists, to the apron strings of the bankrupt theory of bourgeois economics. No doubt Gadgil used many tools of Keynes, Joan Robinson, and such others. But none of them had exposed monopoly capital as Gadgil had done. Gadgil was essentially dealing with the economics of a developing country, India, which had just come out of the political-military clutches of capitalist imperialism. As such he dealt with theory to solve India's problem. And he found that attack on monopoly capital was the king-pin of the whole situation—a conclusion which none of the celebrated economists have put forward so clearly and persistently.

Gadgil, after having found the main enemy, also shows its allies, its tools and instruments, and the way the enemy sneaks into all pores of the national economy and sucks it to fatten itself.

And hence he has to deal with the question of state, bureaucracy, foreign capital, prices, market, land reforms, wages and salaries, small and medium industry, and so on. Gadgil has presented us an integrated picture of Indian democracy, when a new social revolution will have taken place and Indian economy and politics reconstructed after the liquidation of monopoly capital.

I have not yet named the democracy which Gadgil had in his conception. Neither did he. There are many variants of democracy under discussion, but different content and class correlations such as national democracy, people's democracy and socialist democracy, and so on. What we have at present in India is a bourgeois democracy.

But this is a subject which cannot be discussed here. This is not the place for it because Gadgil never raised that question of finding a new name for his conception of democracy. He only raised the question of what new content to put in place of the present monopoly-bureaucrat ridden democracy of India. That new content is put before the reader in the large number of extracts I have given here.

REVOLUTIONARY DEMOCRACY

In my opinion, if you take all the characteristics and content of the new socio-political order which Gadgil proposes, with his ideas of the 'socialistic approach' and 'mixed economy', you may find that he is, in fact, describing the content of 'revolutionary democracy', which will be born only after the overthrow of monopoly capitalism.

Since the end of the Second World War, the newly-liberated countries of Asia, Africa, and Latin America have been throwing up new forms of democracies revealing new economic and political content suitable to their own economic and political correlation of class forces. India also is bound to produce its own new form of democracy after the liquidation of monopoly capital.

It was not an accident that not only Gadgil, but men like professor Bettleheim and Lange also contributed to the economic thinking in the circles of the Planning Commission set up by Nehru. But the tragedy is that all of this remains only as abstract thinking, which when taken to real life, is blown up by the powerful death-dealing hand of monopoly capital and its myrmidons in state power. Unless the working masses make the thinking their own, no force can defeat monopoly capital. I hope, if nothing else, this summary will serve to shed light on the innermost thoughts and feelings of a good and learned man, a serious thinker, and friend of the toiling people of our country.

CRUSADER OF SOCIALISTIC PLANNING

The death of Dr D.R. Gadgil, the well-known economist and chief of planning in the Government of India, in the railway train when he was on his way back home to Poona on 3 May 1971, evoked fulsome tributes from the world of the learned and governmental circles. Everyone said that India had lost a great economist.

That we have lost a great economist is a fact. But very few stated where exactly his greatness lay.

Only a few days ago, the Prime Minister had asked Gadgil to resign as planning chief; and only a day before his death, she had reconstituted her government and put her new planning chief, C. Subramaniam, in the cabinet.

Gadgil was dropped because he was too angular to fit into the framework of the new cabinet and secondly, because he was averse to joining any ministerial set-up. For many years he had refused to join the government despite his active participation in the formulation of plan thinking, as head of the Panel of Economists, since the Second Five-Year Plan in 1955. At one time a proposal to make him the Finance Minister was being unofficially mooted. But he cold-shouldered it and it went to C.D. Deshmukh.

The removal of Gadgil from the leadership of the Planning Commission was not due to any of his disabilities nor was his resignation due to any feeling of frustration on his part. When Y.B. Chavan, the Finance Minister, stated in an interview in Bombay to the Marathi daily *Navakal* on 7 May 1971 that when he met Gadgil on the eve of his departure from Delhi, he did not see any sign of frustration or bitterness in him, he was telling the truth. But then why had the Finance Minister to go out of his way to give such an unusual assurance at all? That it had to be stated means there was something in it!

That something is that Gadgil, though not frustrated, felt his line was defeated. After four years at the head of the Planning Commission, he came to realize that he could not win the battle he had been fighting for the last 15 years as an economist and thinker of Indian planning and India's developing economy.

What was the battle he was fighting and where did he lose it? For a time, he felt he was winning the battle in principle at least. And hence, after his long hesitation, he agreed to head the Commission. But he was too honest, too realistic, and too knowing not to see that those who seemed to agree with him in principle were not taking any rapid strides to translate agreement into honest practice. He came to feel that despite bank nationalization and such other things, the political groupings in power at the centre and in the states had strong elements in the leadership of government who would not allow the vital citadels of monopoly capitalism to be really liquidated. The request to him to resign and all that followed confirmed what he felt.

He bought his ticket for the journey back home, but did not complete it, as if symbolizing the fate of India's journey on the so-called socialist path of our economy at the hands of the ruling gentry.

It is, therefore, necessary to see what was really great in this 'great economist.' It is necessary for our masses, our intelligentsia, to know what he fought for, though all his life he never joined any political party and almost hid himself in the quiet corner of his institute, unless he was dragged out by popular demand to lend his learning to the problems of the democratic masses.

I do not want to go into a life-sketch of Gadgil here. Here I want to confine myself to his writings on the Plan-scheme of Indian economy and his basic approach to that vital question.

RAPID INDUSTRIALIZATION

Gadgil was aware of the fact that if the Indian people were to overcome the poverty in which the British had left them, India must embark on rapid industrialization and a complete overhaul of its agrarian structure. While every school of thought agreed on these basic propositions, there were very vital and fundamental differences on the questions of where to begin and how to begin.

The perspectives of the Second Five-Year Plan, as were opened up by Nehru after the frustrating experience of the post-war period and the First Five-Year Plan, and some of the new faces he saw in the economist group, led Gadgil to agree to participate in the work of the Panel of Economists.

The draft of the Second Five-Year Plan was a complete departure from previous thinking and it disturbed the foreign and Indian monopolists very much. If the whole line of thinking that made the basic structural features of the new Plan-frame were adopted, the entrenched power of foreign and monopoly vested interest was sure to be immensely shaken and a new democratic orientation, not only in the economy but also in the politics of the country, would set in. Hence reactionary vested interests opened up a big offensive against the Second Plan.

The Panel of Economists set up by the Planning Commission invited Gadgil's contribution. He wrote down his views in a memorandum in April 1955 and pursued the subject right till the end. Though the vested interests succeeded in preventing the Second Five-Year Plan being fully given effect to, and also in sidetracking the Third and Fourth Plans, Gadgil never gave up the core of his thinking on the subject, a core which had a revolutionary democratic content and which, therefore, invited opposition from several quarters, including those who professed outward sympathy with his line of thinking.

What was the basic approach of his thinking? He wanted to completely do away with the old foundations of the economy as had been handed down by the British and the six years of rampage that the vested interests enjoyed after Independence.

ABOLITION OF MONOPOLY CAPITAL

What was the first important point he emphasized? *The first and basic point he emphasized was that unless 'monopoly capitalism' was abolished, there would be no rapid progress in India.*

What did he mean by monopoly capitalism in India? Clearly, by that he did not mean all 'private enterprise', which is a comprehensive term including many types of economic activity.

In discussing the Indian situation, at least two distinct types need to be clearly separated. Firstly, there is private enterprise, which may be identified with the type of operation implicit in all classical economic analysis. In this, the number of operators or units of activity in each sphere or field are so numerous and relatively of such size that no single operator could by his action affect either the market for his products or the market for his resources, which he has to acquire in order to produce.

The same is true of sphere of agriculture and primary producers, barring plantations. Similar is the case of small enterprises, cottage industries, commerce, transport and trades and professions.

'There has been never any suggestion from any quarter that this large field of private enterprise should be disturbed or included in the public sector' (Gadgil 1961: 6).

But the propagandists of the monopoly press play upon these millions who handle this sector, frightening them with the bogey of nationalization.

So Gadgil states very clearly that this sector of private enterprise 'will not be part of state-socialistic apparatus.'

Whom then has he in mind for nationlalization or of being taken over in the public sector? As he puts it: *'The dispute arises entirely in the field of what may be correctly described, not private enterprise but monopoly capitalism'* (Gadgil 1961: 7).[1]

'The sphere of operation of this is confined to certain restricted though extremely important sectors of economic activity within the country. These sectors are modern banking and insurance, large-scale machine industry, modern mining, plantation, foreign trade and internal wholesale trade and financial operations such as those on the commodity and stock-exchanges' (Ibid.).

Emphasizing this further, he says: 'The main point to be noticed about this field of economic activity is that though in relation to total occupied numbers and total number of units and establishments, its constituents are small, they are by far the most dominant in political, economic and social terms in the country today' (Ibid.).

Gadgil did not stop at merely describing the phenomenon. He charged the state of adopting policies which built up the octopus of monopoly capitalism. *'State policy has actively helped the full exploitation by the constituents of the field of modern business of their position as monopoly capitalism'* (Ibid.: 9).

And citing an instance known to everyone and which even today operates with full force, he says: 'A study of prices of such commodities as cloth or sugar during the post-war period fully exemplified this' (Ibid.). And further on: 'Modern industry, more than other field in the Indian economy, is sheltered, protected and helped at the cost of the taxpayer and consumer' (Ibid.).

One year later, in January 1956, in a note placed before the National Development Council, Gadgil gave more forthright and positive views. 'A progressive widening of the public sector is an essential prerequisite of any progress towards a socialistic society, particularly in an under-developed area undertaking rapid planned development' (Ibid.: 28).

But the real hit of his thinking is not in this proposition.

One could widen the public sector and make it powerful by starting new units through state investments. That, of course, had to be done. But the first step, according to Gadgil, must be taken by breaking the concentration of economic power that lies in the hands of the private sector in certain fields. Repeating his division of the private sector into two divisions or parts, he demands the nationalization of that division which is occupied by 'monopoly capitalists' who have grown, not by the sweat of their own brow but 'due to the protection of one sort or another given by the State. This division is already the most influential in the country and the high concentration within it increases its ability to exercise power' (Ibid.: 29).

The current phenomenon of a boom on the stock-exchange, the impetus to machine industry production and the prosperity of certain classes in the biggest cities side by side with increasing unemployment, depression in the village and small-scale industries and a general stagnancy, if not decline, of the purchasing power of rural society as a whole throw vivid light on the possible course of investment for development unaccompanied by a proper social policy. (Ibid.)

'*The only real solution to the problem in the long run is that the whole of the division at present occupied by monopoly capitalists should be transferred to the public sector*' (Ibid.).

'Excepting in certain consumption goods industries, all new units in modern industry should be in the public sector. In foreign trade through the establishment of marketing boards, etc., *the exports and imports of all important and strategic goods should be brought into the public sector*' (Ibid.).

APPROPRIATION OF PLAN GAINS

The Second Plan with its big investments, perspectives, and big talk was finally adopted. But there were no effective implementing agencies, no mass participation, no check-up, no democratic consultations or criticisms. The result, as pointed out by Gadgil, was that the monopolists and their supporters, with the help of their agents in the ruling party and in the governmental machinery, particularly in the higher echelons of the bureaucracy, enriched themselves at the cost of the whole society and to the detriment of all other sectors of economy.

Those very elements who had caused the disaster by misappropriating the gains of the Plan to enrich their private and class interests, those who had caused the steep rise in prices, shortage of foreign exchange, scarcity of foodgrains and raw materials, began to blame it all on the big size of the Plan and demanded curtailment, if not the total abolition of this 'adventure'. The Plan, according to them, had failed and should be scrapped.

What was Gadgil's reaction? He said with his characteristic sarcasm: 'There appears, for example, to have been almost an *overfulfilment of the plans in the large private business sector*. This was largely the result of the import license policy' (Ibid.: 71–5). As a consequence, other sectors had suffered.

The claim of monopoly that it is the biggest source of capital formation and hence of continued growth is denied by Gadgil. He blows up the myth that capital formation is done by the owners of monopoly capital, either by means of the old theory of 'abstinence' and self-sacrifice or from their own entrepreneurial activity. He says in his note to NDC in January 1956: 'Already through such devices as the system of Industrial Finance Corporation, and through large scale direct financing of certain large units by government, a substantial portion of the capital required by modern business is being supplied by the state' (Ibid.: 31).

Gadgil gives a devastating picture of what kind of demands are made on resources and lines of production by those very rich operators in the monopoly capitalist division. Vast sources of capital are invested in terylene factories, while cloth for the poor is sabotaged; luxury hotels and houses are built, while ordinary workers housing is denied. Unheard of salary and emolument scales, measured in terms of what is paid abroad in the UK or USA, are introduced, while the miserable minimum earned by others is sought to be frozen; the price market is thrown out of gear and so on.

> The general trend in the technological development, and the operation of the ordinary market forces in modern economics, both lead to continuous centralization of production and of location of population. (Gadgil, 1961: 31)

The result is already there in the concentration of industry and trade in the metropolitan cities like Bombay and Calcutta. The centralization has skyrocketed land values, made housing and expansion difficult, clogging not only transport but social life in all its aspects.

'Unless an attempt is made to evolve a decentralized pattern in the plan of industrialization and in the planning of social and economic overheads such as transport, power generation and distribution, and education and health facilities, the operating trends will prevail' (Ibid.).

The giant public sector alone, with its all-in control of finance and technique, will help industrialization in a new way than mere decentralization and harnessing medium and small industry in the private sector for that task. Only in this way can the ruin of the millions working in the 'private sector' be prevented and harmonious and democratic development of the national economy take place at a rapid rate. Unless the backbone of monopoly capital is broken by nationalization and the ramification of rural financial capital are set aside by co-operativization of the small holder and unless the capitalist market-price mechanism is broken by socialization of wholesale trade in foodgrains and industrial crops and of export-import, our economy and our democracy cannot go forward.

PRICES, WAGES, AND EMPLOYMENT

The same thread leads Gadgil to find solutions to the problems of rising prices and questions of wages and unemployment. Gadgil treats the problem of prices, wages, incomes, and unemployment in an interconnected line of thinking. Development programmes and expenditure are seen to profit the secure and rich areas, while they leave almost unaffected the backward and the poor. All reports point to the same type of differentiation between classes as within an area (Ibid.: 136).

The differentiation between the cities and the villages has widened further. And in the countryside the rich farmer has reaped most of the benefits, while conditions of the agricultural labourer, rural artisan, casual labourer have deteriorated. 'Even the earnings of factory workers have not made any significant progress if 1959 is compared with 1951. ... It is only the traders and the industrialists who appear to have consistently done well, and among them, the bigger and those in the largest cities with the largest organized businesses appear to have done the best' (Ibid.: 137).

'The absolute and relative levels of all incomes received out of the national pool are the concern of the governments and the planning authority. ... Therefore, whether through appropriate tax policy or through direct regulation, *all salaries as well as entrepreneurial incomes must be set at appropriate levels*' (Ibid.: 25–6).

As regards unemployment, he saw its roots in the same phenomenon of concentration of wealth in the hands of a few and the ruination of the poor peasant and agricultural labourer. Beaten by the rural bourgeoisie, unprotected by the governmental policies, which favour the rich, they are forced out from the villages and march to the towns in search of employment.

'In our situation, the adoption, for any purpose, of a technique more capital-intensive than that required for efficient production in any activity in the context of the total plan, is to take away a highly scarce factor from other activities, and is an action which is not only unsocial but also uneconomic' (Ibid.: 152).

He pleads for taking up at least public works programmes, building social-economic overheads all over the country, with the smaller towns at the centre of the picture. Organize at least a 'holding operation' for the traditional industries as employ large numbers and evolve an 'intermediate technology', alongside the giants of modern industry in the public sector, for the employment programme.

In concluding his survey of the prices, income, wages and salaries, and employment problems, Gadgil once again fixes his sight firmly on the nature of the reality of power.

He says : '...the grossly disproportionate share of the national dividend is appropriated by those who wield political and economic power, and by the classes from whom the state and social leaders are drawn' (Ibid.: 26).

It is, therefore, now necessary to go into the question of state power, its class nature, the bureaucracy, and the question of democracy in Gadgil's system of thinking.

CONCENTRATION OF ECONOMIC POWER

It is important to note that actual power is held by a relatively small group, entry into which is becoming increasingly difficult; there is considerable concentration of influence even within its ranks, and effective control has been reduced to a few hands and a very narrow social base. Political and economic power is being concentrated in the hands of selected sections from among the traditional trading communities (Ibid.: 148)

The ruling section of the Congress Party, as of all other political parties in India including the communists, is drawn mainly from the urban educated professional and administrative service class; to these have been added, in recent decades, representatives of certain trading and financial classes who are dominant in modern business. It is the prejudices and interests of these that consciously or unconsciously obstruct the steps needed to bring about a real social revolution. Also, the class composition of the ruling section cuts it off from the rural masses making it less sensitive to their needs as also less sure of enthusing them. (Gadgil 1961: 59)

The necessary efforts for building up the cooperative system and for regulating the activities, in particular, of modern business will not be made. As a consequence, Plan targets will be unevenly fulfilled; an even more dangerous likely result is that social objectives will totally miscarry, and the efficiency of the present Plan and the country's ability to plan for the future will be greatly impaired. (Ibid.: 33)

In November 1960, Gadgil had predicted the coming upheavals. He had said:

'In the not-too-distant future there is bound to be definite confrontation of the actual possessors of the politico-economic power in the country, the large business interests, the top administrative and professional groups and the political parties supported by them, with the mass of the common people...' (Ibid.: xvi)

The great confrontation exploded in 1967 and soon forced the ruling Congress Party to change its positions. And Gadgil, who had all along taken the role of an adviser from afar, agreed to join the Planning Commission as its Vice-Chairman. But neither the new ruling circles led by Smt. Indira Gandhi nor her entourage nor the vested interests would agree to the principles or norms of practice and behaviour that Gadgil had so long preached and now wanted to be acted upon by the government and the Planning Commission. The new regime also, which wanted more of a durbari in attendance in the chief of the Planning Commission than a determined, thinking, uncompromising, anti-monopolist head, could not stomach Gadgil—neither his economics, nor his politics, nor his practice. He was ever prepared to modulate or modify his strong view, up to a point, but not give up his fundamental position against monopoly capital. The bureaucrats, parasites, and charlatans won and the principled thinker lost. He went out of the Commission and out of the world. He had finished his battle. He left his thinking behind in his profound notes on the economy and politics of India, to act as some guide for the builders of revolutionary democracy in a developing economy of a newly-liberated country, still carrying many scars of its past slavery and hopes of its future of democracy and socialism.

NOTE

1. All emphasis in quoted matter is that of the author.

REFERENCE

Gadgil, D.R. (1961) *Planning and Economic Policy in India*, GIPE, Poona.

35

Gadgil's Basic Approach to Indian Development*

H.K. PARANJAPE

With the sudden death of Prof. Gadgil, the country has lost one of the finest scholars of the old liberal academic tradition in India. He not only carried on the tradition set by earlier luminaries like Tilak and Gokhale, but injected a methodological rigour in academic writing, which was somewhat lacking earlier.

Except for a short time at the beginning of his career, and again for about three and a half years at the end, Prof. Gadgil never held an official position.

Essentially, Gadgil was a public-spirited intellectual. The wide range of his knowledge and the catholicity of his outlook and interests were obvious to all those who came in contact with him. He touched upon vast areas of public policy for study and advice at different stages of his long career. While he was mainly known as an economist, not many in the present generation are aware of the deep interest that he took in institution-building of various kinds. Not only did he build up the Gokhale Institute from scratch, but he was also one of those who at a very early stage had envisaged the necessity to create a number of teaching universities and he was in the forefront of a movement for the development of the Poona University. He took keen interest in educational problems. One of the pioneering studies made by him in co-operation with Prof. V.M. Dandekar was in respect of the problem of the lapse into illiteracy of new sections of the population brought under

* Abstract from *Young Indian*, May 1971.

the scope of primary education. His role in building up the Co-operative Movement in the former Bombay Province is somewhat better known. One of his major contributions to the development of the new industrial structure in India was the establishment of the first co-operative sugar factory in Maharashtra. Activities such as these, as well as his association with matters like famine-relief, flood-relief, the organization of the vast network of primary schools developed by the late Shri Bhaurao Patil, and the attempts to formulate local development plans for some of the former princely states like Sangli, Phaltan, and Kolhapur, and later for the Wardha District, were all meant both as grassroots-contact with socio-economic realities and as attempts at pioneering and experimentation in the broad direction of future development which he envisaged and advocated.

DEEP PATRIOTISM

His emphasis on developing empirical analysis by collecting economic and social facts originated from his basic thesis that the idea of a universally applicable body of economic knowledge was in the main fallacious. The tradition of Indian economics in this sense of the term had already been laid down by Mahadeo Govind Ranade, the originator of many ideas that later bore fruit in the life of our country, and Gadgil carried on this tradition with much greater sophistication, based on his deep knowledge of economic and social history and his close acquaintance with the facts of Indian economic, social, and political life.

APPROACH AND APPLICATION

While Gadgil continued to develop and expand particular applications of his basic approach to Indian development right till 1967, when his academic career came to a close, the fundamentals of his approach had been almost evolved in their entirety by 1950. The importance, in the Indian context, of a basic egalitarian approach to incomes had been emphasized by him in his very first publication (1931) under the auspices of the Gokhale Institute. This dealt with the salaries of public servants. He made a strong plea therein both for bringing the emoluments of the higher services to a much more reasonable and lower level in the context of the average income in India, and for transforming the structure of public services by giving up the elitist status given to a generalist group like the ICS. In the context of the development requirements of the country, he had even then pointed out the importance of recognizing the contribution of subject specialists in the service organization of the government. He reverted to this theme over and over again in many of his writings, including his memoranda to the First and Second Pay Commissions. It is a pity that his advice—like the earlier Congress Resolutions on the subject—went unheeded, and continues to go unheeded even in this age of socialism and planning!

In the Patna Lectures, which he delivered in 1940 on Regulation of Wages, he clearly indicated his conclusion that perfect competition and a free market were assumptions that were so irrelevant in the Indian context that any policy orientation based on them could not be of much use. His presidential address at the Indian Economic Conference in 1940 laid down certain propositions that form the core of his policy advice—irrelevance and unsuitability of *laissez faire,* the necessity to regulate the development of economic and technical change so as to reduce the mal-effects of the transition specially on the poorest classes, the importance of balanced regional development, and the necessity of recognizing the public obligations of private industries which grow with special public support such as import tariffs.

POLITICAL CONTEMPLATIONS

Economic planning, for the increase of national wealth and income, was bound to be the major pre-occupation of the future governments in India, he pointed out, and for this it was necessary that the master-plan of economic development must be country-wide. 'The Federal Government must have adequate powers to evolve the general plan of economic development for the whole country, and must also have powers to carry out its essential central features and to supervise and enforce its implementation by the federating units. This is only inherent in economic planning' (Gadgil 1945: 44).

His views about the essentials for a policy-framework for India's economic development were getting crystallized during the forties. The importance of building up a consistent and integrated system of economic controls was advocated by him in his *War and Indian Economic Policy,* published in 1943. As a result of the persuasion, he was able to carry with certain governmental authorities and he came to be closely associated with the building-up of the system of rationing and economic controls that was developed in the then Province of Bombay—a system that compared better with that in any other part of the country and which attempted to provide an element of distributive justice to large sections of the population. Moreover, he was already envisaging that the building-up of such a system would provide an essential basis for the regime of planned economic development in the post-war period. 'Not only in respect of the immediate present, but looking also to the future, economic regulation and the planning of economic life by the State must be taken as having come to stay; and the existence of an efficient and honest public administrative machinery is vital to the operation of these regulations and plans' (Gadgil 1944: 109–10).

This approach he further emphasized through the Reports of the Commodities Prices Board of which he (together with Shri A.D. Gorwala) was a member.

ECONOMIC PROBLEMS

In the period after Independence, Gadgil's writings became more clearly directed towards problems of economic policy and the planning of economic development. One of the very significant criticisms that he had to offer on the Draft Constitution was regarding the little care and attention that had been devoted to Chapter IV containing the Directive Principles of the Constitution, while at the same time considerable attention had been paid to making the Right to Property one which was almost more fundamental than others, 'It would ... appear that the fundamental right guaranteed in Article 13 (1) (g) is more securely founded than the other fundamental rights guaranteed to the citizens' (Gadgil 1948: 28). This might make it difficult for the state to undertake close regulation of economic activity or to embark upon socialistic ventures, he had pointed out. He drew attention to how, even without such specific guarantees, the United States Constitution had hindered state action in respect of regulation of economic activity. He opined that it was not unlikely that very large claims to compensation would arise under the wide guarantee proposed to be given under the Draft Constitution. 'It is in the circumstances incomprehensible why protection to rights of private property and freedom of business should be granted in India in terms much wider than even those guaranteed in U.S.A., the land, par excellence, of free enterprise' (Ibid.: 36).

Subsequent history has indicated how right Gadgil's warnings in this respect were. He had similarly criticized the continuation of the old distinction between agricultural income-tax and income-tax other than agricultural. Not only did such a distinction have no economic or social basis but it would also provide a loophole for tax evasion in addition to causing loss of revenue to the state. This warning also fell on deaf ears (Ibid.: 81).

EDUCATION CAMPAIGN

He, however, played a crucial role through the Panel of Economists regarding the reorientation of public policies that took place at the time of formulating the Second Five-Year Plan. He specially emphasized a wide extension of the public sector, increasing investment in basic and capital goods industries, progress in equalization of distribution and decentralization, and construction of a system of socio-economic regulations which might be brought into operation in appropriate stages. Whatever hopes he had, however, of the new directions to economic policy that seemed possible as a result of the Second Five-Year Plan were soon disappointed. The Second Plan document had no clear statement about the techniques with which the Plan could be effectively implemented. Though a number of direct and indirect instruments had been evolved in the fields of banking, trade, and transport, in none of these had the practice or theory relating to them risen above limited specific objectives (Gadgil 1961: 53).

SCEPTICAL ATTITUDE

In his Laski Memorial Lecture of 1958, he laid bare and criticised the inadequacies of the Planning Commission as it had been organized, and pointed out how it had failed all along the line in essential matters.

His research study on the Industrial Evolution in India (1924) had given Gadgil a good view of the manner in which trade and industry in India had developed. His experience of the operation of the economy in wartime and the manner in which trading and business interests, under different guises, showed profiteering and anti-social tendencies convinced him that these groups have to be kept in check if development planning in the genuine interest of the community had to be undertaken. As time went on, his writings became couched more clearly in terms of class interests and conflicts. He had pointed out in 1959, for example, how, while there was little of free competition in most lines of trade and industry in India and therefore prices were 'administered', as in any oligopolistic situation, the government exercised little or no control over them. Even where the government had given special assistance or privilege, 'the benefits accruing therefrom are compounded into assets of the party assisted by Government without any social claim or public interest being created within it' (Ibid.: 141).

CONCENTRATION OF POWER

Reviewing the whole situation, he had opined that while the monopoly of priestly, intellectual and martial classes had broken down in India, political and economic power was being concentrated in the hands of selected sections from among the traditional trading communities. He even pointed out that the apparently inexpert handling of measures such as state trading in foodgrains might be due not so much to incompetence 'as to the conscious or unconscious desire not to harm dominant interests, through effective operation of policies unwillingly accepted' (Ibid.: 148). Further, in 1960, he had stated that the situation was essentially one of transition. 'In the not too distant future, there is bound to be definite confrontation of the actual possessors of politico-economic power in the country, the large business interests, the top administrative and professional groups and the political parties supported by them with the mass of the common people, and such a confrontation would have very serious results for the Plan and for stability and order in the country' (Ibid.: xvi–xvii). He pointed out that this was essentially a moral crisis and that the mixed economy could prove practicable only if those in power can enjoy moral authority. This they could do only by showing some convincing and overt signs of their sincerity and sacrifice for planned development of India on democratic lines. He had pointed out that the intelligentsia, including the professionals, were fast losing public respect because of their exorbitant claims on the national product and their increasing association with private business. 'The rot (had) progressively spread to political leadership'. If self-discipline could not be accepted by these classes and the implications of democratic development not understood, he had warned that democratic development itself might be jeopardized.

DECENTRALIZATION SOUGHT

Gadgil was a great believer in democratic and decentralized operation of the economic and political system. This in his view was essential if the interests of the common people were to receive proper and full attention. As early as in 1945, he had put forward a plea for the reorganization of federating units so as to bring about linguistically homogeneous provinces or states. This plea he continued to reiterate. He pointed out that the creation of strong and homogeneous primary units was the only lasting basis for the erection of a strong Union, and he also pointed out that the opposition to this approach mainly stemmed from a small number of rootless groups and communities. He believed that such reorganization was an essential part of the development of the Left forces in the country and strong emphasis on federalism was essential in the interests of democracy and the rights of the common people. It is well known how the top political leadership of the country, in spite of the traditional Congress acceptance of linguistic provinces, for long opposed such reorganization of states resulting in much waste of time and energy before this change was brought about.

Gadgil's emphasis on decentralization and democratic development led him to support the development of co-operatives on the one side, and district development planning on the other. In these respects his ideas were close to those of persons like Vinoba Bhave or Jai Prakash Narain. He was, however, a pragmatist and was insistent that no universal panacea was available which would help in all situations. While supporting the Co-operative Movement, both by precept and participation, at the same time he supported the idea of the development of other institutions for the provision of agricultural credit in areas where co-operative institutions could not be expected to develop rapidly. This was clearly brought about both by the Report of the Agriculture Finance Sub-Committee (1944) of which he was the Chairman and, later, of the Rural Credit Survey Committee (1954).

Similarly, while pleading for a consistent overall framework for development planning, he was keenly interested both as a democrat and as a person interested in effective formulation and implementation of development plans in the growth of proper planning machinery in the states and in the districts. The plea for spatial planning which he had hinted at even as early as 1940 was further taken up in the advice he gave in 1966 to the Maharashtra Government regarding Regional Planning and in putting forward the idea of district development planning together with the development of *Panchayati Raj* institutions (Gadgil 1967).

This is not the place to make an evaluation of the man and his work. Some time will have to elapse before one can look at Gadgil's career in perspective and judge his performance as an academic and as a policy adviser. The role that he considered appropriate for himself is very well indicated in his statement that 'it is in the tradition of Indian economists to recognise that problems of national economy are in essence politico-economic problems' (Gadgil 1961: 148). In another but similar context, he had pointed out that many slogans are raised as providing solutions to India's problems. No slogans, he thought, 'can be a substitute for the hard and constant effort required to eradicate the inadequacies in thinking, in attitudes and approaches and in instruments that are the real obstacles to notable economic progress in India. In the circumstances, it becomes one's duty, however tiringly, to draw attention to these persistently, and if possible, persuasively' (Ibid.: 61). That, in essence, was what he tried to do through his writings, policy guidance, and academic and public activities spread over more than four decades.

REFERENCES

Gadgil, D.R. (1944) *War and Indian Economic Policy*, GIPE, Poona.

—— (1945) *Federating India*, GIPE, Poona.

—— (1948) *Some Observations on the Draft Constitution*, GIPE, Poona.

—— (1961) *Planning and Economic Policy in India*, GIPE, Poona.

—— (1967) *District Development Planning*, GIPE, Poona.

36

Gadgil's Impact on Planning, Economic Policy, and Co-operation*

Some Highlights

TARLOK SINGH

Professor D.R. Gadgil first entered the sphere of national economic policy as a member of the Commodity Prices Board which was set up to advise the Government of India shortly after Independence. In mid-1948 when the Government decided to de-control the movement and distribution of food grains, both he and his colleague on the Board, A.D. Gorwala, felt that an erroneous step had been taken and resigned from the Board. Before long, the Government felt obliged to reverse the decision, and the view of the Board was vindicated. Thereafter, in view of the prevailing food deficit, there was much hesitation in modifying the apparatus of controls. The protest by the Board in 1948 had influenced the formulations on price policy advocated in the First Five-Year Plan.

The next significant stage was the setting up of a Research Programmes Committee soon after the First Plan appeared in its final version. The Plan stressed the need for research and investigation into social, economic, and administrative problems through universities and other institutions and made a modest financial provision for such studies. The Research Programmes Committee, with Professor Gadgil as Chairman, marked out three priority areas for study, namely, land reform, rural-urban migration, and surveys of selected cities. A wide range of institutions were involved in these studies. In subsequent years, the programme of research was

* Originally published in *IASSI Quarterly*, Vol. 18, No. 4, 2000.

progressively enlarged. Professor Gadgil had a key role in guiding the work of the Research Programmes Committee which directly led to the setting up of the Indian Council of Social Science Research in 1969.

The formulation of the Second Five-Year Plan with the 'tentative framework' provided by Professor P.C. Mahalanobis brought Professor Gadgil directly into the planning process. This happened through the Panel of Economists which submitted a Memorandum to the Finance Minister as Chairman of the Panel. The work of the Panel was guided by Professor Gadgil. He submitted to the Panel a paper on Policy Decisions in Plan Making. Several of the questions he raised were left unanswered then and still remain to be answered. In particular, he raised questions bearing on the implications of expansion in the public sector, the long-term character of the proposals in the 'plan-frame' and their dependence on foreign aid, priorities within the public sector, deficit financing, controls, and protection of the living standards of the poorer groups.

A major area in which Professor Gadgil had a profound impact related to Co-operation. This came about initially through the Committee of Direction for the All-India Rural Credit Survey, of which he was a member along with A.D. Gorwala and B. Venkatappaiah. The Survey was the first of its kind and a precursor of the series of rural debt and investment surveys carried out in later years by the Reserve Bank of India.

The Rural Credit Survey proposed the principle of state partnership in co-operatives at all levels, including credit, marketing, processing consumer co-operatives and warehousing. To secure viability and improved management, it proposed the merging of smaller village co-operatives into large-sized co-operative societies. The principle was accepted, but it became necessary to reconcile considerations of viability and management with the need to preserve the basic principles of co-operation at the primary level, namely, voluntary participation, close contact, social cohesion, and mutual obligation. Eventually, after the passing of a resolution on Co-operative Policy by the National Development Council, an acceptable solution emerged from the work of the Committee on Co-operative Credit headed by V.L. Mehta. However, the trend towards the reorganization of primary co-operatives continued to be maintained. The nationalization of the Imperial Bank of India and its conversion into the State Bank of India emerged indirectly from the recommendations of the Rural Credit Survey and led to rapid expansion of the Bank's Branches throughout the country.

Professor Gadgil's ideas and practical leadership, beginning with the Rural Credit Survey, led to the steady growth of a vast structure of co-operative institutions. These involved the progressive integration of co-operative credit, marketing, and processing. The first co-operative sugar factory in Maharashtra owed its existence to him.

This was the beginning of development of co-operative sugar factories throughout the country. Co-operatives took up other activities like manufacture and distribution of fertilizers. Eventually, a series of federations emerged at the national level. Maharashtra and Gujarat were fortunate in their reservoir of leadership in the Co-operative Movement and some of the most striking developments in co-operation can be traced to their innovative and organizing abilities in securing the participation of farmers at the village level.

Professor Gadgil's appointment as Deputy Chairman of the Planning Commission placed on him a major responsibility for steering the course of national planning. Whether the suspension of medium-term planning for three years, 1966–67 to 1968–69, was inevitable might still be a moot point. However, following the devaluation of the rupee, lack of foreign aid, and the severe drought in 1966–67 and 1967–68, there was much uncertainty to be reckoned with.

When the Fourth Five-Year Plan for the period 1969–74 finally emerged, significant developments in agriculture through the introduction of high-yielding varieties were already taking place. The nationalization of leading commercial banks was taken into account in the formulation of the Plan. In the main, the Plan reaffirmed the commitments and the broad approach of the earlier Plans, including the emphasis on self-reliance, food self-sufficiency, and institutional development. Its innovative features included the identification of the special problems of drought-prone areas, marginal farmers, and landless labourers. It laid a great deal of emphasis on District Planning and the approach of Growth Areas around promising market centres.

A Five-Year plan is, by its nature, a composite effort. But in its various judgments on crucial issues, Professor Gadgil's influence on the content and strategy of the Fourth Plan is unmistakable. His concern with social objectives was expressed equally in the Report on Organizational Framework for the Implementation of Social Objectives which was prepared under his chairmanship by a Study Group set up by the National Credit Council.

What lent authority to Professor Gadgil's view in every sphere of policy was his frank recognition of problems which had still to be solved, the need to experiment with alternative approaches, and continuous emphasis on the larger social objectives. He was always open to argument, and remained concerned to the very end with the need to understand the ground realities as fully as possible. The combination of fundamental social concerns with the readiness to make practical beginnings wherever opportunities offered themselves and a strong emphasis on integration of various activities in all fields of implementation won ready acceptance and left an enduring impact on national economic and social policy. The major problems which he identified in the course of a lecture in 1968 like the implications of metropolitan growth, uneconomic holdings, landless labour, regional and other disparities, unemployment and underemployment, population, dependence on foreign aid, and the failure of many public enterprises to provide the surpluses anticipated from them still remain to be resolved. In the context of recent changes in economic policy, his searching questions have lost none of their relevance.

37
Gadgil's Vision

K.S. SRIKANTAN

This is the centennial year of the birth of Professor D.R. Gadgil. Not only was he an eminent social scientist but also a pioneer in social action setting up new institutions for socio-economic transformation. His social research and social action programmes were wide ranging and embraced the Co-operative Movement, planning and public administration, and public policy on crucial social and political issues. This is an apt occasion to remind ourselves of Gadgil's vision for India. Perhaps one of his chief contributions to economic development was the establishment of the Co-operative Movement in India. In this paper we attempt to trace the evolution of his ideas on co-operation as an institution for the transformation of the economy and the society.

Gadgil's lectures in memory of Prof. Brij Narayan (Gadgil 1961) outline the origins of co-operative activity and provide a comparative picture of its spread in developed and developing countries. He concludes with a summary of a comparative world review in 1950 on the unequal progress of the Co-operative Movement due to disparities in basic conditions:

> To sum up, in the economically advanced countries the consumer's movement affects one-quarter to one-third of the population and carries on ten per cent to 20 per cent of the national retail trade. Progress in the past ten years has been fairly rapid. Agricultural co-operation affects perhaps two-thirds of the farm population and handles anything from 40 per cent to 90 per cent of the more important agricultural commodities. Progress in countries where co-operation developed early has been relatively slow in the last ten years. In the economically underdeveloped countries the proportions of co-operative membership and trade are much lower, but progress in the last ten years has

been rapid, although not wholly spontaneous, owing much, as will be seen, to the needs and the initiative of the state. (Gadgil 1950: 9–10)

In developing countries, state initiative is often needed to introduce and nurture the Co-operative Movement. In many instances, direct government intervention preceded attempts to establish co-operative activity as a measure of relief and reconstruction. Where mere direct government assistance was not found to provide any permanent solution, the government resorted to the co-operative form of organization involving the affected people.

The development of co-operative institutions in Italy, Japan, Mexico, and Turkey shows how, in various ways, these institutions were adapted to suit the local circumstances. The idea of government participation in the share capital of a primary co-operative is controversial. However, such participation should not be confused with official domination of the movement. It is only the latter aspect which would violate the tenets of co-operation. As regards the size, area, and functions of the primary society, no hard and fast rules could be formulated and applied universally. Gadgil sums up the prospects for the Co-operative Movement in India:

> ... though the existing coverage of co-operative activity and its total performance in India is not impressive, it does not appear that the general structure of the movement or its lines of development are basically unsound. Rapid future development and the ultimate establishment of genuine co-operation depend on the fulfilment of two requirements. These are sound and vigorous complementary official policies in the fields of agriculture and small industry and the encouragement of experimentation and of decentralised local leadership in co-operative activity. If these are forthcoming there is no reason why the rural economy of India should not in an overwhelming measure be soon covered by healthy co-operative effort. (Gadgil 1950: 66)

Gadgil identifies the basic principles of co-operation as open and secular membership, democratic control, and federal, decentralized, autonomous management. Open membership admits of no discrimination on criteria irrelevant to the goals of the primary unit. For instance, credit co-operatives may exclude membership to moneylenders and traders but cannot deny membership on the basis of caste, language, or religion. Voting rights are generally based on membership in the society but not on the quantum of contribution to the share capital. The twin principles of open membership and one-man-one-vote ensure democratic control of the co-operative, minimizing the influence of the rich and preventing the concentration of control. A large number of small units come together to form the co-operative for furthering specific mutual interests. The scope of the co-operative is limited to the common goals. The primary unit has to be generally formed as a local group. Such local groups can be brought together through federal units while maintaining autonomy at the local level in accordance with the principle of federalism.

Co-operative activity may lose its importance with prosperity and progress of the weaker elements. The importance of co-operation to a society which is poor and in which weaker economic units are numerous cannot be overemphasized. However, in many such societies, for co-operation to succeed, it is necessary that it should be supported by appropriate government policies on economic security and progress. Not only is the number of economic units very large in developing countries, but there exists among them great deal of disparity in strength, between the urban and rural sectors, between the technologically modern and traditional units, and in their scales of operation.

Gadgil conjures up a wide ranging image of a Co-operative Commonwealth not only in terms of established co-operative principles but also, more broadly, in terms of co-operative history and philosophy. This is in contrast to the narrower view of many co-operators who are now reconciled to accepting co-operation as an institutional type within a capitalist society. Some have even begun to maintain that, to function effectively, co-operative organization requires the framework of a capitalist society.

Gadgil considers that:

> The wider interpretation has to draw upon all sources, viz., the aspirations and the motivations of co-operative idealists from the days of Owen to those of the Kibbutz, the principles incorporated in co-operative practice and the diverse forms of organization that co-operation has taken in many countries and for different purposes. The attempted synthesis has also to take note of the fact that it is a structure and basis of a new and transformed society that is being considered and not the operation of a sheltered area within a capitalistic or socialistic society. Inevitably, in considering the question in the Indian context, both experience of recent developments in India and traditional values of Indian society will have to be given due weight. (Gadgil 1950: 90–1)

Co-operation would emphasize dispersal and decentralization of activity and would put the small independent enterprise and the primary co-operative unit at the centre of the economic picture. This is consistent with the origins and continued motivation of co-operative activity as being concerned with the protection and strengthening of the small and weak.

On the operational side, co-operation would be distinguished by its approach to economic incentives.

> Belief in co-operation implies accepting the possibility or the established fact that men are not guided in their work solely by hopes of material gain, that they recognize the importance of group and social obligations and are ready to accept voluntary limitations on expectations and rewards and to exhibit restraint in behaviour patterns in pursuit of economic gains, that non-economic incentives such as social recognition and opportunities for social work are of value in motivating them, and that efficiency and sound business are compatible with a regime of deliberately limited economic incentives. Another important operative aspect of co-operation is its deliberate divorce of control from ownership. This is related, in part, to the attitude of co-operation towards incentives; it is also related to the belief that control of economic activity arising out of

concentrated power and in pursuit of private gain has serious disadvantages, and that control operations which are connected only in part with hopes of such gains can both be efficient and socially beneficial. (Gadgil 1950: 92)

Co-operation is based on the universally accepted concepts of equality and democracy. Its philosophy of control and its principle of open membership ensure economic democracy in which all members enjoy equal privileges. Co-operation is against the concentration of control and stands for a diffusion of power through the whole structure by its insistence on the principle of federalism. The insistence from its earliest days of co-operative effort on the responsibility of the primary group for social security and educational and cultural uplift of its members would indicate that the co-operative philosophy is in consonance with the evolution and approach of the welfare state.

After 1918, communist economies resorted to large-scale co-operative organizations to accelerate the pace of socialism, although co-operation appears no longer important except in erstwhile Yugoslavia. Co-operation, however, differs from socialism in not laying the same emphasis on public ownership of means of production. Where the means of production is highly diffused or where it is held by co-operative groups of small independent units, it would be so retained in a co-operative order. In view of the anti-monopoly attitudes of co-operation and its insistence on divorcing control from ownership, co-operation would favour the placing of, at least the control of, large-scale oligopolistic undertakings, chiefly in the hands of public authority. In contrast to co-operation, a large number of socialist economies do not differ radically from capitalism on the issue of economic incentives. Co-operation would also differ from socialism in not attributing the same importance to the state in economic activities. Because of its insistence on decentralization, on small units, on federalism, and on voluntary effort, co-operation would favour a restricted role for the state.

The basic difference of co-operation from capitalism would stem from the former taking a more moral view of economic activity. Co-operation insists on incorporating concepts of social justice and obligations into the structure of the economic society and recognizing ethical values as an inseparable part of economic life. With its insistence on an ethical approach, the attitude of co-operation towards incentives, controls and ownership are in sharp contrast to those of capitalism.

Gadgil proceeds to assess the prospects for establishing a Co-operative Commonwealth in India. The Indian society, rigidly stratified by castes, has neither social cohesion nor a dominant ethos to promote economic development and social mobility. The Gandhian model is directed entirely to the more austere and self-sufficient aspects of economic life and not towards rising aspirations for higher standards of material life.

The Indian economic system is further away from the competitive model of America and Western Europe. The Indian economy is riddled with inequality, privileges, and monopolistic entrenched positions. The normal difficulties of obtaining diffusion of the gains of development encountered in a segmented backward society are intensified in India with its system of hierarchical castes and communities. This leads to the concentration of the economic surplus and power in the hands of a few communities leading to societal imbalances. The economic history of India exhibits the continuous rise in the importance of business communities who have set up successively lower and lower standards of business ethics.

The principles of the so-called liberal economy and competitive capitalism have never been incorporated in our traditional values and they are highly unsuited to our present circumstances. Socialistic views are widely held in India in combination with the *Sarvodaya* philosophy. Co-operation has many values in common with this philosophy. There are, however, two important differences between co-operation and *Sarvodaya.* The former has a much greater concern with rapid economic development and emphasizes organizational effort in ensuring economic progress. In fact co-operation is essentially a philosophy or ideology of organization. Co-operation is a special way of organizing economic activity to be both efficient and beneficent. *Sarvodaya,* in contrast, apparently distrusts all organizational efforts towards economic betterment.

The actual mixed economy of today is neither socialistic nor infused with the ideals of *Sarvodaya,* but grossly capitalistic. In terms of practical policy, the acceptance of co-operation in all appropriate spheres will enable India to move closer to the socialist and *Sarvodaya* ideals that are held widely by the people.

The political, social, and economic scenarios have changed drastically since Gadgil delivered these lectures on his ideal of a Co-operative Commonwealth. The economy is being globalized with the lowering of the tariff barriers, direct foreign capital investment, foreign financial institutions operating in India, and the arrival of multi-nationals on the domestic scene. Political power is getting to be more broad-based and conventional ideals of ethics and morality are breaking down without a new social order taking their place. It is a chaotic time of overwhelming changes in the polity, society, and the economy. It is impossible to make a balanced assessment of these changes in depth and in all the facets as we are still in their chaotic midst. Such a gigantic task has to be the continuing preoccupation of politicians, of social scientists, philosophers, and the media. We will confine ourselves to a few observations on the relevance of Gadgil's ideals of a Co-operative Commonwealth to the current situation in the country.

Plato placed the optimum population for his ideal Republic at a little over 5,000 free citizens. India's population has crossed the billion mark.

If it has to function effectively as a democracy, then a large measure of local self-government has to be introduced in all matters which are of local concern only like education, health, and social welfare of the needy and the poor. Devolution of power, resources, and management to local levels is unavoidable. As the socialist countries discovered, a highly centralized management of production and distribution in the economy under state capitalism led to an inefficient and unwieldy bureaucracy that was unresponsive to local needs and aspirations. Federalism, as espoused by Gadgil, is the salve that heals and binds a large nation like India. Only concerns which are essential for national security and survival, and orderly economic development need to be retained at the centre if we are to progress beyond a viceregal form of administration to which we are traditionally accustomed.

Integration of the rural economy and subsistence agriculture in a global market assumes an even playing field which we do not have at present. Illiteracy, lack of capital and skills place the rural masses at a great disadvantage. The only form of social security for the small farmer is subsistence agriculture but agricultural labour does not have even this shelter. Higher productivity with larger capital investment, higher technology, and commercial farming are reducing the capacity for labour absorption in agriculture. A higher rural population growth rate compared to urban natural growth rate compounds the problem. Large-scale urban migration is the result of these changes. In fact, the backward linkages of modern agriculture to industries are becoming stronger with the use of fertilizers, pesticides, electricity, pump sets, etc. These are mainly urban products generating urban employment. In this situation, unbridled competition can only spell greater misery for the rural masses. Unless there is universal education and occupational training, food security, and affordable health care, the rural population cannot compete in even terms with commercial agriculture and large-scale farming. Co-operative farming and credit to rural agriculture advocated by Gadgil are institutions that can bring about a more gradual and less painful adjustment to the modernization of agriculture. In urban areas, small-scale industries cannot compete on even terms with large-scale industries and multinationals for want of capital, new technology, training in skills, and access to markets and in the face of competitive imports. The co-operative form of organization in this sector would create a more even playing field for economic competition.

India is a land of genetic, ethnic, linguistic, and cultural diversity that has the potential to produce a great civilization. Historically, social stratification has been rigid and water-tight and political power and social prestige have been concentrated in the hands of caste elite. Yet, to fully and fruitfully integrate the society and to benefit from such diversity, social and economic mobility and the diffusion of political power to the people are necessary conditions. The progress towards democracy would be impeded if caste, linguistic, and ethnic barriers are not removed. In the era of globalization, new technological elite, as in the Information Technology sector, have arisen. Unless there is social and economic mobility based on equal educational and employment opportunities such elite have a tendency to entrench themselves in power. Food security, universal education, health care, and social security for minimum needs are essential ameliorative measures that have to be taken along with technological progress. Such measures would prevent wealth and power from being concentrated in the hands of a few and would bring about improvement in the living conditions of the common people. Local institutions like *Panchayats*, based on the principles of the Co-operative Movement, have a great role to play in the diffusion of economic progress and prosperity to the rural areas and weaker sections of the population.

In the final analysis, Gadgil considers the spirit of co-operation as a moral and ethical value. The concept of 'entitlement' developed by the Nobel laureate Amartya Sen, likewise, has an ethical basis in recognizing the innate dignity of human beings and their basic needs. India has a long tradition of compassionate feeling for the weaker sections of the society. But economic incentives do have a role to play in improving efficiency and increasing accountability in productive activities. Moral and ethical sentiments have to be translated into practical terms by developing appropriate institutions like schools, hospitals, life and crop insurance against the risks of accidents and natural calamities, the *Panchayat* system of local self-government, consumer and credit co-operatives, co-operatives for handloom workers, etc. More than in the fields of technology and development, perhaps the weakest link in our culture is the inability to innovate, experiment, and establish appropriate political, legal, health, and educational institutions. The progress and stability of our democracy would ultimately hinge on the attention we pay to institution building.

The birth centenary of Prof. D.R. Gadgil is a fit occasion to recall his contributions to social science research and action programmes, not only because he worked for the betterment of the poor but also because many of his ideas and the institutions he shaped are relevant to bring order and organization to the great political, social, and economic upheaval that we are currently witnessing in our country.

REFERENCES

Gadgil, D.R. (1950) 'The Place of Co-operation in National Economy', in the *Year Book of Agricultural Co-operation*.

—— (1961) *Towards a Co-operative Commonwealth*, Chandigarh: Punjab University Publications Bureau.

38

Towards Radical Social Sciences

*Lessons from D.R. Gadgil**

SUHAS PALSHIKAR

Dhananjaya Rao Gadgil is well known as an economist. What is less well known is that his economics was anchored in sound social science. Since his major professional work was in the field of economics, Gadgil has been mostly assessed in his role of an economist. But he was much more than an economist. True to the times in which he worked, Gadgil functioned both at the academic and the public levels. That Gadgil shared the nationalist ethos and reformist enthusiasm of his times is not very surprising. That was but natural in those times—Gadgil started

* This essay—thin in size and short in substance—has taken too long to complete. It originated, partly, in the speech I gave during the commemoration of Gadgil on his birth centenary, on 9 September 2000 at the Poona College, Poona. About the same time, some of us at the Department of Politics, University of Poona, were already in awe of the scope of Gadgil's sociological work. We were then almost imitating Gadgil; we had planned a socio-economic survey of Pune city and completed the survey in 2000. Other colleagues involved in the survey were Rajeshwari Deshpande and Nitin Birmal. In the course of preparing for the survey instrument, we had an opportunity to have a closer look at the works of Gadgil, confirming our initial regard for the mature and solid nature of his works. In this sense, this essay has grown out of a collective appreciation of Gadgil's social science. I have benefited from discussions with Rajendra Vora and Rajeshwari Deshpande and from comments on the draft by Ramachandra Guha. I should also thank Sulabha Brahme for her persistence in getting this essay out of me and for her uncharacteristic patience in waiting for the essay to be completed. Usual disclaimers apply.

his academic career when the values of the freedom movement were crystallizing and the radical liberal-nationalist intellectual position was in vogue in India. What makes Gadgil, his memory, and his intellectual legacy worth remembering is something different, something much more timeless and impersonal. Gadgil was among the very few intellectuals who seriously attempted to bridge the ever-so-wide gulf between public intellectualism and academic expertise. He was a social scientist and social historian. He was also a founder of systematic empirical sociological inquiry. In this sense, he laid down the foundations of India's social sciences, something that has not been properly appreciated in contemporary social science in the country.

The usual lament about the state of our social sciences is not new to the informed public as well as the practitioners of social sciences in India. To cut the long story short, two limitations of our social sciences are the most prominent: a lack of cross-disciplinary sensibilities and, an utter neglect of the social purpose of the social science endeavour. As far as the institutional context of social science is concerned, the less said the better. For most practitioners of social science in the country, social science is merely a matter of bread and for some, a matter of bread and 'butter'! This other, 'butterly' section of the social science salariat has been busy aping the intellectual fashions of the North and\or becoming part of the establishment of the Indian state. As a young student Gadgil was trained in England and later in his career, he was almost part of the establishment if one looks at the umpteen committees of the Government of India on which he sat. He rose to head the brand new social science research council and also became the deputy chairman of the Planning Commission. But Gadgil held on firmly to his own vision of the social science endeavour, something that can be thought provoking and enlightening even today, after over thirty years since his death.

The intellectual establishment loves to place persons onto the pigeon-holes of simple categories and identify them with short hand identities. This often blurs the real significance of the work of the person concerned. For instance, Gadgil's name is synonymous with the co-operatives and he is classified as an economist. Thus, the non-economist can afford to ignore Gadgil's real worth. It is rarely noted, therefore, that Gadgil's economics was only part of the broad based social science investigation and he had a vision about social scientific exercise, which he exemplified by practice rather than expostulation. Therefore, this essay attempts to sketch the social science vision that Gadgil held, something that informed his work throughout his career. The essay then briefly summarizes the social scientific work that Gadgil undertook and the insights that we can draw from his work.

APPROACH TO SOCIAL SCIENCE

Two themes dominated the social scientific enterprise in India in the first half of the twentieth century: one was the nationalist fervour and the other was the developmentalist perspective. It was the latter that facilitated the transition of Indian social sciences from the British to the American brand of social science in the post-Independence period. Social science became an enterprise directed at the 'development' of a backward but transitional society. What distinguishes Gadgil is that he only mildly subscribed to this prevailing consensus about social science in his time. In his economics, he was undoubtedly motivated by both the nationalist and developmentalist concerns but was more sensitive to ground level situations and the need to evolve a social science that would take into account two other concerns: one was the Indian specificity and the others were the broader concerns of equity and justice. Gadgil's social science was rooted in these two as much as the nationalist and the developmentalist concerns that then dominated the social science establishment in the country. At the same time, Gadgil was not so far removed from the existing consensus as to be branded an 'outsider'. He remained part of the establishment in the sense that the authorities, both in the pre-Independence and the post-Independence period looked upon him for analytical and policy guidance. In other words, Gadgil's social science was not esoteric, drastically revolutionary, or paradigmatically delinked from social science of his contemporaries. The fact that he subscribed to the existing social scientific consensus allowed him to remain part of the social science establishment and yet, the different approach that he employed to his social science made his social science a fresh and critical exercise, distinct from both the establishment and the counter-establishment. (His disciple-cum-critic-cum-biographer, N.V. Sovani has emphasized Gadgil's keen interest in being the 'insider' and working on official committees. However, Sovani completely misses this vital point that Gadgil had a certain relationship of sharing and distance as far as the Indian establishment was concerned. This makes Sovani's discussion smack of malice more than objectivity. For details, see Sovani, 1974. On the other hand, his other close colleague of long duration, who also prided in his objectivity, V.M. Dandekar, was probably too frigid about the social causes Gadgil espoused. Therefore, neither of them situated Gadgil in the larger perspective of the dominant social scientific vision, and his numerous official commitments.)

In terms of methodological approach, Gadgil followed the empirical-positivist method of social enquiry. He looked upon empirical investigation as the tool for gaining social knowledge. At least two observers have noted the significance of the 'survey method' evolved by Gadgil as a method for studying Indian social reality (Apte 2000 and Brahme 2000). Gadgil also believed that social science was not only about description, and as a good empiricist, his investigations were anchored in social and historical materials. We opened this essay by saying that he was a well-known economist. However, his social enquiry extended far beyond the confines of economics. He delved into the social and historical roots of the economy. Implicitly, he believed in the interconnection of the social and the economic. Without taking any ideological position about the *primacy* of the one over the other, Gadgil went on quietly throughout his life investigating the *linkages* between the social and the economic. Though ideologues will not like it, if one wanted a good instance of methodological blending of the Marxian and the Weberian concerns, Gadgil's social science could be almost a textbook example. This unavoidably led Gadgil to a vast territory of social enquiry: from economics to economic history to governmental arrangement to social history to sociological investigations. However, lest this be understood merely in terms of multi-disciplinary activity, Gadgil sought to integrate the methods and findings from this multi-disciplinary exercise, inaugurating the interdisciplinary approach in Indian social sciences. Ramachandra Guha has aptly observed that Gadgil's 'instinct and orientation were interdisciplinary before the term became fashionable' (Guha 2001: 4663).

Many of these points were explicitly made by Gadgil when he spoke at the inaugural ceremony of the Indian Council for Social Science Research (ICSSR), as its first Chairman. In that speech (1969), he emphasized the need for an interdisciplinary approach to the study of social phenomena, the need to undertake study of contemporary Indian scene, and called for interface between academic work and field experience (Gadgil 1981: 419–22). In the same speech, he underlined the need to theorize the peculiarities of the Indian situation. While making clear that he was not opposed to 'intelligent borrowing', Gadgil pointed out that progress in developing descriptive material alone was not sufficient (Gadgil 1981: 421). In a sense, this dilemma is quite central to the social science endeavour in India. The concepts and theories developed in the North often claim universality while the ground level situations obtaining in India are different and do not admit of the same solutions as prescribed by the scholarship in the North. Gadgil himself gives the example of models of economic development. He points out that these are not 'sufficiently rigorous'... to support our practical judgments (Gadgil 1981). Many fields in the social sciences face this problem: global models and theories do not fit, but overemphasis on 'particularities' can deny any generalization in the field of social enquiry. Gadgil does not claim to have any final answer to this problem, but as a true social scientist, he was aware of the problem and suggests that claims of the North need to be taken with a context-sensitive approach.

Two issues are implicit in his plea for theorizing 'our' situation: one is the issue of poverty (an economic issue) and the other is the issue of caste-based social inequalities (a social issue). Gadgil does not elaborate on the caste question much, however, it is clear both from his methodology and subject matters that he was sensitive to the role of caste in any analysis of the Indian society. In fact, at one place, he makes a mention that he was a student of 'our social institutions,' an obvious reference to the caste system (Gadgil 1974: 246). Thus, 'doing' social science would mean incorporating these concerns in social investigations. The interconnection between the two—poverty and caste inequality—can be detected only if we adopt an interdisciplinary approach. Thus, his call for an interdisciplinary study arose from both a methodological approach and sociological necessity.

However, if one looks at the entire body of writings of Gadgil, we realize that there was more to his social science than mere empirical enquiry. In fact, Gadgil never states this, though this point informs all his social scientific work. He was not a social scientist flaunting his command over the 'technique.' He himself did very little 'technical' social science. Social research was a purposive activity for him. The purpose was a humanist egalitarian social order. Gadgil had a measure of the social order. He firmly anchors the assessment of the social institutions on the basis of principles of justice and equity. So much so, that in the conservative atmosphere of social sciences, Gadgil actually appears to be a radical academician! One scholar has in fact referred to Gadgil as an economist following class analysis (Hanson 1966: 236–7). On the other hand, Byres has spent considerable energy (and space) to prove that Gadgil did not follow class analysis (Byres 1998: 58–61; Byres 1998: 35–8). Byres invokes the authority of Dandekar (1971a, 1971b) and Kamat (1974) to prove his point. Ironically, although both Dandekar and Kamat agree on the point that Gadgil was not 'Marxist' in his persuasion, while Dandekar would not see this as a major failing of Gadgil, for the latter, it was certainly Gadgil's failing! Kamat actually comes down very harshly on Gadgil for being a 'radical upper-middle class intellectual' (Kamat 1974: 1028). Interestingly, in this debate over Gadgil's position, one rarely finds any mention of the fact that Gadgil's concerns spanned much beyond economics. Hanson and Byres were of course concerned with the issues of planning and economic debates. Therefore, their neglect of other writings of Gadgil is understandable. What is surprising and telling is the silence of both Dandekar and Kamat over the wide scope of Gadgil's academic activity. Both are almost oblivious to the existence of Gadgil the social scientist. It is, of course, true that Gadgil does not follow class analysis, and it would be inaccurate to ascribe to him pro-Left sympathy. But at the same time, in the tradition of 'value free' social science, Gadgil would certainly appear a bit out of place.

In contrast, more recently, another scholar idolized Gadgil as an intellectual sharing the 'liberal sensibility' (Guha 2001: 4663–4). While the first description might make the leftists uncomfortable (they surely will not admit Gadgil in that self-righteous club of Indian radicals!), the latter does not do full justice to Gadgil himself (more because of the associated meanings of being a 'liberal'. On the other hand, Gadgil was liberal indeed, in the sense that he was non-dogmatic and did not take a deterministic approach.). In a sense, this contrasting evaluation of Gadgil is symptomatic of the unease that Gadgil himself mentioned: the Indian specificity does not fit in the 'Northern' conceptual categories. Hence, the confusion about the intellectual identity of Gadgil. He operated in the atmosphere dominated by a liberal-humanist perspective. However, the modern reformist spirit of social reconstruction dominated this perspective. Besides, the nationalist and Gandhian movements instilled a considerable radical meaning into the liberal thinking, practically moving Indian liberal thinking away from the European liberal cousins. To Gadgil's credit, his constant adherence to the principles of justice and equity did not lead him to a verbose ideological position. Firmly but quietly, he pursued these in his social science. Thus, he continued to remain a social scientist throughout his life. This was an intellectual feat of sorts, particularly in the stagnant atmosphere of Marathi culture, within which he operated. (In contemporary Maharashtra, perhaps throughout the twentieth century, an 'oral' tradition has emerged wherein scholars eschew scholarship in favour of being publicists and then operate as scholars in the public sphere and as public intellectuals in the field of scholarship. Maharashtra loves its publicists more than it cares for the scholars! This has been one of the main reasons for the non-growth of serious and quality social science in Maharashtra in spite of many false starts and enough potential for serious social science scholarship. Incidentally, as Guha has pointed out, Gadgil's Gokhale Institute of Politics and Economics was probably the first social science institute in India, but since then, Maharashtra has not seen any other social science institute in the last eight decades. This is further proof of the frugal interest in serious social science taken by the Marathi culture and society.) To be sure, Gadgil addressed a great many public functions, he was active in the movement for the formation of the Marathi speaking state, he was the founder of and the intellectual spirit behind the Co-operative Movement, and so on. In spite of all this and his constant brush with the field of public activity, Gadgil did not become a publicist as many an academician before and after him. He resolutely remained a 'social scientist' to the core.

How does he then pursue the principles of justice and equity? One part of the answer lies in his constant search for identifying structures of inequality and another lies in the remedies suggested by him to overcome the social problems. In other words, Gadgil's social science has one simple yet difficult message: practice social science as a tool for critical social enquiry. Sociology (in the broader sense of social science) becomes relevant and normatively substantial only when it takes the form of social criticism. It is another matter that this implicit message mostly fell flat on the Indian social science fraternity and the social science institution that Gadgil presided over, Indian Council for Social Science Research, has probably done nothing in the direction of evolving a critical social science in its existence of last three and a half decades. In Gadgil's own works also, the issue of critical social enquiry poses certain tensions, but more about this in the last section.

ACADEMIC CONCERNS

Let us now turn to a brief summary of the themes taken up by Gadgil in his long academic career. Broadly, Gadgil's academic concerns are expressed through three types of articulations: his public addresses, statements, and intervention in public discourse, secondly, the comments, responses, notes submitted by him to various government committees, and thirdly, reports of the research work done and/or steered by him. Through these three, Gadgil concerned himself with economic, political, and sociological matters. As a researcher and academician, Gadgil's contribution lies in two fields mainly. One is the Indian economy and the other is urban sociology. In the former, he dealt with numerous themes as he was frequently called upon to analyse, advise, or recommend on various aspects of the economy. However, the core themes handled by Gadgil were planning, public policy, and salaries of public officials. In the field of Indian economy, he was also interested in issues of co-operative economic activity, decentralized development, and district level planning as instruments of democratic model of development. His concern with political matters was limited: he took interest in federal arrangements—something that tied up with his interest in decentralized planning—and he was actively engaged in propagating the cause of formation of Maharashtra state. This latter concern was mainly a function of his deep involvement in, and engagement with, the society and culture of the Marathi community. At the same time, it was also an expression of his commitment to democratic aspirations. It may not be an exaggeration to say that Gadgil was one of the ideologues of the public movement for state formation.

We get an idea of Gadgil's sociological imagination and rootedness when we look at the range of his social enquiry. This covered a wide spectrum of academic curiosity. His work on Pune city may be considered as a centre-piece of his sociological investigation. As early as in 1937, Gadgil conceived and carried out a socio-economic survey of the Pune city. Modern day sociologists in India have largely ignored this foray into urban sociology. This may be, perhaps, because of the plainness of that study: the 'Poona survey' has a very general framework and its report is not very fashionable by the contemporary standards of jargon in urban sociology. Nor does the report of this study (published much later and in two parts, 1945 and 1952) present any significant formulation about urban social formations. Yet, it must be conceded that Gadgil pioneered studies of cities based on solid fieldwork and empirical investigation. After Pune, Gadgil either participated or promoted studies of Solapur and Kolhapur cities of Maharashtra. By the standards then prevailing, Pune was only a city and not a cosmopolitan centre as it later became and the other cities were in fact only towns. Gadgil realized the potential of these cities and also sensed the significant role the urban centres were likely to play in the future. Therefore, as a sensitive sociologist, he took up studies of these cities to sketch the growth of urban centres. Gadgil also guided a number of studies of smaller localities like Wai in Satara district of Maharashtra. Besides these studies, Gadgil noted the importance of social groups and gave particular attention to the study of business communities, both in historical and contemporary perspectives. His social enquiry led him to social history occasionally. This was not surprising because two of his early works in economics, in fact, dealt with economic history: his early research was on the industrial evolution in India (1924), wherein he covered the period of late nineteenth century and later on he worked on the revenue system in Bombay state (1928). Ever since he became the director of the Gokhale Institute, he steered research in the fields of social and economic enquiry. Without stating so, he integrated the sociological concerns with the economic ones. Another instance of Gadgil's wide-ranging social enquiry is his brief tract on 'Women in the Working Force in India' (Gadgil 1965). At a time when official 'women studies' were not yet launched, Gadgil spoke about the low reporting of women's work and also lower rates of women's participation in the workforce. A keen observer of the sociological pattern, Gadgil refers to the practice among so called upper peasant castes to discourage manual labour among womenfolk (Gadgil 1965: 7, 27). This marriage of sociology and economics made it possible for him to link the historical to the contemporary, the micro to the macro, and the empirical to the theoretical.

The nationalist-developmentalist spirit and Gadgil's own sense of social justice often form the mainstay of his public expositions. But the academician in Gadgil never disappears. Even in his public addresses or public interventions, Gadgil shows an uncanny ability to mould social scientific analyses with public political concerns. This is evident from his speeches on the occasions of convocation addresses (Nagpur University, 1962 and Pune University, 1966), or in his many pamphlets and presentations on the issue of the formation of the state of Maharashtra on the basis of the linguistic principle. In a sense, Gadgil's was an authentic sociological voice in the public discourse on issues with an emotional potential. Political issues often have a tendency to get carried away by populism, demagogy, and subterfuge. Interventions by the likes of Gadgil give substance to the ongoing public debates and help in shaping public reason within the framework of a democratic society. (This point may perhaps be relevant to the claims about Gadgil's liberal sensibilities.) The interface between contemporary political controversies and the social scientific enquiry is thus an essential condition for the shaping of public reason. Such an interface also saves social scientific enquiry from being only technical, from being the prisoner of jargon or a proxy for borrowed imagination.

Gadgil's public interventions and his numerous notes and memoranda to the 'authorities' may be criticized on the ground that they are plain and devoid of emotional or ideological flourish. But they often brought into picture the spirit of scientific enquiry as the basis of public policy and democratic contestations. Gadgil's statements, before numerous committees of the government, were often to the point and non-ideological and non-political in character. However, this does not mean that Gadgil ignored larger issues of macro-level analysis. A champion of planning, he was uncomfortable with the implicit tilt towards the capitalist class in the Second Plan and he was quite forthright in presenting the critique of India's economic policy regime and his own assessment of the political economy of India, though for the most part he reserved these for his public writings or speeches. Perhaps, as someone brought up in the tradition of strict intellectual non-partisanship, Gadgil may have felt that when he was making a presentation before any official forum, he should desist from a macro-level critique of the prevailing policy framework.

CRITIQUE OF POLITICAL ECONOMY

The purpose of the present essay is not to summarize what Gadgil said by way of his sociological works nor is it to evaluate or underscore the 'relevance' of Gadgil's ideas to contemporary India. Neither are we interested in eulogising his steadfast support to co-operatives and decentralization. The modest purpose of this essay is to locate Gadgil as a social scientist who used sociological analysis as a critical instrument. In this context, our central question here is: what kind of social critique does his sociology offer?

To illustrate Gadgil's critical sociology of India, in the following two sections, we shall take two examples at some length and report Gadgil's own formulation on these issues. One is the macro-level understanding of the implications of planned economy as it unfolded in the first decade of planning (later, Gadgil became increasingly associated with the process of planning and yet was unable to push planning in a different direction probably due to the political circumstances—Dandekar, too, notes this fact but does not offer any explanation [see Dandekar 1971b: xxiv]). The other issue is more specific and localized. This is related to the caste question in general but pertains to the role of the Brahmin community in particular.

In his convocation address at the Nagpur University (1962) Gadgil develops a critique of post-Independence political economy. This critique is very close to the 'left' position on India's political economy. Gadgil points out that the concern of the policy makers was to ensure industrial development and protective measures were taken to encourage the private sector, to make it secure from foreign competition, and to provide the private sector with adequate resources. It is noteworthy that Gadgil is not merely complaining about the preference accorded to the industrial sector over and at the cost of agriculture. He is pointing at the advantage this policy accorded to the class of industrialists. He argues: 'All growth of modern industry in India since the early twenties, has been *under a protective regime,* major cost of which has been borne by the Indian consumer ...... Cumulation of gains and the rapid increase of economic resources and power in particular *private hands can thus be described as the deliberate objective of official policy*' (Gadgil 1962: 240–1, emphasis mine). Gadgil is forthright in criticizing that all government operations are based on incentives to the private capitalists. He held that this strategy contributed to the monopoly of some industrial capitalists. On a more general plane, Gadgil also held that it was a mistaken view that production must be increased before distributive measures are taken. 'To put it bluntly, it is a plea for allowing concentration of the ownership of means of production and turning a blind eye to the need for improvement of standards of living ...'. In retrospect, his warning may sound almost prophetic when he correctly anticipates the implication of the pro-capitalist planning that was then adopted. He says, 'It is also very doubtful whether you can continue to concentrate economic power in society in the hands of small groups and yet later expect that they will quietly allow you to take it away or even that a state apparatus dominated by such interests will want to reverse current policy' (Gadgil 1962: 242).

It seems that through the mid-fifties Gadgil had become critical of the effects of post-Independence economic policies and he was agitated over the fact that planning was being used as an instrument for augmenting the domination of the business class. The social scientist in him was aware of the social formations that this process of industrial development was throwing up. After one decade of Independence, he pointed out that two classes were dominant in the rural areas: the trader-moneylender class and landlords and large farmers (who constitute top 10 per cent of the agricultural community). These landlords and farmers were not only economically dominant, but wielded social and political power as well (Gadgil 1962: 56, 1981: 13). The interests of the traders and farmers were sometimes common and on occasions separate. Gadgil goes on to indicate that the traders were representatives of the financial class in the urban areas (Gadgil 1981: 13). While Gadgil was in favour of co-operativization of rural economy, he was not romanticizing the co-operative sector. He was hard-headed enough to realize that co-operatives would diminish the power of the trader-moneylender but unless land reforms take place, co-operatives would further strengthen the large farmers (Gadgil 1981). How did he assess the political possibility of social transformation? Though

Gadgil shared the imagination and dream of the national movement, as an observer of the social processes, he was astute enough to have noted that the 'all powerful' Congress Party was torn from within among heterogeneous groups. He also points out that the Congress Party was drawn from the urban professional and administrative classes and to this were added in the post-Independence period, representatives of financial and business classes (Gadgil 1962: 59).

Thus, Gadgil's stray writings provide us with a class map of India during the fifties and sixties, something that is a treasure as a heuristic tool as also a basis for critical social enquiry, for a student of Indian society. We have noted above that Gadgil's writings glide between the micro and the macro very easily. Therefore, he was able to undertake specific case studies and yet never lost sight of the more general picture of social stratification and inequalities. In an essay written in 1958 he summarizes the Indian social situation. Taking the example of Maharashtra, Gadgil indicates the close correspondence of the ranking in terms of caste, income levels, and educational attainment of three different groups in the society. From this formulation, one gets a clear idea of what conclusions he drew from his empirical studies, for instance the 'Poona study'. He delineates three hierarchical groups: the urban professionals, priests, and traders ; secondly, the peasants and artisans; and thirdly, the Dalits and agricultural labourers (Gadgil 1981: 503). Two observations may be made regarding these writings of Gadgil. One is that these writings clearly show that he was much more than an economist; he was a critical social scientist. The second observation relates to the sociological insights that he provides. They practically form an agenda for contemporary student of Indian society.

CASTE QUESTION

Gadgil, the social scientist, was not unaware of the caste question. He did not specialize in this area, nor was he active as an anti-caste ideologue. However, he was sensitive to the implications of the caste factor in his socio-economic analyses. Dandekar has pointed to the influence of Dr. Ambedkar on Gadgil (Dandekar 1971b: iii). However, it may be more accurate to argue that Gadgil's concern for the caste question was based on his sociological insights and broader interest in justice. Apart from subscribing to the nationalist consensus on the caste question, Gadgil points to the changed relationship between the business class on the one hand and the administrators and the politicians on the other. The administrators, who had discretionary powers of control and regulation over the industry, were in fact looking for opportunities of getting patronage from the industry and the politicians of the ruling party had put themselves in the position of being clients of the business corporations (Gadgil 1962: 243). At another place, Gadgil has also commented upon the social composition of the administrative class. Writing in 1957, he pointed out that the upper bureaucracy maintains the 'monopoly of positions and privileges' of members of the high caste and comments that this is extremely unsuitable for a democratic structure (Gadgil 1962: 54–5). Similarly, his mention of the 'social power' of the emerging class of farmers may also be read to mean the role of the middle castes in the changing circumstance of economic advance of the sections of the middle caste farmers.

But one piece of his writing shows *par excellence* his sensitivity and sense of social responsibility in the matter of caste conflict. Unfortunately for the non-Marathi reader, this was written in Marathi, obviously because the context was Maharashtra's history and society. Let us look at it at some length. Written in March, 1948, the context of this brief essay was tragic and somewhat frightening: Tragic, because this was in the aftermath of Gandhi's assassination. Frightening, because parts of Maharashtra had witnessed somewhat prolonged anti-Brahmin violence, mainly in the rural areas. Gadgil belonged to the Brahmin caste, and among Brahmins, the elite Chitpavan Brahmin sub-caste. The atmosphere was emotionally surcharged. Non-Brahmins were not in a mood to appreciate any Brahmin initiative, while the Brahmins, after having been at the top of the social order for so long, were so accustomed to status and respect that the violence caused a sense of shock and injury among them. It was courageous in such an atmosphere to choose to write on the caste question and more so, to appeal to the Brahmins to follow a certain code of conduct. (As a diversion, one can compare this with the eruption of comparatively very mild anti-Brahmin sentiment in Maharashtra in early 2004, when a controversy arose over the alleged role of Brahmin scholars in providing information to a foreign scholar who made derogatory statements about the parentage of Shivaji. In the prolonged public controversy and atmosphere of unease, no Brahmin scholar or public intellectual could come out with any initiative or imaginative formulation. Most were content with taking recourse to freedom of speech as a figurative intellectual fig leaf.[1]) Titled as 'Future Policy for the Brahmins', Gadgil's essay show-cases not only Gadgil's acute sense of proportion and propriety, but brings out the sociologist in him even in times of emotionally surcharged atmosphere.

He is candid in admitting that for many non-Brahmins there is a conflict of interests between the Brahmins and the non-Brahmins. The onus of breaching the caste-based division lies with those who are the beneficiaries of the caste hierarchy. This implies that Brahmins should abstain from organizing on the caste basis even for benevolent or social service purposes (an advice the Brahmins have not followed). Secondly, Gadgil hits the nail on the head when he says that the superiority of the Brahmins does not rest merely on their traditional ritual status, but rather on the excessive concentration of material and political power in their hands. More importantly, Gadgil comes out with a concrete suggestion: that the

Brahmins should totally abdicate all public power. This was not a plea for 'withdrawal'; Brahmins may, and must, continue to be socially engaged, but not as power holders (Gadgil 1974: 249–54). There is no doubt that Gadgil's comments make eminent sense in the context of Maharashtra. The Peshwa rule was perceived among the public mainly as usurpation of Maratha power by the Brahmins. It was also instrumental in entrenching the Brahmin power in Marathi speaking areas. It was in this background that the non-Brahmin movement had taken place in early twentieth century. In spite of the onward political march of the non-Brahmins since then, cultural and social power continued to be in the hands of the Brahmin community. In the political field as well, the Brahmins were in the forefront of almost all the political parties in the state till the early sixties. Gadgil's suggestion makes sense in this context. But more importantly, this way of looking at the caste question is informed by sociological insight and a sense of justice. Thus, Gadgil's exhortations to the Brahmins need to be seen as founded on his understanding of Indian society in general. In fact, this is evident from his comment that in the case of the Brahmins of Maharashtra, though they are materially well off compared to many other sections, they do not control resources in this part of the country and the Marathas and Bahujans will have to wage separate battles to address economic inequality. He also pointed to the possibility of similar conflict between the interests of the Marathas and Dalits. These observations could not have taken place without having a mature and deep understanding of the operation of caste system in empirical social context.

CONCLUDING REMARKS

The above sections (sections III and IV) indicate that there was a robust moral basis to the social science vision held by Gadgil. He was aware of the implications of the democratic experiment that India had adopted. He believed that planners and administrators must realize the implications of democracy. He wrote in 1958 that democracy requires three things: provision for basic levels of education, keeping economic inequalities under control, and ensuring that the population would be above survival level. This may be understood by some as the 'egalitarian' programme, but Gadgil asserts that this was only an essential precondition of democracy and therefore, the so-called egalitarian programme needed urgent implementation (Gadgil 1981: 512). Given this understanding of democracy, Gadgil does not see any tension between the goals of liberty and equality.

But as we conclude this essay, one cannot but have a sense of unease. This, for two reasons: one, concerning Gadgil's social science and another, about a general methodological issue in the field of social science enquiry. The moral basis of social enquiry that we cull out from Gadgil's writings is somehow not integrated fully with his work in social science. We mentioned two concerns that dominate Gadgil's overall thinking about society: academic curiosity about Indian specificity and concern for justice and equity. The academic work of Gadgil was resolutely focused on socio-economic questions concerning contemporary India. However, the other concern is somewhat weakly present in his scientific enquiry. It is possible to say that in his choice of topics, this concern is implicit. But in his empirical investigations, this issue of social justice and equity, somehow, does not form the core. It is there, and yet is not a central driving force of his enquiry. This would remain a puzzle: was it because of the liberal sensibility that Gadgil kept his moral persuasion away from or at least only weakly implicit in his social science work? In his economics, and more so in his social enquiry, Gadgil stops short of integrating the critical insights into his research questions. He keeps the empirical enquiry distant from questions of contestation and reserves the moral basis for his expostulations mainly in the arena of public forums. In a detailed analysis of Gadgil's economics, none other than Comrade Dange confronted this question. Dange opines that while Gadgil was no doubt opposed to 'monopoly capitalism', he refused to 'cross the line' of established bourgeois economics' (Dange 1971: 2). Perhaps, it was not just bourgeois economics, but the issue of crossing the line of empirical social enquiry and treading in the unknown field of ideological assertion that Gadgil scrupulously avoided. This means that unless we take into account Gadgil's presentations at public meetings and academic seminars, we would miss Gadgil the social scientist. Ironic as it may seem, Gadgil's true worth as a critical social enquirer emerges only from his role as a public intellectual. Or, is it a typical aspect of our typical situation where scholars have to resort to public intellectualism in order to formulate their critical insights?

This leads us to the second, and more general question. How does critical social science shape? Should our moral preferences come as appendages of scholarly expositions? Should the moral preferences be reserved for non-academic platforms alone? One can easily witness two forms prevalent in social science in India. One is where half-baked moralizing masquerades as social science, the researcher wears his ideology on the shirt-sleeve. In this type, we only get moral sermons and non-empirical speculations. On the other hand, and this is more prevalent, social science shines in the 'glory' of value neutrality. Following methodologies, academic rigour, and perfect scientific instruments, one comes across jargon, complex theories, and model-building, but very little sensitivity to contemporary issues. Both these types fail to combine academic soundness with purposive enquiry.

In spite of the unease mentioned above, Gadgil's social science helps us frame the problem and indicates some gateway to integrating moral principles and scientific methods.

NOTE

1. This controversy refers to the work by James Laine (2003). A Sanskrit scholar was initially manhandled for being Laine's collaborator (in another work) and 'informer'. Later, a mob of youth vandalized (January 2004) the library of the Bhandarkar Oriental Research Institute, Pune (which was the place of research for Laine for a long time), on the charge that its Brahmanical management was responsible for spreading the canard about Shivaji. The Marathi press, mostly a citadel of Brahmins, was prompt in its protests against the 'fury of the illiterates' but mostly insensitive to the social perception about the smug superiority of the Brahmin community. So, the debate remained either within the positivist confines of who gave the information or within the vacuous circle of freedom of speech and right of the scholars to do academic work.

REFERENCES

Apte, D.P. (2000) '*Samajik Arthik Abhyasasathi Samshodhan Padhati va Sarvekshanachya Tantracha Vikas: Gadgilanche Yogadan*' (Marathi, 'Gadgil's Contribution to the Development of Survey Method and Socio-economic Research Method), *Arthasamvad*, Vol. 24, No. 2, July–Sept., pp. 110–18.

Brahme, Sulabha (2000) '*Samshodhak Gadgil*' (Marathi, 'Gadgil, the Researcher'), *Arthasamvad*, Vol. 24, No. 2, July–Sept., pp. 156–70.

Byres, Terrence J. (1998) 'State, Class and Development Planning in India', in Terrence J. Byres (ed.), *The State, Developing Planning and Liberalisation in India*, New Delhi: Oxford University Press, pp. 36–81.

——— (1999) 'The Creation of 'The Tribe of Pundits Called Economists', in Terrence J. Byres (ed.), *The Indian Economy: Major Debates since Independence*, New Delhi: Oxford University Press, pp. 20–73.

Dandekar, V.M. (1971a) 'D.R. Gadgil', *Economic and Political Weekly*, Vol. 6, No. 19, 8 May, pp. 938–42.

——— (1971b) 'Dhananjay Ramchandra Gadgil (1901–1971)', *Artha Vijnana*, Vol. 13, No. 2, June, pp. i–xxiv.

Dange, S.A. (1971) *Gadgil and the Economics of Indian Democracy*, Bombay: People's Publishing House.

Gadgil, D.R. (1962) *Planning and Economic Policy in India*, second edition, Pune: GIPE and Bombay: Asia Publishing House.

——— (1965) *Women in the Working Force in India*, Kunda Datar Lecture, 1964. Bombay: Asia Publishing House.

——— (1974) *D.R. Gadgil Lekhsangraha* (Marathi), Collection of Marathi Writings of Gadgil, Vol. 2, edited by Sulabha Brahme, Pune: GIPE.

——— (1981) *Writings and Speeches of Professor D.R. Gadgil on Economic and Political Problems*, edited by Sulabha Brahme, Pune: GIPE and Bombay: Orient Longman.

Guha, Ramachandra (2001) 'The Absent Liberal: An Essay on Politics and Intellectual Life', *Economic and Political Weekly*, Vol. 36, No. 50, 15 December, pp. 4663–70.

Hanson, A.H. (1966) *The Process of Planning: A Study of India's Five Year Plans—1950–1964*, London: Oxford University Press.

Kamat, A.R. (1974) 'D.R. Gadgil: The Last Phase', *Economic and Political Weekly*, Vol. 9, No. 26, 19 June 19, pp. 1024–29.

Laine, James W. (2003) *Shivaji: Hindu King in Islamic India*, New Delhi: Oxford University Press.

Sovani, N. V. (1974) *Majhe Guru: Dhananjyirao Gadgil*, Pune: Deshmukh and Co.

INDEX